Long and
Winding Roads

Long and Winding Roads

The Evolving Artistry of the Beatles

Kenneth Womack

continuum

NEW YORK • LONDON

2007

The Continuum International Publishing Group Inc
80 Maiden Lane, New York, NY 10038

The Continuum International Publishing Group Ltd
The Tower Building, 11 York Road, London SE1 7NX

www.continuumbooks.com

Printed in the United States of America

Library of Congress Cataloging-in-Publication Data

Womack, Kenneth.
    Long and winding roads : the evolving artistry of the Beatles / Kenneth Womack.
        p.   cm.
    Includes bibliographical references (p.   ) and index.
    ISBN-13: 978-0-8264-1745-9 (hardcover : alk. paper)
    ISBN-10: 0-8264-1745-0 (hardcover : alk. paper)
    ISBN-13: 978-0-8264-1746-6 (pbk. : alk. paper)
    ISBN-10: 0-8264-1746-9 (pbk. : alk. paper)
    1. Beatles.   2. Rock music—Analysis, appreciation.   3. Rock musicians—England.   I. Title.

ML421.B4W66   2007
782.42166092'2—dc22

                                                      2007006478

Jeanine,
Pour toi, ma belle

Contents

Chapter 1

The End

Whoever has dreamed of travel and deeds
cannot lower his sails without grieving.
—Bjørnstjerne Bjørnson

Twenty-three seconds.

At the end of the Beatles' career as recording artists, there were twenty-three seconds. There were moments of grandeur and largesse in the studio, punctuated by scenes of acrimony and bitterness staged in business meetings.

There was also Tittenhurst Park, a Georgian mansion with rolling lawns and an assortment of outbuildings. In the spring of 1969, John Lennon purchased the regal, hundred-acre estate to get away from it all, a place to liberate himself from the tumultuous events of the previous year—a period in which he and Yoko Ono had begun to live their lives writ large on the global media stage. Their highly publicized saga had culminated in March with their much-ballyhooed wedding near the rock of Gibraltar. Having vacated the Montague Square apartment in London that he had borrowed from Ringo Starr—Jimi Hendrix would move into the flat soon thereafter—John had fled with Yoko to the greener pastures of rural Ascot.

And for a few hours in the late summer of 1969, the Beatles drifted there as well, eschewing London, with its noise and its pollution, for the countryside, where they posed for a photo session. It was only the latest of a seemingly endless succession of exercises in which they had posed, at times, around bomb craters, in parks and on beaches, on boats and around steamer trunks, or, more recently, as they walked along the zebra crossing on stately Abbey Road in northwest London, where traffic was stayed for ten minutes while the photographer had his way.

Some twenty weeks earlier, the Beatles had strummed the final chords of "Get Back" on the rooftop of their Savile Row office building. Their impromptu concert ended in a moment of ironic caprice as Lennon, wearing a fur coat, his long hair whipping in the wind above the city, grinned at Paul McCartney, with whom he shared a knowing glance, and addressed the smattering of friends, relations, employees, and London Bobbies who had joined them on the rooftop that afternoon: "I'd like to say thank you on behalf of the group and ourselves," he remarked, with an audible wink in his voice. "I hope we passed the audition."

Yet, as they strolled from the main house at Tittenhurst, the Beatles probably had no idea that they were spending one of their final days together. "It was just a photo session," Ringo remembered. "I wasn't there thinking, 'Okay, this is the last photo session'" (*Anthology* 345). Only two days earlier, the band had concluded their final recording session at EMI Studios, where the steely rhythm and blues of "I Want You (She's So Heavy)" dissolved into the sound of raw metal, as the strident chords of Lennon and George Harrison's electric guitars were inflected by the searing white noise of an air machine only to be broken by, of all things, a sudden and ineffable silence.

At Tittenhurst, the Beatles were joined by Yoko, of course, as well as by a heavily pregnant Linda McCartney, who would give birth just six days later to daughter Mary. American photographer Ethan Russell was on hand, as was the *Daily Mail*'s Monte Frisco. The Beatles' steadfast assistant Mal Evans was there, too, shooting amateur film footage, along with Apple press officer Derek Taylor. Even Paul's wooly sheepdog Martha was there at Tittenhurst that day, loping nearby as the group posed for a series of pictures: the Beatles standing in front of the mansion's terraced canopy, pausing along the garden path, loitering near the weathered statue of Diana, with her glowing orbs gazing off into the distance. They posed with a pair of donkeys from the stables, under a spread of Weeping Blue Atlas cedar trees, near the estate's old Victorian assembly hall, with its enigmatic stone busts, and among the four terraced cottages that led back to the main house.

For a while, they stood for the photographers in a paddock of tall grass, an old cricket pitch that had long since lost its purpose, having become overgrown with age and languishing from neglect. Harrison donned a wide-brimmed cowboy hat in comparison with the prim black felt one atop Lennon's head. While Ringo wore a neo-Paisley scarf for the occasion, Paul preferred the simplicity of a nondescript dark suit, tieless in contrast with the red handkerchief around George's neck. Standing amongst the high grass, they looked rather like a family of tourists who had meandered into a novelty shop, hoping to have themselves photographed decked out in the apparel, if not the mythology itself, of the Old West. Seeming tired and withered, the Beatles looked like Butch and Sundance on their last ride. And indeed they were, for all four Beatles would scarcely be together again. It was Friday, August 22nd, 1969.

Chapter 2

The Beginning

*As all historians know, the past is a great darkness,
and filled with echoes. Voices may reach us from it;
but what they say to us is imbued with the obscurity
of the matrix out of which they come; and, try
as we may, we cannot always decipher them
precisely in the clearer light of our own day.*

—MARGARET ATWOOD, *THE HANDMAID'S TALE*

Twenty-seven seconds.

In the beginning, there were twenty-seven seconds. A clutch of muddled guitars. The rhythmic thump of the drums. The hollow tones of a tea-chest bass. And the piercing, nasal vocals of sixteen-year-old John Lennon singing "Puttin' on the Style," the skiffle tune made popular by Lonnie "The King of Skiffle" Donegan.

On Saturday, July 6th, 1957, Bob Molyneux, an amateur recording buff, carried a portable Grundig TK8 reel-to-reel tape machine to St. Peter's Church Hall, Woolton, in Liverpool. The occasion was a garden fête, which began with an afternoon performance outdoors. Led by Lennon, the Quarry Men opened the concert—the George Edwards Band was the main event, although most of the audience had been in attendance for the fête's celebrated dog show—with a flatbed truck as their stage. The band took their name from the motto for Quarry Bank High School, which Lennon and his boyhood friend Pete Shotton both attended: "Quarry Men, strong before our birth." For the evening performance, the concert shifted indoors to the Church Hall, where Molyneux trained his handheld microphone on the stage. Two songs from the Quarry Men's set—"Puttin' on the Style" and Elvis Presley's "Baby Let's Play House"— would survive Molyneux's copying, erasing, and recopying of the original recording, as well as thirty subsequent years of indeterminate storage. Yet all that remains is a poor-quality fragment of twenty-seven seconds—twenty-seven muddy, barely audible seconds—of the Quarry Men's performance on the very legend-making day that John Lennon met Paul McCartney.[1]

With Lennon on lead vocals and guitar, the Quarry Men were rounded out by Shotton on washboard, Eric Griffiths on guitar, Len Garry on bass, Rod Davis on banjo, and Colin Hanton on drums. For its part, Molyneux's recording is all but inaudible. Time and space have decomposed the guitars into a wall of white noise, with a pounding drum kit acting as their solitary guide through the storm. In truth, those twenty-seven seconds could be the sound of any garage band from anywhere, UK, or anyplace, USA—if not, that is, for Lennon's peculiar vocals, soaring high above the drone:

> Well, the young man in the hot-rod car, driving like he's mad
> In a pair of yellow gloves he's borrowed from his dad.
> He makes it roar so lively just to make his girlfriend smile,
> But she knows he's only puttin' on the style.

As with the guitars, the words are almost completely indecipherable. But there it is, in the third line: Lennon's trademark irascibility—the knowing, deadpan humor that would charm George Martin and allow the producer to peer through the haze of uncertain talent, a subpar drummer, and the mind-numbing odds of making it in show business to sign the Beatles to a recording contract. As Lennon sings about the hot rod—and especially the young man deliberately pulsing the engine in order to get a rise out of his girl—he sinks his teeth into the lyric, and, grinning audibly to himself, extends the monosyllabic *sm-i-i-i-i-i-le* for all it's worth.

Before the evening set, Lennon was introduced to the fifteen-year-old McCartney by their mutual friend Ivan Vaughan, an erstwhile member of the Quarry Men himself. Legend has it that the left-handed McCartney borrowed one of the other lads' guitars and, strumming it upside down, played note-perfect versions of Eddie Cochran's "Twenty Flight Rock" and Gene Vincent's "Be-Bop-a-Lula." To everyone's amazement, McCartney knew all of the chords, and, even more remarkably, the lyrics. "I knew all the words and they didn't," McCartney remembered. "That was big currency" (qtd. in Everett, *The Quarry Men through Rubber Soul* 24). Realizing that he had his audience in the palm of his hand, McCartney ended the lesson by teaching Lennon and Griffiths how to tune their guitars. They had previously paid a man in Woolton in order to have the relatively simple procedure done.

It is worth noting that Lennon didn't invite McCartney into the group merely because of their incipient friendship; he intuitively recognized McCartney as a formidable talent. Should he strengthen and improve the group by adding this highly skilled new guy into the band, thereby challenging his own dominance? Or, conversely, should they prattle on into oblivion, with Lennon's superiority intact? John explained his reasoning for inviting Paul to join the Quarry Men in his revealing 1970 interview with Jann Wenner: "Was it better to have a guy who was better than the people I had—obviously—or not? To make the group stronger or to let me be stronger? . . . Instead of going for the individual thing we went for the strongest format. And for equals" (*Lennon Remembers* 133). This incredibly lucid and self-conscious moment—initially experienced by Lennon, incidentally, during the throes of late-afternoon drunkenness—demonstrates the kind of ambition that would characterize the Beatles' creative determination and quest for musical transcendence as songwriters, as well as during the production of their albums. In many ways, the story of John meeting Paul—and the inner conflict that their meeting wrought for Lennon—exists as our first narrative about the Beatles. The stories that they author from that point forward—ever more extended acts of storytelling that climax with *Abbey Road*—are, in and of themselves, rooted in this initial moment of self-awareness and existential uncertainty.

A few weeks after the concert at St. Peter's Church, Shotton was cycling around Woolton and ran into McCartney, whom he invited into the band—no doubt, with Lennon's express permission.[2] After thinking for a bit, Paul readily accepted. But he would miss the group's next gig because he was away with his younger brother at Boy Scout camp, delaying his debut with the Quarry Men until an October 1957 performance at Liverpool's New Clubmoor Hall.

~

The name Liverpool finds its origins in a twelfth-century pool that sat beside the town. It was a sluggish, dirty tidal inlet that joined the River Mersey just south of the Pier Head. The city's name has become synonymous with the delftware and porcelain manufactured in Liverpool in the eighteenth century, and, as an adjective, it has taken on similar meanings connoting filth and a cold, stubborn sensibility. "Liverpool weather," for example, is known for its dank and dirty winds, while hard, nearly inedible biscuits are called "Liverpool pantiles." And then there's the "Liverpool kiss," which connotes a "blow delivered to the head or face"—a head-butt (*OED*).

By the dawn of the nineteenth century, Liverpool had emerged as one of the most prosperous cities in Europe. Borne on the back of the African slave trade, Liverpool's docks served as Great Britain's gateway to Liverpool Bay, the Irish Sea, and, beyond that, the world. Its role as one of the nation's prime shipping hubs was enhanced, as the century wore on, by the growing cotton trade and by the Industrial Revolution, for which the city's shipyards served as a vital engine for importing raw materials and exporting commercial goods. Liverpool's "cast-iron" shores were founded upon the city's proud shipbuilding heritage and the toil of its working-class citizenry—an unruly crew of transplanted Irish immigrants and, even larger in number, its native population of North Country Scousers. Their name finds its origins in a sailor's dish known as lobscouse, a simmering stew of vegetables and table scraps. With their particularized North Country accents and pronunciations, Scousers are known for their intense local patriotism and their unrefined ways.

John Winston Lennon, quite arguably the most famous Scouser of all time, was born on October 9th, 1940, during one of the deadliest and most destructive of the Luftwaffe's nighttime bombing raids on the city. As the home of Great Britain's vital Naval shipyards, as well as of the docklands on the River Mersey from which overseas supplies entered the nation, Liverpool was one of Adolf Hitler's principal English targets—and second only to London in terms of its strategic importance. As the sorties exploded about the city, Julia Stanley Lennon gave birth, honoring her son by drawing his middle name from Great Britain's esteemed Prime Minister, Sir Winston Churchill.

A talented singer, banjo player, and dancer, Julia was known as Judy amongst her family and for her great beauty throughout the city. "Judy was feminine, she was beautiful," a niece recalled. "You never saw her with her hair undone. She went to bed with makeup on so that she'd look beautiful in the morning" (qtd. in Spitz 22). In December 1938, twenty-four-year-old Julia stunned her tightly knit family with the news that she had married a charming twenty-nine-year-old bachelor named Freddie Lennon. After having gone through a succession of odd jobs, Freddie became a merchant seaman in order to support his young bride, with whom he lived in the Stanleys' home at 9 Newcastle Road. As with so many men of his generation, Freddie made his living by putting out to sea on voyages to the Mediterranean, North Africa, and the West Indies—to wherever the shipping lanes would take him. John had no illusions about his origins: "Ninety per cent of the people on this planet, especially in the West, were born out of a bottle of whiskey on a Saturday night, and there was no intent to have children. Ninety per cent of us were accidents—I don't know anybody who has planned a child. All of us were Saturday night specials" (*Anthology* 7).

Not surprisingly, Freddie was at sea on the evening that John was born at the Oxford Street Maternity Hospital. Although his father was away in parts unknown, John was quickly joined by his devoted aunt, Mimi Stanley Smith, who ensured that she was with her sister no matter the risk on that most perilous of nights. "There was shrapnel falling and gunfire," she later recalled, "and when there was a little lull I ran into the hospital ward and there was this beautiful little boy" (qtd. in Spitz 24). By 1942, Julia had tired of staying home in wait for a sea-bound husband, and she began venturing out amongst Liverpool's nightclubs and saloons. Eventually, she took up with Taffy Williams, a Welsh soldier. Pregnant with Williams's baby, Julia gave birth to a daughter, whom she named Victoria, in June 1945 at the Elmswood Nursing Home. The baby was given up for adoption soon thereafter, and Freddie, distraught with his wife's unfaithfulness and his own failings, put out to sea yet again.

Before too long, the still-married Julia set up housekeeping with John Dykins, a Liverpool wine steward. Disgusted with her sister's behavior and determined to provide her nephew with a proper upbringing, Mimi and her husband, George Smith, a dairy farmer, took custody of John. "Julia had met someone else, with whom she had a chance of happiness," Mimi remembered, "and no man wants another man's child. That's when I said I wanted to bring John to Menlove Avenue to live with George and me. I wouldn't even let him risk being hurt or feeling he was in the way. I made up my mind that I'd be the one to give him what every child has the right to—a safe and happy home life" (qtd. in Norman 18). In truth, Mimi saw to it that her nephew was forcibly removed from her sister's home, eventually enlisting the aid of social services after learning that John shared the same cramped bedroom with Julia and her lover. Mimi and George raised John in the middle-class neighborhood of Woolton. Their home, which they nicknamed "Mendips," was a semidetached, wood and stucco house near Penny Lane and across from the Allerton Golf Course. "Mimi told me my parents had fallen out of love," John recalled. "She never said anything directly against my father and mother. I soon forgot my father. It was like he was dead. But I did see my mother now and again, and my feeling never died off for her. I often thought about her, though I never realized for a long time that she was living no more than five or ten miles away" (*Anthology* 7).

During his earliest years at Dovedale Primary School, John was a model student who had developed into an avid reader—he devoured Lewis Carroll and Edgar Allan Poe—as well as a gifted cartoonist. Around this time, John also obtained his first musical instrument: a harmonica. "I can remember why I took it up in the first place," he recalled. "I must have picked one up very cheap. [Mimi] used to take in students, and one of them had a mouth organ and said he'd buy me one if I could learn a tune by the next morning. So I learned about two. I was somewhere between eight and twelve at the time—in short pants, anyway" (qtd. in Babiuk 7). At twelve years old, John moved to Quarry Bank Grammar School, accompanied by Pete Shotton. "We went through it like Siamese twins," Pete later remembered. "We started in our first year at the top and gradually sank together into the subbasement" (qtd. in Norman 23). Indeed, John's life had taken a turn for the worse during his first year at Quarry Bank, especially after his Uncle George died, quite suddenly, from a hemorrhage. During his last years at Dovedale, John ran with a group of friends known for cutting class and pulling off the occasional shoplifting. By the time that he reached Quarry Bank, John had graduated to full-blown rambunctiousness. Within a few years, John and Pete had begun skipping school in order to take the bus to Spring Wood, where Julia now lived. For John, Julia seemed more like an older sister than his mother. "She'd do these tricks just to make us laugh," Pete recalled. "She used to wear these old woolen knickers on her head while she did the housework. She'd open the door to us with the knicker legs hanging down her back. She didn't care. She was just like John" (qtd. in Norman 25).

In addition to rediscovering his mother, John had also discovered skiffle, which Lonnie Donegan had exploded into a national phenomenon with the hit song "Rock Island Line," an up-tempo rendition of Leadbelly's three-chord ditty about a railroad line that brings trainloads of livestock to market in New Orleans. Great Britain's aspiring teenaged musicians loved skiffle for its simple nature, as well as for its relative inexpensiveness. Skiffle's sounds could be easily reproduced with unconventional instruments like kazoos, washboards, or jugs—and, for its more affluent practitioners, sometimes in combination with conventional instruments such as guitars and drums.

With skiffle on his mind—and rock and roll in his heart after first encountering the raw power of Elvis Presley's "Heartbreak Hotel" in May 1956—John finally persuaded Aunt Mimi to purchase a £5 guitar for him in March 1957. It was a steel-stringed instrument that he had spotted in an advertisement in *Reveille* magazine. A Gallotone Champion, the smallish guitar was constructed out of lacquered wide-grain maple. Having talked his friends Eric Griffiths, Ivan Vaughan, and Nigel Whalley to start up a band with Pete and himself, John formed the Black Jacks, which soon morphed into the Quarry Men. Not long afterward, Griffiths introduced them to drummer Colin Hanton. Griffiths remembered the boys' first experiences playing the guitar—and how Julia taught them to play chords: "John's mother had played the banjo, so she retuned our guitars to banjo tuning and taught us banjo chords, maybe three or four at the most. And that was it: instant guitar playing" (qtd. in Babiuk 10). A few months and a couple of personnel changes later, the Quarry Men took their show, which consisted of skiffle tunes along with a dash of imported American rock and roll, on the road. Their first gig, a local qualifying audition for radio and television personality "Mr. Star-Maker" Carroll Levis, was on

June 9th, 1957, at the Empire Theatre on Liverpool's Lime Street. After losing the audition to the Sunnyside Skiffle Group, the Quarry Men played at an outdoor party on June 22nd hosted by Marjorie Roberts, a resident of Roseberry Street who organized the festivities in order to commemorate the 550th anniversary of King John issuing a Royal Charter inviting Liverpool's citizenry to become landowners. The event ended rather badly for the Quarry Men after a local gang threatened to beat them up—especially "that Lennon" (Lewisohn, *The Beatles Live!* 19).

~

The Quarry Men's next gig, the garden fête at St. Peter's Church Hall, brought them into the orbit of Paul McCartney, whose father, Jim, a dancehall pianist and trumpet player, exerted a profound influence upon his son's career as a musician and showman. And in so doing, he would ultimately influence the musical direction of the Beatles.

In the 1920s, Jim led the Jim Mac Dance Band, which made a name for themselves on the local party and dancehall circuit. In addition to his work as a semiprofessional musician, Jim made his living as a cotton salesman. In June 1940—as the air-raid sirens screamed across the Liverpool night—forty-year-old Jim met Mary Mohin, a thirty-one-year-old midwife. By April 1941, they were married. James Paul McCartney was born on June 18th, 1942, at Walton General Hospital, and Paul's younger brother Michael followed in 1944. The boys' youth was marked by the McCartneys' frequent moves from one government-subsidized council house to another—from Anfield to Speke, where they lived on Western Avenue before relocating to Ardwick Road. Paul's formal education began at Stockton Road Primary School, where he received high marks for his work in English Composition and Art. His success on the Eleven Plus exams earned him entrance into the Liverpool Institute, the city's oldest grammar school, where he met Ivan Vaughan, who became one of his closest childhood friends. While he continued to excel in his studies—often after exerting surprisingly little effort in their stead—Paul drifted, rather naturally, toward the performing arts. In one very revealing instance, Paul auditioned for the role of Warwick in the Liverpool Institute's production of George Bernard Shaw's *Saint Joan* and became mortified when he was relegated to a minor role.

By 1955, the McCartneys had departed Speke for the relatively greener pastures of Allerton, where they lived in a council house at 20 Forthlin Road, scarcely a mile away—and just across the golf course—from Mimi Smith's home in Woolton. As Paul entered teenagehood, Jim encouraged him to take piano lessons. For Paul's fourteenth birthday, his father presented him with a nickel-plated trumpet, which the boy struggled to play. While there was always music in the McCartney household—they were one of the few families in their social stratum who owned their own piano—Paul's life was revolutionized by Radio Luxembourg's evening broadcasts of American music.[3] He was particularly entranced by the soulful reverberations of African American R&B, rock and roll's sedimentary bedrock that finds its roots in jazz, gospel, and the blues.[4] Suddenly, Paul's world was ringing with the sounds of Ray Charles, Bo Diddley, Fats Domino, and—one of his all-time favorites—Little Richard. After seeing Lonnie Donegan live at Liverpool's Empire Theatre in 1956, Paul exchanged his trumpet for a Zenith sunburst-model guitar. Before long, Paul realized that, despite the fact that he performed most tasks as a right-hander, he was a left-handed guitar player. After having the strings reversed on his guitar, the instrument, which had initially confronted him with great difficulty, came easily to him. "The minute he got the guitar that was the end," his brother Michael recalled. "He was lost. He didn't have time to eat or think about anything else" (qtd. in Spitz 87).

Although the guitar would change Paul's world forever, his youth was shattered by the breast cancer that overcame his mother throughout the spring and summer of 1956. At first, Mary associated the staggering pain in her chest with a severe bout of indigestion. Yet with her considerable background in nursing, Mary surely realized the perilous nature of her condition. One afternoon—while the McCartney children were away at Boy Scout camp—Mary shared her growing fears with her friend Olive Johnson: "I don't want to leave the boys *just* yet," she cried (qtd. in Norman 29). As summer wore into autumn, her condition took a tragic turn. On October 30th, she underwent an emergency mastectomy, but it was too late. By the next evening, Jim was taking the boys to visit their mother for the last time. Within a few short hours, she was stricken by an embolism and died. Devastated in his grief, Paul could only contemplate the imminent practicalities of his mother Mary's death. "What are we going to do without her money?" he wondered aloud (qtd. in Spitz 90).

"My mother's death broke my Dad up," Paul remembered. "That was the worst thing for me, hearing my Dad cry. I'd never heard him cry before. It was a terrible blow to the family. You grow up real quick because you never expect to hear your parents crying. You expect to see women crying, or kids in the playground, or even yourself crying—and you can explain all that. But when it's your Dad, then you know something's *really* wrong, and it shakes your faith in everything" (*Anthology* 19). As the family settled into their grief, they began, slowly but surely, to acquaint themselves with their new lives without Mary. Jim immersed himself in learning how to run the household, from cooking and cleaning to washing and ironing. Meanwhile, Paul absorbed himself in the power and whimsy of rock and roll, mimicking the sounds of Elvis Presley, Buddy Holly, Carl Perkins, and Chuck Berry. By the summer of 1957, Paul was hooked. All he needed was an audience.

On July 6th, Paul joined Ivan Vaughan at St. Peter's Church Hall. "I remember coming into the fête," Paul recalled. "There was the coconut shy over here and the hoopla over there, all the usual things—and there was a band playing on a platform with a small audience in front of them."[5] His attention was drawn almost immediately to John: "There was a guy up on the platform with curly, blondish hair, wearing a checked shirt—looking pretty good and quite fashionable—singing a song that I loved: the Del-Vikings' 'Come Go with Me.' He didn't know the words, but it didn't matter because none of us knew the words either. There's a little refrain, which goes, 'Come little darlin', come and go with me, I love you darling.' John was singing, 'Down, down, down to the penitentiary.' He was filling in with blues lines, I thought that was quite good, and he was singing well" (*Anthology* 20).

After the Quarry Men completed their afternoon performance, Ivan and Paul visited the band in a nearby Scout hut, where Paul coolly performed renditions of "Twenty Flight Rock," "Be-Bop-a-Lula," and a trio of Little Richard tunes, including "Tutti-Fruitti," "Good Golly, Miss Molly," and "Long Tall Sally." "Right off, I could see John was checking this kid out," Pete Shotton recalled. "Paul came on as very attractive, very loose, very easy, very confident—*wildly* confident. He played the guitar well. I could see that John was very impressed" (qtd. in Spitz 96). And indeed he was. "I was very impressed by Paul playing 'Twenty Flight Rock,'" John remembered. "He could obviously play the guitar. I half thought to myself, 'He's as good as me.' I'd been kingpin up until then. Now I thought, 'If I take him on, what will happen?' It went through my head that I'd have to keep him in line if I let him join. But he was good, so he was worth having. He also looked like Elvis. I dug him" (*Anthology* 12).[6]

While Paul was away at Boy Scout camp in Hathersage with his brother Michael, the Quarry Men played their fourth gig—this time, at Liverpool's Cavern Club on Matthew Street. Owned by Alan Sytner and named after Le Caveau Français Jazz Club in Paris, the Cavern opened its doors in January 1957. As a skiffle group, the Quarry Men found it to be tough going in a club that catered to a jazz-loving audience. After John turned in raucous renditions of Elvis Presley's "Hound Dog" and "Blue Suede Shoes," Sytner sent a note to the stage in which he ordered the band to "Cut out the bloody rock!" (qtd. in Lewisohn, *The Beatles Live!* 20). Sometime before the Cavern Club performance, Shotton quit playing with the group, although his friendship with the band—especially with John—would endure for years. As Pete recalled, "My contribution was totally nonmusical—I just went to make wisecracks and help carry the gear. I never liked going on stage anyway. It gave me the willies." After Pete announced that he was leaving the Quarry Men, John suddenly picked up Pete's washboard and smashed him over the head with it. "We then just laughed until the beer rolled down our eyes," Pete recalled (qtd. in Cross 9).

McCartney's debut with the Quarry Men on October 18th, 1957, at the New Clubmoor Hall in Liverpool's south Broadway section offered a striking contrast to the confidence and skill that he displayed at St. Peter's Church Hall back in July. Stricken with nerves, Paul found himself unable to produce a much-anticipated guitar solo during the Quarry Men's version of Arthur Smith's "Guitar Boogie." It was an inauspicious beginning, to say the least. By early 1958, the Quarry Men's personnel began to shift, as various members left the band to continue their educations or—more likely—in search of stable, full-time employment. Lennon had recently left Quarry Bank for the Liverpool College of Art—a move that allowed him to remain in a group that, for the most part, was still a late-adolescent diversion, a garage band, for all intents and purposes, that had little prospect for success beyond the occasional garden party or local club. By this juncture, the Quarry Men included John and Paul on vocals and guitar, with Garry on bass, Griffiths on guitar, and Hanton on drums. Every so often, John "Duff" Lowe would lend his talents as the Quarry Men's pianist.

On February 6th, 1958, the Quarry Men played Wilson Hall in Garston. The audience included fourteen-year-old George Harrison, an aspiring guitarist in his own right. Paul had known George for a couple of years, dating back to their first meeting on the bus to school. Well aware of George's skills as a guitarist, Paul had suggested that the Quarry Men consider adding him to their ranks. But the band—particularly Lennon—balked at the notion, primarily because of the significant differences in their ages. At seventeen, John could scarcely imagine spending time with the much younger boy who sported a prominent Teddy Boy haircut.

∼

A former steward on the White Star Line, George Harrison's father, Harold, was employed as a Liverpool bus driver. In 1929, he met Louise French, who worked in a grocery shop, and married her the next year. Two children, Louise and Harry, followed in quick succession, and by 1936, Harold brought his seafaring days to an end in order to seek out a more lucrative profession. The long reach of the Great Depression left Harold unemployed for another two years until he landed a position as a bus driver on the Liverpool Corporation's

Speke-Liverpool route. In 1941, the Harrisons' third child, Peter, was born, and on February 25th, 1943, they rounded out the family with George.[7] Harold and Louise's meager occupations ensured that the Harrisons, much like the McCartneys, would scarcely rise above the succession of council houses that life afforded them. Good fortune shined on them, though, when the family was chosen amongst a deep well of housing applicants to relocate from modest Arnold Grove into a new council house on Upton Green in Speke—and less than a mile away from the McCartney abode on Forthlin Road.

Nicknamed Geo (pronounced as "Joe") by his family, George had been a sterling student at Dovedale Primary, yet he had transformed, in his incipient adolescence, into a lackluster, disinterested pupil at the Liverpool Institute. "I felt then that there was some hypocrisy going on, even though I was only about 11-years-old," George remembered. "It seemed to be the same on every housing estate in English cities: on one corner they'd have a church and on the other corner a pub. Everybody's out there getting pissed and then just goes in the church, says three 'Hail Marys' and one 'Our Father' and sticks a fiver in the plate. It felt so alien to me. Not the stain-glass window or the pictures of Christ; I like that a lot, and the smell of the incense and the candles. I just didn't like the bullshit. After Communion, I was supposed to have Confirmation, but I thought 'I'm not going to bother with that, I'll just confirm it later myself'" (*Anthology* 26). George was fortunate, nevertheless, to grow up in a generally convivial environment—no doubt fostered by his mother, Louise, who filled their home with music courtesy of the BBC, and Harold, who, despite his paltry paycheck, was genuinely proud of his work as a bus driver.

As with John and Paul, George's musical passions had been roused by skiffle. In the autumn of 1956, George had attended a Lonnie Donegan concert with his older brother Harold and was mesmerized by the performance. After buying his own copy of "Rock Island Line," George talked his mother into purchasing a three-quarter-sized, Dutch-made Egmond guitar. George's initial attempts at playing the instrument were met with failure. Months later, though, he was buoyed by the imported American sounds of Elvis Presley, and he turned his attentions back on the guitar with a vengeance. With his friend Arthur Kelly in tow, George took weekly lessons from a local guitarist who splayed his talents at a nearby pub known as the Cat. "He taught us a few basic root chords straightaway," Kelly remembered. "The first number we learned was 'Your Cheatin' Heart,' by Hank Williams. We hated the song but were thrilled, at least, to be changing from C to F to G7" (qtd. in Spitz 122). Soon thereafter, George and Arthur formed a skiffle band of their own that they christened as the Rebels. With George's brother Pete on tea-chest bass, they plowed through a handful of songs in George's bedroom. They even played a gig at the local British Legion, where they served as the opening act for a magician.

By this time, George had begun to lose interest in skiffle, having discovered such legendary American guitarists as Chet Atkins and Carl Perkins. George honed his skills by devoting hour upon hour of meticulous practice in order to master the sounds that he heard on Radio Luxembourg and the American records that he and his friends found—and mostly shoplifted—at Lewis's department store on the banks of the Mersey. Meanwhile, George's friendship with Paul began to blossom during their schooldays together at the Liverpool Institute. Before long, Paul was hanging out at the Harrisons' amiable home on weekends. A month after attending the Quarry Men's performance at Wilson Hall, George met up with the group at a skiffle club in West Oakhill Park. As the band looked on, George broke into a slick, note-perfect rendition of "Guitar Boogie," a relatively complicated composition that impressed the group almost immediately. He subsequently wowed them with a painstaking version of "Raunchy." Intuitively realizing that he was in the presence of a budding virtuoso, Lennon overlooked George's age and invited him into the group.

"The Quarry Men had other members," George recalled, "who didn't seem to be doing anything, so I said, 'Let's get rid of them, then I'll join'" (*Anthology* 30). George's emergence in the band quickly spelled the end for Eric Griffiths, who was dismissed when John and Paul intentionally neglected to invite him to a rehearsal, leaving Hanton to inform the guitarist about the change in personnel. Not long afterward, Len Garry contracted tubercular meningitis, and his protracted confinement led to his estrangement from the band. Only Hanton remained from Lennon's original formation of the Quarry Men, but the difference in overall quality was palpable. With John, Paul, and George as the band's trio of burgeoning guitarists, their sound had noticeably brightened, and their creative energy had blossomed like never before. Their garage-band origins were shifting, slowly but surely, into serious musical aspirations.

For this reason alone, George's membership in the Quarry Men should have been a genuine boon for the band. Yet 1958—and, indeed, the first seven months of 1959—saw the group playing only seven gigs, most of which were private parties. Two of the Quarry Men's appearances were made possible by the Harrison family, including the December 20th, 1958, wedding reception for George's brother Harry and, ten days later, a New Year's Day performance at the Wilson Club, for which George's father served as Chairman. All in all, 1958 would be a year of triumph and tragedy for the Quarry Men, a year in which John and Paul discovered themselves as songwriters, only to suffer the mind-numbing pain of inexplicable loss.

Sometime in the early spring of 1958, Paul played his first composition for John, who was now enrolled at the Liverpool College of Art, while his younger friend remained behind at the Liverpool Institute. Entitled "I Lost My Little Girl," the song was written after the death of Paul's mother. Before long, John and Paul were practicing together, often in the McCartneys' front parlor on Forthlin Road or in John's bedroom at Mendips, during every possible free moment. Paul credits Buddy Holly—one of the rare pop singers in the late 1950s who wrote and performed his own material—as the impetus for their genesis as songwriters. They would begin many of their writing sessions by identifying their latest work-in-progress as "a Lennon-McCartney original." But their pretensions didn't stop there. From their earliest days as a songwriting team, John and Paul had much bigger game in mind. As McCartney recalled: "Crediting the songs jointly to Lennon and McCartney was a decision we made early on, because we aspired to be Rodgers and Hammerstein. The only thing we knew about songwriting was that it was done by people like them, and Lerner and Loewe. We'd heard these names and associated songwriting with them, so the two-name combination sounded interesting" (*Anthology* 94). A few of their early titles included "Too Bad about the Sorrows," "Just Fun," "Thinking of Linking," "Keep Looking That Way," and "Like Dreamers Do," a number that was eventually recorded as a cover version by the Applejacks in 1964. In April, they penned "One after 909" and "I Call Your Name," considerably more effective songs, as well as highly conventional rock and roll tunes. John later described "I Call Your Name" as "one of *my* first attempts at a song" (qtd. in Dowlding 65). Over the next several months, early versions of "Love Me Do" and "I'll Follow the Sun" emerged. As Hanton remembered, "Something special was growing between them, something that went past friendship as we knew it. It was as if they drew power from each other" (qtd. in Spitz 135). Yet from their earliest days as songwriters, John and Paul also shared a competitive energy that motivated each boy's desire to one-up the other.

Having glimpsed the creative possibilities of their budding partnership throughout the spring, John and Paul quite naturally embraced the idea of cutting their first record. In June 1958, the Quarry Men—John, Paul, George, Colin, and Duff—pooled their money in order to record a demo at P. F. Phillips Professional Tape and Disk Record Service, a fancy name for a back room in the home of Percy Phillips, who had built a primitive recording studio with a Vortexion reel-to-reel tape recorder, an MSS portable disc-cutting machine, and a trio of microphones. With Phillips's assistance, the group cut a 78-RPM single. The Quarry Men had intended to record several takes in Phillips's studio, but their host was having none of it. For the bargain-basement price of seventeen shillings, they were going "straight to vinyl," which meant that they would be recording directly onto a shellac disc. It also meant that the band had to turn in flawless takes in order to get their money's worth. For their first performance on record, the Quarry Men offered a cover version of Buddy Holly's "That'll Be the Day" with John on lead vocals. The recording is distinguished by the driving force of Lennon's singing, as well as by a rollicking guitar solo from George, who receives an audible shout of encouragement from one of his bandmates to "honky tonk!"

For the record's B-side, Paul suggested that they try out an original composition, "In Spite of All the Danger," which he had written with some musical assistance from George. Composed in the style of Elvis Presley's "Trying to Get to You," "In Spite of All the Danger" was a surprisingly catchy ballad about the anxiety of newfound love, complete with a "doo-wop" backing vocal arrayed against Duff's tinkling piano. Despite its crude production, the band's first recording was a major triumph, particularly given the conditions of Phillips's studio and the haste with which they worked that day. The musicianship is undeniable, as are the energy and enthusiasm inherent in both songs. The Quarry Men agreed to share the record amongst themselves, with each member taking temporary ownership of the prize for a week at a time. John, Paul, George, and Colin duly passed the disc amongst themselves, and when the record was in Colin's custody, the drummer talked his friend Charles Roberts into playing it over the P.A. system in the lounge at Littlewood's gaming hall, where it received a surly response from the staff. The disc next alighted in the hands of Duff, who stowed it away in a linen drawer where it languished for years.[8]

June 1958 was also notable for the Quarry Men's performance at a dinner dance at St. Barnabas Hall in Penny Lane. In attendance that evening was John's mother, Julia, who, in recent months, had rekindled her relationship with her son with a fervor. They enjoyed a closeness that, for John, was rendered all the more special by her new role in his life as a treasured confidante and friend. "Between numbers she was the only person who clapped every time—and loud," Hanton remembered. "If that didn't get things going, she put her fingers in her teeth and whistled. She probably liked us just fine, but she would have done anything to encourage John" (qtd. in Spitz 144).

Yet John and Julia's renewed relationship proved to be short-lived. On the evening of July 15th, John was spending the night at Julia's house with her husband John Dykins, whom John had irreverently nicknamed as "Twitchy." Returning from visiting her sister at Mendips, Julia was hit by a car driven by Eric Clague, an off-duty police officer, as he made a sharp turn around a hedge on Menlove Avenue.[9] By the time that Mimi reached her sister, it was clear that she had perished instantly. Devastated in his grief, John turned inward and buried his pain in silent misery. "It was the worst thing that ever happened to me," John recalled years later. "I lost her twice. Once when I was moved in with my auntie. And once again at seventeen when she actually, physically died. That was very traumatic for me. That was really a hard time for me. It made me very, very bitter. The underlying chip on my shoulder that I had got really big then. Being a teenager and a rock-and-roller and an art student and my mother being killed just when I was re-establishing a relationship with her" (*Anthology* 13). Even music failed to provide a tonic for him, and he was frequently seen drowning his sorrows at Ye Cracke, a local saloon where he salved his wounds with whiskey and beer. Only Paul, it seemed, could draw John out of his stupor, arranging for sporadic gigs and rehearsals in order to rejuvenate his bewildered friend. "That became a very big bond between John and me, because he lost his mum early on, too. We both had this emotional turmoil which we had to deal with, and, being teenagers, we had to deal with it very quickly. We both understood that something had happened that you couldn't talk about—but we could laugh about it, because each of us had gone through it. . . . Occasionally, once or twice in later years, it would hit in. We'd be sitting around, and we'd have a cry together, not often, but it was good" (*Anthology* 19).

Although John and Paul continued to write songs during this period, the Quarry Men were on hiatus for much of the rest of the year, save for the sporadic gigs arranged through the auspices of George's family connections. Meanwhile, John became romantically involved with Cynthia Powell, a fellow art student. With her prim-and-proper appearance and well-mannered middle-class ways, John ridiculed Cynthia by addressing her as "Miss Powell" in an exaggerated posh London accent. After meeting at a Christmas dance in December 1958, John and Cynthia became inseparable, although John found the relationship tough going at first. Still smarting from his mother's tragic death only a few months before, John was an emotional wreck. "He wouldn't give in," she recalled. "He just fought all the time." John's Aunt Mimi surmised that her nephew was afraid of her: "Cynthia really pursued him. He would walk up the road and back until she got tired of waiting and went home" (qtd. in Badman 19). For John, a committed relationship with Cynthia was simply too much to handle. "I was hysterical," he remembered. "That was the trouble. I was jealous of anyone she had anything to do with. I demanded absolute trust from her because I wasn't trustworthy myself. I was neurotic, taking out all of my frustrations on her" (*Anthology* 14). For all of the turmoil that it wrought in his life, his romance with Cynthia also provided him with some of his fondest memories, particularly in terms of George, who idolized his much older friend and bandmate: "When George was a kid," John recalled, "he used to follow me and my first girlfriend Cynthia. We would come out of the art school together and he'd be hovering around. . . . Cyn and I would be going to a coffee shop or a movie and George would follow us down the street two hundred yards behind. Cyn would say, 'Who is that guy? What does he want?' And I'd say, 'He just wants to hang out. Should we take him with us?' She'd say, 'Oh, okay, let's take him to the bloody movies.' So we'd allow him to come to the movies with us" (qtd. in Badman 19).

By early 1959, the future of the Quarry Men had become decidedly uncertain. And after a gig at the Pavilion Theatre in Lodge Lane, the band reached its breaking point. After running through a brisk and professional first set, the group congratulated themselves with several celebratory pints. The result was disastrous, as the second set was an unmitigated drunken mess. On the way home on the bus, Paul erupted, blaming Colin for holding the band back. Pete Shotton intervened, getting off of the bus a stop early with Colin, and his drum set, in tow. And with that, Colin stepped off of the bus—and out of their lives—never seeing nor hearing from his bandmates again. For most of the rest of the year, the group drifted aimlessly. Having turned sixteen, George began working as an electrician, while John and Paul continued pursuing an academic track. At one point, George even auditioned for a spot in another band—the popular Liverpool group Rory Storm and the Hurricanes. Known for the flamboyant antics of their handsome leader Storm (born Alan Caldwell), the explosive sounds of lead guitarist Johnny "Guitar" Byrne, and the slick drumwork of Ringo Starr, the Hurricanes simply felt, as others had before them, that George was too young. After a while, George began performing with other groups, most notably, the Les Stewart Quartet.

The Quarry Men would have lapsed into the silent crevices of history were it not for Harrison's association, brief as it was, with the Les Stewart Quartet, which he had joined after being rebuffed by Rory Storm and the Hurricanes. In August 1959, George and his new bandmates were invited to be the inaugural act at Liverpudlian Mona Best's Casbah Coffee Club. Yet on August 12th, the day of the opening, Stewart and bass player Ken Brown fell into a ferocious argument after Brown had missed a rehearsal in order to help decorate the club. Stewart subsequently refused to perform that evening, and a desperate Brown asked George if he knew anyone who could take the band's place. In short order, George located John and Paul, and the Quarry Men—with Brown on bass—opened the Casbah, where they enjoyed a regular Saturday-night engagement for the foreseeable future. Their performances at the club were especially noteworthy because John and George had recently obtained electric guitars—a pair of Höfner Club 40s—with amplification courtesy of Brown's Watkins Westminster amp. But the band's run at the Casbah would be decidedly short-lived. In October, Brown was forced to miss a performance because of a bad cold. When the Quarry Men received their meager pay at the end of the night, an agitated Paul felt that Brown did not deserve his regular fifteen-shilling cut. Mona Best ignored his protestations and paid the bass player anyway. With that, John, Paul, and George gave up on Brown—and their regular engagement at the Casbah—for good.

In an attempt to rebound from their experience at the Casbah, the Quarry Men refashioned themselves as Johnny and the Moondogs and auditioned, once more, for Carroll Levis. It had been more than two years since their previous appearance before "Mr. Star-Maker," and this time they made it through two trial heats in Liverpool before trundling off to Manchester in November 1959 in order to try their luck yet again. With Paul and George on guitar—John had recently lost or sold his Höfner Club 40—the group performed Buddy Holly's "Think It Over," with John on lead vocals and Paul and George handling the harmonies, in an attempt to vie for the top prize. Forced to leave the venue in order to make the 9:47 train back to Liverpool—the group simply didn't have the money to spend the night in Manchester—Johnny and the Moondogs were long gone by the time that Levis bestowed the honors on the lucky winners. Yet the evening wasn't a total loss, as John landed another electric guitar by stealing an old, tattered cutaway job on their way out of the Manchester Hippodrome. A few days later, George replaced his Höfner Club 40 with a three-pickup Futurama electric guitar. "It was difficult to play," he later recalled, and the strings were about a "half-inch off the fingerboard. . . . but nevertheless it did look kind of futuristic" (qtd. in Babiuk 27). But the future was surely in doubt for the Quarry Men as 1959 came to a close. Their brief revival rocking the Casbah had deteriorated almost as swiftly as it had begun, leaving Johnny and the Moondogs in its highly uncertain wake.

Notes

1. The twenty-seven seconds of "Puttin' on the Style" comprise the only portion of the tape that has made its way into bootleg release. EMI purchased the Molyneux tape, which includes full-length versions of "Puttin' on the Style" and Elvis Presley's "Baby Let's Play House," in September 1994 at a Sotheby's auction for £78,500. Its poor quality likely precluded its selection for the *Anthology* CD or video releases (Winn, *Way Beyond Compare* 1).

2. In various interviews, John claims to have invited Paul to join the Quarry Men the very next day, although this narrative seems apocryphal in light of commentary from both McCartney and Shotton: "I turned 'round to him right then on first meeting and said, 'Do you want to join the group?' And he said 'yes' the next day as I recall it," John later remarked (*Anthology* 12).

3. With its powerful transmitter located in the tiny European nation of Luxembourg, Radio Luxembourg began offering French and English broadcasts in 1933 and was a forerunner of the pirate radio stations that broadcast across England and Europe via ships. Radio Luxembourg reached its influential peak in the 1950s, when it contributed to the popularization of rock and roll in Great Britain.

4. As Jerry Zolten points out, rock and roll originates from "the mass migration of African Americans from the South," which "created a nationwide market for black entertainers of all kinds. In a short time, the whole face of American pop culture would come under the sway of what Langston Hughes called 'black magic,' the alluring mass appeal of African American performance style" (17).

5. A coconut shy is a traditional English game that was often found at festivals and fêtes. To play the game, contestants throw wooden balls at a row of coconuts. If they topple one of the coconuts, players collect a prize, which was frequently the dislodged coconut itself.

6. There is considerable debate about the guitar that Paul played at the garden fête—and whether Paul played the guitar at all on that fateful day. Of the Quarry Men, Hanton, Griffiths, and Davis have no recollection of Paul performing "Twenty Flight Rock." Shotton remembered that "Paul said, 'Well I could play the guitar,' and John said, 'Well go ahead and play this one.' So Paul, being left-handed, took all the strings off and put them back the other way around." In contrast, Garry recalled that Paul brought his own guitar from home. McCartney's own memories seem much more likely—and eminently more practical: "Someone had a guitar," he remembered, but "no one would ever let me change the strings. . . . I could play a couple of songs upside down—providing they only had three chords" (qtd. in Babiuk 13).

7. For much of his life, George believed that he was born on February 25th, 1943, although he claimed in later years that family records proved that he had entered the world on the previous day at 11:50 p.m. While George's birth certificate signifies his date of birth as February 25th, as verified by the *Oxford Dictionary of National Biography* (see Rooksby), *The Beatles Anthology* conspicuously lists the guitarist's date of birth as "February 1943" in contrast with the birthdates of the other three Beatles, for whom it supplies specific days (see *Anthology* 25, 364).

8. Paul purchased the disc from Duff in 1981 for an undisclosed amount. McCartney included "In Spite of All the Danger" as part of his set list for his 2005 US tour. In his remarks before playing the song, Paul joked that "We all shared the recording. I had it for a week, John then had it for a week, then George had it for a week, then Colin had it for a week, then Duff had it for 25 years" (qtd. in Cashmere).

9. Legend has it that Clague was drunk at the time of the incident, a story that John echoes in numerous interviews (see *Anthology* 13). Clague stood trial for Julia's death, but was acquitted. As Clague recalled, "Mrs. Lennon just ran straight out in front of me. I just couldn't avoid her. I was not speeding. I swear it. It was just one of those terrible things that happen" (qtd. in Badman 18).

Chapter 3

A Cellarful of Noise

I can't remember anything
without a sadness
So deep that it hardly
becomes known to me.
—JOHN LENNON, FROM A 1961 POEM
IN A LETTER TO STU SUTCLIFFE

For John, Paul, and George, 1959 had ended almost as despondently as it had started. They were frustrated and confused by their inability to make their way in the world, yet their fortunes were about to change. In January 1960, nineteen-year-old Stuart Sutcliffe, a close friend of John's from the Liverpool College of Art, entered the Second Biennial John Moores Exhibition, and one of his works, *The Summer Painting*, was selected to hang in Liverpool's Walker Art Gallery. Indeed, Moores was so impressed with Stuart's work that he bought the painting himself for a rather lucrative £65. By this time, John, Paul, and George had been regularly practicing in Stu's Gambier Terrace flat. They got on with the talented artist famously, and John knew exactly what to do with his friend's sudden largesse: "Now [that] you've got all this money, Stu, you can buy a [bass] and join our group" (qtd. in Spitz 173). To nearly everyone's surprise, Stu took John up on his offer and purchased a sunburst Höfner 333, after making a £5 deposit, at Frank Hessy's music store.[1] Fellow student Bill Harry recalled his dismay at Stu's decision to join the band. The painter calmed his friend by explaining that he felt their music was an art form in its own right. "And anyway," Stu added, "they're going to be the greatest. I want to be a part of it" (qtd. in Spitz 174).

In February, the Quarry Men rechristened themselves as the "Beatals." Legend has it that Stu suggested the notion of beetles as a reference to the biker gang in the 1953 Marlon Brando vehicle *The Wild One*,[2] although John and Stu later claimed to have chosen the name as an homage to Buddy Holly and the Crickets, changing the spelling from Beetles to Beatals in order to connote the idea of beat music. Paul and George took an immediate liking to the new name, and the days of the Quarry Men were over. The band's future took yet another turn in March, after Eddie Cochran and Gene Vincent's triumphant performance at the Liverpool Empire Theatre. Cochran and Vincent wowed their audience with the feel and power of their amplifiers, not merely relying upon the house's P.A. system. One thing was certain: the Beatals needed amps of their own—and the sooner the better. But lacking the funds to make their dream a reality, John devised a plan via which the Liverpool College of Art would anoint the Beatals as the official college band. Meanwhile, Stu and Bill Harry, as members of the Student Union Committee, proposed that the college purchase a new P.A. system, complete with Selmer Truvoice amplifiers, for the art college dances. In this fashion, the Beatals were outfitted with top-of-the-line, eighteen-inch speakers with which to amplify their new sound. With so much volume at their disposal, they had finally become legitimate rock-and-rollers, shedding their modest skiffle origins once and for all. John, Paul, George, and Stu would never be the same again.

In April, the group gathered at Paul's home at Forthlin Road, where they recorded demos for eight songs on a Grundig reel-to-reel tape recorder that Paul had borrowed from Charles Hodgson.[3] The demos represent some of the band's earliest rehearsals with Stu, who had been struggling with the bass since joining the group. Recorded in the McCartneys' bathroom, the demos include several meandering, largely shapeless instrumentals, and the band's percussion was contributed by Paul's brother Mike. Paul's "Well Darling" offers a rudimentary attempt at merging an instrumental track with words—Lennon and McCartney can be heard improvising the lyrics, "Meanwhile, what do you think? / I think you stink like a sink" (qtd. in Winn, *Way Beyond Compare* 3). The tape includes some fifty minutes' worth of music, and while most of it is valuable simply for its historical merits alone, the instrumental "Cayenne" offers a genuinely haunting piece. The origins of the song's name are uncertain—perhaps being an homage to the capital of French Guiana, or, more likely, to the fiery hot pepper used in cooking spicy dishes. Yet the composition, with its Latin samba rhythm, reveals some intriguing guitar work, especially in the delicate counterpoint delivered by the Beatals' trio of guitarists against the tentative bass line established by Stu in the recording's extreme background.

The Beatals obviously had talent and an innate drive for originality, but what they sorely needed was direction. In the spring of 1960, the Beatals met Allan Williams, the owner of Liverpool's Jacaranda Club, where John, Paul, and Stu took to hanging out after their rehearsals at nearby Gambier Terrace. After staging the Merseyside and International Beat Show in May in collaboration with flamboyant promoter Larry Parnes, Williams had emerged as a central player on the local music scene. The Jacaranda Club had, quite suddenly, become a central hangout for a host of Liverpool bands, would-be managers, and music promoters. During this time, Brian Casser of Cass and the Casanovas happened to witness Paul singing "Tutti-Fruitti," and he couldn't believe his ears. He urged the band to obtain a drummer and to rid themselves of their "ridiculous" name in favor of a moniker that accented the band's leader. Hence, the Beatals refashioned themselves as Long John and the Silver Beetles, which they soon abridged as the Silver Beetles. Meanwhile, Casser presented them with Tommy Moore, a thirty-two-year-old Liverpudlian who worked a forklift at his day job for the Garston bottle works. At their first meeting with the stocky drummer, John, Paul, George, and Stu were put off by his age, but as soon as he got behind the drums, they found that he kept a solid beat without upstaging their frontmen. As luck would have it, only a day later Williams was given the opportunity to promote a nine-date tour of Scotland in support of singer Johnny Gentle (born George Askew). Needing an opening act, Williams offered the Silver Beetles the chance, after a hasty audition, to join the bill—which also included Ronnie Watt and the Chekkers Rock Dance Band—under the management and representation of Jacaranda Enterprises. For the first time in their career, the band had a manager, and, having borrowed the P.A. equipment from the Liverpool College of Art, they were about to embark upon their first concert tour to boot.

For the tour, the Silver Beetles, save for John and Tommy, adopted stage names. Stu dubbed himself Stuart de Staël, as an homage to Nicolas de Staël, the Russian abstract artist. Paul took the name Paul Ramon, while George called himself Carl Harrison in honor of his guitar hero, Carl Perkins. Despite its brevity, the tour was an unqualified success for the Silver Beetles, who exhibited the electrifying stage presence of seasoned veterans. While George and Tommy lingered in the shadows with Stu—who was so uncomfortable onstage that he often played with his back to the audience—John and Paul single-handedly stole the show.[4] "Those two boys operated on a different frequency," Gentle recalled. "I used to watch them work the crowd as though they'd been doing it all their lives—and without any effort other than their amazing talent. I'd never seen anything like it. They were so tapped into what each other was doing and could sense their partner's next move, they just read each other like a book" (qtd. in Spitz 190).

Although the tour left the Silver Beetles dead broke after covering their expenses, they had enjoyed a world of experiences—and more girls, rock and roll, and all-night parties than they could ever have imagined possible. In addition to being penniless, the only blemish from their sojourn in Scotland had been a car accident that left Moore badly shaken, missing several front teeth, and briefly hospitalized until John roused him from his infirmary bed and forced him to rejoin the tour. After the band's amazing first flush of success on the road, Williams booked the group for an array of summer dances on the Wirral peninsula in front of some of the fiercest audiences that the North Country had to offer. Yet their newfound momentum was dealt an unexpected blow when Moore, under pressure from his girlfriend, quit the group. The other members tracked him down to the bottle works, where he refused to climb down from a forklift in order discuss the issue any further. He had simply had it—once and for all. Echoing John's vengeful thievery in Manchester back in November, Paul absconded with Tommy's drum kit, which Moore had conveniently left in the band's care. But without a regular drummer, the Silver Beetles were forced to cancel the remaining summer dances on their docket and had to settle for a succession of down-and-out saloons instead.[5] At one point, Williams even booked them for a week at the New Cabaret Artistes Club as the backing band for a busty stripper known as "Janice."

During this period, the group officially changed the spelling of their name to the Silver Beatles to connote their beat-band origins. The band's only saving grace in July 1960 was a second round of home demo recordings in the McCartney bathroom. The sounds recorded on the Grundig were a considerable improvement over their rudimentary work back in April.[6] Seventeen demos survive, including early versions of the Lennon-McCartney compositions "One after 909," "I'll Follow the Sun," and "Hello Little Girl." The recordings also benefited from Paul's newly purchased Rosetti Solid 7 electric guitar, which punched up the band's sound considerably. In addition to an additional pair of uninspiring instrumentals, the tape also includes generally robust cover versions of several of the songs that comprised their live show during this era, including Eddie Cochran's "Hallelujah I Love Her So," Duane Eddy's "Movin' and Groovin'," Carl Perkins's "Matchbox," Fats Domino's "I Will Always Be in Love with You," Elvis Presley's "That's When Your Heartaches Begin," and Gene Vincent's "Wildcat," among others. Later that month, John and Paul dubbed themselves as the Nerk Twins for a pair of performances at the Fox and Hounds, a pub owned by Paul's cousin Elizabeth Robbins, in Caversham, Berkshire.[7]

Realizing that they had sunk to a new low after achieving so much earlier in the year, the Silver Beatles wasted no time in locating a drummer in the form of twenty-year-old Norman Chapman. Yet after a mere three gigs, Chapman was suddenly conscripted into the National Service, which exported him to Africa for a two-year tour of duty.[8] The Silver Beatles couldn't believe their run of bad luck. Things finally came to a head at the Litherland Town Hall in northern Liverpool. After the performance, a group of local toughs ambushed the Silver Beatles as they carted their equipment back to the van. A violent scuffle erupted in which Stu was furiously kicked in the head, and John subsequently sprained his wrist while attempting to ward off Stu's attackers. "There was blood all over the rug—everywhere," Stu's mother, Millie, recalled. "I was going to get the doctor but Stuart wouldn't allow me to do it. He was so terribly adamant. 'Mother,' he said, 'if you touch that phone, I'll go out of this house and you'll never see me again'" (qtd. in Norman 80).

The Silver Beatles' salvation finally came, from of all places, some seven hundred miles to the east in the port city of Hamburg, West Germany. Williams had sent another Liverpool group, the rhythm and blues combo Derry and the Seniors, to Hamburg for an extended—and highly successful—engagement at Bruno Koschmider's Kaiserkeller Club on the city's notorious Reeperbahn, a street in Hamburg's St. Pauli area, as well as the epicenter of the city's red-light district. In Germany, the Reeperbahn is known as *die sündige Meile*—or "the sinful mile." Determined to import more Liverpool bands into his fold, the diminutive Koschmider approached Williams about other acts in his managerial stable. Rory Storm and the Hurricanes were unavailable, having committed to a summer's worth of gigs at Butlin's holiday camp, while Gerry and the Pacemakers were dead-set against going abroad, leaving Williams with the Silver Beatles as his only hope for satisfying Koschmider's demands. As it turned out, John and Paul were on their last academic legs at the art college, where Lennon had missed most of his spring tutorials and McCartney had failed nearly every course himself. Yet the band still lacked a drummer, the final, necessary ingredient for embarking upon their German adventure. The answer to their problems arrived in the personage of Pete Best, Mona Best's strapping son who played regular gigs with Ken Brown's new band, the Black Jacks, at the Casbah, where the Silver Beatles had been hanging out of late. Pete was born on November 24th, 1941, in Madras, India, where his father, John, served as an army athletic training instructor. They returned to England in 1944, eventually settling into a spacious home in Liverpool's West Derby district. With a two-month booking at Koschmider's Indra Club in the offing, Paul wasted little time inviting Pete— along with his brand new set of Premier drums—to join the group. After a hasty audition on August 12th that he couldn't possibly have failed, Pete was offered membership in the band, provided, that is, that he was willing to go abroad—and soon. In the process, the group dropped "Silver" from their name and settled, once and for all, upon the Beatles as their handle.

Within four days, they were on the road to Hamburg, traveling with Williams's equipment-laden van by ferry across the North Sea to Holland.

During a brief stopover in Arnhem, John shoplifted a mouth organ. Before beginning the final leg of their travels across Europe to Hamburg, the group paused for a photograph taken by Williams's brother-in-law Barry Chang. Sitting around a World War II memorial, the Beatles—save for John, who couldn't be bothered to get out of the van—famously posed in front of the monument's epitaph, "Their names liveth for ever more." They arrived in Hamburg at dusk on August 17th. Having been assigned quarters behind the tainted-yellow screen at the decrepit Bambi-Filmkunsttheater (the "Bambi Kino" for short), their living conditions were simply putrid. As it turned out, the Indra Club was hardly much better. A former strip joint, the Indra had only recently been transformed into a rock and roll club by Koschmider. The Beatles' contract called for five four-and-a-half-hour weekday evening performances, as well as for six hours on Saturday and Sunday, respectively. Their contract also prohibited them from performing at any other venue within a twenty-five-mile radius without Koschmider's express consent. It was during this period—in the midst of the fear and excitement of hedonistic Hamburg—that the band fashioned their famous rallying cry. Inspired by a scene in *Blackboard Jungle* (1955), Lennon recalled that "I would yell out, 'Where are we going, fellows?' They would say, 'To the top, Johnny,' in pseudo-American voices. And I would say, 'Where is that, fellows?' And they would say, 'To the toppermost of the poppermost!'" (*All We Are Saying* 159).

In early October, Koschmider closed the Indra, which was too slatternly for its own good, and transferred the Beatles to the Kaiserkeller. With its rotting stage and its rough clientele, it was only marginally better than the Indra. When the Beatles began to flag after their lengthy evening gigs, Koschmider would encourage them to "Mach schau!"—or to "Make show!" in his broken English. The band—which had taken to swilling beer onstage in combination with the multicolored amphetamine Preludin pills, or "Prellies," that they ingested, save for Pete, to stay awake—responded by evolving a bizarre stage act that included a goose-stepping John, who wore swastikas, shouted "Sieg Heil!" and castigated the audience as a bunch of "fucking Nazis" (qtd. in Lewisohn, *The Beatles Live!* 39).

At the beginning of October, Derry and the Seniors were replaced by Rory Storm and the Hurricanes, and on October 15th, the Beatles made their second record—this time at a tiny Hamburg studio known as the Akustik. In reality, it was nothing more than a private office on the fifth floor of the Klockmann House building in central Hamburg, but the Beatles didn't mind. Joined by two members of the Hurricanes—bassist Lou Walters (born Walter Eymond) and drummer Ringo Starr, who stood in for an absent Pete Best—John, Paul, and George recorded a cover version of George Gershwin's "Summertime," which was subsequently cut as a 78-RPM disc. Meanwhile, Stu had developed a fast friendship with Klaus Voormann, who talked his former girl-friend, artist and photographer Astrid Kirchherr, into visiting the Kaiserkeller to see the Beatles in action. "I fell in love with Stuart that very first night," she remembered. "He was so tiny but perfect, every feature. So pale, but very very beautiful. He was like a character from a story by Edgar Allan Poe" (qtd. in Norman 97). In the coming weeks, Astrid photographed the band in a variety of poses and in a range of locales, but most of her pictures capture Stu, with his ubiquitous sunglasses, shrouded in silence and mystery. Within two months, Stu and Astrid were engaged, much to his family's chagrin. The cou-ple's affection for each other was palpable, but Stu's newfound love was inter-rupted, as time went on, by intense seizures, as well as by paralyzing headaches that left him in a state of utter agony until the pain would finally cease.

Meanwhile, Koschmider's local rival, Peter Eckhorn, had begun luring stage acts away from the Kaiserkeller. In November 1960, the Beatles followed suit by defecting to Eckhorn's Top Ten Club. As they prepared to play the Top Ten, though, the police—perhaps at Koschmider's vengeful urging—inspected Harrison's passport and deported the seventeen-year-old for being ineligible to obtain a work permit. After a few evenings in Eckhorn's employ, Paul and Pete decided to sneak back to the Bambi Kino in order to retrieve the belong-ings that they had left behind in their haste to escape the Kaiserkeller. As a farewell prank, Paul and Pete set fire to a condom and accidentally ignited the rotting tapestry in their quarters behind the cinema. Although the fire quickly extinguished itself in the dampness of the walls, Paul and Pete were arrested and deported from the country in short order. Within a fortnight, John began his own journey by train back to Liverpool, while Stu, with the financial assis-tance of Astrid's family, took a return flight to England in February 1961. His days with the Beatles, it seemed, were numbered. By mid-March, Stu had rejoined Astrid in Hamburg, having made plans to attend the city's prestigious State College of Art.

Back in Liverpool, John, Paul, George, and Pete regrouped in late Decem-ber to play a series of dates at the Casbah. A December 27th, 1960, perform-ance at the Litherland Town Hall proved to be a significant turning point in the Beatles' career. Having been billed by DJ Bob Wooler as "Direct from Hamburg!" the Beatles offered up a searing performance—accented by John's acquisition of a 1958 Rickenbacker Capri 325 electric guitar, with its trade-mark scaled-down neck, back in Hamburg in November. The audience included Mona Best, her son Rory, accounting student Neil Aspinall, and pro-moter Brian Kelly. With Chas Newby standing in on bass for Stu, the concert began with Paul exploding into a powerful rendition of "Long Tall Sally."

"Everyone—the whole lot—surged forward towards the stage," Kelly remembered. "The dance floor behind was completely empty. 'Aye, aye,' I said to myself. 'I could have got twice the numbers in here'" (qtd. in Norman 106).

Quite suddenly, the Beatles had taken Merseyside by storm with their energizing and highly professional post-Hamburg stage act. "It was that evening that we really came out of our shell and let go," John recalled. "This was when we began to think for the first time that we were good" (qtd. in Badman 29). With prodding from Mona Best and with the assistance of Wooler's local connections on the music scene, Ray McFall, the new owner of the Cavern Club, was persuaded to allow the Beatles to return to the tiny stage in the cellar below Matthew Street. Meanwhile, Kelly quickly booked the group for some thirty-six dances over the next few months. By January 1961, Newby returned to his studies in college, leaving the band without a bass player once again. Paul filled the void, initially borrowing Stu's Höfner 333, which he played upside down, before taking up a Solid 7 model. "None of us wanted to be the bass player," Paul remembered. "It wasn't the number-one job: we wanted to be up front. In our minds, it was the fat guy in the group who nearly always played the bass, and he stood at the back. None of us wanted that; we wanted to be up front singing, looking good, to pull the birds" (qtd. in Babiuk 45). For some time, Paul didn't even plug his bass in, slyly depositing the guitar lead in his pocket while he learned the instrument. During the band's next trip to Hamburg, Paul purchased a custom-made, left-handed Höfner 500/1 bass—the violin-shaped instrument with which he is most often associated.

When the band returned to Hamburg for a fourteen-week engagement at the Top Ten Club in April, they decided effectively to end their relationship with Williams by denying him his commission. Williams was understandably infuriated by what he perceived to be a decidedly underhanded move, but the Beatles—still smarting over the incident with Brown back at the Casbah in October 1959—weren't about to pay *anyone* who hadn't worked materially toward the group's success. Ensconced once again at the Top Ten Club, the band played numerous shows with fellow Briton Tony Sheridan (born Andrew Esmond Sheridan McGinnity), a skilled guitarist and vocalist who was known as "The Teacher" amongst his fellow expatriates. "It was great being out there with Tony Sheridan," Ringo recalled. "I was there in 1962 backing him with Roy Young [on piano] and Lou Walters on bass. It was all very exciting. Tony was really volatile. If anyone in the club was talking to his girl, he'd be punching and kicking all over the place, while we'd just keep on jamming. Then he'd come back and join us, covered in blood if he'd lost. But he was a really good player" (*Anthology* 58). For the time being, Stu was temporarily back in the fold, even boldly venturing into the spotlight to sing Elvis Presley's "Love Me

Tender." Initially, he was the talk of the Reeperbahn for his innovative haircut. Astrid had apparently persuaded Stu to change his hairstyle to a "French cut" by shaping his locks to lie atop his forehead rather than towering above it, Teddy Boy style. Although they made fun of him relentlessly, John, Paul, and George eventually followed suit, and the so-called Beatle haircut was born.[9] As it turned out, the last straw in the band's relationship with Stu was Paul, with whom a feud had been simmering for quite some time. Paul had long been critical of Stu's bass playing, and, according to Paul's girlfriend Dot Rhone, "he was jealous of Stu, especially of Stu's friendship with John" (qtd. in Spitz 247). Things came to a head, of all places, on stage, when Stu threw down his bass in the middle of a song and leapt at Paul. The dye had been cast, and within a week Stu informed the others that he was leaving the band.

The Beatles' next opportunity to venture into a recording studio came at the bidding of German bandleader Bert Kämpfert, who caught their act with Sheridan at the Top Ten Club. He subsequently offered Sheridan a contract with Polydor Records and signed up the Beatles as his backup band. For Sheridan's recordings, the Beatles temporarily refashioned themselves as the Beat Brothers. In German slang, *Pidels*, which sounds a lot like *Beatles*, is the plural form of penis. It was a connotation that Kämpfert was entirely unwilling to risk. The three-day session took place in late June 1961, and despite working as Sheridan's supporting act, John, Paul, George, and Pete were thrilled to be making a record—*any* record. For the A-side of Sheridan's single, they recorded a rollicking version of the traditional standard "My Bonnie (Lies over the Ocean)," with George on lead guitar and harmonies by John, Paul, and George. For the B-side, they recorded yet another standard, "When the Saints Go Marching In." To their great delight, they were also allowed to record "Cry for a Shadow," an instrumental that George and John, with his whammy bar in full force, had composed as a parody of the work of Cliff Richard and the Shadows, who were enjoying enormous success in Great Britain at the time. On the final day of the sessions, Sheridan offered renditions of Jimmy Reed's "Take Out Some Insurance on Me Baby" and Hank Snow's "Nobody's Child." For the Beatles, though, the highlight was their own recording of "Ain't She Sweet," which featured a kinetic lead vocal performance from John.

Having just completed a highly successful engagement in Hamburg and energized by their first experience in a professional recording studio, the band was poised for bigger and better things—and Liverpool was ready to welcome the boys home with open arms. Upon their return, an Astrid Kirchherr photograph of the band was featured on the cover of the second issue of Bill Harry's *Mersey Beat*. Their popularity led to numerous cover stories thereafter, including the famous issue in which Harry entreated John to explain the genesis of the Beatles' name: "It came in a vision," John wrote in a July 1961 *Mersey Beat* article entitled "Being a Short Diversion on the Dubious Origins of Beatles." "A man appeared in a flaming pie and said unto them, 'From this day on you are Beatles with an A.' 'Thank you, Mister Man,' they said, 'thanking him.'"[10] While John's attempt at fashioning one of the Beatles' legends was purely comical in its origins, by the summer of 1961 they had established themselves as a bona fide North Country phenomenon. By this juncture, Neil Aspinall had joined the band as their first roadie, transporting their equipment to and from each venue in his Commer van and setting it up and dismantling it for each performance. On August 18th, Ringo Starr sat in for Pete yet again. "One day, Pete Best went sick," Ringo recalled. "A car came for me and the driver asked if I would play drums for the Beatles at a lunchtime session down at the Cavern. What a laugh it turned out to be. We all knew the same numbers, but we did them differently. I didn't fit in well at first" (qtd. in Badman 33).[11] Over the course of the next few years, the Beatles settled in for more than 280 performances at the Cavern, the springboard from which they finally made their name—at least in the region. In the summer of 1961, George changed guitars yet again—this time, retiring his Futurama and buying a Gretsch Duo-Jet, complete with a Bigsby vibrato bar.

August 1961 also saw the Polydor release of the 45-RPM single "My Bonnie" b/w "The Saints," credited, as promised by Kämpfert, to Tony Sheridan and the Beat Brothers. The song eventually earned the fifth spot on the West German charts and sold more than one hundred thousand copies. "My Bonnie" quickly made its way, along with the man on the flaming pie, into the Beatles' growing legend. On October 28th, 1961, a patron named Raymond Jones reportedly entered NEMS (North End Music Stores)—the largest record outlet in Liverpool and throughout the North Country—and requested a copy of the Beatles' "My Bonnie" from the store's owner, twenty-seven-year-old Brian Epstein.

∼

Born to Harry and Malka "Queenie" Epstein on September 19th, 1934, Brian Samuel Epstein operated two NEMS outlets in Liverpool, including stores on Great Charlotte Street and Whitechapel, the latter of which was less than two hundred yards away from the Cavern Club. Epstein had been educated at a succession of schools before settling upon Wrekin College in Shropshire. In 1950, Brian entered the business world as a furniture salesman in his father Harry's prosperous department store on Walton Road. After a stint in the National Service, Brian returned to Liverpool, and Harry subsequently assigned his son to manage the record department.[12] With his wide-ranging knowledge of classical music, Brian transformed it into a profitable business in short order. Yet to his parents' great chagrin, he decided to leave Liverpool in order to pursue an actor's life at London's Royal Academy of Dramatic Art (RADA). After dropping out of the RADA in his third term, he returned to his hometown once again. His indefatigable father then opened Clarendon Furnishings, an upscale furniture store on the Wirral peninsula, and installed Brian as manager. In 1958, Harry decided to capitalize on the booming record business by opening up the NEMS store at Great Charlotte Street under Brian's management. Although his early years had been distinguished by a general inability to fit in—he was homosexual, which was criminalized in Great Britain at the time—Epstein had proved highly adept at consolidating NEMS's success, and within a few years, he was in charge of the family's entire record operation.[13] With the August 3rd, 1961, issue of *Mersey Beat*, Epstein had even begun authoring a regular column entitled "Record Releases by Brian Epstein of NEMS."

In his autobiography *A Cellarful of Noise* (1964), Brian claims to have been unfamiliar with the Beatles before Jones's visit on that fateful day: "The name 'Beatle' meant nothing to me though I vaguely recalled seeing it on a poster advertising a university dance at New Brighton Tower, and I remembered thinking it was an odd and purposeless spelling" (94–95). Given his association with *Mersey Beat*—and its regular cover stories about the band—it is doubtful that the Beatles had so thoroughly eluded his notice.[14] In any event, on November 9th, he attended a lunchtime performance by the group at the Cavern in the company of his assistant manager at NEMS, Alistair Taylor. They descended into the cellar, where the club's DJ, Bob Wooler, announced that Mr. Brian Epstein of NEMS was in attendance. Mesmerized by their performance, Epstein met with the Beatles backstage, where he was greeted by George: "Hello there. What brings Mr. Epstein here?" As with so many others who encountered the group, Epstein enjoyed their charm and good humor. But more importantly, he was impressed with the reaction that they garnered from the kids in the audience. "They gave a captivating and honest show and they had very considerable magnetism," he wrote in his autobiography. "I loved their ad-libs and I was fascinated by this, to me, new music with its pounding bass beat and its vast engulfing sound" (98–99).

Even as he walked away from the Cavern that day, Epstein was already thinking about managing the band. After an initial meeting on December 3rd with the group—sans Paul, who was allegedly at home taking a bath—Epstein began to make inquiries about the Beatles. Not surprisingly, Allan Williams warned him about what he believed to be the band's lack of ethics. "I wouldn't touch 'em with a fucking barge pole," he told Epstein (qtd. in Spitz 274). But

Brian was once and truly hooked, and at a meeting on December 10th, the Beatles accepted Epstein as their manager. They signed a formal, five-year contract with him on January 24th, 1962, at Pete Best's house. Epstein pointedly declined to sign the contract in order to allow his clients to withdraw from the agreement at any time. Over the next few months, he entreated the band to improve their demeanor on stage—no more swearing, no more eating between songs. For his part, he ensured that their regular fee at the Cavern Club was doubled, and he vowed, more importantly, to win them a record deal with a major label. Without missing a beat, Brian began expanding his contacts throughout the music world. To this end, Epstein had played "My Bonnie" for Ron White, the Marketing Manager for the monolithic EMI (Electric and Musical Industries), as well as to Tony Barrow, the *Liverpool Echo*'s music reporter who also served as a publicity representative for Decca Records. Brian was known for the brash confidence that he brought to such meetings, often touting the Beatles' destiny as being "bigger than Elvis." For his part, Barrow contacted Dick Rowe, Decca's chief A&R (Artists and Repertoire) man, and Rowe dispatched one of his producers, Mike Smith, to Liverpool. On December 13th, Smith visited the Cavern and was duly impressed with the energy and charisma inherent in the Beatles' performance. Later that evening, Smith told Epstein that "we've got to have them down for a bash in the studio at once. Let's see what they can do" (qtd. in Spitz 285).

On New Year's Eve, the Beatles made the nine-hour trek to London in a driving snowstorm. Just before 11 o'clock in the morning of Monday, January 1st, 1962, the band members, understandably nervous and grumpy, arrived at Decca's Russell Square recording studios. They performed fifteen songs for the label's consideration, including several staples from their stage act—"Till There Was You," "The Sheik of Araby," "Three Cool Cats," and "Besame Mucho"—as well as three original numbers, including "Like Dreamers Do," "Hello Little Girl," and "Love of the Loved." As Lennon later reported, "I remember when we made our first recording. We didn't sound natural. Paul sang 'Till There Was You' and he sounded like a woman. I sang 'Money,' and I sounded like a madman. By the time we made our demos of 'Hello Little Girl' and 'Love of the Loved,' we were okay, I think" (qtd. in Winn, *Way Beyond Compare* 7). Yet, for all of their concern and unease, Smith seemed pleased with their performance. "I can't see any problems," he told them as they left the studio. "You should record" (qtd. in Spitz 287).

Yet, to everyone's surprise, EMI's Ron White sent his formal rejection of the band in mid-January, asserting that the label already had plenty of vocal groups under contract at the time. Finally, on February 1st, Dick Rowe offered Decca's response, curtly reporting that "groups with guitars are on the way out." Besides which, Rowe added, the Beatles "sound too much like the Shadows" (qtd. in Spitz 293). In a symbolic gesture that demonstrated their increasing estrangement from their drummer, the other Beatles didn't bother to inform Pete about the Decca rejection for several days. But the Decca saga was hardly over. Fearing that Decca would lose their precious retail record contracts with NEMS, Rowe turned up at the Cavern on February 3rd in order to hear the band for himself. Rowe arrived in Liverpool during a deluge, and when he finally reached the club's entrance, he couldn't make his way through the throng of kids packing themselves into the Cavern's sweaty archways to see the Beatles. Rowe returned to London, where, several days later, he met with Epstein yet again in order to assuage the manager, who felt as though he had been slighted by the music conglomerate. "You have a good record business in Liverpool," Rowe told him. "Stick to that" (qtd. in Spitz 294).[15] Having now been rejected by EMI and Decca, as well as by two other major British record firms, Pye and Philips, Epstein was crestfallen as he left Decca House. With nothing to lose, he sought out Bob Boast, who managed London's HMV record store on Oxford Street. Although Boast was unimpressed with the Decca audition tapes, he suggested that Epstein cut an acetate of the best tracks in order to present his product more effectively to the city's A&R men. While Brian waited, sound engineer Jim Foy cut the acetate in the studio below the HMV. Liking what he heard, Foy introduced Brian to Sid Colman, who worked as the General Manager of Ardmore and Beechwood, the influential London music publisher. As with the HMV, Ardmore and Beechwood were members of the EMI corporate family, and Colman felt that it was in the company's best interest to avoid losing the Beatles to their competitors. Recognizing that few, if any, of the EMI in-house producers would be willing to take on the Beatles, Colman directed Epstein to George Martin at Parlophone, the bottom of the proverbial barrel amongst EMI's numerous subsidiary labels.

∽

At first glance, Martin's partnership with the Beatles would seem like an unlikely pairing; the classically trained, thirty-six-year-old producer would appear to have little in common with four Liverpool Scousers. Born on January 3rd, 1926, in Holloway, North London, Martin taught himself to play piano in his youth. By the age of sixteen, he was an active member of his school's dance band. During World War II, he served in the British Navy's aviation unit, where he achieved the rank of Lieutenant. Paul credits Martin's military service with the leadership abilities that would assist the producer in shaping the Beatles as his musical protégés: "I think that's where George got his excellent bedside manner. He'd dealt with navigators and pilots. He could deal with us when we got out of line" (qtd. in Houston). In 1947, Martin enrolled in London's Guildhall School of Music, where he specialized in piano and oboe and pursued his studies in composition and classical music orchestration.

After graduating in 1950, the twenty-four-year-old Martin landed his first job at the BBC Music Library before finding employment at the EMI Group's Parlophone Records, where he worked as an assistant for company head Oscar Preuss. Parlophone had been founded in Germany by the Carl Lindstrom Company before the outbreak of the First World War. In 1923, the British division of Parlophone was created under the leadership of Preuss, who served as the branch's first A&R manager. During the label's early years, Preuss established Parlophone as one of the United Kingdom's most successful jazz labels. Parlophone's association with EMI finds its roots in the Columbia Graphophone Company, which had purchased a controlling interest in the Carl Lindstrom Company in 1927. Four years later, Columbia Graphophone merged with the Gramophone Company, one of the UK's oldest recording firms, and EMI was born. At Parlophone, Martin's initial responsibilities included managing the label's catalogue of classical recordings. In 1955, Preuss retired, and Martin was appointed as head of the label at the relatively youthful age of twenty-nine. In the ensuing years, Martin served as producer for a variety of artists, ranging from Cleo Laine and Stan Getz to Humphrey Lyttelton and Judy Garland. He also made a name for himself producing a number of popular comedy records by such luminaries as Peter Ustinov, Peter Cook, Dudley Moore, and Spike Mulligan and Harry Secombe's Goons. Martin scored his most impressive sales, at least in terms of comedy, through his work with Peter Sellers, who emerged, with his strange array of characters and verbal machinations, as a bona fide star. Quite suddenly, Parlophone was making a name for itself—and generating significant profits for their parent company in the process. "We had gone from being known as a sad little company," remarked Parlophone producer Ron Richards, "to making a mint of money" (qtd. in Spitz 297). Nevertheless, Parlophone had scored only a single top-ten hit under Martin's tutelage—a comedy selection by the Temperance Seven entitled "Stop, You're Driving Me Crazy." In the early 1960s, Martin—having tired of Parlophone's lowly place on the EMI food chain in spite of its spate of recent successes on the comedy charts—planned to expand the label's catalogue by venturing into the evolving world of pop music.

With absolutely nothing to lose, Epstein made an appointment to meet Martin on February 13th, the day after making the acetate at the HMV. The manager delivered his usual bombastic pitches about the Beatles—that they would be "bigger than Elvis," that they were poised to conquer the world—

before offering Martin a sampling of the Decca sessions. For the most part, Martin was unmoved. Yet he found himself impressed with Paul's voice, an occasional harmony, and some of the boys' guitar work. "There was an unusual quality—a certain roughness," Martin recalled. "I thought to myself, 'There might *just* be something there'" (qtd. in Norman 153). But he wasn't willing to stake his reputation on the band without having properly auditioned them. "It's *interesting*," he told Brian, "but I can't offer you any kind of deal on this basis. I must see them and meet them. Bring them down to London, and I'll work with them in the studio" (qtd. in Spitz 301). For the time being, Brian decided to forgo Martin's offer. He was determined to present the band with a recording contract—particularly after the disappointment that they had experienced after being rejected so soundly by Decca. With that, Brian resolved to continue working the London record labels.

While he had yet to land a record deal, the Beatles' new manager possessed an innate sense about how to repackage the group for the wide world beyond Liverpool and the North Country. Ridding them of their notoriously unkempt hair and their leather jackets and blue jeans, he re-styled the band's image with more exacting grooming and brand new suits. They introduced their new look before a live audience on March 7th, 1962, at Manchester's Playhouse Theatre, where they were recorded in concert for their radio debut on the BBC program *Teenager's Turn: Here We Go*.[16] "Brian was trying to clean our image up," Lennon recalled. "He said we'd never get past the door of a good place. He'd tell us that jeans were not particularly smart, and could we possibly manage to wear proper trousers? He didn't want us suddenly looking square. He let us have our own sense of individuality. We stopped chomping at cheese rolls and jam butties on stage. We paid a lot more attention to what we were doing, did our best to be on time, and we smartened up, in the sense that we wore suits instead of any sloppy old clothes" (qtd. in Babiuk 62). Brian also proceeded to ban Cynthia and Dot—John and Paul's longtime girlfriends—from attending the band's performances because he was afraid that their female fans would become alienated if their idols were perceived as being romantically unavailable.

The Manchester show turned out to be a smashing success. Buoyed by the prospect of being broadcast on the BBC, the Beatles attacked each number with raw power and enthusiasm. As a gesture to their fans, Brian had talked the Beatles into riding the bus back home with the Liverpool faithful. After crossing the parking lot and boarding the motor coach, John, Paul, and George watched in silence as a throng of girls mobbed Pete—always a fan favorite for his moody good looks—in their wake. When Pete finally boarded the bus, Paul's father, Jim, angrily rebuked the drummer for having upstaged his bandmates. The growing distance between Pete and the other members of the group was as palpable as ever. Meanwhile, the Beatles were scheduled to return to Hamburg for an April–May 1962 engagement at the Star-Club, a brand-spanking new venue on the Reeperbahn, where the dance floor alone could accommodate nearly one thousand people. Yet their visit was marred from the outset by an unexpected tragedy. Astrid met their plane on April 11th and reported that Stu had died of a brain hemorrhage the day before, after complaining for months on end about a relentless series of headaches.[17] The Beatles—particularly John—were devastated by the news. John spent much of their seven-week engagement working out his grief and sorrow in an alcohol- and speed-driven barrage of fistfights. His stage antics reached new levels of madness. At one juncture, he punctuated his Nazi goose-stepping act—with its "Sieg Heil!" salutes—by parading across the stage clad only in his under- wear with a toilet seat resting about his neck. For all of John's exploits, the band continued to hone an exciting live show that swelled with a selection of new numbers—Ritchie Barrett's "Some Other Guy," the Marvelettes' "Please Mr. Postman," the Shirelles' "Baby It's You," and Smokey Robinson and the Miracles' "You Really Got a Hold on Me," among a host of others. At one point during their visit to Hamburg, Epstein invited pianist Roy Young to be the fifth member of the Beatles, although he ultimately declined: "I looked at my position. I had a three-year contract with a car written into it, everything that people would love to have, I had it all there. I was making great money, and I think up until then the Beatles weren't making much money. Not that money was the only reason, we all loved to play" (qtd. in Babiuk 65).

There could be little doubt that Epstein knew how much the Beatles loved to play, but he also knew how distraught they had become about taking the next big step in their careers. By the time that he returned to England, Epstein had become absolutely desperate to prove himself to his clients—especially Paul, who intimidated Brian to no end. On May 9th, he made one last effort to win a contract from Parlophone. During a morning appointment with Martin at EMI Studios in St. John's Wood, London, Epstein toned down the overcon- fident approach that he had employed back in February. To Brian's genuine surprise, Martin agreed to provide the Beatles with a recording contract with- out having met them, much less auditioned them. In truth, the contract sad- dled EMI with very little in the way of risk—the Beatles' contract would only become binding if Martin was satisfied with the audition; otherwise, it wasn't worth the paper upon which it was printed. But Epstein was ecstatic. After arranging for the Beatles' audition at EMI Studios on June 6th, he telegrammed the Beatles in Germany: "Congratulations, boys. EMI request recording session. Rehearse new material." He posted a second message to the

Mersey Beat that same day in which he announced that the Beatles had secured a recording contract from Parlophone. In both instances, he neglected to account for the extremely provisional nature of the agreement with Martin.[18] As Elvis Costello notes, the Beatles, with their North Country roots, were fortunate to have a contract—*any* contract—at all: "The fact that four young musicians from Liverpool were assigned to the EMI comedy imprint, Parlophone, and the staff producer responsible for the comedy output, gives us a glimpse of a number of casual regional assumptions and the hierarchies of early '60s England" (x). But no matter: the Beatles' sojourn to Hamburg had begun with tragedy, yet it had seemingly ended—finally—with the makings of a very lucky break.

Notes

1. Stu's bass is often incorrectly identified as a Höfner President. Sales records from Frank Hessy's music store indicate that it was a Höfner 333 (Babiuk 30).

2. In *The Wild One*, Chino (Lee Marvin) refers to the Beetles, an all-girl biker gang in the film, while pleading with Johnny Strabler (Brando): "You know I miss you. Ever since the club split up, I miss you. We all missed you. . . . The Beetles missed you. All the Beetles missed you. Come on Johnny, let's you and me go inside and have a beer." In his editorial note for Lennon's *Mersey Beat* article "Being a Short Diversion on the Dubious Origins of Beatles," Bill Harry argues that *The Wild One* couldn't possibly have acted as an influence for the group's name because the "movie was banned in Britain until the mid-1960s, and the Beatles never saw it in those early days."

3. Known as the "Kirchherr Tape," the surviving copy of the April 1960 recordings was given by Stu to his fiancée Astrid Kirchherr. In 1994, she presented it to George (see Winn, *Way Beyond Compare* 3).

4. While Beatles folklore attributes Stu's stage posture—playing either sideways or with his back to the audience—to shyness, Paul alleges that, in truth, the bassist, and his bandmates, didn't want anyone to realize that he couldn't play his guitar properly. "We sometimes used to tell him to turn away when we were doing pictures because he sometimes wasn't in the same key we were in. We always used to look. I still do. . . . That was one of the things we loved about guys in the audience. The girls would look at us, the guys would look at the chords" (qtd. in Babiuk 29).

5. Babiuk alleges that McCartney briefly assumed the role of drummer for the Silver Beatles after Moore quit the band. By June, though, the experiment had apparently run its course, when he replaced his Zenith with a Rosetti Solid 7 (32).

6. Known as the "Braun Tape," the recordings survived in the possession of Hans-Walther "Icke" Braun, one of the band's Hamburg friends, who was entrusted with the tape in the spring of 1961 (see Winn, *Way Beyond Compare* 4).

7. When they were children, Paul and his brother Mike occasionally performed before their relatives as the Nerk Twins. Years later, Mike performed under the stage

name Michael McGear, and he enjoyed a number of hit singles in the UK with the Scaffold, a trio that included McGear, Roger McGough, and John Gorman.

8. Enacted in 1939, the National Service ended on December 31st, 1960, thus sparing any of the Beatles from mandatory conscription.

9. According to Kirchherr, "All that shit that people said, that I created their hairstyle, that's rubbish! Lots of German boys had that hairstyle. Stuart had it for a long while and the others copied it" (qtd. in Badman 34). Jürgen Vollmer was in fact responsible for creating the Beatles' haircut. A German photographer whom they had met in Hamburg in 1960, Vollmer first shaped John and Paul's distinctive hairstyles a year later in Paris, where the duo had traveled in order to celebrate John's twenty-first birthday. As Vollmer remembered, "John and Paul visited me and decided to have their hair like mine. A lot of French youth wore it that way. I gave both of them their first Beatle haircut in my hotel room on the Left Bank" (qtd. in Miles 77).

10. In May 1997, McCartney released a studio album entitled *Flaming Pie*. In the title track, he alludes to Lennon's fabrication, proclaiming that "I'm the man on the flaming pie."

11. As fate would have it, Ringo later worked as Pete's substitute on February 5th, 1962, when the drummer became ill and was forced to miss a lunchtime session at the Cavern and an evening performance at Southport's Kingsway Club.

12. Brian only completed half of his two-year term in the National Service. At one point, he was charged with impersonating an officer after being saluted, incorrectly, by a sentry. As a result, he was confined to barracks and later discharged on "medical grounds."

13. Brian's homosexuality forced him to lead a double-life. Given his elite social status in Liverpool, he was often the target of blackmailers and consequently enjoyed few genuinely happy love affairs. As Philip Norman points out, Brian was "attracted to what homosexuals call the rough trade—to the dockers and laborers of whom their kind go in greatest mortal terror. Those who sought the rough trade in Liverpool in 1957 paid a high price, even in that currency of damnation. Rebuffed or accepted, they still went in fear. If there were not a beating up, then there would probably, later on, be extortion and blackmail" (132).

14. In addition to the *Mersey Beat*'s lavish attention upon the band, the Beatles were featured on numerous posters throughout Epstein's record stores. As Bill Harry pointed out, "He would have had to have been blind—or ignorant—not to have noticed their name" (qtd. in Spitz 266). A number of music historians have gone so far as to suggest that Epstein manufactured Raymond Jones out of thin air (see Lewisohn, *The Complete Beatles Chronicle* 34). Yet in Epstein's defense, Spencer Leigh recently located the elusive Raymond Jones, now retired and living in Spain. As Jones remarked, "No one will ever take away from me that it was me who spoke to Brian Epstein and then he went to the Cavern to see [the Beatles] for himself" (qtd. in Leigh, "Nowhere Man?" 21).

15. Mark Lewisohn contends that Decca's decision may have had its roots in geography. It turns out that Mike Smith auditioned two groups on January 1st, 1962, the

Beatles and Brian Poole and the Tremeloes, but Rowe only allowed Smith to sign one of the bands: Smith "chose the latter group," Lewisohn writes, "not because they were more promising but purely and simply because they were based in Barking, just eight miles from his office. They would be far easier, and cheaper, to work with than a group based 200 miles away. So Decca Records let the Beatles go, and, more than coinciden- tally, began their slide into oblivion" (*The Beatles Live!* 91–92).

16. The band had auditioned less than a month before at the Playhouse Theatre before BBC staff producer Peter Pilbeam on February 12th. Pilbeam offered a curt response to the Beatles' vocal potential: "Paul McCartney: NO; John Lennon: YES" (qtd. in Winn, *Way Beyond Compare* 8).

17. It is an accepted fact among many Beatles scholars that Stu's untimely death was related to the head injuries that he sustained during the scuffle in the Litherland Hall parking lot. The autopsy declared the official cause of death as "cerebral paralysis due to bleeding into the right ventricle of the brain" (qtd. in Harry, *The Ultimate Beatles Encyclopedia* 638).

18. Lewisohn's meticulous research has unearthed an EMI "red form" indicating that the Beatles were already under contract—and, hence, not required to audition during a so-called "artist test"—at the June 6th session. When confronted with the evidence by Lewisohn, Martin refused to reconsider the circumstances of his first meeting with the Beatles: "Why on earth would I have signed a group before I even saw them? I would never have done that, it's preposterous" (qtd. in Lewisohn, "The Day of Reckoning" 46). Yet additional testimony from Ken Townshend underscores Lewisohn's conclusion: "The difference between an artist test and a commercial test is that the former are not paid to undertake the test," Townshend recalled, "but the Beatles were paid official MU (Musicians Union] rates for that session" (qtd. in Ryan and Kehew 346).

Chapter 4

And the Band Begins to Play

Before they walked in, I thought to myself,
"Well, here comes another nothing group."
—NORMAN SMITH, EMI SOUND ENGINEER

On Wednesday, June 6th, 1962, the Beatles—with Neil Aspinall behind the wheel of his trusty van—made their circuitous way to 3 Abbey Road, the august address of EMI Studios.[1] They had difficultly locating the facility at first—nestled, as it is, amongst the stately Edwardian homes of London's St. John's Wood. Built in 1830 as a luxurious residence that included five reception rooms, nine bedrooms, a wine cellar, a substantial garden, and servants quarters, the home was purchased by the Gramophone Company in 1929. It officially opened its doors in November 1931—scant months after Columbia Graphophone had merged with the Gramophone Company and formed the EMI Group. In the early 1930s, English composer Edward Elgar conducted the historic recording sessions at EMI Studios for *Pomp and Circumstance*, the series of five marches that would immortalize his name—the march entitled "The Land of Hope and Glory" emerged as a British sporting anthem, while "The Light of Life" became the signature melody for American graduation ceremonies.[2] The EMI complex is comprised of four studios, the largest of which is Studio One, where much of the facility's orchestral recording occurs (Harry, *The Ultimate Beatles Encyclopedia* 4). On that fateful day in June 1962, the Beatles were ushered into Studio Two. As sound engineer Geoff Emerick describes it, "Studio Two was unusual at the EMI complex—in fact, unusual anywhere in the world—in that the control room was on the floor above the larger studio area where the musicians sat, overlooking it instead of being on the same level. Access between the two was navigated by a narrow flight of wooden stairs, and communications from the control room were transmitted over a pair of large speakers that hung on the far wall of the studio, directly over the emergency exit" (41). For the balance of the afternoon, the band rehearsed their entire stage act—some thirty-two numbers—for staff producer Ron Richards, who was decidedly underwhelmed by their performance. "I probably wouldn't have signed the Beatles," Richards later admitted (qtd. in Spitz 317). As far as the band was concerned, they were warming up for their first EMI recording session, as opposed to auditioning in order to earn their contract.

Richards had been tasked by Martin with choosing four songs to record for the Beatles' audition. His first selection, a cover version of "Besame Mucho," was followed by three original Lennon-McCartney compositions, "Love Me Do," "P.S. I Love You," and "Ask Me Why." After a dinner break, Martin joined the band in Studio Two, and his initial reaction mirrored Richards's dismal assessment. "They were rotten composers," Martin decided, and "their own stuff wasn't any good" (qtd. in Spitz 318). Joined by engineer Norman Smith and the Beatles, Martin explained various rudimentary aspects of the recording process before launching into a fairly unvarnished critique of their performance, chastising them, in particular, for their choice of original material and, at one point, even working to improve Pete's abilities as a time-keeper by entreating him to play the bass drum with his left foot—indeed, his work on "Love Me Do" had been conspicuously marred by an irregular drum pattern. To the band's great surprise, Martin also exhorted John and Paul to switch their vocals on "Love Me Do" in order to allow John to transfer to his harmonica with more dexterity. As Paul recalled:

> I'm singing harmony then it gets to the "pleeeaase." STOP. John goes, "Love me . . ." and then put his harmonica to his mouth: "Wah, wah, waahh." George Martin went, "Wait a minute, wait a minute, there's a crossover there. Someone else has got to sing 'Love Me Do' because you can't go 'Love me waahhh.' Now you're going to have a song called 'Love Me Waahhh'! So, Paul, will you sing 'Love Me Do'!" God, I got the screaming heebegeebies. I mean he suddenly changed this whole arrangement that we'd been doing forever. . . . We were doing it live, there was no real overdubbing, so I was suddenly given this massive moment, on our first record, no backing, where everything stopped, the spotlight was on me. . . . And I can still hear the shake in my voice when I listen to that record! I was terrified. . . . John did sing it better than me, he had a lower voice and was a little more bluesy at singing that line. (qtd. in Everett, *The Quarry Men through Rubber Soul* 126–27)

When Martin concluded his lengthy, scathingly candid diatribe, he asked the Beatles if there was anything they didn't like, to which George famously responded, in perfect deadpan: "Well, for a start, I don't like your tie." Quite suddenly, the room, which had lapsed into an unearthly silence, erupted with laughter. "During that one conversation," Richards remarked, "we realized they were something special" (qtd. in Spitz 318). When the group left the studio later that evening—having cut acetates of all four songs—the producer told them he would begin scouting new material for the band. As far as Martin was concerned, the Beatles were now worth the risk of a recording contract.[3] On June 26th, Ron White—as if to echo Martin's optimism—posted a letter of apology to Brian for his snubbing of the band back in January: "George Martin tells me that he has been suitably impressed and has made certain suggestions to you which in his view may improve them still further" (qtd. in Winn, *Way Beyond Compare* 10).

One of those suggestions would end up transforming the Beatles' chemistry forever. While Martin liked the band's raw potential and their acerbic sense of humor, he wasn't fond of the work of Pete Best, whom he felt that the band should replace—at least in the recording studio, that is. But for Epstein and the Beatles, Best had now become expendable. For quite some time, Pete had been estranged from his bandmates—preferring not to fraternize with them, for the most part, nor to adopt their hairstyles or irreverent mannerisms. There is little question, moreover, that they were jealous of Pete's popularity among the band's growing legion of female fans. But the final straw was clearly his musicianship. He could maintain a steady, pounding beat in a dancehall, to be sure, but his skills had proven to be remarkably limited in the recording studio, where subtlety and finesse, rather than his ham-fisted drumming style, were more suitable. The June 6th recording of "Love Me Do" is resoundingly clear in this regard—particularly during the bridge, as Pete's cadence very perceptibly lags before lumbering back into the chorus.

Between the EMI audition on June 6th and the end of July, Epstein booked the Beatles for a staggering sixty-one gigs over a period of eight weeks. By the time that August arrived, Pete's fate was sealed. His final performance with the band occurred at the Cavern on the evening of August 15th. The group felt that it was Epstein's duty, as manager, to do the dirty work. The next morning, Brian summoned Pete to his office and dismissed him from the Beatles. "The boys want you out," Epstein told him, "and it's already been arranged that Ringo will join the band on Saturday" (qtd. in Spitz 330). In a state of utter shock, Pete nursed his wounds in a sea of ale at the Grapes, a pub across Matthew Street from the Cavern, in the company of Neil Aspinall.[4] Pete was flummoxed, understandably, by his bandmates' betrayal. After all, he had been in the group for just over two years, and before Epstein's arrival, he took it upon himself to handle most of their booking and managerial responsibilities. His mother, Mona, had worked indefatigably on behalf of their ambitions to boot. It is difficult, then, to deny that Best's ousting was underhanded and deceitful.

When Neil offered to quit the band's employ in protest, his friend graciously talked him out of it in spite of his own unfathomable despair.[5]

Amazingly, Epstein asked Pete if he wouldn't mind playing the remaining three gigs before Ringo's inaugural performance—and even more amazingly, Pete agreed. By the time of the next show, though, he had clearly rethought his decision, and Johnny Hutchinson, the drummer for the Big Three, sat in for him. The Big Three were enormously popular in Liverpool at the time, and Epstein had reportedly invited Hutchinson to join the band before bothering to invite Ringo into the fold. Hutchinson declined for the simple reason that he didn't like the Beatles' cheeky and derisive attitudes. For John and Paul, the choice was simple. At dawn on the morning of Wednesday, August 15th, they had driven up to the seaside resort of Skegness, where Rory Storm and the Hurricanes were playing yet another extended run at Butlin's holiday camp.[6] Knocking on the door of the trailer Ringo shared with Johnny "Guitar" Byrne at 10 o'clock that morning, John and Paul didn't waste any time. "Pete Best is leaving," John announced, "and we want Ringo to join" (qtd. in Spitz 328). Rory was understandably upset, but realizing that Ringo had the opportunity to play in a band that had an EMI recording contract, he quickly yielded— albeit with two provisos: first, that Ringo perform in the Hurricanes' two remaining shows scheduled for that week; and, second, that Ringo cede his pink stage suit to Gibson Kemp, his sixteen-year-old replacement, who was still in school. All in all, it was a very small price to pay to join the Beatles.

~

As history well knows, Ringo Starr was the stage name for Richard Starkey, who was born to his father, Richard, a bakery worker, and mother, Elsie, on July 7th, 1940, in Liverpool's notoriously rough and impoverished Dingle neighborhood. The family's surname had originally been Parkin—that is, until Ringo's paternal grandmother remarried to a man named Starkey, and the entire family adopted her new last name. Ringo's parents were married in 1936, having met in the Liverpool dancehalls. Known as "Big Ritchie" after his son's birth, Ringo's father was entirely unprepared for the responsibilities of fatherhood, preferring instead to continue making the rounds of the dancehalls where he and Elsie had begun their courtship only a few years before. Within a year of their son's birth, the Starkeys had separated. By 1943, they had divorced, leaving Elsie to raise Ringo—or Ritchie, as he was called—by herself. Eventually, Elsie found employment as a barmaid, while devoting nearly all of her free time to her son, upon whom she doted. Sadly, most of the boy's childhood was overshadowed by illness. On July 3rd, 1947, Ritchie was felled by sharp pains in his abdomen, and he was hospitalized for appendicitis. In the aftermath of his surgery, Ritchie developed peritonitis, a severe inflammation of the lining of the abdominal cavity, and slipped into a coma from which he awoke—lucky to have survived at all—on his seventh birthday. Ritchie spent the remainder of the year recuperating at the hospital. By the time he returned to school, Ritchie had fallen woefully behind his classmates. For the next several years, Ritchie made little improvement at school, although he benefited greatly from the efforts of family friend Marie Maguire, who served as the boy's tutor at his home on Admiral Grove. Before long, he was even beginning to advance at reading. "He made incredible progress," Marie recalled. "It seemed like we were *that* close to bringing him up to proper school standards when he got sick again" (qtd. in Spitz 337).

In 1952, Ritchie was stricken with tuberculosis, which had reached epidemic proportions in Liverpool—particularly in the Dingle. Eventually, the boy ended up at Royal Liverpool Children's Hospital, where he convalesced in the sanitarium. During his lengthy stay at the hospital, Ritchie was encouraged to keep his mind alert by participating in the makeshift hospital band, which consisted of young patients playing rudimentary percussion along with prerecorded music. Ritchie joined in by tapping a pair of cotton bobbins on the cabinet beside his bed (Spitz 338). For the first time in his life, Ritchie felt a spark. The art of drumming came naturally to him. In the autumn of 1953, Ritchie finally went home to the Dingle, where he found himself lagging even further behind in school, which he eventually stopped attending altogether. Ritchie's salvation arrived in the form of Harry Graves, a bachelor who had left London after a failed marriage only to find his true love in Ritchie's mother. Harry worked as a Liverpool Corporation housepainter, and his one abiding passion—in addition to Elsie, that is—was music. He shared his wide-ranging tastes—from vocal stylists like Dinah Shore and Sarah Vaughan to pop stars in the vein of Frankie Lane and Johnnie Ray—with Ritchie, who became Harry's stepson in April 1954, when Elsie and Harry got married.

Over the next few years, Ritchie went through an assortment of jobs. First, he tried his hand working for the British rail, although he was laid off in short order. Next, he took a position working as a waiter on daily boat trips from Liverpool to North Wales. Before long, Harry found Richie a job at Henry Hunt and Sons, a gymnastics equipment company, where he performed a range of chores. It was at Henry Hunt and Sons that Ritchie met Eddie Miles. A budding guitarist in his own right, Eddie was the leader of the Eddie Miles Band, which evolved into Eddie Clayton and the Clayton Squares. Using an old washboard for percussion, Ritchie joined the group, which specialized—as with so many other bands across the UK—in the primitive musical sounds of skiffle. In December 1957, Harry presented his stepson with a used drum kit, which he had bought in London for £10. With Ringo's drum set in tow, the Eddie Clayton skiffle group began booking a series of small-time local engagements. Soon, Ritchie had even started playing rock and roll with Al Caldwell's Texans. In 1958, he left Eddie behind as the band transformed into the Raging Texans, which became Jet Storm and the Raging Texans before settling in for the long haul as Rory Storm and the Hurricanes. Having borrowed £46 from his grandfather, Ritchie purchased a proper set of drums—a new Ajax drum kit, complete with pigskin heads.

As a member of Rory Storm and the Hurricanes, Ritchie came into his own. He quickly emerged as one of the group's most popular musicians, and his image was enhanced by the many rings that adorned his fingers. Before long, he became known as "Rings," which morphed into "Ringo." Likewise, Starkey was abbreviated into "Starr," and a stage name was born for the ages. Eventually, the band turned the spotlight on their drummer, who occasionally sang a song, and, during "Starr Time," he began playing extended drum solos. Like the Beatles, Rory Storm and the Hurricanes served an apprenticeship in Hamburg, where Ringo got to know John, Paul, and George in 1961. As with his earlier years, though, Ringo had begun to develop a sense of wanderlust. At one point, he even pondered emigrating to Texas, where his blues idol, Lightnin' Hopkins, plied his trade. He went so far as to write a letter to the Houston Chamber of Commerce, but became dismayed by the mountain of registration forms that came in the return post. After playing drums behind Tony Sheridan in Hamburg, Ringo rejoined Rory Storm and the Hurricanes for their annual run at Butlin's holiday camp in the summer months of 1962. But what he really wanted was to be the drummer for the Beatles, and in August 1962, his dream came true.

Philip Norman contends that "the plot to oust Pete dates right back to 1961, when Ringo joined the Beatles as a backing group" for the 78-RPM recording of "Summertime" (162). That plot finally came to fruition on August 18th. After only two hours of rehearsal, John, Paul, George, and Ringo took the stage at a Horticultural Society Dance at Hulme Hall, where a crowd of five hundred filled the venue beyond capacity. The Beatles' first performance with Ringo at the Cavern on the evening of August 19th was marred by an uproar from Pete's numerous fans, who were heard chanting, "Pete Best forever! Ringo never!" George was subsequently given a black eye—head-butted with a Liverpool kiss—as he walked from the bandroom and into the mêlée that was brewing inside the club.[7] On August 22nd, the Beatles' new lineup was first captured on film by Manchester's Granada TV for the *Know the North* program. Introduced by an ebullient Bob Wooler, they performed rollicking versions of

"Some Other Guy" and the medley "Kansas City/Hey-Hey-Hey-Hey!" The Granada footage—despite its grainy textures and its relatively poor sound quality—offers magnificent testimony to the energy and excitement that the Beatles were experiencing during that most transformative of moments in their career.[8] As Walter Everett astutely observes: "Given everything that was to happen afterward, it is difficult to imagine what August 1962 would have been like for the Beatles. But it was the single most crucial crossroads of their career. Virtually unheard of outside of a pair of port cities, they were turning the corner rapidly toward inescapable fame." After years of toil amongst less-talented and, almost as significantly, far less-motivated musicians, John, Paul, and George had finally met their match in Ringo. "They were leaving behind a weak drummer for a great one," Everett adds, and "they were just entering a partnership with the rare producer who could steer them toward a number-one pop hit and artistic statement in the same gesture" (*The Quarry Men through Rubber Soul* 118).

As if to underscore how complicated the boys' lives had truly become, John married Cynthia on the day after the Granada TV performance. His longtime girlfriend had recently become pregnant, and, after their civil ceremony—an event that John's Aunt Mimi refused to attend—Epstein ensconced the newlyweds in his flat on Falkner Street, secreting them away from the Beatles' growing legion of fans. "I thought it would be goodbye to the group, getting married," John later remarked. "None of us ever took girls to the Cavern as we thought we would lose fans (which turned out to be a farce in the end). But I did feel embarrassed, walking about, married. It was like walking about with odd socks on or your flies open" (*Anthology* 73).[9] Dot Rhone had also become pregnant that year, and Paul was ready for a hasty marriage of his own. But when Dot miscarried after three months, Paul excused himself from the relationship—and, essentially, from Dot's life—forever. Although Paul had been eminently prepared to do the right thing on Dot and his unborn child's behalf, her miscarriage must surely have effected a genuine sense of relief in the young man, a welcome feeling of liberation as his career was just beginning to unfold before him. Yet for Paul, this moment of good fortune followed on the heels of a number of highly self-conscious instances of unrelenting ambition over the past few years. While John's aspirations had paved the way for Paul's entrance into the ranks of the Quarry Men way back in the summer of 1957, Paul's own purposefulness had been in high gear during the intervening years. He had, after all, orchestrated George's ascendance as the Quarry Men's lead guitarist, thus displacing Eric Griffiths' place in the lineup, and he had applied the necessary pressure to force Colin Hanton's departure from the band not long afterward. As Dot herself noted, Paul maneuvered to replace Stu as the Beatles' bassist, and, as Bill Harry observed, Paul—with the enthusiastic assistance of George Harrison—played a central role in causing Pete's alienation and ultimate severance from the group. Although George Martin provided the Beatles with the requisite professional excuse, Paul "plotted to oust Pete Best against the wishes of Brian Epstein and a reluctant John," according to Harry. "In hindsight, Paul's determination to hone the group was crucial, and these changes would help make up the right chemistry for what would be a unique quartet." But make no mistake about it, Pete's departure shifted, once and quite possibly for all, the Beatles' delicate balance of power, and the result was to "effectively change the Beatles from John's group to Paul's group" ("When We Were Very Young" 17). As with the narrative of the Beatles that had begun at the churchyard in Woolton, the story of the group is impossible to convey without acknowledging the fundamental roles of self-consciousness and ambition in their emergence.

~

On Tuesday, September 4th, 1962, the Beatles arrived at EMI Studios for their first official Parlophone recording session, but their producer was nowhere in sight. Instead, they were greeted by Ron Richards, who led them through a rehearsal of "How Do You Do It," a song that Martin had carefully selected for the band's initial single release by going down to Tin Pan Alley and attempting to find the hit song that would make the group's name. Written by well-known British songwriter Mitch Murray, the number didn't appeal to the Beatles, but, at Epstein's urging, they reluctantly agreed to learn it anyway. "It doesn't matter if you don't like it," the manager told his charges. "Just do it" (qtd. in Cross 398). When Martin finally arrived, he took the Beatles out for an Italian dinner before getting down to business in Studio Two, where they recorded "How Do You Do It" in one take, with a second take used to overdub a series of handclaps. After listening to the playback, John offered a blunt rejoinder to Murray's composition. "Look, George," he said, "I have to tell you, we really think that song is crap. . . . We want to record our own material, not some soft bit of fluff written by someone else" (qtd. in Emerick 44–45).

In many ways, Lennon's remarks comprised a signal moment in the band's career, a turning point, in a sense, in terms of the industry's approach to the previously inflexible relationship that it maintained between songwriters and recording artists—indeed, amongst all aspects of the record business. The existing model during that era in the history of popular music was a highly prescriptive process in which songwriters composed songs, producers oversaw their recording, and vocalists and musicians rehearsed them in order to capture them on tape for the record-buying public. Under this system, the so-called recording artists would reap the lion's share of their own profits by going on tour in support of their latest record. It was a rigid model that most record companies—the EMI Group included—were loath to unsettle. Yet since 1958, John and Paul had imagined themselves as more than a measly stage act—as more than mere puppeteers for other composers' tunes. For them, the act of songwriting was a performative experience in which the composers themselves self-consciously brought their art to life. And with that, the Beatles scrapped "How Do You Do It" and returned their producer's attention to "Love Me Do," the original composition that had fared relatively poorly during their first visit to EMI Studios in the company of Pete Best. Although the song had greatly improved with Ringo behind the drums, "Love Me Do" required some fifteen takes for the band to get a handle on the rhythm track. As John Winn points out, "More than anything, it was probably this struggle that caused him [Martin] to have second doubts about Ringo's drumming" (*Way Beyond Compare* 14). As the Beatles' first session came to a close, engineer Norman Smith—whom John had affectionately nicknamed "Normal"—edited a basic track of the song from several of the early takes. Martin mixed both songs into mono recordings and cut an acetate for closer scrutiny in advance of their next session, which had been scheduled for one week hence. The historical proceedings of September 4th were captured on film by photographer Dezo Hoffmann, whose pictures of George Harrison find the guitarist still sporting a black eye from the incident at the Cavern Club.

For Ringo in particular, the recording session on September 11th proved to be entirely disheartening. "I was nervous and terrified in the studio," Ringo said. "I saw a drum kit that wasn't mine, and a drummer that most definitely wasn't me! It was terrible. I'd been asked to join the Beatles, but now it looked as though I was only going to be good enough to do ballrooms with them. They started 'P.S. I Love You' with this other bloke playing the drums and I was given the fuckin' maracas. I thought, that's the end. They're doing a Pete Best on me. And then they decided to record the other side again ['Love Me Do'], the one on which I'd originally played the drums. I was given the tambourine this time" (qtd. in Cross 399). Dissatisfied with Ringo's musicianship on September 4th—his drumming lacked "drive," according to the producer—Martin booked top London session drummer Andy White to play on "Love Me Do" and "P.S. I Love You." John's mouth organ work on "Love Me Do" was inspired by Delbert McClinton's harmonica playing on Bruce Channel's "Hey! Baby"—and, as Martin had surmised, the shift in vocalists had improved his delivery of the harmonica part. For "P.S. I Love You," John, Paul, and George fashioned an exquisite three-part harmony in which they accented the lyrics on "treasure," "words," and "home," key phrases in a simple romantic vignette about lovers anticipating their reunion. Inspired by the Shirelles' "Soldier Boy," "P.S. I Love You" would be the first in a long line of songs over the next few years that would explore the tension between absence and presence, between separation and reconciliation.[10] "Love Me Do" and "P.S. I Love You" also saw the recording debut of John and George's new Gibson "Jumbo" J-160E electric-acoustic guitars. The September 11th session ended with a rehearsal of "Please Please Me," a slow number that John had styled after Roy Orbison's "Only the Lonely (Know the Way I Feel)." The song found its origins in Bing Crosby's "Please," which John's mother, Julia, sang to him during his youth. John's imagination was piqued by the song's homonymic quality—"Please lend your ears to my pleas"—a conceit that he mimicked with the repetition of "please" in his new composition. But Martin felt that "Please Please Me" was "much too dreary" in its current state, and he encouraged the boys to prepare a more vigorous, upbeat version for their next session.

Released as the Beatles' first official single on October 5th, 1962, "Love Me Do" needed all of the promotion that it could get.[11] From his years at NEMS, Epstein knew that record-company juggernauts like EMI didn't put many advertising dollars behind new acts like the Beatles—particularly new acts on the lowly Parlophone label. First, he hired Tony Barrow to do some freelance publicity work. Barrow had contacts in the music trade papers, including the *New Musical Express* and *Melody Maker*. At Brian's urging, Barrow crafted a press kit with biographical material—some of which was fallacious—about the band members. The issue of garnering radio time for the new single was another matter altogether. "It was a hell of a job trying to get 'Love Me Do' on the radio," Ron Richards remembered. "At that time, there weren't many programs on the BBC where you could get a pop record played" (qtd. in Spitz 356). To the company's credit, EMI purchased air time for "Love Me Do" on the influential Radio Luxembourg, and the song slowly crept up the charts. Meanwhile, back in Liverpool, the single sold thousands of copies—and legend has it that Epstein bought ten thousand copies himself in order to bolster sales revenues and prod EMI into pushing the record even harder. Eventually, "Love Me Do" peaked at #17 on the British charts, and the Beatles—although not quite the "toppermost of the poppermost"—were a top-twenty sensation. Yet as Ian MacDonald observes, "Love Me Do" signifies a paradigm shift, of sorts, in the world of popular music. "The first faint chime of a revolutionary bell, 'Love Me Do' represented far more than the sum of its simple parts," he writes. "A new spirit was abroad: artless yet unabashed—and awed by nothing" (43).

Not content to rest on his laurels, Epstein saw to it that the Beatles were in constant motion. On October 25th, they recorded their first performance for radio broadcast on the BBC. Their selection of songs included Tommy Roe's "Sheila," "Love Me Do," Bobby Scott and Ric Marlow's pop standard "A Taste of Honey," and "P.S. I Love You."[12] Throughout October and November 1962, the band played numerous dates, as usual, at the Cavern, while adding in an assortment of dancehalls and even an additional fourteen-day stint at the Star-Club in Hamburg, where they logged another forty-nine hours' worth of stage experience. On November 26th, they returned to EMI Studios to meet with Martin, who, at least at the time, was still considering the release of "How Do You Do It" as the Beatles' next single. But then he heard the band's revivified version of "Please Please Me," and everything changed. "We've revamped it," they informed him (qtd. in Spitz 358). And indeed they had. Gone were the malingering shadows of Roy Orbison, which the Beatles had replaced with heavy doses of raw energy and the kinetic nuance of musical ornamentation. The up-tempo version of the song, with its catchy, suggestive lyrics, opens with John's brisk harmonica melody before Lennon and McCartney sing the number's familiar opening lines, "Last night I said these words to my girl / I know you never even try, girl." Much of the track's vigor emerges from the guitar accents with which, at the producer's urging, George embellishes the lyrical breaks, as well as from Ringo's lightning-quick attacks on the drum heads of his Premier kit. For the newest member of the band, "Please Please Me" was a moment of great redemption. Despite the apparent simplicity of his drumwork, Ringo possesses a unique, nonchalant playing style that acts, in its subtlety, as his musical signature:

> I used to get put down in the press a lot for my silly fills, as we liked to call them, and that mainly came about because I'm a left-handed right-handed drummer; that means I'm left-handed but the kit's set up for a right-handed drummer, so if I come off the hi-hat and the snare . . . any ordinary drummer would come off with the right hand . . . so if I want to come off, I have to come off with the left hand, which means I have to miss a . . . miniscule of a beat . . . I can go around the kit from the floor tom to the top toms, which are on the bass drum easy, but I can't go the other way because the left hand has to keep coming in under the right one. (qtd. in Everett, *The Quarry Men through Rubber Soul* 121)

For Martin, the recording of "Please Please Me" was simply transformative. Not only did he realize the band's considerable commercial potential, but he also recognized the awesome power of their original material. There would be no more talk of "How Do You Do It" in the wake of "Please Please Me." "The whole session was a joy," Martin remembered. "At the end of it, I pressed the intercom button in the control room and said, 'Gentleman, you've just made your first number-one record'" (qtd. in Everett, *The Quarry Men through Rubber Soul* 131).

Two additional songs were recorded on November 26th, including "Tip of My Tongue"—a McCartney composition, the recording of which doesn't survive—and "Ask Me Why," which was chosen as the future B-side for the "Please Please Me" single. With its easygoing Latinate rhythm, "Ask Me Why" features a lead vocal by Lennon and harmonies by Paul and George that invoke the band's numerous cover versions of 1950s pop standards. But the real gem that day was unquestionably "Please Please Me," which Brian played for Dick James at the music publisher's Charing Cross Road office. Utterly dissatisfied with Ardmore and Beechwood's lackluster efforts to promote "Love Me Do," the manager was determined to find a new firm to handle the Lennon-McCartney publishing rights. After listening to the acetate of "Please Please Me," James telephoned Philip Jones, the producer behind *Thank Your Lucky Stars*, one of the UK's most influential television shows. James played the song for Jones over the phone, and, with that, the Beatles had earned a spot on an early 1963 episode of the program. It was a major promotional coup, but James had much more in mind. Why not create a new publishing company, he suggested, that would handle all of the Lennon-McCartney publishing rights? Entitled Northern Songs in order to connote John and Paul's North Country roots, the company would split the songwriters' royalties evenly after deducting James's ten percent fee. The deal that they concocted required Northern Songs to purchase Lenmac Enterprises, a holding company that Epstein had established earlier in the year that already owned the rights to fifty-nine original Lennon-McCartney compositions. The new agreement with Northern Songs required the songwriters to produce six new numbers per year over the next four years—a period in which they would literally compose hundreds of songs.[13]

The Beatles spent the last few days of the year in Hamburg, where their concerts on December 28th and 31st were recorded by Star-Club sound man Adrian Barber, who also played guitar for the Big Three. Several of the tapes ended up in the hands of Ted "Kingsize" Taylor, who later claimed that John gave him the rights to the live recordings in exchange for a round of drinks (Winn, *Way Beyond Compare* 21).[14] Barber's tapes are, for the most part, largely inaudible—particularly in terms of the vocals. Yet the recordings, for all of their crudity, reveal the band at the top of their game. Their rendition of Cynthia Weil and Barry Mann's "Where Have You Been All My Life"— recorded on New Year's Eve—is especially telling, particularly in comparison with the Granada audio for "Some Other Guy" and most of the other tapes in the Beatles' early recorded corpus. There is a sense of precision inherent in their version of "Where Have You Been All My Life"—an imprimatur of deliberateness, of exactitude that would undergird much of their work in the years hence. This is especially evident in Harrison's guitar solo, which takes up the baton from Paul's walking bass maneuvers and delivers—with electric, staccato clarity—a wicked report of sixteenth notes. In truth, the Beatles didn't want to be in Hamburg at all that December: "We didn't really want to go back," John remarked. "If we had our way, we'd have just copped out on the engagement, because we didn't feel we owed them fuck all!" (qtd. in Badman 47). Although the Beatles were reluctant to fulfill their contract for their final performances at the Star-Club in December 1962, it is impossible to deny the significance of their apprenticeship in Hamburg in terms of the larger calculus of their career as recording artists. By putting in thousands of hours' worth of stage time, they honed the style that would serve as the bedrock for Beatlemania, while also developing the interpersonal chemistry and musicianship that undoubtedly rewarded them with the confidence to let their imaginations run wild in the studio. They would share this very innovative style and rock and roll panache with a national television audience on the January 19th episode of *Thank Your Lucky Stars*. Recorded on January 13th at Alpha Television Studios in Birmingham, the Beatles mimed a performance of "Please Please Me." Dizzied by the raw power and energy of the song, the studio audience absolutely erupted in response to the Beatles' mere presence.

George Martin was determined to capture the exhilaration of a Beatles concert for the band's first long-playing record. "It was obvious, commercially, that once 'Please Please Me'—the single—had been a success, we should release an LP as soon as possible," the producer remembered (qtd. in Lewisohn, *The Complete Beatles Recording Sessions* 24). For a while, he contemplated the notion of recording a live album at the Cavern before realizing that the venue's acoustics—given the building's unforgiving cement edifice—would make it all but impossible to achieve the necessary balance for the recording process. Instead, Martin came up with the idea of approaching their first studio album as though it were a Beatles concert in itself. Along with the four songs that comprised the band's first two singles, they would assemble a selection of Lennon-McCartney compositions and an assortment of cover versions in order to reproduce the rhythm and musical range of a live show, albeit with the opportunity to refine their performances in the studio. The only problem was that, given the tight schedule that existed at EMI Studios during that era, they only had a single day in which to bring the project to fruition. On February 11th, 1963, the Beatles arrived at Studio Two, where they had some ten hours in which to record the album. To make matters worse, John had been felled by a bad cold, which he had contracted during the band's recently completed tour with Helen Shapiro, the sixteen-year-old British pop sensation. When the tour began, Helen was the headlining act, while the Beatles were fourth on the bill. By the end of the tour, though, "Please Please Me" had worked its magic, and they were pop stars in their own right. As the *New Musical Express*'s Gordon Sampson later reported, the Beatles ended up dominating the last several concerts on the tour, so much so that "the audience repeatedly called for them while other artists were performing" (qtd. in Spitz 370).

At the band's request, a jar of Zubes throat lozenges and two packs of Peter Stuyvesant cigarettes were placed atop the piano in Studio Two, thus beginning a Beatles tradition that would continue for years. Martin was determined to complete the basic tracks for the entire album that day—the mixing process could be carried out later outside of the group's presence. In addition to the practical dilemma of booking studio time, Martin was also confronted with the fact that the Beatles were due to play for a youth-club dance at the Azena Ballroom the following evening in Sheffield, Yorkshire. The sessions began at 10 o'clock on the morning of February 11th, and the Beatles, for the most part, were all business—deadly serious, in contrast with the jocularity that Martin had witnessed on previous occasions. Over a period of some 585 minutes, the band recorded eleven songs using EMI Studios' two-track recording desk, ten of which would be included on their first album. It was an incredible pace, but the workmanlike Beatles—hardened after thousands of hours on stage on the Reeperbahn, in the Cavern, and in damned near every dancehall in the North Country—were clearly up to the task.

Of their ten studio albums, *Please Please Me* would seem to be an anomaly, then, given the hurried aspect of its production, the comparatively primitive nature of their songwriting capabilities at this juncture, and the limited flexibility inherent in the available recording equipment at this stage of their career. But even at this remarkably early moment in its evolution, the Beatles' art—or, at the very least, an intelligible *outline* of the Beatles' art—is clearly in evidence. When interpreted as a simulated concert that ranges from "I Saw Her Standing There" through "Twist and Shout," *Please Please Me* underscores the energy and excitement of the Beatles' first extended studio foray. Also on exhibit are the three primary artistic thrusts that will develop throughout the group's career: the manner in which ideas of authorship impinge upon the songwriters' approach both to their craft and to their working relationship within the band; the powerful effects of nostalgia as the group's fundamental literary and musical *métier*; and the irony of distance that informs their incipient textual interrelationship with their listening audience.

This latter aspect of the Beatles' art is evinced, most notably, by the explosive introduction of the album's opening track, "I Saw Her Standing There," which had gone under the working title of "17" over the past few years. Beginning with Paul's brisk count-off—"one, two, three, four!"—"I Saw Her Standing There" inaugurates the Beatles' first album-length recording in arresting fashion.[15] Written years before in Paul's front parlor on Forthlin Road, "I Saw Her Standing There" offers a prescient example of the manner in which John and Paul shared in the crafting of each other's lyrics. Paul had originally written the song's initial phrases as "Well, she was just seventeen / Never been a beauty queen." In John's revision, the lyrics take on an entirely different aspect altogether—"Well, she was just seventeen / You know what I mean"—thus informing the composition with an ironic, knowing sense of suggestiveness in contrast with the speaker's fairly innocent experience. By making such an explicit, third-person gesture toward their audience, the Beatles effectively shrink the distance between themselves and their listeners. Paul's opening lyric echoes Chuck Berry's "Little Queenie"—"too cute to be a minute over seventeen"—and he borrows his walking bass line directly from Berry's "I'm Talking about You." This incidence of petty musical theft is a critical aspect of the Beatles' songwriting proclivities, as well as of popular music and the creative arts in general.[16] Lennon and McCartney were hardly shy about the intercollaborative nature of their compositional practices: "We were the biggest nickers in town," Paul admitted. "Plagiarists extraordinaires" (qtd. in MacDonald 144).

Yet, as Anne Bogart has demonstrated in the postulation of her revolutionary acting methodologies, all art involves the "repetition" of existing creative artifacts, and the Beatles are no different. "It is significant," she writes, "that the French word for rehearsal is *repetition*" ("Violence" 25).[17] Indeed, the act of iteration, in itself, involves the exploration of familiar territory. Yet through the process of repetition—of rehearsing the existing rock and roll master texts of their era—the Beatles succeeded in moving beyond iteration and creating new art. With their near-encyclopedic knowledge of pop music, they drew their inspiration from all corners of the musical world. Rather than simply dismissing such deeds as the work of crass copyright infringers, we might more profitably understand their textual borrowings as the result of two songwriters—*authors*, even—having become fully immersed in the larger world of their craft. They self-consciously reached out and embraced that world by engaging it on its own terms and then—transported by their initial inspiration—succeeded in transforming it.

～

Not surprisingly, the vast majority of the band's songs on their first few albums concern love's trials and tribulations. Nearly all of their early tunes address romance as a low-impact sport, as a venue for fun and games, as opposed to a pursuit that might produce emotional anguish or misery. "I Saw Her Standing There" depicts the speaker in the act of discovering love and just as quickly taking the beloved's place in his world for granted: "Now I'll never dance with another / Since I saw her standing there," McCartney sings. The song also features a middle-eight, the musical trait that becomes one of John and Paul's writerly signatures as composers. A portion of a song that includes four, eight, twelve, or sixteen bars sandwiched between two iterations of the chorus, the middle-eight affords their compositions with a refreshing change of pace in contrast with pop music's standard verse-chorus, verse-chorus structure. In Lennon-McCartney compositions, the middle-eight often represents a pointed lyrical departure from the rest of the song. This aspect shares much in common with the "turn," or volta, of a sonnet, the transitional moment that denotes an appreciable shift in tone or mood. For "I Saw Her Standing There," the middle-eight provides the song with a powerful burst of energy as the speaker strolls toward his beloved across the dance floor and— thunderstruck by her beauty—falls in love at first sight: "Well, my heart went boom / When I crossed that room / And I held her hand in mine." Despite the speaker's lascivious demeanor—"You know what I mean"—he is happy and content merely to hold his beloved's hand.

As Tim Riley remarks, songs like "I Saw Her Standing There" consider nothing more (or less) than "the simple but penetrating rush of adolescent desire" (51). Riley's assertion is equally valid for "Misery," the album's second track. Originally written for Helen Shapiro, "Misery" offers a splendid example of the ways in which youth's unvarnished optimism proves impossible to quell. At the same time, though, this aspect of the composition prevents the songwriters from achieving a sense of unity between the song's heartbreaking subject matter—"I've lost her now for sure"—and the upbeat manner in which John and Paul opt to sing the number. In "Misery," the speaker, suffering from the understandable woes of a failed romance, maligns his gloomy present in contrast with the ostensibly joyful times of a rapidly fading past: "I'll remember all the little things we've done," he tells us, suggesting that his blissful memories of happier days might function as curatives for his broken heart. The song's implicit irony, of course, is that the speaker's nostalgic longings for his beloved serve to establish a vicious circle of sorts in which his miserable state will continue to plague him indefinitely. The song benefits, moreover, from an early example of Martin's knack for using studio trickery in order to achieve new-fangled soundscapes. In the case of "Misery," the producer superimposed a piano over the existing guitar introduction, played in 6/8 time, during an overdubbing session on February 20th—while the Beatles were across town performing on a live BBC broadcast from the Playhouse Theatre, no less. Years before, Martin had developed the technique of recording a piano at half-speed by itself or in unison with a guitar track that had been recorded an octave lower (Emerick 60). Played back at regular speed, the piano introduction assumes a quasi-harpsichord or music box effect, which Martin hailed as the "wound-up piano."

After devoting numerous takes to "Hold Me Tight," a Lennon-McCartney composition that failed to make the album's final cut, the Beatles turned to Arthur Alexander's "Anna (Go to Him)," which was recorded in a comparatively economical three takes. In another example of the meticulous nature of the band's cover versions, "Anna" features a lockstep duet between Harrison's Duo-Jet and Ringo's hi-hat. Although their arrangement deviates perceptibly from Alexander's original, the Beatles make the song their proverbial own by imbuing it with the precision and familiarity of a band that has performed the tune on far too numerous occasions to count. The same could easily be said for the album's next number, Gerry Goffin and Carole King's "Chains," a Brill Building-era composition that features George Harrison on lead vocals. At two key junctures, John's guitar part becomes heavily distorted—perhaps because of a poor electrical connection (Everett, *The Quarry Men through Rubber Soul* 155). This uncorrected blemish underscores the swiftness with which *Please Please Me* was produced. Ringo takes the microphone on the next track, a cover version of Wes Farrell and Luther Dixon's "Boys" that was recorded in a single take. The song, with its "bop shoo-op" chorus, would become a fan favorite during the Beatles' live performances throughout 1963.[18]

The album's next four tracks—"Ask Me Why," "Please Please Me," "P.S. I Love You," and "Love Me Do"—comprise the contents of the band's first two singles. But they also characterize the nature of the Beatles' easy romantic attitude in their early work. "We were just writing songs à la [the] Everly Brothers, à la Buddy Holly," John later recalled. "Pop songs with no more thought to them than that—to create a sound. And the words were almost irrelevant" (qtd. in Dowlding 23). In each instance, the songs' speakers ponder the feel and veracity of true love. In "Ask Me Why," romantic love affords the speaker with the pure, unadulterated knowledge that "I should never never never be blue," yet his happiness—his *happiness*, no less!—still causes him to weep in unchecked desolation. As with "Misery," though, the speaker's gloom is belied by the glee with which John sings the lyrics. In "Please Please Me," the speaker laments in the middle-eight that "there's always rain in my heart" because his beloved won't reciprocate his feelings—or, perhaps even more despairingly, his aggressive sexual advances. As Alan Pollack notes, "This song is also emotionally quite gripping, not only because of its apparently incessant drive, but even more so for the very human way in which the hero appears to waver in the amount of self-control he can muster—starting out urgently insistent yet trying to appear controlled; talking through clenched teeth in a forced-polite voice, even while his façade is continually cracking to reveal the true heat and impatience behind it." While "P.S. I Love You" offers the sincere, one-dimensional prose of a love letter, the song's earnestness is trumped by the romantic spirit of the Beatles' first single. In "Love Me Do," the speaker effortlessly promises to "always be true" with nary a care in the world. From the melancholic "Ask Me Why" and the brusque insistence of "Please Please Me" through the blind faith of "P.S. I Love You" and "Love Me Do," the Beatles play the game of love as a weightless trifle in spite of the comparatively hefty freight of their lyrics.

Featuring a celesta solo that had been overdubbed on February 20th by their producer, "Baby It's You" was a veteran number from the band's stage act. The song's lazy rhythm exists in dramatic contrast with the up-tempo "Do You Want to Know a Secret," which features George on lead vocals. For "Do You Want to Know a Secret," John drew his inspiration from Walt Disney's *Snow White and the Seven Dwarfs* (1937). In the film, Snow White offers a spoken introduction to the movie's first song, "I'm Wishing": "Wanna know a secret?" she asks a clutch of adoring doves. "Promise not to tell?" John had recently composed the song in the Liverpool flat that he and Cynthia were borrowing from Brian Epstein. In contrast with its superlative counterparts in "I Saw Her Standing There" and "Please Please Me," the middle-eight for "Do You Want to Know a Secret" is decidedly underwhelming: "I've known the secret for a week or two / Nobody knows, just we two," George sings. Lacking either the unabashed positivism or the tongue-in-cheek depravity of the album's other songs, "Do You Want to Know a Secret" suffers from, of all things, too much earnestness for its own good.

As with the other cover versions recorded that day—and, indeed, over the next few years—the Beatles' nonoriginal recordings are marked by lockstep precision, often in contrast with the comparatively loose renditions offered by their precursors. For "A Taste of Honey," which had previously been popularized by crooner Tony Bennett, Paul double-tracked his vocal by recording a second version along with the original, thus creating a layered effect and, hence, a fuller sound. *Please Please Me*'s penultimate track, "There's a Place," was actually the first number to be recorded during February 11th's marathon session. "There's a Place" was inspired by Motown rhythm and blues, and John borrowed the title from "Somewhere," the song from the musical *West Side Story* (1957), in which Tony and Maria sing dreamily that "there's a place for us" beyond the bitter turmoil of their feuding families. "There's a Place" provides listeners with an intriguing early portrait of John and Paul's embryonic sense of nostalgia as a restorative experience. In the song, the speaker imagines an otherworldly space where "there's no sorrow" and "no sad tomorrow." More likely a state of being as opposed to an actual physical locale, this personally inscribed place allows Lennon's speaker to be alone and, rather significantly, to be liberated from the socially dislocating forces of the workaday world. Yet as with so many other Lennon-McCartney songs written during this period, the lead vocalist's optimism belies the lyrics' multifarious shades of blue. While these early compositions are often sorely lacking in musical unity, it makes little difference at this stage of Lennon and McCartney's nascent career as songwriters. As John Lahr astutely reminds us, "Rock and roll legislates by joy, not by reason" (80).

In contrast with "There's a Place," Lennon achieves liberation of a decidedly different kind in "Twist and Shout," the raucous cover version of the old Isley Brothers tune that closes the album. It would be the last song that the Beatles recorded on that fateful day. As the studio personnel prepared to close around 10 p.m., a shirtless John settled in for one more number. With his voice cut to shreds—Martin described the performance as a "real larynx-tearer"—John captured the vocal on the first take (qtd. in Spitz 375). A second attempt at the song proved to be a nonstarter, and the band decided to call it an evening, having completed their work on *Please Please Me* in a little under ten hours' worth of studio time. As more than a mere rehearsal of the group's contemporary set list, the album begins with the relatively innocent handholding of "I Saw Her Standing There" and concludes with the sexual abandon inherent in John's screaming lead vocal on the final cut. "Sure, I'm a cynic," John remarked in April 1963. "What we play is rock and roll under a new name. Rock music is war, hostility, and conquest. We sing about love, but we mean sex, and the fans know it" (qtd. in Badman 57). In itself, the Beatles' recording of "Twist and Shout" is one of rock's primal events, yet so, too, is the album, which finds the group on the cusp of realizing their artistic promise and possibility in the studio. In many ways, Angus McBean's cover photograph for *Please Please Me*—with the bandmates' fresh faces peering down the stairwell at London's EMI House—says it all.[19] The Beatles were well-poised to embark upon a creative journey that—for John and Paul, at least—they had been dreaming of since teenagehood. It was a heady moment indeed. "We were performers," John told *Rolling Stone*'s Jann Wenner. "What we generated was fantastic when we played straight rock, and there was nobody to touch us in Britain" (*Lennon Remembers* 20). For the Beatles, the recording studio was a revelation. It was ground zero for their art. "We gradually became the workmen who took over the factory," Paul remarked in later years. "In the end, we had the run of the whole building. It would be us, the recording people on our session, and a doorman. There would be nobody else there. It was amazing, just wandering around, having a smoke in the echo chamber. I think we knew the place better than the chairman of the company because we *lived* there. I even got a house just 'round the corner, I loved it so much. I didn't want ever to leave" (*Anthology* 93). And, as history has so resoundingly demonstrated, he never really would.

Notes

1. EMI would rechristen the complex as Abbey Road Studios in 1970.

2. While the Beatles are clearly responsible for the renown that Abbey Road Studios enjoys across the globe, the Greater London Council "blue plaque" affixed to its entry-way commemorates the work of "Elgar, Sir Edward (1857–1934)." Aside from the ubiquitous graffiti on the complex's front wall, Abbey Road Studios offers no external commemoration for the work of its most famous clients.

3. Although they recorded all four songs, only the discs for "Besame Mucho" and "Love Me Do" survive. The audition tape for "Love Me Do," with its shaky drum patterns and inconsistent beat, most likely spelled Pete's doom—at least to Martin's ears. A version of the song with Pete behind the drums is included on *Anthology 1* (1995).

4. Neil's relationship with the Best family had become highly complex by this juncture. In addition to his close friendship with Pete, Neil had lived in John and Mona Best's house as their lodger. On July 21st, 1962, Mona gave birth to Vincent Roag Best—and though the birth certificate ascribed his parentage to John and Mona Best, the newborn's father was twenty-one-year-old Neil Aspinall (Spitz 331). Leigh argues, moreover, that Pete was hardly conciliatory about the idea of Neil maintaining his relationship with the Beatles. "When Pete was sacked," Leigh writes, "he told Aspinall to leave the house if he was to continue as the band's roadie." According to Leigh, Roag's recent birth had complicated their friendship rather dramatically, and Neil's decision to continue working for the Beatles "further soured an already fragile relationship" ("The Axe Files" 36).

5. For Pete, the Beatles' incredible success would overshadow the rest of his life. As an act of consolation, Epstein found work for Pete as the drummer for the Liverpool group Lee Curtis and the All-Stars. Renamed Pete Best and the All-Stars after Curtis's exit in 1964, the band released an unsuccessful single, "I'm Gonna Knock on Your Door," for Decca. In 1965, he reportedly attempted suicide by gassing himself. Over the next several years, he led the Pete Best Four and later the Pete Best Combo, which released an album entitled *Best of the Beatles* (1966). By the end of the decade, he was working as a Liverpool baker before embarking upon a career as a civil servant. In 1978, he was hired as a technical advisor for the ABC television production of *Birth of the Beatles*, and, in later years, he has emerged as a regular staple at Beatles conventions.

6. In Ringo's memory, Brian Epstein invited him by telephone to join the Beatles (*Anthology* documentary).

7. In an interview with Mark Lewisohn, Paul suggested that the story about George's black eye had nothing at all to do with Pete's dismissal: "He'd been bopped in the Cavern by some guy who was jealous over his girlfriend!" (6).

8. Granada TV returned to the Cavern on September 5th in order to retape the audio—using three microphones instead of two—for "Some Other Guy" and "Kansas City/Hey-Hey-Hey-Hey!" At the end of "Some Other Guy," John can be heard saying, "We'll probably have to do it again" (qtd. in Winn, *Way Beyond Compare* 15). While the new audio track was dubbed onto the film, the footage was never aired by Granada. The band's performance of "Some Other Guy" is available on the Beatles' *Anthology* documentary (1995).

9. John ultimately denied that the Beatles were explicitly attempting to veil the marriage in secrecy: "We didn't keep it a secret. It's just that when we first came on the scene nobody really asked us. They weren't interested whether we were married or not" (*Anthology* 73).

10. As Craig Cross observes, "John always claimed that Paul wrote it ['P.S. I Love You'] as an answer-song to the Shirelles' hit 'Soldier Boy' because there was a tradition—common in the sixties, but less common these days—of 'replying' to other people's hits" (424). Cross identifies "Can't Buy Me Love" as another answer song—in this instance, to "Money (That's What I Want)," the 1959 hit single penned by Berry Gordy and Janie Bradford, which the Beatles subsequently cover on *With the Beatles* (1963).

11. Given Martin's initial concerns about Ringo's musical skills, early pressings of the single rather ironically featured Ringo's drumwork on "Love Me Do," while the version of the song including Andy White on the drums appeared on *Please Please Me*, where Ringo can clearly be heard playing the tambourine.

12. The Beatles would begin their semi-regular appearances on the BBC's *Saturday Club* program, hosted by Brian Matthew, on January 22nd, 1963. The BBC recordings are commemorated in the 1994 release *Live at the BBC*, which features selections from their broadcasts from 1963 to 1965.

13. Initially, Northern Songs handled all of Lennon and McCartney's songs, as well as early composing efforts by Harrison and Starr, who later formed their own publishing companies—Harrisongs and Startling Music, respectively. The problems with Northern Songs began in 1965, when the company went public in order to save money on capital gains tax. Lennon and McCartney each maintained 15 percent ownership of Northern Songs, Epstein held 7.5 percent, Harrison and Starr owned some 1.6 percent, and James (along with his business partner Charles Silver) held a whopping 37.5 percent. The remaining shares subsequently traded on the London Stock Exchange.

14. Several of the songs recorded during the 28 and 31 December performances would be released in 1977 as *Live! At the Star-Club in Hamburg, Germany, 1962* on CBS's Lingasong label. Although the sound quality is questionable throughout, the album is of considerable historical value, given that it comprises their fifth and final extended engagement on the Reeperbahn.

15. For Greil Marcus, McCartney's count-off was even more risqué: "It was the most exciting rock and roll I'd ever heard (with Paul's one/two/three/*fuck!* opening—how in the world did they expect to get away with that?)" (180).

16. In this sense, popular music often functions as an intercollaborative process—a rich and creative environment in which artists respond to one another's work through

imitation, response, and revivification. In the past few decades, such intercollaboration has resulted in music sampling, in which an element from one recording is employed in another. The advent of the Internet has seen the emergence of the so-called "mash-up," which is generally considered to be a "website or web application that seamlessly combines content from more than one source into an integrated experience." In terms of popular music, the mash-up is most often understood as a form of "bastard pop," which is a "musical genre which, in its purest form, consists of the combination (usu-ally by digital means) of the music from one song with the *a cappella* from another" (*Wikipedia*). In Hank Handy's widely Internet-dispersed "Beatles Mash-Up Medley," the track includes dozens of Beatles songs that have been combined via digital means. The song's first movement, for example, consists of four Beatles songs transformed into a single textual entity, including Paul singing "I've Just Seen a Face" against a musical backdrop that includes George's acoustic guitar motto from "Here Comes the Sun" and Ringo's drum cadence from the "Sgt. Pepper's Lonely Hearts Club Band (Reprise)." Prepared by George Martin and his son Giles, *Love* (2006) employs a series of authorized Beatles mash-ups—or "soundscapes," in the Martins' parlance—as the soundtrack for the hit *Cirque du Soleil* production. The concept of intercollaboration doesn't excuse out-and-out plagiarism, of course, a phenomenon that can be usefully illustrated by George's 1971 chart-topping solo hit "My Sweet Lord," which was deter-mined to be an instance of unintentional plagiarism because of its striking similarities to the Chiffons' 1963 hit song, "He's So Fine." With personal grace and good humor, George revisited the fiasco in his 1976 composition "This Song," as well as in his Monty Pythonesque spoof "The Pirate Song," which was broadcast in December 1976 on the BBC's *Rutland Weekend Television*.

17. In *The Viewpoints Book: A Practical Guide to Viewpoints and Composition* (2005), Bogart and Tina Landau discuss the role of repetition in the creative process. In the act of composition, repetition is a necessary aspect of artistic creation. Indeed, the act of creation, in and of itself, is the repetition of previous compositional acts by precursory artists. Repetition, then, involves the act of rewriting preexisting texts (200–01).

18. "Boys" continues to be a staple in Ringo's live repertoire, including Ringo Starr and His All-Starr Band's 2006 tour, which featured a cover version of the song on its set list.

19. George Martin had originally suggested that the group entitle the album *Off the Beatle Track* and that the cover photo be taken in front of the Insect House at the London Zoo, an idea that was jettisoned when the zoo's director objected to the photo shoot. Martin was so fond of the title, though, that he eventually used it for the 1964 anthology of Beatles instrumental covers that was credited to "George Martin and His Orchestra."

Chapter 5

Rock and Roll Music

Sexual intercourse began
In nineteen sixty-three
(Which was rather late for me)—
Between the end of the Chatterley *ban*
And the Beatles' first LP.
—PHILIP LARKIN, "ANNUS MIRABILIS"

But *Please Please Me*, of course, was only the beginning. The explosive power of the Beatles was ignited before a national television audience of some fifteen million viewers on the evening of October 13th, 1963, when the band performed on the popular British variety show *Val Parnell's Sunday Night at the London Palladium*. The group played a four-song set that included three new tunes—"From Me to You," "I'll Get You," and "She Loves You"—and concluded with "Twist and Shout." The scene at the Palladium was pure pandemonium. By the end of the show, more than two thousand frenzied fans had collected outside on Oxford Street. "Screaming girls launched themselves against the police—sending helmets flying and constables reeling," the *Daily Herald* reported. The next morning, the Beatles dominated the London headlines, with the *Daily Mirror* trumpeting "BEATLEMANIA!" on newsstands across the nation (qtd. in Spitz 427–28).[1]

Released on March 22nd, 1963, *Please Please Me* quickly assumed the number-one spot on the UK charts—a position that it held it for an astonishing thirty weeks. After a second appearance on *Thank Your Lucky Stars* and yet another brief stint on the road with Helen Shapiro, it was time for the band to record their next single. "Brian Epstein and I worked out a plan," George Martin recalled, "in which we tried—not always successfully—to release a new Beatles single every three months and two albums a year. I was always saying to the

Beatles, 'I want another hit, come on, give me another hit,' and they always responded" (qtd. in Lewisohn, *The Complete Beatles Recording Sessions* 28). The group returned to the recording studio on March 5th. John and Paul had written the band's next single, "From Me to You," on the tour bus on February 28th. The idea had come to them while discussing the regular *New Musical Express* column "From You to Us," which Paul decided to personalize by refashioning the phrase in the first-person as "From Me to You." This allowed them to speak directly to their audience, as they had previously done with "I Saw Her Standing There." It was a brilliant posture for the Beatles to take with their listeners, who were being explicitly invited to identify with the speakers in their compositions. The song's middle-eight, for example, contrasts the speaker's pledge to give his girlfriend anything she wants with a more intimate, more mutually rewarding gesture: "I've got arms that long to hold you, and keep you by my side / I've got lips that long to kiss you, and keep you satisfied." The notion of "longing"—of enjoying the sweet thrill of reuniting with one's beloved—is a mainstay of popular music, yet it is also an early Beatles hallmark that establishes an identificatory relationship between the vocalists and their growing horde of female fans. As Paul later recalled in an interview with Mark Lewisohn:

> We knew that if we wrote a song called "Thank You Girl" that a lot of the girls who wrote us fan letters would take it as a genuine thank you. So a lot of our songs—"From Me to You" is another—were directly addressed to the fans. I remember one of my daughters, when she was very little, seeing Donny Osmond sing "The Twelfth of Never," and she said "he loves me" because he sang it right at her off the telly. We were aware that that happened when you sang to an audience. (9)

In the early years, they rehearsed their new compositions in Studio Two in front of Martin, who sat above them on a tall stool. While they readily ascribed this position of authority to their producer, the group intuitively recognized the importance of their collaboration with the elder Martin, who—despite his many producing spoken-word and novelty records—possessed a genuine knack for recognizing and crafting hit songs. "The Beatles had marvelous ears when it came to writing and arranging their material," Ron Richards observed, "But George had real taste—and an innate sense of what worked" (qtd. in Spitz 386). When he first heard "From Me to You" with its original guitar introduction, Martin suggested that John and Paul sing the opening motto—"da-da-da da-da-dun-dun-da"—along with an overdubbed harmonica part by John. Having forgotten his harmonica that day, John borrowed one from Malcolm Davies, a disc-cutter at EMI Studios. For the Beatles, it was a bold gesture to even consider singing the introduction to a rock and roll song, yet in its uniqueness, the vocal overture makes for one of the song's most innovative features.

"From Me to You" was clearly superior to "Thank You Little Girl," another composition that John and Paul had recently prepared. Retitled as "Thank You Girl," it was relegated to the single's B-side. In contrast with the disjunctive emotional moods established in "Misery" and "There's a Place," with their gloomy lyrical outlooks and their incongruously buoyant vocals, "Thank You Girl" offers a pure, unified vision of unfettered romance, as well as an intriguing early Beatles example of literary enjambment—"only a fool would doubt our love," John sings. "And all I've got to do / Is thank you girl, thank you girl." The upbeat music and saccharine lyrics exist in direct relation with one another. In this fashion, "Thank You Girl" provides an early example of the band's capacity for creating musical unity, albeit of the variety that will find many listeners looking away in embarrassment in the face of so much unblemished puppy love. Two other songs were recorded that day, including "One after 909," a Lennon-McCartney composition that dates back to April 1959, and "What Goes On." The former recording had improved only slightly over the July 1960 recording of the song in the McCartney family's bathroom. After five takes and various edits, the Beatles remained unsatisfied with "One after 909," particularly in terms of George's unimaginative stabs at producing a guitar solo.

With "From Me to You" winging its way to the top of the charts, where it would join *Please Please Me*, the group took a much-needed holiday from a breakneck routine that found them performing at bars, two-bit dance clubs, and ballrooms across the UK. But on April 18th, they added the esteemed Royal Albert Hall to their résumé, and, with their final Cavern performance on August 3rd, their days of such modest venues were once and truly over. For Paul, the Royal Albert Hall appearance brought him into the orbit of Jane Asher, already a renowned stage actress at the tender age of seventeen-years-old. As Cynthia Lennon recalled, "Paul fell for her like a ton of bricks. He was obviously as proud as a peacock with her. She was a great prize. The fact that she was already an established actress of stage and screen, very intelligent, and beautiful gave an enormous boost to his ego" (qtd. in Cross 89). But for John, April may have been one of the most transitory periods in his entire life. On April 8th, his son Julian was born in Liverpool. John first laid eyes on the newborn a few days later at the Sefton General Hospital, where the Beatle doted on his son. "Who's going to be a famous little rocker like his Dad then?" John boasted (qtd. in Spitz 395).[2] But in truth, John must have felt suffocated by marriage, by fatherhood, and, perhaps most confoundingly, by the first flush of fame. In recent weeks, he had been regularly seen in the company of raven-haired beauty Ida "Stevie" Holly, and, when it came time to get away from it all, John accompanied Brian Epstein on a two-week jaunt to Barcelona, while the rest of the Beatles relaxed on the beaches of Tenerife at Klaus Voormann's family cottage.

In Spain, John and Brian behaved like the pair of tourists that they were— shopping by day, wining and dining themselves by night at the city's stylish restaurants and nightclubs. "Cyn was having a baby," John remembered, "and the holiday was planned, and I wasn't going to break the holiday for a baby and that's what a *bastard* I was" (qtd. in Cross 89). In Brian's rented car, the travelers motored up and down the Costa Brava. Eventually, Brian became more openly gay with John. "I watched Brian picking up boys," John recalled, "and I liked playing it a bit faggy—it's enjoyable." In Sitges, John and Brian's relationship became more personal—although the degree of their intimacy remains uncertain. "It was almost a love affair," Lennon remembered, "but not quite. It was not consummated. But it was a pretty intense relationship" (qtd. in Spitz 403–04). Pete Shotton offered a slightly more concrete recollection in his memoirs: "I let him toss me off," John told him (73).[3] Whether John acted out of curiosity, impulsiveness, or sheer desire, his Spanish excursion with the Beatles' manager possessed larger implications for McCartney beyond his songwriting partner's sexuality. From "Love Me Do" and *Please Please Me* through the "From Me to You" single, their songs were pointedly credited to "McCartney-Lennon." Paul alleged that John plotted to reverse the order of their names during his vacation with Brian, who later asserted that the reversal resulted from their collective effort to simplify the cadence of Lennon and McCartney's authorial designation and create brand-name recognition—a tactic that clearly succeeded beyond their wildest dreams. According to Paul, Lennon "had the stronger personality, and I think he fixed things with Brian" (*Anthology* 94). From thence forward, the duo's songs were officially credited to "Lennon-McCartney," a practice that began with the release of the Beatles' next single, a little ditty entitled "She Loves You." At the end of April 1963, the Beatles established brand-name recognition of a similar sort when Ringo and Brian ventured out to London's Drum City in order to replace his tattered Premier drum kit with a new set of Ludwig drums. After Ringo selected an oyster-black pearl finish for his new kit, Epstein demanded that the store's owner, Ivor Arbiter, prepare a logo for the head of Ringo's bass drum. Without hesitation, Arbiter created the Beatles' world-famous drop-T logo, with its exaggerated capital B, on the spot.[4]

By July 1963, Brian Epstein had emerged as a genuine rock and roll impresario, and George Martin and his once lowly Parlophone label were the happy recipients of his sudden largesse. Over the next several years, Epstein's Liverpudlian acts scored one hit song after another. Gerry and the Pacemakers topped the UK charts with "How Do You Do It"—only to be dislodged by "From Me to You"—proving that Martin's intuition about the song's hit potential was right on the money. Billy J. Kramer and the Dakotas would reach the upper echelons of the UK charts with "Do You Want to Know a Secret," while Cilla Black, a former cloakroom attendant at the Cavern Club, enjoyed modest success on the UK charts in 1963 with the Lennon-McCartney composition "Love of the Loved," and reached the top of the charts with the Burt Bacharach-Hal David song "Anyone Who Had a Heart" the following year. The Fourmost would score a hit of their own in 1964 with "A Little Loving."

When the Beatles themselves arrived at EMI Studios on July 1st, they came armed with the raw material for a single that would make pop-musical history. "I was sitting in my usual place on a high stool in Studio Two when John and Paul first ran through the song on their acoustic guitars, George joining in on the choruses," Martin remembered. "I thought it was great but was intrigued by the final chord, an odd sort of major sixth, with George doing the sixth and John and Paul the third and fifths, like a Glenn Miller arrangement. They were saying 'It's a great chord! Nobody's ever heard it before!' Of course, I knew that wasn't quite true!" (qtd. in Lewisohn, *The Complete Beatles Recording Sessions* 32). Begun by Lennon and McCartney during the previous week in a Newcastle-upon-Tyne hotel room and completed the following night at Forthlin Road, "She Loves You" was inspired by the call-and-response structure of Bobby Rydell's recent hit "Forget Him," which counsels his young female fans to be wary of dubious male suitors: "Don't let him tell you that he wants you / 'Cause he can't give you love which isn't there." In addition to offering the inaugural performance of the Beatles' famous "yeah yeah yeah" vocal stylings, "She Loves You" is significant for the different points of view that it affords their male and female listeners, respectively. In one sense, the speaker provides gentle and much-needed reassurance to a wayward boyfriend—and, indeed, to a growing male audience—when he sings, "She said you hurt her so / She almost lost her mind / But now she says she knows / You're not the hurting kind." Yet at the same time, the speaker comforts the distraught girlfriend with his feelings of consolation and understanding, two facets that she is sorely lacking in her current romantic relationship. As with "From Me to You," such lyrics—splayed against the optimistic, upbeat backdrop of John and Paul's vocals and the band's equally buoyant music, particularly informed by the guitar ornamentation of George's recently acquired Gretsch Country Gentleman—find the Beatles speaking, quite literally, to their massive contingent of female listeners. Safe—but not *too* safe—the bandmates occupy a unique space in their fan's mindset: "The Beatles come across as being 'acceptable,'"

Sheila Whiteley writes, "as ideal boyfriends who are sexy but tuned into a girl's perspective, thus allowing them both to enjoy and to explore their own sexuality through association with their respective idols" (61). It was this decidedly nonthreatening sort of intimacy that would win their audience over through a deft combination of acceptance, sincerity, and style.[5]

For the B-side of "She Loves You," the Beatles recorded "I'll Get You," which had gone under the working title of "Get You in the End." In contrast with the single's A-side, "I'll Get You" offers an immodest celebration of true love's capacity for triumphing over every possible obstacle. In the world of "I'll Get You," which was pointedly influenced by Joan Baez's folk rendition of "All My Trials," love is a miracle that can be realized through the simple act of faith and fantasy: "Imagine I'm in love with you / It's easy 'cause I know / I've imagined I'm in love with you / Many, many, many times before / It's not like me to pretend / But I'll get you, I'll get you in the end." While Ian MacDonald rightly acknowledges the song's subterranean cheekiness—with its "mock-naïve love framed by sardonic 'oh yeahs'" and an "air of dry self-sendup" (65)—it's easy to imagine that most, if not all, of the group's listeners during that era and beyond might be easily swept up in the sincerity that lingers on the surface of "I'll Get You."

As "She Loves You" poised itself for runaway success on the UK charts—becoming the group's first single to sell a million copies—the Beatles began recording their second album. As with *Please Please Me*, *With the Beatles* intermingles a variety of new compositions with a smattering of cover versions from their live act over the past few years. Like "She Loves You" and many of their original songs circa 1963, the tracks on their new album rejoice, for the most part, in the transcendent power of carefree young romance. As with so many of their early compositions, the Beatles' songs during this era witness them in the act of trying on different personalities while simultaneously enduring the trials and tribulations of romantic love. These identities allowed them to comment upon particular aspects of human experience without necessarily assuming the more transparent guise of their autobiographical selves. Thus, a song's speaker—having been vocalized by John, Paul, George, or Ringo—becomes the *de facto* performer of the particular identity on display. The singer, then, gives voice—with the appropriate musical accompaniment—to Lennon and McCartney's various textual stances. The Beatles' early work finds John and Paul directing rudimentary, first- and second-person gestures at their listening audience—regularly adopting the pronominal perspective of an arbitrary "I" singing songs of love and adoration (or, conversely, despondency and loss) about an indiscriminate "you."

Recorded, for the most part, over eleven sessions from July through October 1963, *With the Beatles* continues the unabashed romantic sincerity inherent in their first album. For the speakers in many of their original songs—and, indeed, in several of their cover versions—the notion of romantic love exists as a powerful, life-altering experience. In its manifestation in a number of early Beatles songs, this form of love involves qualities associated with Eros, an object-centered, generally rational love for another individual. But it also features aspects associated with Agape, which connotes a subjective, unconditional, and—in contrast with Eros—irrational sense of love. The instances of love at first sight that leave so many of Lennon and McCartney's speakers thunderstruck in the face of love would seem to be erosic, yet Lynne Pearce contends that the first flush of love often presents a hybrid form of Eros and Agape. Such an amalgam, Pearce writes, "allows for the possibility of romantic love *beginning* erosically (*x* is arrested/seized by some attractive quality in *y*) and then becoming agapic (*x* now loves *y* in the involuntary/unconditional way in which one might love God)" (5). The romantic admixture of Eros and Agape in the songs of the early Beatles makes perfect sense when one takes into account the prevailing view of love during that same era, a period in which the would-be lovers of the day grappled with similar emotions of erosic certainty coupled with rash and involuntary feelings of unconditionality. During the late 1950s and early 1960s, Western culture "appears to have been swithering between a new agency and bravado, on the one hand, and an ongoing postwar impotence and existential despair, on the other," Pearce observes. "Women, in particular, still struggled to find a meaningful sense of selfhood, and this led, according to proto-feminists like Betty Friedan, to a strained overemphasis on femininity and sexuality" (164). This phenomenon resulted in a complicated double-bind in which conservative 1950s-era social values collided with a growing sense of sexual freedom in the early 1960s. And for the Beatles—whose music during this period enjoyed a massive audience of receptive female listeners—this highly complex sociocultural tension manifested itself in the relatively simplistic message that romantic love was both a totalizing erosic experience of steadfast commitment and an unconsidered state of infinite certainty.

It is hardly surprising, then, that *With the Beatles* erupts into being with "It Won't Be Long," a song that sets the album's unswerving romantic tone into motion. With the exception of "Till There Was You" and "Not a Second Time," the Beatles' instrumentation for *With the Beatles* would be remarkably consistent, with John on his Rickenbacker 325, Paul on his Höfner violin bass, and George playing his trusty Gretsch Country Gentleman. Musically, "It Won't Be Long" attacks the listener with the brute force of unwavering confidence. As Harrison picks out a series of descending guitar figures, Ringo's backbeat and John's rhythm guitar propel the song ever forward. Lyrically, the track begins with a burst of energy: "It won't be long," Lennon sings, before cascading, along with Paul and George, into the call-and-response chorus of "yeah, *yeah*, yeah, *yeah*, yeah, *yeah*." As with "P.S. I Love You" and "From Me to You," the speaker longs to return to the reassuring company of his beloved. Yet in contrast with those songs, the speaker in "It Won't Be Long" feels a stronger urgency, a lonely sense of disconnectedness in his lover's absence. The middle-eight underscores this point as the music and lyrics retreat, if only briefly, from the pulsing beat of the chorus: "Since you left me I'm so alone / Now you're coming, you're coming on home / I'll be good like I know I should / You're coming home, you're coming home." The speaker can scarcely imagine risking the pure bliss of his current relationship for a dalliance with another—"I'll be good like I know I should"—for the simple reason that the utopian dream of their romantic love might come to an end. "It won't be long," the speaker sings, aglow with the self-assurance that only true love can furnish, "till I belong to you." In so doing, Lennon and McCartney craft a clever pun that juxtaposes the speaker's temporal longing with the literal notion of *belonging* to his soulmate, who lingers somewhere offstage, despite her considerable presence in her lover's consciousness.

With "It Won't Be Long," romantic love exists as an all-purpose, all-consuming antidote for the intervals and pauses that prevent us from experiencing life on our own terms—and, more significantly, without the frustration of postponing the satiation of our desires. Written with Smokey Robinson and the Miracles on his mind, John's "All I've Got to Do" offers a soothing rejoinder to the delays that send the speaker of "It Won't Be Long" into his not-so-protracted loneliness. With the telephone as the instrument of his release, the speaker in "All I've Got to Do" can realize his romantic gratification with the turn of the dial on his rotary telephone. "When I want to kiss you," he sings. "All I've got to do / Is call you on the phone, / And you'll come running home, / Yeah, that's all I've got to do." Such spellbinding immediacy is entirely unavailable for the speaker in Paul's "All My Loving," who must console his beloved in advance of the journey that will separate them on the morrow. As with so many of the Beatles' songs about romantic reunion, "All My Loving" depicts its speaker in the act of affirming his love, promising that his feelings will remain true and unwavering during his absence from her world. "I'll pretend that I'm kissing / The lips I am missing / And hope that my dreams will come true," he proclaims. "And then while I'm away, / I'll write home every day, / And I'll send all my loving to you." Musically, "All My Loving" is one of the Beatles' most intriguing early compositions. As MacDonald points out, the song benefits from its "elegant simplicity," as well as from McCartney's double-tracked vocal, which is "irresistibly joyous" (72). Recorded in thirteen takes in a single session on July 30th, the song features neatly bookended verses. Shrewdly positioned instances of stop-time between them bring the track to a sudden halt, only to be reawakened by Paul's buoyant singing and, in one memorable instance, Harrison's Carl Perkins-inspired guitar break.[6] With its country-and-western, perhaps even slightly Hawaiian, flavor, the twangy guitar interlude provides the song with an air of carefree abandon, reassuring listeners that the adoring couple's love will indeed remain forever true. No song encapsulates the pure joy and exuberance of the early Beatles quite like "All My Loving." It revels in unmitigated elation and the sheer magic of being alive.

The same can hardly be said for Harrison's "Don't Bother Me," the guitarist's inaugural recording as a songwriter. In "Don't Bother Me," the speaker contends with his wayward lover's absence by plunging himself into self-imposed isolation in order to wallow in his all-encompassing pain. With its appropriately stern musical demeanor, "Don't Bother Me" finds its speaker, not surprisingly, at erosic and agapic cross-purposes: "I know I'll never be the same / If I don't get her back again," he sings. "Because I know she'll always be / The only girl for me." On the one hand, his love remains unconditional— involuntary, unexplainable—yet on the other, his broken heart can only be mended by the highly individualized expression of her particular love. By contrast, the next track, "Little Child," seems positively frivolous. By concocting one-dimensional metaphors for narrating youthful experience during this period, Lennon and McCartney engaged in a series of language games—verbal experiments, if nothing else—that derive little, if any, genuine meaning. Inspired by British folk singer Elton Hayes's "Whistle My Love" and recorded in some twenty takes over three different sessions, "Little Child" finds John singing the line "I'm so sad and lonely" with pure gusto and abandon. As if his bombastic vocal weren't enough, the music's upbeat phrasings belie his lyric's *faux* melancholy at nearly every turn. In "Hold Me Tight," the Beatles' next original composition on the album, the speaker objectifies his beloved as both the tonic for his loneliness and the antidote for his desire. Resuscitated from the *Please Please Me* sessions, "Hold Me Tight" features a tight rock and roll groove in which the singer seduces his girlfriend by amplifying the power of her love to slake his yearnings. "You don't know what it means to hold you tight," he sings. "Being here alone tonight with you" and "making love to only you," he adds, will bring his world into a perfect, comforting repose. There is no denying the speaker's overarching self-involvement. As one of the early Beatles' most blatantly sexual compositions, "Hold Me Tight" hints at a subjective reorientation away from the beloved and toward the more adult self that will begin to characterize their work in 1964. As Pearce observes, it is the self— in both its social and sexual manifestations—that "is truly the limit-point of love; which is why the sexual act, and its temporary oblivion, is its most consummate metaphor. Love which ends with the self and not with the other," she cautions, "is also, inevitably, the end of the story, the end of the relationship" (141). And, not surprisingly, it also signals the end of puppy love's idealized fantasy.

As with *Please Please Me*, *With the Beatles* features a selection of cover versions from the band's rapidly decaying stage act, including "Please Mr. Postman," "You Really Got a Hold on Me," and "Money (That's What I Want)," which Paul Du Noyer describes as "Lennon's Motown trilogy" (80). A tight, surprisingly lifeless remake of the Marvelettes' hit single "Please Mr. Postman" pales in comparison to John's inspired, soulful vocal on Smokey Robinson's "You Really Got a Hold on Me," which, like "Twist and Shout," actually improves on the original recording. With George Martin's Steinway piano helpfully guiding the melody, John offers one of the most moving vocal performances of his career. As with so many of their cover versions, the Beatles' recording of "Money" transforms the original, with its comparatively relaxed air, by punching up the song's structure with a relentless backbeat and a driving vocal performance—in this case, a powerful duet by Lennon and McCartney. The band's rendition of Berry Gordy and Janie Bradford's composition brings the album to a close in much the same fashion as "Twist and Shout" does on their first album. Along the way, the Beatles offer three additional remakes, including the Broadway standard "Till There Was You," which Paul croons with unflinching sincerity.[7] A song from Meredith Wilson's hit Broadway show *The Music Man* (1957), "Till There Was You" features George's note-perfect Spanish-inflected solo on his nylon-stringed José Ramírez classical guitar, as well as Ringo on the bongos. No doubt inspired by Jim McCartney's own penchant for show tunes, Paul's performance of "Till There Was You" underscores the musical eclecticism that will define much of his unparalleled career in popular music. The cover versions on *With the Beatles* are rounded out by George's lead vocals on a tepid rendition of "Devil in Her Heart"— fashioned after the Donays' 1961 hit "Devil in His Heart"—and, far more impressively, Chuck Berry's "Roll over Beethoven," which had been a staple of the band's live act since the Quarry Men days of the late 1950s.

With the Beatles features two additional original compositions, including "I Wanna Be Your Man," which figured prominently in the band's growing friendship with an up-and-coming rhythm and blues quintet that called themselves the Rolling Stones, and "Not a Second Time," a song that heralded the Beatles' abrupt arrival into the high-minded world of serious musical scrutiny. With Ringo on lead vocals and Martin playing EMI Studios' Hammond organ, the group's version of "I Wanna Be Your Man" offers a serviceable rock and roll hook with just enough panache to earn the tune, with its relatively meek sexual come-on, a regular place on their set list through the summer of 1966. The Beatles first met the Rolling Stones back in April at London's Crawdaddy Club, and a chance encounter in September between Lennon and McCartney and the Stones' manager and publicist Andrew Loog Oldham brought "I Wanna Be Your Man" into the fledgling band's orbit. John and Paul actually finished the composition, which was inspired by Benny Spellman's "Fortune Teller," in the presence of Oldham and the Rolling Stones, whose version of the song features Brian Jones on slide guitar and a comparatively uninhibited lead vocal performance by Mick Jagger. The Stones' "I Wanna Be Your Man" ultimately peaked at a respectable #12 on the UK charts. While Lennon and McCartney's "I Wanna Be Your Man" enjoys obvious historical significance for its role in the Stones' emergence on England's rock and roll scene, "Not a Second Time" marked the first instance in which the Beatles received songwriting accolades beyond the low culture of the pop-music press. In a December 1963 article in the *Times*, William Mann famously saluted John's composition for its deployment of an Aeolian cadence, a feature that Mann likened to the chord progression that concludes Gustav Mahler's *The Song of the Earth* (1907–1909).[8] Years later, Lennon remarked that "to this day I don't have *any* idea what [Aeolian cadences] are. They sound like exotic birds." Yet way back in 1963, John could barely contain his excitement at Mann's sophisticated response to the band's work, going so far as to have the article framed: "That was the first time anyone had written anything like that about us" (qtd. in Dowlding 57). For Lennon and McCartney, the stakes of authorship were slowly but surely growing in significance, and their friendly writerly competition was poised for a transformation that neither of them could have expected. For Mann, the Beatles were already making an innovative and vital contribution to popular music: "They have brought a distinctive and exhilarating flavor into a genre of music that was in danger of ceasing to be music at all," he remarked. It makes "one wonder with interest what the Beatles, and particularly Lennon and McCartney, will do next."

～

And soon, with the dark clouds of an international tragedy and a most fortuitous hit single, the Beatles would be sharing their distinctive and exhilarating sound with an American record-buying public who had succeeded in resisting their charms throughout the early throes of British Beatlemania. In addition to their triumph at the London Palladium, October 1963 witnessed the group's first four-track recordings. Previously constrained by EMI Studios' two-track tape machines, the band frequently had to resort to the recording technique known as "bouncing down," the process in which multiple tracks are mixed and then recorded on an unused track, thus allowing the original tracks to be erased and made available for additional instruments.[9] Yet all that changed on October 17th, when they recorded two new compositions, the second of which was "This Boy," a gentle, three-part harmony in 12/8 time that bespeaks of lost love and loneliness. But the real story of that fateful day was the recording of "I Want to Hold Your Hand," a song that Lennon and McCartney wrote after Epstein urged them to aspire for a distinctly American sound. Working at the piano in the basement of Jane Asher's house on London's Wimpole Street, John and Paul—sitting "eyeball to eyeball" at the keyboard—were singing, "Oh you-u-u . . . got that something," when Paul happened upon a B-minor chord. "That's *it!*" John exclaimed. "Do that again!" (*All We Are Saying* 138).[10] And with that, a classic was born. A pleasing blend of African American rhythm and blues, West Coast surf music, and high-octane rock and roll, "I Want to Hold Your Hand" detonates into the collective consciousness with Harrison's driving lead guitar, which affords the song with doses of energy and intensity that pilot it through the subtle arpeggios of the middle-eight and the commanding flourish that brings it home. Lyrically, the track continues the thematic conventions of *With the Beatles*, in which the idea of love offers a totalizing utopian dream, an idyll in which unconditionality and desire live in perfect compatibility. As Tim Riley remarks, "The love relationship extends beyond one specific lover" in "I Want to Hold Your Hand" to "the idea of love itself and an affirmation of all it can offer" (89). It was a winning combination that no one—not even those unsuspecting fans in the New World—could resist for long.

As with the heady days of August 1962, the first blustery weeks of winter 1963 loom large in the Beatles' story. In the company of Neil Aspinall and their recently acquired roadie Mal Evans, a former bouncer at the Cavern Club and a one-time postal engineer, the group played a quartet of songs for their Royal Variety Command Performance on November 4th at the Prince of Wales Theatre. Before closing their set with "Twist and Shout," John audaciously remarked to the venue's regal audience, "For our last number, I'd like to ask your help. The people in the cheaper seats, clap your hands, and the rest of you, if you'd just rattle your jewelry" (qtd. in Spitz 434).[11] Within a week, Brian Epstein traveled to New York in order to meet with American television personality Ed Sullivan. As luck would have it, the Beatles had come into Sullivan's orbit on the morning of October 31st, having just landed at London's Heathrow Airport. Sullivan had flown in from the United States to scout out talent for his popular CBS variety show, when he and his wife Sylvia encountered the thousands of ecstatic fans who had gathered at the airport to welcome their idols home. On November 11th, Epstein met with Sullivan in New York City, and the dueling impresarios quickly struck a deal: for $10,000, plus expenses, the Beatles would perform on three consecutive installments of Sullivan's program. Wasting little time, Brian set his sights on Capitol Records, the EMI subsidiary that, for the balance of 1963, had refused to consider releasing the Beatles stateside. Afforded the right of first refusal by their parent company, Capitol had given the band a listen way back in January 1963 before scuttling them to their growing pile of rejected British imports. Having been rebuffed by Capitol, the group's wares had been considered, and passed on, by such American music luminaries as Columbia, RCA, Mercury, and United Artists before finding a home at Chicago's tiny Vee-Jay Records. But fate was clearly not on the Beatles' side. As EMI prepared the group's recordings for their conveyance to Vee-Jay, the company's president, Ewart Abner, had flown to Las Vegas to celebrate his fortieth birthday. Within a week, he had accumulated massive losses at the tables that left Vee-Jay on the cusp of bankruptcy and without the necessary operating capital to promote the Beatles (Spitz 388-89). Released without fanfare in February and March, respectively, Vee-Jay's single versions of "Please Please Me" and "From Me to You" languished in American obscurity, while their Parlophone counterparts topped the charts across the Atlantic.[12]

By the time that Epstein arrived in New York City, Capitol Records had been ordered by EMI's managing director L. G. Wood to release the Beatles' next single without delay. Having racked up nearly three hundred thousand advance orders for *With the Beatles* alone, EMI could simply no longer wait for its American subsidiary to come around. With the band slated to perform on the *Ed Sullivan Show* on February 9th, 1964, promoter Sid Bernstein signed them for a pair of shows at Carnegie Hall that same week. Having originally planned to press a mere five thousand copies of "I Want to Hold Your Hand," Capitol earmarked the impressive sum of $40,000 to promote the single in the United States (Spitz 443–44). As history would so resoundingly prove, it would go down as one of the most astute investments in the annals of popular music. On November 22nd, Parlophone released *With the Beatles* to the hungry ears of the British record-buying public. With its shadowy cover photograph by Robert Freeman, the album pointedly depicted the band as serious musicians, rather than mere pop sensations. In England, the sheer joy inherent in the record's release was palpable. Yet meanwhile, back in the States, President John F. Kennedy was felled by a lone gunman in Dallas, and, to borrow a phrase from William Butler Yeats, "all changed, changed utterly" (84). Nothing could have prepared Americans—indeed, the world—for the devastation of the Kennedy assassination and its attendant effects upon a nation's belief in itself and its possibilities for the future. But then, like a proverbial breath of fresh air, the Fab Four arrived on the scene in February 1964, and a nation in mourning became transfixed by "I Want to Hold Your Hand" and the notion—pleasant relief that it was—of meeting the Beatles.

Notes

1. Canadian journalist Sandy Gardiner is often erroneously credited with coining the term "Beatlemania," which appeared in his *Ottawa Journal* article entitled "Heavy Disc Dose Spreads Disease in England" on November 9th, 1963—nearly a month after the *Daily Mirror*'s headline made its way into print in London.

2. After the media finally discovered the existence of John and Cynthia's secret marriage in late 1963, Epstein persuaded the Beatles to "make the best of it," according to Peter Brown and Steven Gaines: "A married Beatle with an adorable baby son [Julian] was wholesome enough for their image—as long as none of the newspapers pointed out that Cynthia was obviously pregnant before John married her" (102).

3. Allegations of John and Brian's intimacy reached their fever pitch at Paul's twenty-first birthday party in Liverpool on June 18th, 1963. Bob Wooler, one of the band's long-time confidants and supporters, made a sarcastic remark about John and Brian's "honeymoon in Spain," and Lennon thrashed him within an inch of his life: "I was beating the shit out of him," John recalled, "and for the first time I thought, 'I can kill this guy'" (qtd. in Spitz 415). With that—and a fairly modest out-of-court settlement—the Cavern DJ who had been instrumental in the group's early success was effectively out of their lives. John's April 1963 holiday with Brian is explored in Christopher Münch's film *The Hours and Times* (1992).

4. As Gerry Evans, the manager of Drum City, later recalled, "The Beatles logo that we know today with the drop-T was created in our store by Eddie Stokes, the songwriter who used to do the front of the bass-drum heads for us. He would come in during his lunchtime because he had worked locally. Ivor Arbiter drew the Beatles logo on a pad of paper, then had Eddie put what he had sketched on the drum head.... I think we charged £5 extra for the artwork" (qtd. in Babiuk 88). The logo was registered as the Beatles' official trademark by Apple Corps, Ltd. in the late 1990s (see Babiuk 89).

5. As Jane Tompkins points out, the Beatles "didn't protect themselves with sophistication or righteousness or sheer masculinity; they tried vulnerability and it worked, so they tried it some more. What a relief! Their voices didn't have that authoritarian baritone of a lot of male singers who declared, with every note, the supremacy of the male point of view. And though young, they weren't empty-headed *vitelloni* with tans and white teeth and tight bathing suits who had never had a thought and never would have one. There was something new about the Beatles. The newness wasn't only generational; it had to do with gender and authority and showing your feelings and being vulnerable and wanting to change the world. They believed in love.... They had compassion, and wonder, and delight" (216–17).

6. According to the Center for Black Music Research, stop-time finds its origins in African-American popular music, with notable examples occurring in such compositions as Scott Joplin's "The Ragtime Dance" and Jelly Roll Morton's "King Porter Stomp." In addition to affording space for soloists, stop-time provided audiences with moments in which to share their enthusiasm and applause ("Project Stop-Time").

7. McCartney was known to introduce "Till There Was You" as a number "by our favorite American group, Sophie Tucker," although the Beatles employed this running gag with other songs as well, including their performance of "I Want to Hold Your Hand" on the *Ed Sullivan Show* on February 16th, 1964.

8. Mann's allusion to Mahler coheres rather appropriately with Lennon and McCartney's sustained textual analyses of nostalgia. As Michalis Lapidakis observes, Mahler's modernism connotes a certain "quality of nostalgia that provides his music with [its] characteristic tragic tone" and its "paradigmatic manifestation of musical pluralism."

9. Bouncing down ultimately results in a generational loss with each successive bounce. As Kevin Ryan and Brian Kehew observe, "Several tracks on *With the Beatles* ('Little Child,' 'Devil in Her Heart,' 'Money [That's What I Want],' and "I Wanna Be Your Man') saw three overdub bounces, meaning the final mix of each song was four generations removed from the initial take. In most cases, though, they generally tried to limit overdubs to a single bounce if possible" (359).

10. Paul lived on the top floor of the Ashers' home on London's Wimpole Street from 1964 to 1966, when he moved into his own residence in St. John's Wood near EMI Studios. Jane's father, Richard, was a revered psychiatrist who enjoyed renown for identifying and naming the Munchausen Syndrome, in which patients manufacture illnesses in order to receive attention from medical professionals. Jane's brother Peter achieved fame as a member of Peter and Gordon, a pop duo that scored a hit single with the Lennon-McCartney composition "A World without Love."

11. During the band's rehearsals for the performance, John claimed that he intended to ask the audience to "rattle your fucking jewelry," a threat that left Epstein absolutely paralyzed with fear. "You could almost hear him exhale," the group's publicist Tony Barrow later recalled, after Lennon had delivered the line without using the expletive (qtd. in Spitz 434).

12. Tollie Records, a subsidiary of Vee-Jay, released single versions of "Twist and Shout" and "Love Me Do" in the spring of 1964.

Chapter 6

The Biggest Showbiz Town Ever

*We were in Paris when a telegram came through from
Capitol Records saying that "I Want to Hold Your
Hand" had gone number one in America. We just
jumped on each other's backs and screamed the whole
place down. The cheekiest thing the Beatles ever
did was say to our manager that we didn't want
to go to America until we were number one.*

—Paul McCartney

It is almost impossible to imagine what it was like to be at ground zero of
American Beatlemania on February 7th, 1964, when the group landed at New
York City's John F. Kennedy International Airport, which had been renamed
some fifty days earlier in honor of the fallen leader. The band's Pan Am flight
was met with the screams and fanfare of some five thousand people, whom the
Beatles claimed to have heard—incredible as it may seem—even as the plane
was taxiing along the runway. As Stephen Glynn presciently remarks, "The
spirit of Camelot, shot down in Dallas, Texas, had flown over from Liverpool,
England, and the unprecedented euphoria that greeted the group seemed part
of an expiation, a nation shaking itself out of its grief and mourning" (61).[1]
There is little question that the Beatles' timing in the history of the United
States was uncanny, as well as a welcome respite from the national malaise, but
one cannot overlook the power of marketing in a new media era unlike any
that the postwar world had ever seen. Capitol Records had saturated the city
with posters announcing "The Beatles Are Coming," while New York's WMCA
and WINS radio stations had given away T-shirts—and, rumor has it, one dollar each—to thousands of teenagers who greeted the Beatles that Friday afternoon on the JFK tarmac.[2] Released in December 1963 by Capitol, "I Want to
Hold Your Hand" had sold more than one million copies by mid-January, an

astounding feat for a group that had been largely unheard of on American shores scarcely a month before.[3] On Sunday, February 9th, the Beatles launched into a spirited rendition of "All My Loving" on the *Ed Sullivan Show* before some seventy-three million television viewers, a figure that accounted for nearly forty percent of the population of the United States at that time. During one memorable week in April, the Beatles occupied the top five spots on the Billboard Hot 100, including "Can't Buy Me Love" at #1, "Twist and Shout" at #2, "She Loves You" at #3, "I Want to Hold Your Hand" at #4, and "Please Please Me" at #5. In Australia, some three hundred thousand fans greeted the Beatles' arrival, while baseball owner Charlie Finley paid the band an unprecedented $150,000 fee for a single performance in Kansas City, Missouri.[4] It was a year, in short, in which the group's unparalleled level of success—of becoming, indisputably, the "toppermost of the poppermost"—trumped their wildest dreams at nearly every turn. As Lester Bangs astutely observed, the phenomenon of the Beatles was "not simply a matter of music, but of event" (qtd. in Marcus 181).

Yet the giddy days of 1964 and the Beatles' conquering of America—which Paul later described, tongue-in-cheek, as "the biggest showbiz town ever"—were not without strife (*Anthology* documentary). There was the evening of February 11th, for instance, in which the group accepted their countrymen's invitation to visit the British Embassy in Washington, DC. The occasion was a benefit for the National Society for the Prevention of Cruelty to Children, the favorite charity of Lady Ormsby-Gore. The Beatles arrived at around one o'clock in the morning, having spent the evening performing in the round at the Washington Coliseum, where they were being filmed by CBS for a March closed-circuit telecast in American cinemas. After every third song, Mal Evans shifted Ringo's drum riser so as to allow the group to face another quadrant of the audience. It was a maneuver that worked fairly well until the drum riser became stuck, thus causing an irritating delay in the otherwise festive proceedings. Nevertheless, it was an ecstatic, bravura performance in spite of the venue's awful acoustics. By the time that the Beatles arrived at the embassy, they were understandably exhausted. Ushered into a party room with some three hundred guests, the group found themselves besieged by British glitterati. "We want autographs!" they shouted, with one woman asking aloud, "Can they really write?" As Canadian journalist Bruce Phillips remembered, "There was more than a hint of the master-servant relationship in one [embassy official's] voice when he said: 'Come along, you there, you've got to come and do your stuff.'" As if to make matters worse, one of the diplomat's wives surprised Ringo by sneaking up behind him and, with her nail scissors at the ready, snipping a sizable lock of his hair as a souvenir. "What the hell do you think you're doing?" the usually affable drummer demanded. Photographer Harry Benson was struck by the group's reaction as they left the embassy. "They were very sad. They looked as if they wanted to cry, John, in particular. They weren't pugnacious. They were humiliated" (qtd. in Spitz 478). It was yet another reminder, as Ringo was fond of putting it, that the four lads from the North Country would always be, at least in many upper-class eyes—and, worse yet, perhaps even in their own—"shitkickers from Liverpool" (*Anthology* documentary). As a result of the British Embassy fiasco, the Beatles sternly rebuked Epstein for accepting the invitation in the first place, and they insisted, moreover, that they would never submit themselves to such degradation ever again. It was a pledge that would prove, in time, to exact far-reaching consequences.

The Beatles' privacy and any hope of anonymity notwithstanding, the first casualty of their near-global fame would be their once-vaunted stage act, which had devolved from its highly professional state at the beginning of 1962 into twenty-five-minute scream-fests by early 1964. "We were out of tune," Paul remembered, but "it didn't matter—we couldn't hear it, nor could they." As Ringo recalled, "I couldn't do anything clever. I couldn't do drum kicks or rolls or fills. I just had to hang onto the backbeat all the time to keep everybody together. I used to have to follow their three bums wiggling to see where we were in the song."[5] In spite of their monumental lack of free time and personal space—racking up tens of thousands of air miles on tour, going from one mind-numbing press conference to another, pining away in hotel rooms in cities they would never really see—their musical artistry continued on its upward swing. Yet for all of their creative strides in 1964, their work as recording artists that year had begun with a thud, albeit a very fleeting one. On the morning of January 29th, George Martin waited in vain for the Beatles to join him in Paris's Pathé Marconi Studios. He had traveled to Paris, along with Norman Smith and a translator, to prepare German-language versions of "I Want to Hold Your Hand" and "She Loves You" for distribution by West Germany's Odeon label, an EMI subsidiary that had been pressuring their parent company for a Beatles release in their mother tongue. Relaxing in their suite at the George V Hotel, the band had decided not to go to the session after all. Martin was livid, to say the least:

> I barged into their suite, to be met by this incredible sight, right out of the Mad Hatter's tea party. Jane Asher—Paul's girlfriend—with her long red hair, was pouring tea from a china pot, and the others were sitting around her like March Hares. They took one look at me and *exploded*, like in a school room when the headmaster enters. Some dived into the sofa and hid behind cushions, others dashed behind curtains. "You are bastards!" I screamed, to which they responded with impish little grins and roguish apologies. (qtd. in Lewisohn, *The Complete Beatles Recording Sessions* 38)

Within minutes, the Beatles were on their way to the studio, where they dubbed German-language vocals in order to create the tracks that would be known as "Komm, Gib Mir Deine Hand" ["I Want to Hold Your Hand"] and "Sie Liebt Dich" ["She Loves You"]. But the sessions at Pathé Marconi would achieve renown for a very different reason—namely, a new McCartney composition, "Can't Buy Me Love," that the group recorded that day in just four takes. Having arrived in Paris for an extended run at the Olympia Theatre, the band spent much of their free time writing new songs for their first feature film, which Epstein had negotiated with United Artists back in October. "Can't Buy Me Love" had only recently been completed, and, after less than an hour in the studio, the song had evolved from a blues effusion with a backing vocal that perfunctorily echoes the lead to a tight rock number. George Martin cleverly suggested that the band reorient the song's structure. "We've got to have an introduction," he remarked, "something that catches the ear immediately, a hook. So let's start out with the chorus" (qtd. in Cross 327). In so doing, the Beatles crafted a track that captures the senses with its trademark chorus overture. Played on his Gretsch Country Gentleman, George's guitar solo is a masterwork of energy and style that benefits, in eerie fashion, from the guitarist's earlier attempts at the solo, which can be heard leaking into the mix in the extreme background. The song's central tenet—that the essence of true love cannot be bartered with material goods—coheres with Lennon and McCartney's romantic idyll, a fantastical view of love that had begun to wane, rather precipitously, with their most recent spate of compositions.

Recorded on February 25th back at EMI Studios in St. John's Wood, John's "You Can't Do That" was written with Wilson Pickett on the songwriter's mind. It also marks the beginning of the end for the Beatles' miniature narratives about puppy love's untenable contrivance of erosic and agapic qualities. With his newly acquired Rickenbacker twelve-string guitar at the ready, Harrison imbues the song with its insistent drive, while Lennon turns in a guitar solo with the appropriate rhythmic intensity to underscore the speaker's anxiety over his beloved's uncertain affections: "Well, it's the second time I've caught you talking to him / Do I have to tell you one more time I think it's a sin? / I think I'll let you down / And leave you flat / Because I told you before / Oh, you can't do that." The song's middle-eight demonstrates the speaker's growing concerns that his beloved's infidelities will expose him as a cuckold in front of his friends. Interestingly, his fear seems more rooted in the notion that he will be embarrassed before his peers—who admire him for landing such a delectable girlfriend—than in the reality that she has so easily betrayed him. "You Can't Do That" was slated as the B-side of the "Can't Buy Me Love" single, which became an international smash hit in March, when it sold more than two million copies during its first week of release in the United States. The February 25th sessions also witnessed the emergence of two additional compositions, "And I Love Her" and "I Should Have Known Better"—each of which was written in haste for the still-untitled feature film, which was scheduled to begin principal photography on March 2nd. The title was delivered from the lips of Ringo, who, after a particularly long and difficult day in Beatledom, was said to have uttered, "It's been a hard day's night."[6] With the name of the film in hand, Lennon penned the title track in breakneck fashion. Recorded on April 16th, "A Hard Day's Night" opens in unforgettable style with Harrison's distinctive, chiming chord—a G7-suspended played on his Rickenbacker twelve-string: "We knew it would open both the film and the soundtrack LP," Martin recalled, "so we wanted a particularly strong and effective beginning. The strident guitar chord was the perfect launch" (qtd. in Lewisohn, *The Complete Beatles Recording Sessions* 43). The album *A Hard Day's Night* was released on July 10th, 1964, and it finds the group at a musical crossroads from which they'd never look back. It also marks the first Beatles album comprised entirely of original compositions, with nary a cover version in sight.

The title track spins what seems—in the style of "It Won't Be Long" and "All My Loving"—like yet another yarn about star-crossed lovers yearning for pure romantic reunion. But in truth, it's nothing of the sort. The lovers are divided alright, but by nothing more than the drudgery of the nine-to-five workaday world. And while they may, indeed, be in love, their relationship is highly conditional—contemporary in every possible way—and chockfull of material and sexual expectations. "It's been a hard day's night, and I've been working like a dog," John's speaker tells us. "It's been a hard day's night, I should be sleeping like a log." Toiling all the day long "to get you money to buy you things," he sings, "it's worth it just to hear you say you're going to give me everything." By day, the speaker's beloved receives her material reward; by night, he derives the sexual gratification that brings him release, solace, even well-earned romantic calm. With Paul's harmony booming into the vocal stratosphere, the middle-eight finds the couple enjoying a romantic connection, albeit one whose bedrock is founded upon a well-honed set of adult-oriented needs: "When I'm home, everything seems to be right / When I'm home, feeling you holding me tight—tight, yeah." Introduced by a raspy shriek of inhibition from John, Harrison's guitar solo affords the song with an elegant interlude amidst all of the number's energy and desire. It also represents a signal moment in the Beatles' corpus, given that it would be all but impossible for George to reproduce the solo on stage.[7] If the band could hear above the din of their screaming fans—a near-impossibility in and of itself—the group could reasonably hope to produce a note-perfect rendition of "Can't Buy Me Love" in concert. Yet the sheer velocity of the solo in "A Hard Day's Night," achieved via Martin's wound-up piano effect, resulted in a guitar figure that could only find flight in the recording studio. With the producer "doubling" George's guitar solo on Studio Two's upright piano, sound engineer Geoff Emerick rolled the tape at half-speed in the control room above. With only one free track available on the mixing desk, Emerick watched the "two Georges—Harrison and Martin—working side by side in the studio, foreheads furrowed in concentration as they played the rhythmically complex solo in tight unison on their respective instruments" (84).[8]

In contrast with the title track, "I Should Have Known Better" hearkens back to the band's *With the Beatles*-era notions of romance. In the middle-eight, the speaker revels in the undiluted power of love as a mechanism for self-revelation: "When I tell you that I love you, / You're gonna say you love me too. / And when I ask you to be mine, / You're gonna say you love me too." With its driving harmonica introduction and John's Jumbo acoustic engaged in a rhythmic duet with Harrison's emphatic Rickenbacker accents, "I Should Have Known Better" can't help but warm even the most cynical of hearts, although love's romantic spell is quickly broken by the tortured passion play inherent in "If I Fell." Later described by Lennon as a turning point of sorts in his work as a songwriter—"that's my first attempt at a ballad proper" (qtd. in Dowlding 69)—"If I Fell" tells the story of a bewildered soul whose character, lost amidst his very worldly fears, is brought to life by one of Lennon and McCartney's most beautiful and heartrending harmonies on record. In the song, the speaker seems to be making tentative steps toward a new romantic relationship, although his attitude regarding his former lover belies his alleged emotional growth: "I must be sure from the very start, / That you would love me more than her," he cautions his prospective girlfriend, conspicuously reminding her that his erstwhile love "will cry when she learns we are two." At one of life's great crossroads, the speaker finds himself—as with the narrator in Robert Frost's "The Road Not Taken"—in a beguiling quandary. He may recognize, as in Frost's poem, that he may eventually be telling his story "with a sigh / Somewhere ages and ages hence," but for now, the speaker in "If I Fell" can only contemplate the possibilities of new love and their potential ramifications (1). The only thing that is certain, it seems, is that neither choice—neither of the metaphorical roads that lie before him—will ever restore the lost romantic world that he once shared with his estranged lover.

In itself, "If I Fell" underscores the explicit disparities between the innocent narratives of the early Beatles of 1962–1963 and their mature, eminently more fractured and authentic counterparts in 1964 and beyond: "I've been in love before," John and Paul sing, "And I found that love was more / Than just holding hands." In the end, it is the speaker's ego—his wounded pride—that spells the difference between heartbreak and bliss: "'Cause I couldn't stand the pain / And I would be sad if our new love was in vain." In short, there are winners and losers in the "real" love of "If I Fell," and it is knowing which one you are that matters in the very complicated, painful game of adult romance. It is a brutal, excruciating truth that love's calculus often dictates the manner in which one person's happiness can only be gained through another's despair. By way of contrast, "I'm Happy Just to Dance with You" offers a throwback to a simpler time when the sock hop was the one and only romantic proving ground. Explicitly written by Lennon for George to undertake as lead vocalist—"I couldn'ta sung it," John later confessed (qtd. in Dowlding 70)—"I'm Happy Just to Dance with You" finds its speaker achieving divine contentment by merely basking in his beloved's company: "I don't want or need to hold your hand / Well, it's only try and understand / 'Cause there's really nothing I would rather do / 'Cause I'm happy just to dance with you." With its "Bo Diddley rhythm guitar pattern," in MacDonald's words, the song achieves its resolution when the speaker, with no great surprise betrayed in his voice, discovers "I'm in love with you" (87).

For all of the chaos in their lives, the Beatles enjoyed a reasonable working pace in the studio during the production of *A Hard Day's Night*. The album was recorded sporadically over several sessions between February 25th, earlier if you count their stint at Pathé Marconi, and June 2nd. After completing "I'm Happy Just to Dance with You" at the beginning of March, the Beatles turned to a pair of songs intended for summer release in the United Kingdom on their *Long Tall Sally* EP, including "I Call Your Name," a Lennon-McCartney composition that had been ceded to Billy J. Kramer and the Dakotas as the B-side to their "Bad to Me" single, which had also been written by the Beatles' songwriting duo. A pulsing rocker with nifty guitar work by Harrison and Lennon, "I Call Your Name" is distinguished by John's middle-eight guitar solo, which he later revealed to be a rudimentary attempt at ska, a form of Jamaican music that merges elements of calypso with American jazz and rhythm and blues. The Beatles also recorded a blistering version of Little Richard's "Long Tall Sally," a cover version that had been in their stage arsenal for ages. With George Martin offering a thrashing, note-perfect piano part, the group succeeded in immortalizing the rousing encore to their live set for all time. Later, on June 1st, they recorded covers of Larry Williams's "Slow Down" and Carl Perkins's "Matchbox" to complete the quaternion of tracks required for the *Long Tall Sally* EP.[9]

After "I'm Happy Just to Dance with You," *A Hard Day's Night* resumes with "And I Love Her," for which the band easily assumes a stirring Latin beat.

Ornamented with Harrison and McCartney's flamenco-like guitar arpeggios, "And I Love Her" swells with the rhythmic intensity of Ringo's bongos and Harrison's intermittent claves. For McCartney, "And I Love Her" is nothing short of a watershed moment—the coda even features an arresting key change that brings the song to fruition. "With one stroke," Riley writes, Paul "gains the status of standard balladeer composer" (104). McCartney's enormous catalogue of romantic melodies and ballads finds its origins in "And I Love Her," and the discerning fan can draw a line from its composition to the emergence of such classic tunes as "I'll Follow the Sun," "Yesterday," "Michelle," "Let It Be," and "The Long and Winding Road." While Paul would later confess to being embarrassed by the simplicity of the song's lyrics, "And I Love Her" draws its power from its effortless minimalism: "Bright are the stars that shine, / Dark is the sky," he sings. "I know this love of mine / Will never die / And I love her." With all of the rapture and verve of an early 1960s girl group, "Tell Me Why" finds the Beatles at the zenith of their unabashed sincerity: "Well, I gave you everything I had, / But you left me sitting on my own, / Did you have to treat me oh so bad? / All I do is hang my head and moan." In itself, the chorus is a study in the innocuousness of faithless love: "Tell me why you cried," John sings, "and why you lied to me." As Lennon's Jumbo jangles toward its resolution in "Can't Buy Me Love," the album's first side comes to a close, only to be resurrected by the staccato drumbeat salute that inaugurates "Any Time at All." A spirited rock and roll tune with no-nonsense lyrics about steadfast, unremitting love, the song witnesses John in one of his most earnest guises on record. "If you need somebody to love, just look into my eyes, / I'll be there to make you feel right," he sings. In the world of "Any Time at All," love is all you need. Musically, the song features an artful solo in which Paul's piano and George's guitar create a clever opposition. Played with conspicuous classical overtones, the piano begins in a lower register and travels upward, while the guitar journeys, in converse fashion, from high to low. The result offers a breathtaking study in pop-music counterpoint.

In contrast with the hopeful romantic gesture inherent in "Any Time at All," the quintet of songs that conclude *A Hard Day's Night* find the Beatles engaged in a more nuanced study of love's capacity for engendering bewilderment and loss. Recorded on June 1st, "I'll Cry Instead" narrates its speaker's manic response to heartbreak against a driving country and western backdrop. "I've got a chip on my shoulder that's bigger than my feet, / I can't talk to people that I meet," John sings. "If I could see you now, / I'd try to make you sad somehow, / But I can't, so I'll cry instead." The speaker's anguish makes for a signal moment in the Beatles' corpus, given that he's not merely heartbroken, but hungry for revenge in the bargain. Turning inward, he begins by weeping for his own failures and insecurities, yet he vows to return one day to avenge his disconsolate heart: "And when I do, you better hide all the girls," he threatens. "I'm gonna break their hearts all 'round the world." The brute force of the song's transition—and the larger shift in the Beatles' previously unswerving veneration of womanhood in their aesthetic—is telling, especially when the speaker, with the bitterest of ironies in his voice, promises to "show you what your loving man can do." It's a moment of pure menace commingled with despair—and not that dissimilar to the speaker's somber and very calculated realization, in "Things We Said Today," that the convivial present that he shares with his beloved exists as the mere prelude to an uncertain future about which he harbors serious doubts. Love may be blind (and blinding) in the here and now, Paul sings, but "someday when we're dreaming, / Deep in love, not a lot to say, / Then we will remember things we said today." All in all, it's a deeply foreboding composition, and the lover's tone—far more than the song's lyrics—speaks volumes about his inner feelings of distrust and skepticism regarding the notion of true love. When the speaker announces that "love is here to stay / And that's enough" in the middle-eight, we'd be fools to believe him, particularly when he no longer believes in love's tonic himself. As the last song recorded for the album, "When I Get Home" tells the story of the speaker's urgent return to his beloved. His anxiousness and agitation are at work in every fiber of the song, from the forceful bass and guitar fusion that undergirds the composition to the ferocity with which Lennon voices the lyrics. "I got a whole lot of things to tell her," he promises, "When I get home." While it would be reasonable to assume that he's imagining a passionate reunion with his lover, his language and tenor suggest something more sinister, something unsettled that exists between them and that threatens to devastate their bliss. At one point, he even rebukes himself for loitering in the company of a third party—another woman perhaps?: "Come on, let me through, / I've got so many things I've got to do, / I've got no business being here with you this way." The speaker's crucial phrase—"*this way*"—turns out to be the crux of the matter, hinting, as it does, at the compromising situation in which he has placed his wayward heart. Only a swift return to his darling, it seems, can salve his growing remorse, as opposed to any burning desire that he may have for romantic return.

A Hard Day's Night comes to an unexpectedly forlorn close—particularly in comparison with "Twist and Shout" and "Money (That's What I Want)," the rockers that drove their first two albums home. Inspired by Del Shannon's "Runaway," "I'll Be Back" makes for a darker manifestation of the earlier, less-threatening "This Boy." For Lennon and McCartney, nostalgia assumes an embittered guise in "I'll Be Back," wherein the song's speaker, supported by a clutch of bristling acoustic guitars, offers what appears to be a fairly routine dirge about the emotional traumas of lost love. Yet, rather interestingly, the speaker learns an excruciating lesson about the fleeting nature of romance. Claiming that "I'll be back" because "I'm the one who wants you," he discovers the agonizing truth about his lover's immutable discontent. Believing all the while that she would reciprocate his love, he "got a big surprise" instead. Will the speaker usurp the past and finally prove to his beloved that he has changed emotionally, or will he proffer an engagement ring, or is he referring to something sinister—her desire for a vengeful breakup perhaps? MacDonald fittingly describes the song as "a surprisingly downbeat farewell and a token of coming maturity" (94). The composition's explicit reference to the potentially sad realities of romantic love demonstrates the songwriters' recognition of the complex interpersonal relations that occur when the self engages emotionally—and more fully—with the world. And its positioning as the album's final cut, as *A Hard Day's Night*'s self-consciously authentic finale, acts as a telling compass for the balance of the Beatles' dazzling recording career.

∼

Based on a screenplay by Alun Owen and produced on a budget of some $350,000, the movie *A Hard Day's Night* was filmed at London's Paddington Station, Twickenham Film Studios, and various other locations in March and April, premiering on July 6th at the London Pavilion in Piccadilly Circus. Directed by Richard Lester, the movie grossed $11 million worldwide and $1.3 million in the first week of its American release—both of which were astounding figures for that era. It was a defining moment for the Beatles in terms of its commercial success, as well as for its myth-making power. When Epstein negotiated their contract with United Artists for *A Hard Day's Night* in October 1963, they wanted to make the movie "for the express purpose of having a soundtrack album," according to the film's producer Walter Shenson (*You Can't Do That*). In one instance, Lennon even told Epstein that "we don't fancy being Bill Haley and the Bellhops, Brian" (qtd. in Barrow, "*A Hard Day's Night*" 5). By the end of February 1964, they came to envision the film as an opportunity for blazing trails into new marketing vistas well beyond the teenage demographic. For the Beatles, the world of film afforded them with a means for securing control of themselves as a commodity and for establishing the self-image that would fuel their marketing engine. As Jacques Attali remarks in *Noise* (1985), the popular music industry's economic emergence in the 1950s and beyond spawned a new, media-driven era of production in which acts of representation and repetition serve as the mechanisms for engendering and sustaining success. The evolution of this multiplicative marketing phenomenon "fundamentally changes the code of social reproduction," Attali writes, and consumers—the recipients of iteration after iteration of deftly constructed signs and messages—begin responding to the "mysterious and powerful links [that] exist between technology and knowledge on the one hand, and music on the other" (146, 147). As this awe-inspiring marketing machine developed throughout the latter half of the twentieth century, its promoters, amongst whom Epstein functioned as a pioneer, came to understand that the art of any effective media campaign originates in its capacity for communicating its message to a target audience. With *A Hard Day's Night*, the Beatles accomplished this end by adeptly crafting images for each of the band members that their later films, in one fashion or another, would attempt to echo. It was, pure and simple, an act of guileless mythology.

The idea of mythology finds its roots in our desires to tell stories about ourselves. We do this, of course, in an effort to make sense of our experiences, to imbue our lives with meaning. The act of myth-making possesses a peculiarly social dimension as well. By mythologizing our experiences, we establish a narrative frame through which people may contextualize their own lives in relationship with other human beings. In this way, we introduce points of convergence in our various mythologies that allow us to create spaces of interaction. These moments of intersection can be genuine instances of our longing for human connection. Yet they can also be calculated maneuvers to control—indeed, to manipulate—the ways in which audiences come to perceive the mythologized subject. The stories that we tell about ourselves assume much greater power when placed in a public context driven by media, marketing, and economic imperatives. At the same time, our identities become obscured, subservient to myth's machinery, a legend-making mechanism that, by virtue of its very existence, must tell and retell story after story in order to keep our dreams of a comprehensible, unified narrative alive. Quite obviously, the Beatles themselves—as human beings and as artists—sought to establish their own micro-stories within their real, workaday lives. As we know from the juggernaut of Beatles-related paraphernalia, these personal myths were ultimately subsumed by the awesome myth-making power of Beatlemania. Yet can we really perceive the genuine nature of their personae in such a surreal context? Clearly, the screaming fan at a random American concert in 1964—tears running down her cheeks as she pushes her way to the front of the pack in an effort to touch the hem of Paul McCartney's suit coat—was looking into the mythologizing frame of Beatlemania in an effort to catch a glimpse of the "real" Paul. Surely, this fan would have wanted no truck with the less fantastic stories that McCartney might tell about himself, stories that bear little resemblance to the plasticine image of him as a lovable, nonthreatening Mop Top.

Rather, she hoped—as so many of us do—to encounter the mythologizing accoutrements that she had already projected onto him via Capitol Records' media-generated desire to "meet" the Beatles. In short, Beatlemania's grand illusion accrued its power through the financially advantageous collision between a growing international fan base's need for a facile mythology and the willingness of the Beatles' relentlessly regenerating marketing engine to sustain the Fab Four's media-friendly story.

Yet these are not artfully created narratives. As a highly constructed socio-cultural text, the Beatles—in concert with legions of marketeers and a compliant global audience—appropriated their pre-existing pop-cultural personae in order to cobble together a film that merges their mythological identities with the cinematic tropes in which their audience was already well-versed. Hence, *A Hard Day's Night* capitalizes on each band member's image as it had been established by their adeptly choreographed press conferences and their appearances on such popular fare as *Thank Your Lucky Stars* and the *Ed Sullivan Show*. Perhaps even more significantly, the audience for the Beatles' films would already have been well-schooled in the generic, myth-making conventions of the pop musical by such movies as *The Girl Can't Help It* (1956) and *Rock Around the Clock* (1956), not to mention Elvis's various cinematic forays. The audience's desire to see their heroes fulfill their preconceived roles as the Fab Four allows them to anticipate—and thus share in the construction of— the existing characters and plot mechanisms inherent in *A Hard Day's Night*. As with the Beatles cartoons that would premiere on ABC in September 1965, *A Hard Day's Night* assisted the band in promoting the mythology about their different personalities that lingers to the present day.[10] As a pop musical that splices together micro-narratives about each band members' experiences during a "hard day's night," the film features various montages and performance pieces devoted to the six new Beatles songs recorded explicitly for the movie. Bob Neaverson contends that films such as *A Hard Day's Night* attempt to draw their audiences into a voyeuristic relationship with their subjects, to afford their spectators with a glimpse into the band's constructed "lives": "The audience is allowed to see a pop group in intimate, 'behind-the-scenes' scenarios which are essentially 'real,' or at least, realistic," Neaverson writes. "Ultimately, [the film] enabled them to leave the cinema feeling that they had come to 'know' (and love) the group as 'real' people, rather than that they had merely been 'entertained' by a pop group acting out a totally fictitious plot" (*The Beatles Movies* 21). But, of course, a fictive and self-consciously constructed text is exactly what audience members experienced.

In addition to marketing the band as a happy-go-lucky group of unthreatening young men, *A Hard Day's Night* concretized the Beatles' individual images for the present generation and—thanks to videocassettes, DVDs, and cable television—generations to come.[11] Henceforth, John became known for his sarcastic intelligence; Paul for his boyish charm and good looks; George for being the "quiet one"; and Ringo for his genial personality and good-natured humor. The movie underscores the very result of such myth-making opportunities in the concert scene, where "the camera moves rapidly between the faces of the Beatles and their audience," Stephen Glynn writes. "Close-ups of the latter show girls in tears, in ecstasy, but clearly mouthing the name of their favorite Beatle" (45). Robert Freeman's cover photographs for *A Hard Day's Night* offer a revealing study in identity creation. The album's cover art features five playful shots of each Beatle mugging for the camera. Lennon can be seen striking slyly introspective poses, while Harrison's various guises underscore his reputation as the quiet Beatle—one of his photographs even depicts him with his back to the camera in monochromatic silhouette.[12] McCartney is portrayed in the act of pursuing innocent and unself-conscious antics, while Starr seems intentionally muted. His photos make him appear bland and unobtrusive, as if more palpable characteristics might shatter his good-natured image. Paramount to the construction of the Beatles' media personalities was the notion that none of them be perceived as being romantically involved. As Lester remembers, "It was an instinctive thing that fans would be quite happy with them as four available people as opposed to, I suppose, the Elvis Presley pictures, where there was always a love interest" (qtd. in Neaverson, *The Beatles Movies* 25). After the release of *A Hard Day's Night* in the summer of 1964, John, Paul, George, and Ringo became household words. As Roger Ebert observes, "After that movie was released everybody knew the names of all four Beatles—*everybody*" (*You Can't Do That*). As Epstein and the Beatles had intended, *A Hard Day's Night* allowed them to establish inroads into demographic bases well beyond the teenagers who worshipped them after the *Ed Sullivan Show*. In short, the Beatles had won over, in Neaverson's words, the "non-believers" (*The Beatles Movies* 27).

As if the Beatles' film debut weren't enough, the "non-believers" would find themselves equally challenged by John's sudden entrance into the literary world. Published by Jonathan Cape in March 1964, Lennon's book *In His Own Write* demonstrates the literary pretensions that would characterize the Beatles' finest work, while also contributing to the lyrical and musical strides that would grace their vastly more nuanced and intricate later albums. In his analysis of the volume, John Wain likened Lennon's prose to the novels of James Joyce, especially in terms of the writer's penchant for language games in *Ulysses* (1922) and *Finnegans Wake* (1939): "The first thing any literate person will notice on reading through Mr. Lennon's book is that it all comes out of

one source, namely the later work of James Joyce." Although John was relatively unfamiliar with Joyce's novels at this juncture in his life, his subsequent
readings of the Irish master proved to be a revelation. It was like "finding
Daddy," he remarked (qtd. in Harris 119).

∼

On August 28th, 1964, the Beatles encountered a father figure of an altogether
different sort when they met Bob Dylan in New York City. It was a momentous
event, to say the least, because of its far-reaching effects upon the group's
evolving approach to their art. They were already serious musicians, to be sure,
but their search for something deeper, something more profound was clearly
amplified after coming into contact with Greenwich Village's prince of peace
and protest. John was especially influenced by his relationship with Dylan,
who had already achieved, at a mere twenty-three-years-old, growing national
renown for his work as America's reigning folk poet, a singer-songwriter with
fire in his heart and social change on his mind. Paul had purchased a copy of
The Freewheelin' Bob Dylan (1963) before the Beatles left for their stint in the
French capital, and, according to John, "for the rest of our three weeks in Paris
we didn't stop playing it" (qtd. in Spitz 533). Having listened obsessively, albeit
very attentively to Dylan's work—particularly *The Times They Are a-Changin'*
(1964)—the Beatles "realized that entire albums of boy-meets-girl songs were
now, at one blow, outmoded" ("Bob Dylan"). The group finally encountered
Dylan in the flesh in their suite at the Delmonico Hotel after performing a
concert at Forest Hills. "When I met Dylan I was quite dumbfounded," John
later admitted. But the Beatles warmed up to him quickly, especially after he
declined their offer of amphetamines, suggesting instead that they turn their
tastes to marijuana. With their penchant for Scotch-and-Cokes tempered by
uppers—a habit accrued over the years after their initiation in Hamburg—the
Beatles had never, to Dylan's great surprise, experienced the intoxicating powers of the devil weed. "But what about your song—the one about getting
high?" Dylan asked, referring to "I Want to Hold Your Hand." "And when I
touch you, I get high, I get high," Dylan crooned, to which John interjected,
"Those aren't the words. It's 'I can't hide, I can't hide.'"[13] After Dylan helpfully
rolled a joint for their consumption, the Beatles expanded their conscious-
nesses in ways they had never quite imagined. At one point, Paul demanded
that Mal Evans record his psychotropic thoughts for posterity. Despite his self-
assurance that marijuana had driven him to experience moments of pure
genius, Paul was aghast to learn the next morning that the result of his fecundity was the arcane notion that "there are seven levels" (qtd. in Spitz 535–36).

While marijuana drove the group into laughing fits of hysterics, it clearly deepened their appreciation for the surreal. And their relationship with Dylan—a serious thinker who deployed his music as a lacerating form of self-expression—would change their art forever.

Released on December 4th, 1964, *Beatles for Sale* arrived at the tail-end of an unprecedented and incredibly hectic year. "They were rather war-weary during *Beatles for Sale*," Martin recalled. "One must remember that they'd been battered like mad throughout 1964, and much of 1963. Success is a wonderful thing, but it is very, very tiring. They were always on the go" (qtd. in Dowlding 82). As it turned out, the Beatles had very little to offer in the way of new material by that period. Although many of the band's critics—and even their producer—malign *Beatles for Sale* as one of their weakest efforts, there is little doubt that it contains moments of profound change and insight. While the album includes eight original compositions, it is rounded out by a whopping six cover versions—the most amongst any of their studio albums. Despite their paucity, *Beatles for Sale*'s original compositions find the songwriters, especially John, in their most revealing and self-analytical guises to date. In contrast with *A Hard Day's Night*, the Beatles had very little time in the studio to complete *Beatles for Sale*. After recording "Baby's in Black" on August 11th, the Beatles devoted six additional sessions at EMI Studios during the production of the album, with seven days allotted in the control room for the mixing and mastering processes associated with *Beatles for Sale*. Not since *Please Please Me* had the Beatles been so rushed to churn out a new product—and, starting with their next album, they would never be hurried in quite the same fashion again.

The album begins with the trio of songs that Beatles scholars have dubbed the "Lennon trilogy" in an effort to reflect the progressive nature of the group's work—and Lennon's work as songwriter, in particular—on "No Reply," "I'm a Loser," and "Baby's in Black." When read progressively, the trilogy presents a thematic whole, with John's speaker shifting amongst three stages of evolving self-awareness, including the post-breakup stupor of "No Reply," the intense realization of personal culpability in "I'm a Loser," and the somber resignation of "Baby's in Black." For John, "No Reply" represented a considerable moment of personal and professional growth. He was especially pleased when renowned music publisher Dick James saw fit to compliment his latest composition: "That's the first complete song you've written where it resolves itself" (qtd. in Everett, *The Quarry Men through Rubber Soul* 261). Inspired by the Rays' 1957 hit "Silhouettes" and recorded on September 30th, "No Reply" takes the essence—at least in the beginning, as John strums his Jumbo—of a lazy bossa nova. But the lilting intro is well-played deception, as with the thematic construction of the song itself, in which the speaker waits in vain for his estranged girlfriend to answer the telephone and acknowledge his existence. But all he gets, of course, is "no reply," even as he watches from a distance as she walks "hand in hand / with another man." The effect is debilitating, as the speaker realizes his sudden irrelevance in her life—even, ironically, as she becomes even *more* relevant to him by virtue of her looming absence in his world. "I nearly died," John sings in the refrain, with the low-rumble of George Martin's piano accents lingering in the background and Ringo's cymbal crashes underscoring the darkness and depth of the speaker's internal crisis. The middle-eight is a masterpiece of ferocity and regret, as the speaker seems to threaten his wayward lover in the very same breath in which he vows forgiveness: "If I were you I'd realize that I / Love you more than any other guy," John sings. "And I'll forgive the lies that I / Heard before when you gave me no reply." The song eventually "resolves itself," to borrow Dick James's words, by affording listeners with a miniature portrait of the speaker's self-delusion and despair, as well as of the deathly silence that greets his futile cries for recognition. When the speaker claims that "I saw the light," he suggests that he's enjoyed an epiphany of sorts about his quandary. But the bitter truth is that the only light he actually sees is shining from his former beloved's bedroom, a world that has become suddenly and irrevocably closed to him.

Incredible as it may seem for a pop song, "No Reply" also finds Lennon in the act of creating the Beatles' first explicitly unreliable narrator. According to Wayne C. Booth in *The Rhetoric of Fiction* (1961), the unreliable narrator is a literary device, frequently contrived in the first-person, in which the narrator operates from a compromised perspective. Whether as the result of a precarious psychological state or a self-conscious effort to deceive the audience, the narrator's unreliability challenges readers (or in the Beatles' case, listeners) to interpret the story in spite of the ambiguities provoked by the narrator's lack of credibility. In "No Reply," the speaker desperately attempts to align himself with his audience by convincing them of his own victimization even as he stalks his erstwhile lover, forcing her friends and family to lie on her behalf. In itself, the unreliable narrator of "No Reply," and of the Lennon Trilogy in its entirety, offers a pointed example of the Beatles' latent modernity. Although the unreliable narrator enjoys a long literary lineage—reaching as far back as the enigmatic narrator of Chaucer's General Prologue to *The Canterbury Tales*—the device deepens and matures with such twentieth-century modernist masterworks as Ford Madox Ford's *The Good Soldier* (1915), William Faulkner's *The Sound and the Fury* (1929), and Vladimir Nabokov's *Lolita* (1955), among others. Modernism refers to the general culture of, roughly, the first part of the twentieth century in which artists were known for their experimental and highly subjective aesthetics. While modernism involves a rejection of nineteenth-century—and, in particular, Victorian—traditions and mores, its prevailing value systems originate from generally accepted ethical centers such as community, family, and religion. Modernism's rallying cry—"Make it new!"—is often associated with American poet Ezra Pound, who challenged the writers and thinkers of the early twentieth century to devise innovative forms of artistic expression that broke with the traditions of their Victorian precursors. As the 1960s move ever forward, the Beatles—namely, Lennon and McCartney—reveal themselves to be working against the grain of their antecedents as well, exploring new vistas of storytelling and musicality, while positing larger questions about the ethical landscapes both within and beyond the textual worlds of their creation.

As with several of the compositions on *A Hard Day's Night*, many of the songs on *Beatles for Sale* explore the convoluted nature of human identity construction (and, in some cases, its deconstruction and reconstruction). In "I'm a Loser," John explodes the narcissistic mask of his character's inner self. "I'm a loser," the speaker reports, "and I'm not what I appear to be." While the track loosely concerns itself with romantic dissolution, Lennon's lyrics suggest something even more conflicted: "My tears are falling like rain from the sky," he sings. "Is it for her or myself that I cry?" With its country and western veneer, "I'm a Loser" effects a lighthearted ambience that undercuts, at times, the song's sobering message about the vexing relationships that so often exist between our selves and the world. For John, the song's confessional aspects underscore a key instance in his creative development. "That's me in my Dylan period," he later remarked. "Part of me suspects I'm a loser and part of me thinks I'm God almighty" (qtd. in Dowlding 83). "I'm a Loser" is poorly served by the song's fadeout, which feels premature and ultimately rushed, bringing an otherwise effective composition to a somewhat dissatisfying end. With its waltz-like Sauteuse structure, "Baby's in Black" brings the trilogy to a close, tracing the story of a woman who has become wedded to an immutable past—and the man who left her to mourn his loss forever. In the song, the speaker waits in frustration for her to rejoin the living, breathing present. As John and Paul sing in one of their most exquisite harmonies: "Oh, how long will it take, / Till she sees the mistake she has made?" As with "No Reply" and "I'm a Loser," "Baby's in Black" depicts a speaker lost in the throes of his own uncertain selfhood and waiting in vain for some external other to see the light. The speaker has matured, of course, but at what cost?

Generally considered to be merely another chestnut among McCartney's vast catalogue of silly love songs, "I'll Follow the Sun" similarly concerns itself with the nature of sorrow and loss. A refugee from his earliest days as a songwriter,

Paul's song brims with a sense of deeply felt nostalgia, as if the speaker were intensely self-conscious about his fleeting place within the temporal moment: "One day you'll look to see I've gone," Paul croons, while calmly strumming his Epiphone Texan. "For tomorrow may rain, so I'll follow the sun." The song's speaker is content simply to leave his beloved in the dead of night—and thus damning her to a lifetime of ambiguity about why her lover departed in such a sudden and unexpected manner. The speaker's fondest hope, it seems, is for his old girlfriend to realize the extent of her loss after years of contemplating his absence. Is Paul's speaker in "I'll Follow the Sun" the second incarnation of the tortured soul in Yeats's "When You Are Old" who "loved the pilgrim soul" in his beloved only to flee and hide "his face among a crowd of stars"? (14). As with its counterparts on *Beatles for Sale*, "I'll Follow the Sun" offers an intentionally revealing portrait of the byzantine ways in which we divulge ourselves, often unsuspectingly, to our societies.

The album's plethora of cover versions includes John's rather uninspired reading of Chuck Berry's "Rock and Roll Music," a time-worn staple of the Beatles' road show. With Martin "rocking that piano" and the group "going like a hurricane," the recording took exactly one take to reach fruition. Perhaps John's surprisingly ordinary vocal was the result of cover-version fatigue from a songwriter, who, along with his partner, was understandably more interested in the process of his own self-expression? In Lennon's case, Riley observes, "These grand old rock-and-rollers don't say it all for him anymore: he's beginning to say things better for himself" (122). In comparison with "Rock and Roll Music," the group's rendition of "Mr. Moonlight" is arguably one of the weakest, most insipid moments in the entire text of the Beatles. Written by Roy Lee Johnson and popularized by Dr. Feelgood and the Interns, "Mr. Moonlight" finds Ringo thumping his bongos, George pitching in with an African drum, and John singing his guts out for a composition that hardly merits the effort. Left off of *Beatles for Sale* in favor of "Mr. Moonlight," "Leave My Kitten Alone" would have doubtlessly emerged as one of the album's standout tracks, at least amongst its cover versions. Written by Little Willie John, Titus Turner, and James McDougal, as well as a 1961 hit single for Johnny Preston, the Beatles' recording of the song wasn't even mixed for release until 1984. In "Leave My Kitten Alone," Lennon's vocal is steely perfection, while Harrison's energetic guitar work defines the relentless, hard-driving sound of the early Beatles to a tee. The song's unrestrained nature would be echoed on the band's tumultuous May 1965 recording of Larry Williams's "Bad Boy." *Beatles for Sale*'s cover versions are rounded out by Carl Perkins's "Honey Don't," Buddy Holly's "Words of Love," and Paul's unflinchingly marvelous work on "Kansas City"/"Hey-Hey-Hey-Hey!" Based upon the medley originally performed by

Little Richard, the track was yet another well-honed veteran from the group's stage act. For "Honey Don't," Ringo offers a spirited vocal turn on Perkins's country-rock song, while "Words of Love" witnesses the band in the act of effecting a note-perfect imitation of their songwriting idol's two-part harmony. If Holly had lived to see the day, it would have made for the sincerest form of flattery indeed.

Beatles for Sale carries on with "Eight Days a Week," a Lennon-McCartney original that exudes charm from every nook and cranny. Often erroneously attributed to Ringo, the genesis of the song's title finds its origins in one of Paul's road trips from London to suburban Weybridge to visit John. "I remember asking the chauffeur once if he was having a good week," Paul recalled, and the chauffer said, "'I'm very busy at the moment. I've been working eight days a week.' And I thought, 'Eight days a week! Now there's a title'" (qtd. in Everett, *The Quarry Men through Rubber Soul* 262).[14] With its brisk, upbeat harmonies, its infectious melody, and its well-placed handclaps—"Hold me, love me! Hold me, love me!"—the song became a runaway American hit in the early spring of 1965. After putting the finishing touches on "Eight Days a Week" on October 18th, 1964, the Beatles turned to a new composition, "I Feel Fine," which they intended to release as their next single. The song represents the first intentional use of feedback on record, a fact about which John, the tune's primary songwriter, was especially proud. He was equally buoyant about the highly inventive guitar riff that he crafted for the track. Yet in his own recollections about the song's origins, George disputes John's memories and, in so doing, provides intriguing commentary about the corporate nature of musical composition:

> A lot of Lennon-McCartney songs had other people involved, whether it's lyrics, or structures, or circumstance. A good example is "I Feel Fine." I'll tell you exactly how that came about: We were crossing Scotland in the back of an Austin Princess, singing "Matchbox" in three-part harmony. And it turned into "I Feel Fine." The guitar part was from Bobby Parker's "Watch Your Step," just a bastardized version. I was there for the whole of its creation—but it's still a Lennon-McCartney. (qtd. in Everett, *The Quarry Men through Rubber Soul* 265)[15]

With John and George's nifty guitar picking, Ringo's masterful drum-breaks, and the song's unabashedly joyful lyrics, "I Feel Fine" was a surefire hit and easily notched the group's seventh number-one single in a row for Parlophone. The song's B-side, "She's a Woman," was a catchy, Little Richard-inspired blues number in which Paul sang lustily about his lover, who "turns me on when I get lonely." As John later recalled, "We were so excited to say 'turn me on'—you know, about marijuana and all that, using it as an expression" (qtd. in Everett, *The Quarry Men through Rubber Soul* 266).

As with "I'm Happy Just to Dance with You" on *A Hard Day's Night*, *Beatles for Sale*'s "Every Little Thing" is an early Beatles throwback that celebrates love's everlasting simplicity and fulfillment: "When I'm with her I'm happy / Just to know that she loves me," John sings. As if to underscore the speaker's faith in love with all due deliberateness, the song finds Ringo pounding a tympani to punctuate the chorus: "Every little thing she does [boom! boom!] she does for me, / And you know the things she does [boom! boom!] she does for me." The simple romantic clarity inherent in "Every Little Thing" represents a far cry from John's "I Don't Want to Spoil the Party," which offers a decidedly realistic and eminently more subtle rejoinder to the public tantrum depicted in Lesley Gore's 1963 smash hit "It's My Party." As John later remembered, "That was a very personal one of mine" (qtd. in Dowlding 90). While "I Don't Want to Spoil the Party" depicts its speaker wallowing in self-pity, the manner in which the lyrics question the narrator's place in the world ultimately speaks volumes about Lennon and McCartney's transition into more expansive ways of thinking about existence and identity. "There's nothing for me here," Lennon concludes, "so I will disappear." As with the harmony that adorns "Baby's in Black," the middle-eight in "I Don't Want to Spoil the Party" finds John and Paul engaged in a delicate duet about the tender vicissitudes of vulnerability and hope: "Though tonight she's made me sad, / I still love her," they sing. "If I find her I'll be glad, / I still love her." With its artful electric guitar and bass figures, as well as a bluesy vocal courtesy of Paul, "What You're Doing" offers a telling preview of the newfangled textures that will characterize the band's work in the coming year. For all of its invention and musicality, *Beatles for Sale* limps rather meekly to the finish line with a cover version of Carl Perkins's up-tempo "Everybody's Trying to Be My Baby." Although George's lead vocal, lost amidst an unruly sea of echo-ridden tape delay, affords the track with as much gusto as he could hope to muster, the net result provides a relatively feeble ending for a transitional project that otherwise flowers with grace and meaning.

Devin McKinney shrewdly describes *Beatles for Sale* as "half a great album; but that half is so great it shoots energy through the rest and elevates the field" (398). The album's cover photograph—shot by Robert Freeman at dusk near London's Hyde Park—depicts the Beatles amidst the autumnal colors of late fall. Like the trees shedding their leaves in the cover's background, the band was clearly caught up in their own transitional state. From its heady beginnings in Paris through the band's sessions at EMI Studios at the end of the year, 1964 was a signal moment in the group's career. They had succeeded in reinvigorating their musical and lyrical aesthetic by taking more creative risks, on the one hand, and strengthening their vice grip on their massive international audience, on the other, by generating a seemingly endless series of hit songs—and with apparent ease, no less. It was a bountiful period that would reap artistic dividends in the ensuing years, an era in which the band would be forced to contend with a growing dis-ease with life on the road and a fervent desire to improve their art with every passing composition. As Thomas Mac-Farlane observes, "The Beatles' early period (1962–1964) is characterized by a consolidation of composition forms inherited from previous musical eras (rock, blues, country), which the group then proceeded to integrate into a highly distinctive personal style" (26). It would be no simple task, to say the least, but there is little doubt that the group's early musical forays were paving the way for a larger, more complex form of expression that existed just beyond their collective grasp. For the Beatles, the times were truly a-changin' indeed.

Notes

1. In "'The Beatles Are Coming!': Conjecture and Conviction in the Myth of Kennedy, America, and the Beatles," Ian Inglis questions the Kennedy assassination's role in the group's North American success: "After all, in the six months that followed the assassination, a number of other memorable and controversial episodes were to take place: Cassius Clay's defeat of Sonny Liston in February marked his first steps on the path to becoming the century's most influential and celebrated sportsman; Malcolm X announced his departure from the Nation of Islam in March to found the Organization for Afro-American Unity; in April, Sidney Poitier's Oscar for his role in *Lilies of the Field* was the first time a Black actor had received the Academy Award for Best Actor; the Pulitzer Committee in May decided that there was no fiction, music, or drama worthy of its annual prize; Lenny Bruce was tried in New York for obscenity in June. Should we grant Kennedy's death responsibility for these incidents, too, simply because of their proximity?" (105).

2. The promotional giveaway was the brainchild of Nicky Byrne, Epstein's advance man in New York City who was in charge of Seltaeb [Beatles spelled backward], the North American merchandizing arm established by NEMS Enterprises. While the Beatles grossed an enormous amount of money in the United States in 1964—including sales of more than thirty-two million records—Byrne was responsible for one of the greatest financial blunders in the band's brief history. Reliant Shirt Corporation paid Seltaeb nearly $48,000 for the exclusive rights to manufacture Beatles T-shirts. After hawking their wares for a mere three days, Reliant had sold more than a million T-shirts (Badman 79). The fiasco involving Byrne's mismanagement of the Beatles' merchandizing rights dissolved into a series of lawsuits that weren't untangled until 1967, by which time the group had lost an estimated $100 million in revenue (Brown and Gaines 149). T-shirts, lunchboxes, Beatles wigs, and board games were available everywhere, and Epstein's management team had, for the most part, given it all away: "The vaguest representation of insects, of guitars, or little mop-headed men had the power to sell anything,

however cheap, however nasty," Norman writes. "And so, after one or two minor prose-cutions, the pirates settled down, unhampered, to their bonanza" (207–08).

3. When Capitol Records finally opened the floodgates on Beatles releases in the United States, their eagerness to distribute the band's music knew no bounds. Capitol ultimately repackaged the Beatles' first seven English albums—from *Please Please Me* (1963) through *Revolver* (1966)—as ten separate recordings for American release. Although the Beatles' pre-1967 English record releases featured an average of more than forty-five minutes of music per album (or approximately fourteen songs), their American albums during that same era scarcely averaged more than thirty minutes (or approximately ten songs). Capitol's repackagings resulted in a slew of unofficial album releases, including *Meet the Beatles!* (1964), *The Beatles' Second Album* (1964), *Something New* (1964), *Beatles '65* (1964), *The Early Beatles* (1965), *Beatles VI* (1965), and *Yesterday . . . and Today* (1966). Meanwhile, Capitol's US releases included significantly different versions of *Help!* (1965), *Rubber Soul* (1965), and *Revolver* (1966). United Artists' American soundtrack release of *A Hard Day's Night*, with its healthy selection of incidental film music, also represented a considerable divergence from the original English album. After the release of *Sgt. Pepper's Lonely Hearts Club Band* in 1967, Capitol's unofficial releases included two additional entries, the *Magical Mystery Tour* LP (1967), which Parlophone originally released as an EP in the UK, and *Hey Jude* (1970). Released in 2004 and 2006, respectively, *The Capitol Albums, Volume 1* and *Volume 2* reproduce the American releases with stereo and mono versions of every track. For additional discussion regarding the discrepancies between the British and American releases, see Kenneth Womack's "Editing the Beatles: Addressing the Roles of Authority and Editorial Theory in the Creation of Popular Music's Most Valuable Canon."

4. The Beatles' unprecedented reception in Adelaide, Australia, would not be in the company of Ringo, who had collapsed on June 3rd during a photo session with the *Saturday Evening Post*. Felled by acute tonsillitis, Ringo was replaced temporarily by drummer Jimmy Nicol on the band's upcoming tour of Northern Europe and the South Pacific. Ringo would rejoin the band on June 14th in Melbourne, Australia.

5. As Mark Lewisohn observes, "After six years of musical progression on stage, the Beatles now became more stilted with every concert they played" (*The Complete Beatles Chronicle* 93).

6. John employed Ringo's malapropism in "Sad Michael," a short story collected in his 1964 book *In His Own Write*. Alan Clayson perceptively notes that, with all due deference to Ringo, the phrase had more likely come into the Beatles' universe by way of Eartha Kitt, whose song "I Had a Hard Day Last Night" was the B-side of her 1963 single "Lola Lola" (380).

7. This byproduct of the group's evolving studio complexity is demonstrated on the recording of the Beatles performing "A Hard Day's Night" on *Live at the BBC* (1994). According to producer Bernie Andrews, the band initially hoped to reproduce the intricate solo on stage with Martin's musical assistance. When Martin couldn't make it for the BBC session, Andrews opted to splice in the pre-recorded wound-up piano effect that Martin had created in the studio with the Beatles (see Russell 291).

For the group's 1964–1965 live performances of "A Hard Day's Night," Harrison improvised a contrastingly simplistic guitar solo that mimicked the song's melody.

8. The manner in which the Beatles differentiated between the two Georges in the studio exemplifies their cheeky sense of humor. As Geoff Emerick recalled, "Because there were two George involved in the recording sessions—Harrison and Martin—George Martin was usually referred to as 'George H,' since his middle name was Henry. It was an arrangement I always found a little odd, since George Harrison was also a George H" (6).

9. Of the Beatles' thirteen EP releases in the United Kingdom, only two would be composed of new material that had not been culled from one of their albums—*Long Tall Sally* and the 1967 UK release of the *Magical Mystery Tour* EP.

10. The brainchild of King Features Syndicate producer Al Brodax, the Beatles Cartoons aired as a half-hour production from September 15, 1965, through September 7, 1969. Financed by toy magnate A. C. Gilmer, the ABC series became an instant hit in the Nielsen Weekly Ratings for its Saturday morning time slot. Each show consisted of two musical numbers, which formed the basis for every episode's plot. The first of the series's thirty-nine installments featured "I Want to Hold Your Hand" and "A Hard Day's Night." In each episode, the lyrics appeared on the screen in order to encourage viewers to sing along with the band. The voices of the Beatles' cartoon personae were supplied by Paul Frees (John and George) and Lance Percival (Paul and Ringo). The animation for the Beatles cartoons was produced by TVC Animation of London and Astransa, an Australian firm. TVC would later perform the bulk of the animation duties for the Beatles' feature-length cartoon *Yellow Submarine*. In a 1972 interview with Roy Carr, Lennon warmly recalled that "I still get a blast out of watching the Beatles cartoons on TV." During a 1999 interview with Timothy White, Harrison remembered that "I always kind of liked [the cartoons]. They were so bad or silly that they were good, if you know what I mean. And I think the passage of time might make them more fun now" (qtd. in Axelrod).

11. In one of the most interesting examples of the band's efforts to cement their media-created personalities in the public mindset, the Beatles authorized the publication of a novelization of *A Hard Day's Night* in July 1964. Written by John Burke, the volume purports to be an insider's look at "the Beatles as nobody ever before has known them." The book's dust-jacket promises that "in this fabulous new novel you'll get the chance of a lifetime to spend a whole, fantastic day with them. Loving and romancing, twisting and singing, cutting up and cutting out—here are Ringo, Paul, John, and George at their irresistible best. Yeah, yeah, yeah!"

12. One of the great misnomers of the Beatles myth concerns George's allegedly "quiet" demeanor. As his friend David Hedley fondly recalled: "He was such a private man, but not a quiet one. He didn't like fame and the irrational behavior that fame brings, but he was a very outgoing person and a very lovely man. He was hugely sociable and would talk on equal terms with everybody" (qtd. in Barlow).

13. Lennon's inspiration for the repeated phrase "I can't hide" finds its origins in an album by a French experimental composer whose work was introduced to the Beatle

by photographer Robert Freeman. The album featured the jarring effect of a needle skipping at the end of a record, a phenomenon that John attempted to imitate via the reiteration of "I can't hide" in "I Want to Hold Your Hand."

14. "Eight Days a Week" offers yet another example of a purported "Ringoism." Credited as the originator of various malapropisms like some kind of rock and roll Yogi Berra, Ringo has also been inaccurately credited as the source for the aforementioned "A Hard Day's Night." Perhaps his well-known—and correctly attributed—title for *Revolver*'s "Tomorrow Never Knows" has prompted his biographers to toast him as pop music's King Malaprop with broad, uncritical strokes?

15. Walter Everett points out, however, that George's historical memory about the occasion of the composition of "I Feel Fine" may, in fact, be in error: "The Beatles did not take this trip across Scotland until *after* the recording of 'I Feel Fine.' (Perhaps they were instead returning to London from the far-northern Hull, a trip that directly preceded the session in question?)" (*The Quarry Men through Rubber Soul* 265).

Chapter 7

Yesterday and Today

Our finest hope is finest memory;
And those who love in age think youth is happy,
Because it has a life to fill with love.
—GEORGE ELIOT, *FELIX HOLT, THE RADICAL*

Life is a game, and true love is a trophy.
—RUFUS WAINWRIGHT, "POSES"

In the songs of the early Beatles, love was a many-splendored thing. But by 1965, and the advent of their fifth studio album, *Help!*, it was a many-conflicted and interpersonally vexing thing as well. By this juncture, the joys and conundrums of the heart—with a decided accent on the *joys*—had been Lennon and McCartney's principal songwriting theme. But there was a paradigm shift in the offing, and there is no denying that the Beatles' transformation owed a considerable debt to the influence of Bob Dylan, their recent experiences with marijuana's intoxicating effects, and the growing personal and professional space that they had begun devoting to their art in spite of the frantic pace of their lives. Yet, as Mark Lewisohn astutely points out, "This was a curious year for the Beatles, one in which they consolidated all the successes and excesses of 1964 by virtually repeating everything already achieved" (*The Beatles Live!* 182). Indeed, in 1965, they would produce two additional albums and a feature film, while also embarking upon a European tour, followed by a summer trek across the United States, and concluding with a nine-day blitz through the UK. John would publish yet another book—*A Spaniard in the Works*—and the Beatles would reprise their legendary 1964 appearance at the Hollywood Bowl with a pair of concerts at that esteemed venue at the end of August.[1] For the band, it must have been like *déjà vu* all over again.

But there were some palpable differences as well. On February 11th, Ringo married the former Maureen Cox, an eighteen-year-old hairdresser from Liverpool who had met her future husband, rather fittingly, nearly three years earlier at the Cavern Club. Later, on June 11th, it was announced that the Beatles would be ordained as Members of the British Empire (MBE), an honor that resulted in the return of several MBE medals by previous recipients who felt that the Beatles were unworthy of such lofty recognition. The Beatles received their medals on October 26th from Queen Elizabeth II at Buckingham Palace. On July 28th, BBC television broadcast its *Songwriters* program, which celebrated the work of Lennon and McCartney. In November, Granada Television produced yet another tribute, entitled *The Music of Lennon and McCartney*. As with Mann's 1964 *Times* article about the band's deployment of Aeolian cadences, such encomiums would only serve to ratchet the stakes of authorship ever higher between the songwriting duo. During the sizzling summer of 1965, the Beatles virtually invented the arena rock and roll tour after playing to an audience of some 56,000 at Shea Stadium on August 15th. Less than a fortnight later, they met Elvis Presley, the King himself, at his home in Bel-Air. Fresh from shooting *Blue Hawaii* in Honolulu, Elvis entertained the Fab Four, who overcame their initial awkwardness—"if you guys are just gonna sit there and stare at me, I'm goin' to bed," he reportedly told the group—and joined their host in renditions of such Presley classics as "That's All Right (Mama)" and "Blue Suede Shoes" before turning to the Beatles' "I Feel Fine." Although the band's publicist Tony Barrow ensured that the press was showered with clippings in which the Beatles lauded their idol to no end, John, for one, was unimpressed. "It was a load of rubbish," he remarked. "It was just like meeting Englebert Humperdinck" (qtd. in Spitz 583). Way back in 1956, Elvis was the King of Rock and Roll, and, in Lennon's eyes, "Heartbreak Hotel" had been the great revelation of his youth. But now, nearly a decade later, John was clearly in search of something more substantive to tame his unruly heart.

And while 1965 witnessed the Beatles in the act of recording two albums— a feat that they had already accomplished during each of the previous two years—they would be two new studio albums' worth of material that would set their career on a very different trajectory. For good measure, the group polished off a landmark single—"We Can Work It Out" b/w "Day Tripper"—that brilliantly prefigured their work in 1966 and beyond. The former album would serve as the soundtrack for their second feature film. Originally entitled *Eight Arms to Hold You*, the screenplay had been written as a vehicle for Peter Sellers, who turned it down in order to star in *What's New Pussycat?*, a movie in which he portrayed a sex therapist for an inveterate ladies' man played by Peter O'Toole. Rechristened as *Help!*, the screenplay had been tailored to fit the Beatles' on-screen personae, and it received an ample budget of some $600,000. With *Help!*, the Beatles cemented the collective, carefree image that they began fashioning in *A Hard Day's Night*, while also creating additional opportunities for deepening the highly orchestrated nature of their public "personalities." Directed by Lester and filmed between February 23rd and May 11th in such diverse locations as the Bahamas and London's Twickenham Film Studios, *Help!*'s narrative relies upon the same zany humor as *A Hard Day's Night*. In contrast with the band's earlier film, *Help!* employs a James Bond-inspired spy text as its central crisis: Ringo, it seems, has come into the possession of an exotic diamond ring that is coveted by various desperate people, including a cult of Eastern mystics, hit men, and mad scientists, among a host of others. Numerous car chases and skiing shenanigans ensue as the drummer's mates attempt to rescue him from his predicament. In *Help!*, one can glimpse the future of such equally screwball oddities as the Monkees and the Banana Splits in the film's campy ridiculousness. As with *A Hard Day's Night, Help!* labors to maintain the mythology of the group's collective identity. In one unforgettable scene, the Beatles return home to four adjacent row houses. After unlocking each of their separate doors in unison, each member enters what turns out to be a single, gigantic flat that they all share. For the bandmates themselves, the irony of that scene must have been simply staggering at the time. As Ann Pacey, a critic for the London *Sun*, observes, the Beatles seem "as trapped as four flies" in *Help!* (qtd. in Neaverson, *The Beatles Movies* 42). Fittingly, the soundtrack's cover art features a Robert Freeman photograph of the group flashing a distress signal of their own—"LP US" in semaphore—to an unsuspecting world.

∼

While the movie *Help!* was an exercise in pleasantly diverting, albeit vacuous, comedy, the eventual album turned out to be nothing of the sort. Released on August 6th, 1965, *Help!* was recorded over several lengthy sessions in mid-February and mid-June, with an additional pair of sessions conducted on April 13th and May 10th. Yet for all of the album's strides, *Help!* was a hodgepodge in terms of its overall content. There were moments of unparalleled beauty ("You've Got to Hide Your Love Away" and "Yesterday") in the midst of some of the band's feeblest of efforts ("Act Naturally" and "You Like Me Too Much"). But there was clear musical growth in evidence as well. Having picked up where *Beatles for Sale* left off, the album offered Lennon and McCartney's first sustained analyses of nostalgia and the past—the core subjects, along with love itself, that would form the Beatles' recorded narrative for all time. While the concept of nostalgia hails from a protracted lexical history, its current usage is relatively fresh in terms of the wide world of language. As Kimberly K. Smith points out, our contemporary notions of nostalgia first came into being through various nineteenth- and twentieth-century conflicts over the political significance of the past. According to Smith, nostalgia finds its origins in the historical transition from the relative stability of an agrarian society to the mounting anxiety of a largely industrial world. In this sense, nostalgia emerges as a means for recontextualizing the past in terms of the present, as a form of social constructivism in which the past accrues greater meaning because of its significance and desirability in contrast with an uncertain and highly volatile contemporary moment. "To experience a memory nostalgically is not just to have certain feelings along with that memory," Smith suggests, "but to adopt a particular attitude towards it: to understand the memory and its associated feelings as the product of a psychological propensity to romanticize the past, and to value it as a vehicle for a Proustian sort of heightened sensibility or self-awareness" (509). In this way, nostalgia exists as an acculturated behavior through which we develop a perspective toward the past as a place where we might fulfill our collective longing for an "archetypal paradise" (514).[2]

There is little question that music enjoys a powerful capacity for eliciting a nostalgic response in its audience. When the conditions of the listening experience evoke nostalgic yearnings for the past, music clearly succeeds in exerting a psychological impact upon our emotional states of being. "Music seems to be profoundly connected to our emotional life," Martha C. Nussbaum observes, "indeed perhaps more urgently and deeply connected to the life than any of the other arts. It digs into our depths and expresses hidden movements of love and fear and joy that are inside us" (254). Psychologists have identified a compelling interrelationship between music and mood, arguing, for the most part, that the nature of lyrics and tonality often serves to arouse an affective and similarly directed emotional response in listeners. In their studies of the intersections between psychology and music, Valerie N. Stratton and Annette H. Zalanowski demonstrate that the "general style of Western music has established a relationship between various components of music, such as pitch, speed, and intensity, and moods." Perhaps even more interestingly, "the presence of other mood-altering stimuli, including the [listener's] thoughts and memories, may alter the manner in which the music is interpreted and even whether it is responded to at all" (126). In short, music becomes ineluctably associated with our moods and our memories, and our aesthetic experiences with music act as the driving forces behind our cognitive responses to particular musical texts. Inextricably bound up with our memories and our psychological states of being, music enjoys a natural relationship with the feelings of nostalgia that subsequently shape—indeed, *re*-shape—the emotional texture and sentimentalized quality of our personal museums of recollection.

But whose nostalgia are we ultimately experiencing? Is it the artist's nostalgic yearnings through which, séance-like, we channel our memories, or does music merely serve as the catalyst for summoning forth our own deep-rooted feelings of nostalgia? Composed, for the most part, on April 4th by Lennon and McCartney, "Help!" is about the very loss of the "archetypal paradise" of which Smith speaks. The song's nostalgia emerges from John's wistful yearnings for a simpler past. Flummoxed by the traumas and excesses of Beatlemania, he later described this era of his life as his "fat Elvis period." Married and isolated in the London suburbs, he felt alienated and lost, with "Help!" becoming his literal cry for emancipation and assistance. Musically, the song is a structural masterpiece. Originally a slow-tempo composition that evoked the anxiety of Lennon's lyrics, the song was intentionally sped up; after all, it was the title track for a zany comedy, and the up-tempo design made commercial sense. But, rather fittingly, the tempo shift served to further underscore the speaker's growing desperation. The song opens with the chorus, in which the speaker announces his desolation to a shower of descending sixteenth notes from Harrison's lead guitar, a distinguishing feature that was added on the track's twelfth and final take. Paul resumes this motif with a descending bass figure of his own during the verses. In addition to the composition's innovative call-and-response backing vocals, the song's confessional quality is highlighted in the latter third of the song, as Lennon returns to the first verse—"When I was younger so much younger than today," he sings. "I never needed anybody's help in any way." George's electric guitar and Ringo's drums disappear temporarily into stop-time, creating an inverted terraced effect, of sorts, in which John's vocal accompanies the gentle strumming of his Framus twelve-string "Hootenanny" acoustic: "But now these days are gone I'm not so self-assured / Now I find I've changed my mind and opened up the doors."

As a knowing study of the human condition, "Help!" explores the manner in which people carry the potential for evolving into pseudo-selves, or those individuals, according to psychotherapists Charles P. Barnard and Ramon Garrido Corrales, who remain unable to maintain any real stasis between their inner feelings and their outward behavior (85–87). The song's musical phrasings contribute to the band's unnerving depiction of the speaker's malaise. As Tim Riley observes, "Since Paul and George anticipate nearly every line Lennon sings in the verse, the effect is of voices inside the same head, prodding, goading [the listener] to chilling consequences. By the time Lennon sings 'open up the doors,' the voices are completely caught up in the nightmare" (139).[3] Although the speaker in "Help!" is pointedly reaching out for support, the song offers little in the way of genuine comfort or hope. Instead, he can only contemplate a distant past in which he was allegedly more happy, more secure. This notion is addressed in similar fashion with "Yes It Is," the B-side of "Ticket to Ride." Performed in the darkish hues of a minor key—so dark, in fact, that listeners might understandably wonder if the speaker's former love had died, rather tragically, in youth, instead of merely dumping him summarily—"Yes It Is" cautions his beloved's successor that wearing a red dress will conjure up powerful memories of the past, a painful nostalgia for which he has no antidote. "I could be happy with you by my side," he admits, while claiming that his indefatigable pride in the face of a public breakup apparently prevents him from moving forward. Played in an hypnotic, heartrending 12/8 time signature, "Yes It Is" clearly exists as one of the Beatles' more mature pre-1966 compositions about nostalgia's potency. Alan W. Pollack praises the song for the "manner in which the tyrannical, debilitating power of . . . memory is contrasted with the simple, mundane objects and sensations of life which are capable of triggering such hot flashes."

The group presents mundanity of another sort with Paul's "The Night Before," one of the album's weaker cuts. On the one hand, it offers a refreshingly cynical take on romance in comparison with the pure, unadulterated love of the *Please Please Me*-era Beatles. Yet on the other, it is one of the band's most obvious throwaway, or "filler," tracks, as is "Another Girl," which is a carbon copy of "The Night Before"—even down to its depiction of a speaker who responds to his lover's inattention and insincerity by satiating himself with the charms of another. Yet "The Night Before" exists as a landmark of sorts, given that the track marks the first appearance of the Epiphone Casino, the electric guitar that would impact the Beatles' sound for the rest of their career. By 1966, it would virtually supplant the Rickenbacker 325 as John's axe of choice. With its distinctive f-holes, the archtop hollow-bodied instrument features a highly resonant tonality. Paul was the first Beatle to use one on a Beatles recording, with Harrison and Lennon ordering Casinos of their own the following year in advance of the *Revolver* project. In contrast with "The Night Before" and "Another Girl," McCartney achieves a decidedly more authentic response to love's trials and tribulations on the Little Richard-inspired "I'm Down," the throat-wrenching B-side for "Help!" With John's pulsing Vox Continental organ and George's edgy guitar work, the song provides a tormented retort to the speaker's girlfriend, an unrepentant liar and cheat.

"You've Got to Hide Your Love Away" explores torment of an entirely different kind. While the composition is generally understood to be John's coy allusion to Brian Epstein's homosexuality—and the associated pain that comes from secreting the very truth and nature about oneself from the world—

"You've Got to Hide Your Love Away" also exists as the Beatles' most complex literary narrative to date.[4] Doing his best Dylan impersonation, John sings about loneliness and the bitter effects that it stamps upon its victims: "Here I stand head in hand / Turn my face to the wall," he sings. "If she's gone I can't go on / Feelin' two-foot small." It's a tortured and sympathetic portrait, to be sure, with the speaker—courtesy of one of the Beatles' happy accidents in the recording studio—merging "two-foot tall" with the idea of feeling "small" in order to connote his brittle self-esteem. Our empathy for his predicament—and his seeming compliance in its construction—is heightened by the speaker's paranoia about the laughter and stares of his persecutors. But who are they? Are they the stuff of the speaker's grief-stricken imagination? Or, worse yet, are there actually people staring at him and laughing at his malaise? John's composition finds him crafting a narrator who, in the tradition of Robert Browning's "My Last Duchess," offers a dramatic monologue about his quandary. In Browning's poem, the Duke of Ferrara directs our attention to the image of his late wife: "That's my last duchess painted on the wall, / Looking as if she were alive." As the poem continues, we learn the truth about the jealous Duke's role in her demise—specifically, his complicity in ensuring that "all smiles stopped together"—and, in so doing, he gives himself away (25, 26). In Browning's dramatic monologues, his speakers work from ironic stances in which they reveal, often unintentionally, aspects about their inner nature and true proclivities. This is entirely the case with "You've Got to Hide Your Love Away," the lyrics of which find John's speaker engaged in winning our sympathy in the same instant in which he exposes his derision for the world—with his stolid defiance assuming the place of his earlier compliance:

> How could she say to me
> "Love will find a way"?
> Gather 'round all you clowns
> Let me hear you say,
> "Hey, you've got to hide your love away."

It's a magnificent moment in which John's narrator can no longer stomach his own passive-aggression. Suddenly—like all of us—he finds himself slipping neatly into the double-bind of real life: on the one hand, we all want to cut sympathetic portraits, yet on the other, we can scarcely hold our tongues about what we perceive to be life's inequities and inherent unfairness. As the song comes to a close, John and George's acoustic guitars give way to a plush wall of flutes—recalling the first movement from Stravinsky's *The Rite of Spring*—and the composition draws to a hasty finish, tying a neat bow around Lennon's tender fable about loneliness and its all too real capacity for engendering self-effacement (Pollack). In his deft arrangement for "You've Got to Hide Your Love Away," Martin's score calls for a concert flute to be played an octave above an alto flute, thus affording the track with its layered, velveteen effect.

For George Harrison, *Help!* proved to be a boon, given that two of his compositions, "I Need You" and "You Like Me Too Much," were featured on the album. With the assistance of a guitar effects pedal, "I Need You" establishes an ethereal mood, although the song's ineffectual lyrics seem rather pedestrian in comparison with its fairly innovative music. As with "You Like Me Too Much"—which, with its unrestrained sentimentality and Martin's ersatz barrelhouse piano, is arguably Harrison's most ineffectual Beatles recording—"I Need You" concerns the guitarist's budding relationship with Pattie Boyd, the British fashion model whom he had met on the set of *A Hard Day's Night*. "George was in love," Cynthia Lennon recalled. "Pattie, on the other hand, was well and truly involved with a very steady boyfriend. George proceeded to work to a plan of campaign to woo Pattie away from her steady and make her his own" (qtd. in Badman 96). George's scheme apparently succeeded, and he married Pattie in January 1966, leaving Paul as the only remaining bachelor among the Beatles. Ringo's contribution to the album, a cover version of the Buck Owens cowboy tune "Act Naturally," equals "You Like Me Too Much" in terms of its mediocre result. "Act Naturally" was a late addition to *Help!*'s lineup in place of the Lennon-McCartney original "If You've Got Trouble," an up-tempo pop number, vocalized in pure deadpan by Ringo, that hearkens back to the whimsy of the early Beatles. Yet another Lennon-McCartney composition, "That Means a Lot," was recorded on the same day as "If You've Got Trouble" and was similarly scrapped. As with "If You've Got Trouble," its lack of musical innovation and lyrical inanity—"Love can be deep inside / Love can be suicide," Paul sings—found the Beatles going in the opposite direction of their finest work during this period. Recorded during the album's final session, "Act Naturally" would be the last of the Beatles' cover renditions for the balance of their career, a fact that speaks volumes about the remarkable creative momentum that they had begun to harness by the summer of 1965.[5] John's rasping interpretation of Larry Williams's "Dizzy Miss Lizzy" would bring *Help!* to a noisy close. It would also be the final installment in the Beatles' increasingly stale tradition of employing rollicking cover versions—memorable as they may have been in achieving closure on *Please Please Me* and *With the Beatles*—in order to conclude their albums.

As *Help!* would so clearly demonstrate, the group had more ambitious things on their minds than simply replicating their own recorded past year in and year out. As much of the Western world followed their lead and produced amplified guitar music at an incredible pace, the Beatles progressively turned to the acoustic feel of folk melodies such as "It's Only Love," "Tell Me What

You See," and "I've Just Seen a Face." Written under the working title of "That's a Nice Hat (Cap)," John's "It's Only Love" is a redaction, less than a year later, of romantic love's lilting simplicity in "Every Little Thing." With a folksy pastoralism that presages several key (and, more frequently than not, superior) tracks on *Rubber Soul*, "It's Only Love" depicts the inherent difficulty of maintaining human relationships, rather than the breathless peace of mind that they afford: "It's only love, and that is all," John sings to his own gentle Hootenanny accompaniment. "But it's so hard loving you. / Yes, it's so hard loving you." With the simple musical palette of his electric piano and George's Gretsch Tennessean, Paul's "Tell Me What You See" approaches the kind of existential self-awareness that prefigures much of *Rubber Soul* and *Revolver*. Yet, in their present manifestation, the lyrics exist on a basal level, one human being to another, in which the songwriters—in this instance, McCartney—can only make furtive gestures at the larger, waiting world just beyond their reach: "Open up your eyes now, tell me what you see." In terms of capturing the simple passion and conviviality of the band's music, few tracks equal the ebullience inherent in Paul's "I've Just Seen a Face," which had gone under the working title of "Auntie Gin's Theme."[6] With its stirring acoustic introduction, the composition pointedly eschews the perfunctory stories about love in so many early Beatles songs, instead providing listeners with an abrupt, imagistic portrait of the first flush of heart-stopping romance: "I've just seen a face, / I can't forget the time or place / Where we just met," Paul sings. "She's just the girl for me / And I want all the world to see / We've met." Magisterial, overwhelming, and with a minimum of verbal fuss, "I've Just Seen a Face" is the uncomplicated representation of love that the Beatles had been striving toward throughout their career. And they found it just in the nick of time.

Whereas "I've Just Seen a Face" offers tender portraiture about love's first blush, "You're Going to Lose That Girl" is about what happens when shame has all but lost its place amongst our virtues. In "She Loves You," John and Paul proffered advice and reassurance for a diffident male friend about the uncertainty of new love. In "You're Going to Lose That Girl," their words of encouragement and support have been replaced by threats, the no-nonsense language of confidence, and the surety of not-so-friendly betrayal: "If you don't take her out tonight, / She's going to change her mind," they sing. "And I will take her out tonight, / And I will treat her kind." John and Paul vocalize the number with the same kind of high-gloss congeniality that undergirds "Misery" and "There's a Place," but "You're Going to Lose That Girl" is about a different world altogether—a world unfettered by the utopian niceties of the early Beatles, as well as a social milieu in which the needs of the individual inevitably come first. The notion of raw selfishness similarly exists at the core of "Ticket to Ride," a composition that music historians often cite for its proto-metal origins.

Indeed, it's difficult not to hear the thunder of hard rock bristling at the song's unruly core. It's a place where a girl can accept a ticket to ride and feel emancipated enough to enjoy the journey itself, while remaining blissfully ambivalent, noncommittal even, about the company. The speaker tries every angle that he can imagine in order to cleave her to him, to win her love, and, at the very least, bargain for sex. When the speaker's threats fall on deaf ears—"She ought to think twice, / She ought to do right by me"—he resorts to the time-honored cheap trick of earning her sympathy by confessing his sadness, his sensitivity. Neither method succeeds, of course, and the music's tension fittingly never ebbs—seeming, instead, to increase as the guitars grow faster, more urgent and destructive, as the speaker repeats "My baby don't care" with no relief in sight.

Although John would later malign (and, in all likelihood, under-represent) Paul's contribution to "Ticket to Ride" as "the way Ringo played the drums," there is no question about the sheer care and inventiveness that McCartney brought to the composition of "Yesterday," the Beatles' most universally revered ballad (qtd. in Dowlding 102). Paul had originally written the song during the band's January 1964 sojourn in Paris, and for more than eighteen months, "Yesterday" had existed in the ether of his dreams—initially, as half-baked lyrics bespeaking an enduring love for "Scrambled Eggs," and later, as a tune that felt so fresh and original that the songwriter was certain that somebody else had composed it.[7] But all along—from its earliest moments in his authorial custody through the fateful June 1965 day when it came into recorded being at EMI Studios—Paul knew that he had something special on his hands:

> It fell out of bed. I had a piano by my bedside and I must have dreamed it, because I tumbled out of bed and put my hands on the piano keys and I had a tune in my head. It was just all there, a complete thing. I couldn't believe it. It came too easy. In fact, I didn't believe I'd written it. I thought maybe I'd heard it before, it was some other tune, and I went around for weeks playing the chords of the song for people, asking them, "Is this like something? I think I've written it." And people would say, "No, it's not like anything else, but it's good." (qtd. in Dowlding 105)

After Paul had finally settled down to record the song—all by his lonesome with his Epiphone Texan—George Martin suggested that his solo performance might benefit from a string accompaniment. Paul was initially skeptical, believing that a classical arrangement would be too precious for a Beatles' record. They were a rock and roll band, after all, and a string quartet might detract from the image that they had been cultivating since teenagehood. But the producer was not to be deterred. Eventually, Paul settled down at the piano with Martin, and they hammered out a suitably tasteful arrangement to the Beatle's liking.[8] For the producer, it proved to be the most transformative moment in the group's career. As Martin recalled in *All You Need Is Ears* (1979):

That was when, as I can see it in retrospect, I started to leave my hallmark on the music, when a style started to emerge which was partly of my making. It was on "Yesterday" that I started to score their music. It was on "Yesterday" that we first used instruments other than the Beatles and myself. On "Yesterday," the added ingredient was no more nor less than a string quartet; and that, in the pop world of those days, was quite a step to take. It was with "Yesterday" that we started breaking out of the phase of using just four instruments and went into something more experimental, though our initial experiments were severely limited by the fairly crude tools at our disposal, and had simply to be molded out of my recording experience. (166–67)

It is an amazing thing to consider—given the musical worlds that the Beatles would eventually explore—that a classical arrangement was the height of experimentation for the group. Yet it was a crucial barrier that, once eclipsed, changed the way in which they approached their craft.

In itself, "Yesterday" is arguably the Beatles' only thoroughly sad song—a true masterwork of musical unity, given the exquisite parallelism of the composition's words and music. The song's speaker experiences deeply felt connotations with a sense of pastness that he finds impossible to transcend, just as he remains unable to reconcile himself with the personal fact of lost love. In the speaker's memory, yesterday's shadow never ceases, displacing him once and for all amongst the tall grass of an immutable past: "Yesterday, / Love was such an easy game to play," he sings. "Now I need a place to hide away, / Oh, I believe in yesterday." The song also demonstrates Lennon and McCartney's interest, time and time again, in performing nostalgia. William Faulkner famously wrote in *Requiem for a Nun* (1951) that "the past is never dead. It's not even past" (80). In John and Paul's hands, the Beatles' musical effusions for the balance of their career demonstrate that they understand the spirit of Faulkner's words intuitively. With "Yesterday," the notion of an enduring past is made abundantly clear when the speaker remains unable to escape the heartbreaking life in which he finds himself sequestered. The concept of "yesterday" itself denotes a sense of looking backward into an increasingly distant past, as well as a self-consciousness about a certain "shadow hanging over me" in the irreducible present. The shadow, of course, involves the speaker's unfathomable sense of loss. His beloved has robbed him of everything except the possibility of experiencing an unquenchable nostalgia for their romantic heyday. As Andreea Ritivoi reminds us, nostalgia "is constantly and painfully aware of loss," and it functions primarily to define what Ritivoi identifies as the "critical discrepancy between the present and the past" (6, 30). This "critical discrepancy" is precisely what the speaker in "Yesterday" experiences—and is damned to continue experiencing for the foreseeable future. It is the very sort of transfixing memory, with its intensely traumatic and emotional implications, from which John and Paul would never shy away in their work. As a musical achievement, the moment was not lost on the esteemed BBC critic Deryck Cooke, who, echoing Mann's sentiments during the previous year, branded Lennon and McCartney as "serious" composers of a "new music" (199).[9] With "Yesterday," the Beatles had suddenly alighted on a much wider international stage that had granted them an audience of all ages *for the ages*. In this way, Paul's masterpiece of sorrow and simplicity would radically transform the nature and direction of the band's career. The dye had been once and truly cast, and for Lennon and McCartney, the days of "She Loves You" were over for good.

Amazingly, on the same day—June 14th—that McCartney recorded the vocal for "Yesterday," he also sang the lead on the folksy "I've Just Seen a Face" and the throat-gnashing "I'm Down." It was an incredible feat that the group would begin and, for the most part, complete such a jaw-dropping trio of songs during the same session. At the end of the first take of the raucous "I'm Down," Paul famously described the band's sound as "plastic soul, man"—an ironic reference to the sonic textures of American rhythm and blues that the Beatles had become veritable masters at emulating (qtd. in Winn, *Way Beyond Compare* 342). As their cover versions of American rock and roll had demonstrated throughout their recording career, the group's peculiarly British performances of R&B had afforded the genre with an exacting sense of precision and buoyancy in place of the improvisational and soulful elements evinced by their American counterparts on the original compositions. The concept of "plastic soul," then, refers to the Beatles' chameleonic penchant for transforming a musical form in their own image, retaining its fundamental qualities in the process of making it their own.[10] As the group's valentine to their American rock and roll roots, *Rubber Soul* draws upon the notion of "plastic soul" as its musical firmament. The group recorded the album during multiple sessions in October and November 1965, having taken the month of September off after completing their latest American concert tour. On November 16th, Martin concocted the running order for the album's tracks. Pointedly, it would be one of the last times that he undertook such a role without the Beatles' express input. As Paul had predicted, the workmen were indeed taking over the factory.

~

Released in December 1965, the band's sixth studio album witnesses Lennon and McCartney as they continue to experiment with the intriguing interstices between memory and narrative. In contrast with their early albums, the Beatles' later efforts reveal them to be fully engaged as storytellers in the act of meaning-making. While it is genuinely difficult to establish a turning point in which they dismiss puppy love's vacuous simplicity in favor of more elaborate analyses of the human condition, their work on *Rubber Soul* demonstrates a considerable lyrical and musical leap from their previous efforts. With songs like "Norwegian Wood (This Bird Has Flown)" and "In My Life," the Beatles' aesthetic clearly shifts from boy-band whimsy into narrative and impressionistic overdrive. The release of *Rubber Soul* was a groundbreaking musical and lyrical event in the larger scope of their career as songwriters. As John Covach points out, the album—particularly in songs such as "Nowhere Man" and "Michelle"—finds Lennon and McCartney discarding the standard patterns of their early "craftsperson" years, a fecund period in their development made possible by virtue of their creative approach, which "privileges repeatable structures." With *Rubber Soul*, Covach writes, John and Paul emerged as full-fledged "artists" who eschew repetition in favor of "adopting and adapting notions of inspiration, genius, and complexity" (38, 39). And the Beatles would be the collective medium for Lennon and McCartney's craft, the venue from which they would unfold astonishing stories about the nature of our condition, our memories, and our dreams.

Rubber Soul begins with the ear-catching flourish of George's bluesy guitar, which kick-starts "Drive My Car" into life. With Paul's relentless bass and Ringo's cowbell propelling the rhythm, "Drive My Car" challenges the highly gendered expectations of the Beatles' mid-1960s audience. As "Drive My Car" emphatically demonstrates, the everygirl from the songs of the early Beatles was very quickly transforming into an everywoman, complete with an ego and agenda that wasn't playing second fiddle to any masculine other. As with the woman in "Ticket to Ride," the female character in "Drive My Car" is all business, all the time. In itself, the song is loaded with sexual innuendo, with "baby, you can drive my car" being one of the Beatles' more obvious come-ons. Even more intriguingly, McCartney's lyrics, with considerable assistance from Lennon in the studio, devise a rather provocative superstructure in which the woman and the man exchange power positions; in the beginning, she's looking for a literal and figurative vehicle in order to obtain wealth and celebrity—"I wanna be famous, a star of the screen"—yet by the end of the song she's in the proverbial driver's seat herself: "I've found a driver and that's a start." For Paul, there was little question about the woman's intentions: she was a "bitch," he reported, who had no use for romance or the pursuit of true love (qtd. in Dowlding 114). "Working for peanuts is all very fine," she tells her car-driving suitor, "but I can show you a better time." Rather than allowing her now ecstatic driver to maintain the upper hand, she performs an exercise in self-empowerment by taking firm control of the reins of their relationship: "Baby, you can drive my car, and maybe I'll love you." The couple's elation—

short-lived as it may indeed prove to be—is represented by an inspired moment of onomatopoeia in which the car's horn announces their jubilation: "Beep-beep, beep-beep, yeah!"

With its meticulous forward momentum and pulsating rhythm, "Drive My Car" was the clear precursor for "Day Tripper," the B-side of the Beatles' next single, which was recorded during the very next session. As with "I Feel Fine," "Day Tripper" was inspired by Bobby Parker's "Watch Your Step." As John later recalled about the genesis of "Day Tripper": "That's mine, including the lick, the guitar break, and the whole bit. 'Day Tripper' is just a rock and roll song. Day-trippers are people who go on a day trip, right? Usually, on a ferryboat or something" (qtd. in Badman 194). For John, a day tripper is a "weekend hippie," a roustabout who travels from place to place with little, if any, plans for the future. In the context of the song, the day tripper emerges as a woman, a provocateur who refuses to surrender to the speaker's desires: "She's a big teaser, she took me half the way there," he sings. Originally written as "she's a prick-teaser," the lyrics underscore the speaker's confusion regarding the woman's suggestive behavior. Eventually winning her sex, the speaker becomes perplexed by her lack of interest in a committed relationship: "Tried to please her," he complains, but "she only played one night stands." The single's A-side, "We Can Work It Out," finds the Beatles' speaker experiencing a vastly similar form of frustration in which his beloved refuses to yield.[11] As a true collaboration by Lennon and McCartney, the song is often misread as the musical representation of an ongoing conflict between the songwriters' personalities. This misinterpretation, as it turns out, finds its roots in the words of John himself: "You've got Paul writing 'we can work it out,' real optimistic, you know, and me, impatient, 'Life is very short and there's no time for fussing. . .'" (*Anthology* 199). While McCartney may have been optimistic and Lennon impatient in the reality of their biographical lives, the song was about nothing of the sort. Although the composition's title rather blatantly refers to the idea of reconciliation, "We Can Work It Out" is really about the sheer force of human will. In Paul's passage, the speaker pleads with his discordant lover to "Try to see it my way, / Do I have to keep on talking till I can't go on?" And when she refuses to acquiesce, he inveigles her with threats: "While you see it your way, / Run the risk of knowing that our love may soon be gone." The song's only authentically hopeful space exists in the chorus, in which the speaker reports that "we can work it out," only to be belied by John's middle-eight, in which the speaker reminds his lover— his opponent, no less!—that "Life is very short, and there's no time / For fussing and fighting, my friend." When considered in tandem, John and Paul's passages offer two aspects of the very same passive-aggressive self. With its jaunty musical atmosphere, tempered only by the relative intensity and seriousness of the middle-eight, "We Can Work It Out" is a masterpiece of writerly deception. As with the speaker, who disguises himself as a peacemaker in contrast with his inner obstinacy, the song offers a knowing representation of the ways in which human beings engage in social subterfuge in order to conceal their internal failings behind attractive walls of seeming equanimity.[12]

Along with "Drive My Car," "Norwegian Wood (This Bird Has Flown)" was described by McCartney as one of *Rubber Soul's* two "comedy numbers."[13] And like "Day Tripper" and "We Can Work It Out," the humor finds its origins in the divine comedy of the human condition. As with the speaker in "Drive My Car," the joke in "Norwegian Wood" is squarely at the expense of the protagonist. On *Rubber Soul*, the Beatles effectively signaled the expansion of their musical horizons via Harrison's well-known experimentation with sitar music.[14] George had first come into the orbit of the sitar on the set of *Help!*, which featured a scene in which a band of Indian musicians performed an instrumental version of "A Hard Day's Night." After listening to the sitar work of Ravi Shankar, the renowned Bengali-Indian virtuoso, George was hooked:

> I had bought a very cheap sitar in a shop called India Craft in London, and it fitted on to the song ["Norwegian Wood"] and it gave it that little extra thing. Even though the sound of the sitar was bad, they were still quite happy with it. At the same time as I played the sitar, very badly, on the Beatles' record, I began to hear Ravi Shankar's name. The third time, I thought, "This is an odd coincidence." I went out and bought some of Ravi's records, put them on, listened to them and it hit a certain spot in me that I can't explain, but it seemed familiar to me. The only way that I can describe it was my intellect didn't know what was going on and yet this other part of me identified with it. It just called on me. (qtd. in Badman 190)[15]

In "Norwegian Wood," which went under the working title of "This Bird Has Flown," the exotic, microtonal flavor of Harrison's sitar lines accent the flourishes of Lennon's haunting acoustic guitar, which he played in waltz-like 12/8 time on his capoed Jumbo. They also provide a curious palette for Lennon's confessional tale about an extramarital affair.[16] Lennon's lyrics—far from underscoring love's everlasting possibilities—hint at something far more fleeting, even unromantic: "She asked me to stay and she told me to sit anywhere / So I looked around and I noticed there wasn't a chair." Compare the words of "Norwegian Wood" with such earlier phraseology as "I ain't got nothing but love, babe / Eight days a week," and Lennon and McCartney's development as poets and storytellers becomes resoundingly clear.

In "Norwegian Wood," the speaker ponders the nature of a past affair, particularly in terms of the ironic and, in hindsight, confounding difference between his and his lover's expectations for the liaison: "I once had a girl, / Or should I say, / She once had me." After relaxing in her flat, sharing a bottle of wine, and talking into the wee hours, she coolly announces that "it's time for bed." Is it an emotionless come-on for a little rough-and-tumble, or, conversely, is it the curt declaration that their evening together has met its end? "She told me she worked in the morning and started to laugh," the speaker reports. "I told her I didn't and crawled off to sleep in the bath." The woman's tempestuous laugh offers a clear signal about her obvious control of the situation, and it is highly suggestive, moreover, that she intends to take carnal possession of the speaker on her own fiercely independent and uninhibited terms. The scene is eerily reminiscent of the lascivious behavior of Calixta, the heroine in Kate Chopin's *fin-de-siècle* short story "The Storm," who takes a lover, Alcée, while her husband is away, riding out a hurricane with their son in another vicinity of Grand Isle. As Alcée leaves her side, Calixta "lifted her pretty chin in the air and laughed aloud" (285). In "Norwegian Wood," the woman delivers an unforgettably lusty laugh of her own—a brawny, derisive chortle of self-satisfaction. The next morning, the speaker wakes up alone. He's been *had* alright, and by a woman who, without the faintest hint of passion, devises an emotionless, antiromantic one-night stand. "And when I awoke / I was alone, / This bird had flown," the speaker laments. His lover—his adversary, more accurately, in the bitter game of love—has extinguished any seeds of romance before they even took root. Seething in anger and resentment, the speaker exacts his revenge by burning the woman's stylish wooden furniture in the fireplace: "So I lit a fire, / Isn't it good / Norwegian Wood?"[17]

The sexual crimes described in "Norwegian Wood" are quickly erased by the self-absorbed misdemeanors depicted in Paul's "You Won't See Me," a playful, up-tempo song about the unfeeling, unresponsive object of a frustrated would-be boyfriend's romantic interest. Featuring an all but inaudible Hammond organ played by Mal Evans, the song bears a strong resemblance to the Four Tops' "It's the Same Old Song," from which Paul borrowed the three-chord sequence that undergirds "You Won't See Me." In addition to the sitar, *Rubber Soul* introduces listeners to Nowhere Man, the band's first genuinely literary character. In so doing, the Beatles also acquaint us with Nowhere Land, their first explicitly literary setting. As a literary construct, Nowhere Land shares much in common with Sir Thomas More's conception of *Utopia* (1516), the Grecian title of which literally signifies as "in or at no place." Although it is a decidedly gentler and eminently more caring form of cultural critique than More's novel, "Nowhere Man" situates its protagonist in similarly unforgiving environs. Being in Nowhere Land is like being in no place at all— it is, quite literally, the equivalency of being an "insignificant, unsatisfactory, or worthless person, thing, [or] state" (*OED*). Sadly, Nowhere Man is clearly a long way from going anyplace significant or from experiencing meaningful human interconnection. Although his name demands little, if any, exegesis, Nowhere Man also suffers from the same pangs of loneliness that will impinge upon nearly every one of the band's literary characters. Living alone in Nowhere Land, he whiles away the hours "making Nowhere plans for nobody." The only antidote for his malaise, it seems, would be the experience of human interrelationship—when "somebody else / Lends you a hand," Lennon sings.[18] It's a panacea that, in the Beatles' construction of nostalgia and pastness, will never sate the weary souls of their protagonists. As Riley perceptively remarks, "No one can make it through life's difficulties alone, the music seems to be saying, and the best crutches are other people" (162). For John and Paul, Nowhere Man—as with the speaker in "You've Got to Hide Your Love Away"—is but the first of many in a long line of desolate souls whose loneliness threatens to corrupt his sense of well-being and destroy him from within.

Musically, "Nowhere Man" offers a deep, trebly sound that the Beatles achieved through the studio trickery that would become their standard *modus operandi* in 1966. As Walter Everett observes: "John and George ran their Strats through several sets of faders so the engineers could boost the treble to the utmost, multiple times, to enhance their silvery doubled part in 'Nowhere Man,' the solo of which culminates in the first natural harmonic featured in a Beatles recording" ("Painting Their Room in a Colorful Way" 80). The composition's intentionally shrill musical sheen heightens our sense of the Nowhere Man's plight, as if his social alienation has left him on the cusp of a totalizing psychological break with a world that has no use for him nor any interest in his well-being. With Paul's fuzz-bass effect throbbing in the foreground, Harrison's "Think for Yourself" witnesses the lead guitarist in the act of cultivating the shrewdly, coldly analytical, and slightly misanthropic persona that will pilot many of his songs throughout his career. Having gone under the working title of "Won't Be There with You," the track masquerades as the story of a contemptuous speaker who has made the awful discovery that his beloved is blithely unoriginal and—worse yet—unthinking, to boot: "Although your mind's opaque, / Try thinking more if just for your own sake," Harrison sings. "The future still looks good / And you've got time to rectify / All the things that you should." At its core, the composition is the inaugural entry (with shades of "Don't Bother Me") in Harrison's existential philosophy, later to be adumbrated by Eastern religion and thought, about the mind-numbingly automatic and insensate manner in which human beings undertake their lives in the workaday world—a vacuous place in which real life remains indelibly subservient to the accumulation of wealth and perfunctory consumerism. The album's next track, "The Word," seems positively naïve in

the wake of Harrison's hard-edged social critique. With Martin on harmonium, Paul's composition offers a bouncy, utopian romp about the simply
joys inherent in the act of repeating a certain word: "Say the word and you'll
be free / Say the word and be like me / Say the word I'm thinking of / Have
you heard the word is love?"

The carefree spirit of "The Word" is quietly doused by the opening acoustic
guitar phrases of "Michelle," a song whose seemingly unquenchable wistful-
ness will characterize John and Paul's nostalgic forays for years to come. With
nostalgic feelings, Fred Davis remarks, "the emotional posture is that of a
yearning for return, albeit accompanied by an ambivalent recognition that
such is not possible" (21). In Paul's "Michelle," a home demo of which first
surfaced way back in July 1963, the yearning for romantic fruition is tempered
by his star-crossed lovers' inability to eclipse the language barrier that threatens to destroy their love, even in its embryonic state. Musically, the composition finds its roots in Chet Atkins's instrumental "Trambone," while Paul's
vocal stylings emerge relatively unscathed, at John's suggestion, from Nina
Simone's "I Put a Spell on You." McCartney was assisted on the song's French
phrases by Ivan Vaughan's wife Jan, the language teacher who helpfully translated Paul's existing lyrics, "These are words that go together well," as "*Sont des
mots qui vont très bien ensemble.*" With Paul on his Texan and John and George
on their Jumbos, all three capoed acoustic guitars establish a sobering founda-
tion for one of the band's most peculiar meditations on loss. The lyrics for
"Michelle" reveal an implicit nostalgia in which the song's speaker confesses
his love for his would-be French paramour even as he already espies the death
of love in their future. While McCartney's lyrics concentrate on providing the
object of the speaker's affections with romantic "words that go together well,"
the Beatles' music—particularly the song's contemplative bass lines—establish
a sorrowful subtext with undeniably gloomy portents for the couple's future.
In so doing, Paul exposes one of nostalgia's fundamental and most seductive
mythologies about engendering hope and renewal. In "Michelle," the speaker
is engaged in the act of glancing backward at a relationship that he's never
even had—and, most likely, never will experience in the first place. The
speaker has fallen victim, like so many of us, to nostalgia's cruelest trick.

Recorded on the same day as the band's blues instrumental "12-Bar Original," which went unreleased until the *Anthology* project during the 1990s,
"What Goes On" was chosen as Ringo's vocal showcase for *Rubber Soul* and
credited to Lennon-McCartney-Starkey after the drummer helped out with
the lyrics—"about five words," Ringo later recalled (qtd. in Turner 95). With
its loose rockabilly structure, it is also quite arguably the weakest and most
incongruous track on the album. Yet the song is memorable for the Beatles'

first instance of self-referentiality. "It's so easy for a girl like you to lie," Ringo sings. "Tell me why." In the extreme background, John can be heard responding, "We already told you why." In one sense, he is making an explicit reference to the Lennon-McCartney composition "Tell Me Why," which was included on *A Hard Day's Night*. Yet in another sense, he is answering Ringo's former question about why "it's so easy for a girl like you to lie." Indeed, much of the Beatles' post-*A Hard Day's Night* corpus has functioned as a response to the aspects of human duplicity that so often complicate love's skirmishes and render its battlefields into combat zones where anything goes. Lennon's recognition of the larger sweep of the band's music signals a patent realization of the growing interconnectedness inherent in their work. In itself, it gestures toward a new level of artistry that the Beatles had not previously traversed.

In contrast with "What Goes On," Paul offers a more complex analysis of romantic deceit in "I'm Looking through You," a song that finds its origins in an argument that the songwriter had with Jane Asher. As Paul recalled, "I knew I was selfish. It caused a few rows. Jane went off and I said, 'Okay then, leave. I'll find somebody else.' It was shattering to be without her. That was when I wrote 'I'm Looking through You'" (qtd. in Badman 193). Interestingly, an earlier version of the song is pointedly despairing and proceeds at a more desolate pace. Lyrically, "I'm Looking through You" finds Paul questioning the veracity of true love and, in a larger sense, the cultural elevation of romance. "Why, tell me why, did you not treat me right?" he sings in the middle-eight. "Love has a nasty habit of disappearing overnight." With Ringo playing the Vox Continental organ and Martin on piano, the song also marks the first recorded appearance of Paul's Rickenbacker 4001S, a maple, full-bodied bass that was superior to the lighter-weight Höfner violin model in terms of the instrument's solid sustain and its clear, precise tonality. As Tony Bacon and Gareth Morgan point out, the Rickenbacker offers tighter string tension, affording "a better focus to each note" and providing a "more tangible bass-end to the sound, in contrast to the warm, woody thud of the Höfner" (45). With the Rickenbacker's expansive sonic possibilities literally at his fingertips, Paul would virtually redefine the bass's melodic role in popular music.

In addition to being one of *Rubber Soul*'s standout tracks, "Girl" is, quite possibly, the Beatles' most callous attack on humanity's penchant for engaging in blinding self-interest. In the eyes of the speaker, his girlfriend—perhaps another metaphor for the universal everygirl in the mid-Beatles repertoire—is simply irresistible, yet cunning in the degree to which she confounds conventional gender expectations. John punctuates the chorus with deep, contemplative sighs that illustrate the speaker's aching heart. The song's middle-eight, with Paul and George providing irreverent vocal percussion by singing "tit-tit-

tit-tit" as their backing vocal, is pure, unadulterated verbal laceration: "She's the kind of girl / Who puts you down when friends are there, / You feel a fool." But the speaker's deception at the hands of his girlfriend is only a prelude to the final verse, where Lennon provides a sizzling reproach of the girl, of her society, of the culture of romance itself. It is the most brutalizing lyric in the Beatles' corpus:

> Was she told when she was young that pain would lead to pleasure?
> Did she understand it when they said
> That a man must break his back to earn his day of leisure?
> Will she still believe it when he's dead?

It is a well-known cliché that a fine line exists between love and hate, but with "Girl," John suggests that an even finer line exists between romantic love and self-love—and that in the end, we all too frequently serve the desires of the self before ministering to the needs of others, even when those others are ostensibly the most cherished, most beloved members of our personal worlds. The song's caustic conclusion is underscored by the instrumental solo that Harrison fashions for the finale. Simulating a bouzouki-like sound on his Hootenanny, George plays an intricate Greek melody that affords the track with an Old World resonance, implicitly reminding us that the song's arguments about the discrepant realities between love and devotion are genuinely timeless dilemmas.[19]

Arguably *Rubber Soul*'s most significant and lasting composition, John's "In My Life" likely originated from the songwriter's youthful reading of Charles Lamb's eighteenth-century poem "The Old Familiar Faces": "For some they have died, and some they have left me, / *And some are taken from me*; all are departed; / All, all are gone, the old familiar faces" (21). With "In My Life," Lennon deftly examines the power and inevitable failure of memory. While some places and people remain vivid, others recede and disappear altogether. "Memories lose their meaning," John sings, although he knows that "he'll often stop and think about them," referring, yet again, to the past's elaborate layers of character and setting. Fittingly, "In My Life" features Martin's wistful piano solo, which he later described as his "Bach inversion." With its Baroque intonations, the piano interlude participates in establishing the track's nostalgic undercurrents. The song's closing refrain—"In my life, I love you more"—suggests obvious romantic overtones, as well as a lyrical posture in which the speaker commemorates the all-encompassing power of romantic love. Yet it also underscores our vexing relationship with the past, which exerts a powerful hold upon the present, in one sense, while slowly fading from memory and metamorphosing into other, perhaps more pleasing or less painful memories with each passing year. As Maurice Halbwachs reminds us, "The past is not preserved but is reconstructed on the basis of the present" (qtd. in Kimberly K. Smith 517–18). With its haunting melody and moving lyrics, "In My Life" is one of the group's finest exercises in creating pure musical beauty.[20]

Perhaps even more important in terms of the Beatles' recording career, "In My Life" represents one of Lennon and McCartney's most complicated instances of writerly dispute. As John remembers, "It was, I think, my first real major piece of work. Up till then it had all been sort of glib and throwaway. And that was the first time I consciously put my literary part of myself into the lyric" (*All We Are Saying* 178–79). The Beatles recorded the track in a mere three takes on October 18th, 1965. Four days later, Martin went to EMI Studios before the band members arrived in order to record the keyboard solo, which was made possible via his wound-up piano effect and which replaced the Vox Continental organ solo that he had recorded earlier as a space-saver (Lewisohn, *The Complete Beatles Recording Sessions* 202–03). The very fact that Martin felt free and confident enough to contribute to the song's musicality renders the Beatles' authorial practices even more cloudy, while also underscoring his substantial and continuing role in orchestrating their musical direction. Yet Martin's contribution in this instance also demonstrates the manner in which multiple authorship frequently characterized the band's songwriting practices. In the case of "In My Life," documentary evidence offers a number of revealing clues about the song's lyrical composition. The testimony would seem to be in favor of Lennon, who recalls writing a first draft of the song in which he "struggled for days and hours trying to write clever lyrics" (*All We Are Saying* 193):

> "In My Life" started out as a bus journey from my house on 250 Menlove Avenue to town, mentioning every place that I could remember. And it was ridiculous. This is before even "Penny Lane" was written and I had Penny Lane, Strawberry Field, Tram Sheds—Tram Sheds are the depots just outside of Penny Lane—and it was the most boring sort of "What I Did on My Holiday's Bus Trip" song and it wasn't working at all. (*All We Are Saying* 152)

In John's estimation, the song's lyrics improved after he began waxing nostalgically about the friends, lovers, and places of his Liverpudlian past. Lennon pointedly recalls that "the whole lyrics were already written before Paul even heard it. In 'In My Life,'" he adds, "[Paul's] contribution melodically was the harmony and the middle-eight itself" (*All We Are Saying* 153).

McCartney's recollections about the composition of "In My Life" vary to a considerable degree from Lennon's version of events. Paul remembers a writing session in which John had already completed the song's opening stanzas:

"But as I recall, he didn't have a tune to it." McCartney allegedly devoted half an hour to composing the song's musical structure in its entirety:

> And I went down to the half-landing, where John had a Mellotron, and I sat there and put together a tune based on Smokey Robinson and the Miracles. Songs like "You Really Got a Hold on Me" and "Tears of a Clown" had really been an influence. You refer back to something you've loved and try and take the spirit of that and write something new. So I recall writing the whole melody. And it actually does sound very like me, if you analyze it. I was obviously working to lyrics. The melody's structure is very me. (qtd. in Miles 277)

While they often dispute Robinson's influence on the composition of the song's musical structure, a number of musicologists agree that "In My Life" evinces a McCartneyesque flavor. The song's "angular verticality, spanning an octave in typically wide—and difficult—leaps, certainly shows more of his touch than Lennon's, despite fitting the latter's voice snugly," MacDonald writes. "As for the middle-eight, there isn't one, [with] the song alternating between its verse and an extended chorus" (136–37).[21] By categorically asserting that he wrote the tune's evocative melody, Paul suggests that "In My Life" was a joint effort. And, as with the likes of "Help!" and "Yesterday," it was certainly a song over which claiming authorship was a worthy goal indeed. John and Paul's postmortem conflict regarding the authorship of "In My Life" was a revealing episode about the manner in which they approached their particular contributions to the Lennon-McCartney catalogue. There was clearly a shifting tide in Beatledom, and it would define the balance of their career as collaborators.

Following "In My Life," *Rubber Soul* is rounded out by "Wait," "If I Needed Someone," and "Run for Your Life"—a trio of songs that demonstrates, rather insistently, that the Beatles' most accomplished album to date doesn't end nearly as well as it had begun. A holdover from the *Help!* sessions, "Wait" is the album's must uninspired track, and its artless lyrics are a full step backward from the musical strides achieved by compositions such as "Norwegian Wood" and "Nowhere Man": "Wait, till I come back to your side," John and Paul sing. "We'll forget the tears we've cried." As with the lyrics, the song simply doesn't go anywhere. With Martin on harmonium, "If I Needed Someone" is vastly superior to its precursor. The mid-tempo composition features Harrison's distinctive shimmering guitar introduction—played on his capoed Rickenbacker 360—which was inspired by the Byrds' "The Bells of Rhymney." Lyrically, it doesn't begin to measure up to "Think for Yourself," and even George mocked its lack of musical sophistication: "'If I Needed Someone' was like a million other songs written around one chord. A D chord actually." George caused a minor controversy when he ridiculed the Hollies' cover version of the song: "I think it's rubbish the way they've done it. They've spoilt it," he reported. The Hollies' Graham Nash didn't mince words in his retort: "I'd back any of us boys against the Beatles musically any time!" (qtd. in Badman 193). *Rubber Soul* concludes with John's acerbic "Run for Your Life," which was, ironically, the first song recorded for the album. John unabashedly based his composition on Elvis Presley's "Baby Let's Play House," which had been written by Arthur Gunter, a Nashville preacher's son who fashioned the song around Eddy Arnold's 1951 country and western hit entitled "I Want to Play House with You." With "Run for Your Life," the speaker coldly threatens his beloved with knee-jerk homicide if she strays from their relationship and, even more discomfiting for the speaker, beyond his steely-eyed control: "I'd rather see you dead, little girl / Than to be with another man," Lennon sings. "You better keep your head, little girl / Or I won't know where I am." John later confessed to being embarrassed by the lyrics' brutishness, but there's no denying the beastly honesty inherent in the boorish speaker's wrath. He means business alright, and he won't be shielding his intentions behind the pretty words of romantic love.

Although "Run for Your Life" serves as an unfortunate coda for *Rubber Soul*, the album was truly a watershed moment—an unmistakable harbinger for innovative and even more provocative works of musical art. In 1965, the Beatles had clearly turned the corner into a new level of creative promise and possibility—and they had actually grown their fan base considerably in the bargain. As Gary Burns notes, Lennon and McCartney's nostalgic ventures in such songs as "Michelle" and "In My Life" during this era "softened and humanized" their recordings, thus "increasing their mass appeal." Rather than being politically motivated, he adds, "this was a benign use of nostalgia" (186). In short, the Beatles were employing nostalgia for nostalgia's sake—drawing upon its perpetual allure as a comforting mechanism for their listeners and, perhaps even more tellingly, for themselves. *Rubber Soul*'s eye-catching cover was the last to feature the work of Robert Freeman. Shot in the garden of Kenwood, John's Weybridge estate, the photograph was intentionally distorted at the group's request. In itself, the warped vision of the four Beatles on the cover was a hint of things to come—an arresting and skewed image of ambiguity for a new musical age. *Rubber Soul* was released on December 3rd, the same day that the Beatles embarked upon a nine-day tour of the United Kingdom. On December 12th, the curtain closed in front of the band at the Capitol Cinema in Cardiff, Wales. The show ended with a blistering performance of "I'm Down," which, amidst the tumult of screams, no one in the audience, much less the band, really heard. And what nobody knew, save for the increasingly weary lads from Liverpool, was that it was the last song of the last concert on the last tour that the Beatles would ever play in their homeland.[22]

Notes

1. Lennon's third book, *Skywriting by Word of Mouth and Other Writings*, would be published posthumously in 1986.

2. Smith argues that the dangers of a politically engendered nostalgia extend well beyond our futile dreams of an "archetypal paradise": "If nostalgia is universal, even a return to pre-industrial society won't help. We are convinced that whatever it is we long for wasn't actually there, that we are longing for something—community, stability, the feeling of being at home—that is unattainable anywhere. Thus, not only has industrialization obliterated agrarian society, but its accompanying theory of nostalgia has destabilized our individual and collective memories of our pre-industrial past" (522–23).

3. In its American release, the song was introduced by a brief instrumental known as the "James Bond Theme." Riley rightly argues that this introductory piece unnecessarily mitigates the feelings of panic and crisis inherent in the song's lyrics. The "pseudo-James Bond music . . . puts the song in huge nonthreatening parentheses," he writes (138).

4. John's empathy for the plight of homosexuals would later manifest itself in the famous limerick that he contributed to Len Richmond's landmark anthology *The Gay Liberation Book* (1973): "Why make it sad to be gay? / Doing your thing is okay. / Our body's our own, so leave us alone / And play with yourself today" (95).

5. After "Act Naturally," the Beatles would record one more nonoriginal composition—the traditional nineteenth-century Liverpool ballad entitled "Maggie Mae," which was copyrighted to John, Paul, George, and Ringo as the composition's songwriters.

6. The working title was in honor of Paul's Aunt Gin, who adored "I've Just Seen a Face." The youngest sister of Paul's father Jim, Gin was later referenced, along with Paul's brother Michael and the Everly Brothers, in the 1976 Wings' hit "Let 'Em In": "Sister Suzie, brother John, / Martin Luther, Phil and Don, / Brother Michael, Auntie Gin, / Open the door, and let 'em in."

7. There have been two principal theories about the inspiration for "Yesterday." British musicologist Spencer Leigh contends that McCartney was inspired by Nat King Cole's 1953 hit song "Answer Me, My Love," while Italian producer Lilli Greco suggests that "Yesterday" finds its roots in an 1895 Neapolitan composition entitled "Piccerè che vene a dicere." See "Beatles' 'Yesterday' a Cover of Old Neapolitan Song, Producer Claims." Regardless of the song's origins, McCartney debuted "Yesterday" during a live television broadcast on Sunday, August 1st, 1965. Some two years before, Rory Storm's sister Iris Caldwell had broken up with Paul, relaying a message to the Beatle through her mother in which she claimed that he "had no feelings." Shortly before the broadcast, Paul telephoned Mrs. Caldwell: "You know that you said that I had no feelings?" he asked her. "Watch the telly on Sunday night and then tell me that I've got no feelings" (qtd. in Turner 84).

8. During Martin's years as the band's producer, the Beatles were unable to read or write musical notation due to their lack of formal training. (McCartney became somewhat adept at understanding musical notation during his later years as a solo artist.) Hence, Martin would function as the Beatles' arranger and assist them in crafting the particular sounds that they wanted to achieve in their songs. See Martin, *All You Need Is Ears* 137–40.

9. In his discussion of the origins of "Yesterday"—the subject of more cover versions than any other song in the history of popular music—Lennon gracefully admits to having "had *so* much accolade for 'Yesterday.' [But] that's Paul's song and Paul's baby. Well done. Beautiful—and I never wished I'd written it" (*All We Are Saying* 177). John offered a parodic version of "Yesterday" during an outtake from the *Walls and Bridges* sessions in 1974: "Suddenly, I'm not half the man I used to be," he sings. "'Cause now I'm an amputee." See Lennon's *Anthology* (1998).

10. As Bob Spitz points out, the term also finds its origins in the remarks of an American blues musician, who reportedly referred to the Rolling Stones as "plastic soul" (592).

11. Technically, "We Can Work It Out" was the single's A-side, according to Parlophone. Yet the single was released as a so-called "double A-side" in which both songs were slated for considerable airplay and promotion. It turned out to be a shrewd move on Parlophone's part, given that both "Day Tripper" and "We Can Work It Out" became number-one hits in England and the United States, respectively.

12. "We Can Work It Out" allegedly finds its roots in Paul's frequent disagreements with his girlfriend, Jane Asher, a rising star on the London theater scene who was hardly ready to settle down, even if her beau was a Beatle, no less. "They were like two speeding trains," John Dunbar remarked, "running on opposite tracks. Paul liked having Jane on his arm—when it suited him. But you could see he was gradually losing patience" (qtd. in Spitz 588).

13. For Bob Dylan, the song's humorous underpinnings were inherently obvious, and he famously parodied "Norwegian Wood" in his song "4th Time Around" from his *Blonde on Blonde* (1966) album. Yet as Michael Gray observes, "4th Time Around" moves beyond simple parody by offering "a cold, mocking put-down of a woman and a relationship untouched by love. For extra sarcasm's sake, it is set against a backing of fawning, schmaltzy guitar-work" (147). John reported being initially bemused by Dylan's parodic gesture, likely overreacting to its sarcastic aspects in lieu of enjoying Dylan's keen recognition of the sexual dynamics that Lennon had crafted for the original song. Although John respected Dylan's work immensely, he admitted that the songwriter often made him feel "paranoid" (qtd. in Badman 191). On "Satire 1," a home recording that John made in the Dakota in 1979, he poked playful fun at Dylan's music and mannerisms: "Lord, take this makeup off of me. / I said, 'lordy, lordy, lordy, take this makeup off of me.' / It's bad enough on the beach, / But it's worse in the sea. / Because I'm knockin' on heaven's door, / Because I'm lookin' for my Ma." See Lennon's *Anthology*.

14. As Norman Smith points out, recording the sitar at EMI Studios proved to be difficult, given the instrument's unusual sonic properties: "It is very hard to record because it has a lot of nasty peaks and a very complex wave form. My meter would be going right over into the red, into distortion, without us getting audible value for money. I could have used a limiter but that would have meant losing the sonorous quality" (qtd. in Lewisohn, *The Complete Beatles Recording Sessions* 65).

15. Eventually, Shankar became George's mentor. In 1974, his band, Ravi Shankar and Friends, served as the opening act for Harrison's "Dark Horse" concert tour.

George lent his musical talents on several of Shankar's solo compositions, including "Memory of Uday" and "Friar Park."

16. Lennon admitted to having an affair with a "prominent journalist," who has been widely speculated to be Maureen Cleave, a frequent contributor to the *London Evening News* and the *London Evening Standard* (qtd. in Dowlding 115).

17. In his explanation of the origins of the composition, Paul takes credit for the song's vengeful dénouement: "Peter Asher had this room done out in wood, a lot of people were decorating their places in wood. Norwegian wood. It was pine, really cheap pine. But it's not as good a title, 'Cheap Pine.' It was a little parody, really, on those kind of girls who, when you'd get to their flat, there would be a lot of Norwegian wood. It was completely imaginary from my point of view, but not in John's. It was based on an affair he had. She makes him sleep in the bath and then, finally, in the last verse, I had this idea to set the Norwegian wood on fire as revenge. She led him on, then said, 'You'd better sleep in the bath.' In our world, the guy had to have some sort of revenge, it meant I burned the fucking place down" (qtd. in Badman 190).

18. Lennon's lead vocal on "Nowhere Man" offers an exemplar of the manner in which the Beatles' North Country pronunciation affects their delivery of gerunds—words with -ing endings, as in "sitting in his Nowhere Land" from "Nowhere Man." In this phenomenon, their Scouse pronunciation patterns occur when the velar nasal [ŋ] is succeeded by a hard [g] sound. Their North Country accents find them pronouncing words like *sing* as [sɪŋg], in contrast with the more conventional [sɪŋ].

19. Lennon felt that "Woman," a hit single from his *Double Fantasy* (1980) album, was the mature version of "Girl": "My history of relationships with women is very poor—very macho, very stupid, but pretty typical of a certain type of man, which I was, I suppose: a very insecure, sensitive person acting out very aggressive and macho. Trying to cover up the feminine side, which I still have a tendency to do, but I'm learning" (*All We Are Saying* 226). Lennon pointedly dedicates "Woman" to the "other half of the sky," echoing the words of Mao Tse-Tung regarding the plight of women under gendered Western socioeconomic systems.

20. The ethereal beauty of "In My Life" is rather brusquely (and intentionally) contrasted by the Bran Flakes, a self-described "sound collage" band from Seattle, Washington, that recorded a pointedly sterile, disconcerting, and emotionless version of "In My Life."

21. Walter Everett, for one, disagrees with MacDonald's somewhat definitive conclusion about McCartney's musical contributions to "In My Life." Everett argues that "John and Paul had such a long history of writing 'into each others' noses' that the origins of even such Beatles-marking details can't be securely placed with one or the other" (*The Quarry Men through Rubber Soul* 320).

22. With the exception of January 1969's rooftop concert, the Beatles made their final live appearance in England on May 1st, 1966, when they performed a five-song set for the *New Musical Express*'s Annual Poll-Winners' All-Star Concert at the Empire Pool in Wembley. The Beatles' set included "I Feel Fine," "Nowhere Man," "Day Tripper," "If I Needed Someone," and "I'm Down."

Chapter 8

The End of the Road

We must be still and still moving
Into another intensity
For a further union, a deeper communion
Through the dark cold and the empty desolation,
The wave cry, the wind cry, the vast waters
Of the petrel and the porpoise. In my end is my beginning.
—T. S. ELIOT, *FOUR QUARTETS*

It's hard to describe, even with the clarity of memory,
the moment the apple falls. The thing will start moving
along at a speed of its own, then you wake up at the end
of it and have this whole thing on paper, you know?
—JOHN LENNON

Where *Rubber Soul* is about the Beatles' self-conscious redefinition of them-selves and their art, *Revolver* is about taking those newfangled models of themselves and their art out for a proverbial spin. The album is about revving up the engines of their musicality, about admiring the chrome of their lumi-nous and seemingly immutable talent. But *Revolver* is also about the Beatles' desire to push the boundaries of their achievement, to experiment with their abundant and endlessly fecundating sound. In so doing, they have created their most thematically coherent project to date. *Revolver*'s eclectic collection of songs engages in an "intra-album dialogue," to borrow a phrase from Rus-sell Reising, that examines the ceaseless interplay between life and death, as well as the divergent forms of consciousness that we experience in our lives and afterlives ("'It is not dying'" 235). "*Revolver* is a very serious and a very heady album, both in terms of its sonic experiments as well as in its lyrical drift," Reising writes. "Even the love songs (and there are no 'silly love songs' on *Revolver*) relate deeply and seriously to its darker, more tragic elements" (*"Vacio Luminoso"* 127). In short, the album addresses the human conception of life and death in their many guises—real or imagined, spiritual or romantic. Released in August 1966, *Revolver* finds the Beatles in full flower as they emerge as vibrant and imaginative storytellers with a particular interest in investigating the philosophical nature of pastness as it relates to the simultaneously more and less pressing dilemmas of the here and now. While albums such as *Help!* and *Rubber Soul* offer cogent gestures toward the nature of the Beatles' evolving aesthetic, *Revolver* is an uncompromising work of art in its own right.

In many ways, *Revolver*'s remarkable sonic textures are what made the art work possible in the first place. In March 1966, John remarked in an interview that "Paul and I are very keen on this electronic music. You make it clinking a couple of glasses together or with bleeps from the radio, then you loop the tape to repeat the noises at intervals. Some people build up whole symphonies from it. . . . One thing's for sure," he added. "The next LP is going to be very different" (qtd. in Ryan and Kehew 408). Anticipating the album's revolutionary soundscapes, Paul commented in the June 24th, 1966, issue of the *New Musical Express* that "I for one am sick of doing sounds that people can claim to have heard before" (qtd. in Alan Smith 3). And while the album's astonishing textual worlds first found their being in the Beatles' fertile imaginations, it was nineteen-year-old Geoff Emerick who brought those very sounds and visions to life. Emerick had joined the staff of EMI Studios as an assistant engineer at the tender age of sixteen. His second day on the job was September 4th, 1962, the very date of the evening session, all those years ago, in which the Beatles recorded "How Do You Do It" and "Love Me Do." He also worked the July 1963 session in which the group first unveiled "She Loves You" for George Martin's consideration, and he later took part in the equally historic recording sessions for "I Want to Hold Your Hand" and "A Hard Day's Night." For quite some time after that— as the young EMI staffer was promoted from assistant engineer to lacquer cutter to mastering engineer to balance engineer—the Beatles worked outside of Emerick's earshot. But his lucky break came in 1966, when Norman Smith was promoted to become a full-fledged producer at EMI Studios; in the process, he also became head of Parlophone, replacing the recently estranged George Martin. Smith's first project was *The Piper at the Gates of Dawn*, the debut album by a fledgling band from the "London Underground" scene known as Pink Floyd.

With Smith's absence, Martin wasted no time in inviting Emerick, whom the EMI staff affectionately nicknamed "Golden Ears," to be the Beatles' engineer for *Revolver*. But the project nearly didn't happen—at least not in the same fashion as history has foretold. In fact, the Beatles had originally considered recording the album in the United States after learning that Dylan had made his latest LP *Blonde on Blonde* (1966) in Memphis. With Brian Epstein handling the negotiations, the band mulled over the possibility of working at either Detroit's Motown Studio, Memphis's Stax Studio, or New York City's Atlantic Studio. They even tinkered with the idea of having their next album produced by legendary soul guitarist Steve "The Colonel" Cropper, who was thrilled with the prospect of recording the Fab Four. Life had become complicated in the Beatles' camp, it seems, and a change of scenery—and possibly even in recording personnel—would "shake things up," in George Harrison's reasoning (qtd. in Spitz 599). Things had indeed been shaking up since August 1965, when Martin had severed his official ties with EMI, shed his A&R duties with Parlophone, and became an independent producer who could record any act in any venue of his choice. Over the past few years, Martin had become fed up with the EMI Group, which paid him a paltry £3,000 for his work in 1963—a year in which the records he produced held the number-one position on the British charts for a phenomenal thirty-seven weeks. Soon thereafter, Martin established AIR (Associated Independent Recording) Studios in London, and his liberation from EMI was complete. Meanwhile, Epstein's dealings with Cropper had disintegrated almost as quickly as they had begun. But it hardly mattered in the slightest to the Beatles: the group's plans to record in the United States, and perhaps even with a different producer at the helm, had already become moot. By the time that Epstein was ready to ink a deal with an American studio, the Beatles and Martin—in their typical breakneck fashion—had already finished recording much of the next album.

The creative team involving the Beatles, Martin, and Emerick was a veritable *tour-de-force*, and *Revolver* would be their proving ground. Emerick ultimately succeeded in masterminding the sound of *Revolver* by violating EMI Studios' highly proscriptive rules. As with the EMI Group itself, the studio was known for its austerity and tradition. Indeed, the production staff, from lowly assistant engineers on up, were required to wear white laboratory coats at all times. But Emerick was determined to test the limits of the recording studio, and the Beatles were the perfect vehicle for trying out his radical ideas. By placing microphones within inches of the group's amps and Ringo's drums, for example, Emerick defied EMI's stipulated recording distances yet created a host of new sounds in the bargain. No matter how outlandish the group's requests, he made every effort to accommodate the Beatles' desires for formulating new sounds. When John would come up with an outrageous metaphor for how he wanted his vocal to sound—"Give me the feel of James Dean gunning his motorcycle down the highway"—Emerick never hesitated in dreaming up the necessary studio trickery with which to bring the songwriter's creative visions to life (qtd. in Emerick 8). In addition to Emerick's innovative engineering techniques, the band benefited from the invention of Automatic Double Tracking (ADT) by EMI Studios' maintenance engineer Ken Townshend, who had devised the system at John's behest. Fed up with the laborious task of double-tracking his voice on the Beatles' recordings, John wanted a mechanism that could accomplish the job automatically. In contrast with double-tracking, which requires musicians to synchronize their voices or instruments with a pre-existing track, ADT employs two studio tape decks that automatically feed the same signal through both decks, as well as through the mixing desk. In Townshend's design, ADT simultaneously duplicates the sounds of voices or instruments in order to create a layered effect. Townshend's system also enables its users to manipulate the second track by a few milliseconds in order to create a more expansive, trebly texture. When John asked how ADT worked, Martin couldn't resist the opportunity to bamboozle him with nonsense, given Lennon's legendary inability to comprehend the nature of studio technology: "It's a double-bifurcated sploshing flange," the producer informed him, without a hint of irony (*All You Need Is Ears* 156). John subsequently took to calling the process "flanging."

The use of Townshend's invention on multiple *Revolver* tracks and beyond established ADT as the *de facto* Beatles sound. With unlimited studio time at their disposal and the timely advent of ADT, the group was well-poised to eclipse the artistry of their earlier efforts. Produced over a series of intense sessions in April, May, and June, *Revolver* was compellingly prefigured by the milestone single "Paperback Writer" b/w "Rain," which was recorded during the *Revolver* sessions and released in June 1966.[1] A revolutionary track in which McCartney allows his melodic bass to act as the lead instrument, "Paperback Writer" was recorded in a marathon eleven-hour session in mid-April. Paul's lighthearted composition tells the story of a dime novelist who flaunts his lack of literary ambition in favor of cheap and tawdry fame. "Dear Sir or Madam, will you read my book?" the speaker implores. "It took me years to write, will you take a look?" His artistic indifference is magnified by his baser concern for turning a buck at any cost. The speaker is nothing more than a hack for hire, he willingly admits, who will tailor his wares for any interested party who can pay his fare: "I can make it longer if you like the style, / I can change it 'round and I want to be a paperback writer." Lyrically, the song takes on incredible metatextual thematics when one considers the remarkable ease with which the Beatles concocted chart-topping hits by 1966. As with the speaker in "Paperback Writer," they "could make a million for you overnight"—and hardly begin to flex their creative muscles in the process. Musically, the song signals a breathtaking leap forward in terms of the band's ability to imagine new vistas of sound—and this is in comparison with their transformative work in the latter months of 1965, no less. Where *Rubber Soul* is buoyant, smart, and folkminded, "Paperback Writer" is bright, colorful, and crisp. John, Paul, and George's soaring three-part *a cappella* harmonies—fashioned after the Beach Boys' latest album *Pet Sounds*—give way to the fuzzy introductory guitar riff that Harrison strums on his Epiphone Casino, only to be followed by McCartney's peripatetic bass lines. Inspired by recent recordings by Otis Redding and Wilson Pickett in which the bass had figured prominently—as well as by the groundbreaking bass work of Paul's Motown idol James Jamerson—McCartney's roving, fluid bass is brought vividly to life by Emerick, who employed a loudspeaker as a microphone for the Beatle's Rickenbacker. The resulting effect renders the bass's already precise tonality even more dynamic and evokes an expansive and vibrant sound from the instrument. McCartney's bass playing and Emerick's engineering had come together in a recorded performance that would hearken a radical shift in terms of the bass guitar's role in popular music.[2]

As with the "comedy numbers" on *Rubber Soul*, "Paperback Writer" undercuts its own musical virtuosity with impish humor. Witness, for example, John and George's comic backing vocals in which they sing "Frère Jacques" in broken falsetto. Their unbridled silliness acts as an ironic counterpoint to the Paperback Writer's own narrative, which elevates droll melodrama and mindless pop fiction over any semblance of a more exacting (and lasting) literary art: "It's the dirty story of a dirty man / And his clinging wife doesn't understand," the speaker reports. "It's a thousand pages, give or take a few, / I'll be writing more in a week or two." Were the Beatles mere artists for hire like the Paperback Writer, or were they driven by larger artistic motives? Or both? With "Rain," the B-side of "Paperback Writer," the band crafts a canny response to these very timely questions. Given that the group's identity as stage-oriented musicians— as a proverbial working, hard-driving rock combo—had all but dissolved by the summer of 1966, the Beatles had mutated into a band that existed for the express purpose of recorded performance. Born in songwriterly isolation, their compositions took flight in the spaces of the studio, the artificial environment in which the ability to reproduce their work in concert no longer mattered.[3] "Rain" is a powerful case in point. As with "Paperback Writer," the vocals materialize from the ethereal haze of ADT—the source of that peculiar "Beatley" sound, as Eric Clapton later described it. Like "Paperback Writer," "Rain" dispenses with the world of reality and embraces the realm of the imagination, where illusion and artifice coalesce in the mind.

In itself, "Rain" is an odd collaboration of styles: John's meandering vocals merge with Ringo's insistent drums, George's flange-like strumming of his Gretsch SG Standard, and Paul's lively bass runs to evoke the murky palette of an impressionistic painting. Emerick's studio trickery rendered this effect possible by recording the rhythm track and Lennon's vocal at a faster speed, then slowing them down during the mixing process to create the song's purposefully idiosyncratic sound. Walter Everett likens John's distinctive singing on the chorus to a Hindustani *gamak*, an ornamental vocal embellishment that is delivered in a forceful, oscillating style. His vocal, as with several tracks on *Revolver*, evinces an Eastern flavor that affords the Beatles' music with a more exotic sheen in contrast with their American rock and roll heritage. With five staccato beats of his snare drum, Ringo sets "Rain" into motion. For Ringo, it was a watershed moment: "I was possessed!" he later remarked about his favorite drum work on record (*Anthology* 212). With "Rain," Ringo's drum playing offers more than mere time-keeping. It's a bravura performance that enriches and accentuates the song's other instrumental adornments—namely, Lennon's lead vocal. In turn, John's indeterminate lyrics enhance the music's imagistic aspects and, in so doing, challenge listeners to fill in the blanks with their own readings of the composition's intentionally uncertain properties. "If the rain comes, they run and hide their heads. / They might as well be dead," Lennon sings. "When the sun shines, they slip into the shade / And drink their lemonade." While they eschew any semblance of a conventional storyline, John's lyrics explore humankind's tendency to dispense with self-awareness and slip into the unconscious selves with which we visit the workaday world. After an instrumental break in which Paul's bass and Ringo's snare engage in spontaneous duet, John's voice—recorded backward—repeats the composition's opening phrase, "If the rain comes, they run and hide their heads." As "Rain" prepares to disappear into the ether of its fadeout, the track literally reverses itself via John's backward vocal. In this sense, it ends in nearly the same manner in which it had begun before sliding into infinitude.

~

The Beatles expand on this evolving "sense of an ending" with "Taxman," the song that conjures *Revolver* into being. With the possible exception of *A Hard Day's Night*—which evaporates into the twilight in heartrending fashion with "I'll Be Back"—the placement of the group's tracks on their albums had been motivated almost entirely by strict commercial designs. George Martin's philosophy for structuring a recording for the pop-music marketplace dictated that an album hook its listeners with a dynamic opening track and conclude with a knockout punch: "My old precept in the recording business was always 'Make side one strong,' for obvious commercial reasons," he remarked. "Another principle of mine when assembling an album was always to go out on a side strongly, placing the weaker material towards the end but then going out with a bang" (*With a Little Help from My Friends* 148–49). And while "Taxman" most certainly affords *Revolver* with a strident opening track, the album's thematic arrangement suggests that the Beatles had something more substantial in mind. To this end, "Taxman" begins with a moment of *faux* spontaneity, an overtly constructed instance in which the Beatles simulate the sounds of a band in the act of warming up for a performance. But their simulation is intentionally skewed toward the unreal, with Harrison deliberately counting "one, two, three, four" out of rhythm and off-tempo. On the surface, the intro to "Taxman" seems like mindless studio noise—McCartney can be heard coughing in the background, and one can even make out the ambient sound of one of the Beatles (George perhaps?) idly sliding his fingers about the fretboard of an electric guitar. Yet the song's mock-overture draws explicit attention to the fact of its studio creation, as opposed to any origins in live performance.

In short, "Taxman" identifies itself—and, hence, the album—as the self-conscious stuff of pure invention and creative caprice. As Shaugn O'Donnell remarks, the song "acts as a frame or doorway, a boundary between reality and the mystical world of *Revolver*" (81). The reality of the Beatles' mythology—as the Fab Four, the Mop Tops, and the four lads from Liverpool, *ad nauseum*—hardly matters in *Revolver*'s soundscapes of unreality. When the doorway finally opens, "Taxman" reveals itself, at least initially, as an energetic rock number in the lockstep fashion of "Drive My Car" and "Day Tripper." Harrison's cutting lyrics about the taxman's callous disregard for his victims is remarkably consistent with the earlier compositions' irreverent depictions of their female protagonists, in Paul and John's words, as a "bitch" and a "prick-teaser," respectively. Harrison's satirical lyrics about the perils of taxation—particularly for those in the most elevated of tax brackets—reach their malevolent climax in the call-and-response duet that emerges between John and Paul's backing vocals and George's lead:[4]

> (If you drive a car), I'll tax the street.
> (If you try to sit), I'll tax your seat.
> (If you get too cold), I'll tax the heat.
> (If you take a walk), I'll tax your feet.

As with the "comedy numbers" that inaugurate *Rubber Soul*, "Taxman" seems to exist for the purpose of its humorous overtones. But then Paul's high-octane guitar solo interrupts the proceedings, and any resemblance between

"Taxman" and its 1965-era precursors dissolves in the solo's ferocity. Played, *raga*-like, on his Epiphone Casino with a characteristic Indian flavor and tempo, McCartney's solo is, quite simply, like nothing else in the Beatles' corpus to date; for that matter, it hardly bears any resemblance to anything in the history of recorded music. And neither do Paul's looping bass lines, which increase in complexity and finesse as the song moves ever forward—matching the guitar solo in terms of their sheer musicianship. With "Taxman," the Beatles announce a sweeping shift in the essential nature of their sound. But *Revolver* was only just beginning.

The silence in the wake of "Taxman" is quickly shattered by John, Paul, and George singing "Ah, look at all the lonely people" in three-part harmony, accompanied by a stirring string octet. Along with "In My Life," "Eleanor Rigby" is one of the two central instances of authorial dispute within the Lennon-McCartney corpus. Martin created the song's haunting string arrangement—ostensibly after receiving detailed instructions from McCartney—during the lengthy first session on April 28th, in which Lennon and McCartney conversed with the producer via the studio's intercom system (Lewisohn, *The Complete Beatles Recording Sessions* 219). Paul had seen the name "Rigby" on a storefront in Bristol, where Jane Asher was starring in a production of John Dighton's *The Happiest Days of Your Life*. His protagonist's first name found its inspiration in Eleanor Bron, the British actress who played one of the Eastern cult leaders in *Help!* As for the song's musical origins, Paul recalls that "I wrote it at the piano, just vamping an E-minor chord; letting that stay as a vamp and putting a melody over it, just danced over the top of it. It has almost Asian Indian rhythms" (qtd. in Miles 281). With the threads of the melody in hand, he began tinkering with a variety of different lyrics: "I was just mumbling around and eventually came up with these words: 'Picks up the rice in a church where the wedding has been.' Those words just fell out like stream-of-consciousness stuff, but they started to set the tone of it all, because you then have to ask yourself, what did I mean?" (qtd. in Miles 282). After establishing the character of Eleanor Rigby as one of the song's central characters, Paul opted to turn the song over to John "because I hadn't finished all the words" (qtd. in Miles 283).

In sharp contrast with McCartney's recollections, Lennon remembered composing some "70 percent" of the lyrics for "Eleanor Rigby." Paul's response? "Yeah. About half a line" (qtd. in Dowlding 134–35). Lennon admits that McCartney and Harrison invented the song's familiar chorus—"Ah, look at all the lonely people"—during the first session: "He and George were settling on that as I left the studio to go to the toilet, and I heard the lyric and turned around and said, 'That's *it!*'" Otherwise, John attributes the first verse to Paul, while claiming that "the rest [of the lyrics] are basically mine" (*All We Are Saying* 139, 140). Yet Pete Shotton agreed entirely with McCartney's memories about the composition of "Eleanor Rigby." Shotton visited the studio during the session in which the song was first recorded: "Though John was to take credit, in one of his last interviews, for most of the lyrics," Shotton averred, "my own recollection is that 'Eleanor Rigby' was one 'Lennon-McCartney' classic in which John's contribution was virtually nil" (qtd. in Dowlding 134–35). It is worth noting that Lennon's own memories of the session were considerably tainted by what he perceived to be McCartney's intentionally hurtful behavior:

> Well, he knew he had a song. But by that time he didn't want to ask for my help, and we were sitting around with Mal Evans and Neil Aspinall, so he said to us, "Hey, you guys, finish up the lyrics."
>
> Now I was there with Mal, a telephone installer who was our road manager, and Neil, who was a student accountant [and the Beatles' personal assistant], and I was insulted and hurt that Paul had just thrown it out in the air. He actually meant he wanted *me* to do it, and of course there isn't a line of theirs in the song. But . . . that's the kind of person he is. "Here, finish these lyrics up," like to *anybody* around. (*All We Are Saying* 139)

At the risk of indulging in amateurish psychoanalysis, it might be logical to factor Lennon's injured feelings into the authorship equation. Perhaps his residual pain—still smarting more than fourteen years after the *Revolver* sessions—played a not-so-subtle role in his recollections about the composition of "Eleanor Rigby," one of the most fully realized songs in their corpus. As Lennon remarked about McCartney during a September 1980 interview, "How *dare* he throw it out in the air like that?" (qtd. in Everett, *Revolver through the Anthology* 11). Isn't it possible to assume that John, aggrieved as he so clearly was by Paul's insensitivity, felt that "Eleanor Rigby" warranted more flattering origins, that such a magnificent song deserved better treatment?[5]

As with "In My Life," "Eleanor Rigby" was a songwriting gem worth fighting over—the sort of composition, like "Yesterday," that continued to enlarge the group's audience beyond Beatlemania's horde of ecstatic teenagers. According to John, Paul's idea for a string accompaniment for "Eleanor Rigby" came via Jane Asher, who had recently introduced him to the work of Vivaldi. As McCartney later recalled, "I thought of the backing, but it was George Martin who finished it off. I just go bash, bash on the piano. He knows what I mean" (qtd. in Dowlding 135). For his arrangement for "Eleanor Rigby," Martin claimed to have drawn his inspiration from Bernard Herrmann's recent orchestral score for François Truffaut's *Fahrenheit 451* (1966).[6] As the composer behind the terrifying soundtrack for Alfred Hitchcock's *Psycho* (1960),

Herrmann might seem, at first blush, like an unlikely model for the musical arrangement of a pop song. Yet in retrospect, Martin's choice was a stroke of genius. With its razor-sharp tempo, Martin's arrangement imbues McCartney's narrative about the perils of loneliness with an appropriately chilling veneer. Instructed by Paul to establish a "really biting" sound, Emerick attempted to capture the songwriter's vision by placing the microphones unusually close to the string octet, which consisted of four violins, two violas, and two cellos. The studio musicians were visibly irritated by the idea of playing in front of microphones that were as little as an inch away from their strings. As Emerick recalled, "The musicians were horrified! One of them gave me a look of disdain, rolled his eyes to the ceiling, and said under his breath, 'You can't do that, you know.'" When Emerick returned to the control room, he could clearly hear the studio musicians sliding their chairs away from the microphones that he had just set up. The musicians finally complied with Emerick's mic placement, but only after Martin ordered them to remain in position (127). As for Paul's vocal, the singer double-tracked his voice, which occurs in the right channel of the mono recording, only to return to both channels when John and George join him for the chorus. It makes for a genuinely eerie effect that is bolstered by Martin's haunting arrangement.

As with "Nowhere Man," "Eleanor Rigby" explores the disquieting power of loneliness as a source of isolation and despair that, in its human deprivation, leaves its victims in virtually inconsolable states of hopelessness.[7] But Eleanor is not alone in her grief. In many ways, she is but one person among the crowd, a throng of alienated humanity evincing Henry David Thoreau's dictum in *Walden* that "the mass of men lead lives of quiet desperation" (6). In the song, Paul's speaker functions as the narrator, assuming a detached, nonjudgmental posture. With "Eleanor Rigby," the band creates vivid memorial images that ask pointed questions about the failure of interpersonal relationships as a tonic for healing the soul. Eleanor's name, with its origins from Helios, the Greek god of the sun, connotes a sense of radiance, of health, of shimmering beauty (Long 36). Her surname, a variant of Rigsby, suggests a wanton woman, or, as the *OED* tells us, a "romping girl." But in "Eleanor Rigby," she is nothing of the sort—neither radiant nor romping in the slightest. McCartney's timeless elegy depicts Eleanor as an aging spinster. Loneliness consumes his protagonist, whom society has ignored—even deplored for her inability to conform. Waiting at the window, she camouflages her despair by "wearing a face that she keeps in a jar by the door." She "lives in a dream," the narrator reports, with her public and private selves in ceaseless contradiction. In the song, Paul juxtaposes her impoverished persona with that of Father McKenzie, who busies himself "writing the words of a sermon that no one will hear." The congregation cannot heed Father McKenzie's homily because they're not really listening to him—or to anyone or anything else, for that matter—having become insensate themselves. In addition to its origins in a legume, the name McKenzie connotes a sort of friend or advocate, a person who will lend moral support on behalf of another, less-fortunate person (*OED*). And this is precisely what he attempts to do in the song, albeit to no avail. After Eleanor pointedly dies alone—and in the church, no less—Father McKenzie buries his parishioner, forgotten along with her name, in the churchyard. "Wiping the dirt from his hands as he walks from her grave," he realizes the awful truth of Eleanor's predicament—and, indeed, of his own. In the end, the narrator reports, "no one was saved"—not Eleanor, not society, not even ourselves. As the song comes to fruition, the chorus resurrects its prevailing, rhetorical, and seemingly unanswerable questions: "All the lonely people, where do they all come from? / All the lonely people, where do they all belong?"

Whereas "Eleanor Rigby" addresses the larger effects of society's unconscious ways of living, Lennon's "I'm Only Sleeping" urges his listener to experience a different form of (un)consciousness altogether—the dreamworld of sleep. Punctuated by John's deep yawns, the bright, ringing quality that he achieves on his Jumbo with the assistance of ADT, Paul's pensive bass lines, and George's otherworldly backward guitar solo on his Fender Stratocaster, "I'm Only Sleeping" establishes an appropriately ethereal mood. "When I wake up early in the morning / Lift my head, I'm still yawning," John sings. "When I'm in the middle of a dream / Stay in bed, float upstream." In comparison with the album's closing track "Tomorrow Never Knows," in which John exhorts us to "float downstream" in a conscious embrace of the death-drive, "I'm Only Sleeping" implores us to "float upstream" through our dreams and into the world of the living, if only as soporific bystanders: "Keeping an eye on the world going by my window," the speaker reports.[8] As songs that underscore the ways in which sleeping and death proffer different phenomenologies of consciousness, "I'm Only Sleeping" and "Tomorrow Never Knows" act as *Revolver*'s polar philosophical opposites, yet they each perform different aspects of the human life cycle.

With Harrison's "Love You To," the Beatles take a sharp musical turn into the world of Eastern sound. The song begins with an unhurried Hindustani overture—featuring the Asian Music Circle's Anil Baghwat on tabla and Ayana Deva Angadi on sitar—before launching into a full gallop in which Harrison examines the fleeting nature of existence.[9] Given that George famously disliked the task of composing song titles, "Love You To" went under the makeshift title of "Granny Smith" during the recording process. In "Love You To," the speaker identifies the animus that exists all around us: "There's people standing 'round / Who'll screw you in the ground," George sings. "They'll fill you in with all their sins, you'll see." Yet the speaker's cautionary words seem selfishly motivated by the pleasure principle in which he seeks immediate sexual gratification. "Each day just goes so fast," he warns his would-be lover, so "love me while you can / Before I'm a dead old man." The song's sexual come-on—"I'll make love to you / If you want me to"—finds the speaker in "Love You To" offering up an orgiastic feast of love and liberation for the woman of his desires: "Make love all day long / Make love singing songs." As a sentence fragment, the title itself is syntactically interesting, given the world of possibility that it seems to offer in the absence of a tangible direct object. "Love You To" diverges from being a love song in any conventional sense, and, if anything, it exists as a rallying call to accept our inner hedonism and release our worldly inhibitions—while we still can, that is. The album's next cut, "Here, There, and Everywhere," exchanges George's voice of possibility for Paul's words of promise and certainty. Inspired by "God Only Knows" from the Beach Boys' *Pet Sounds* album, "Here, There, and Everywhere" was *Revolver's* penultimate recording, produced during a pair of sessions in mid-June. Paul's vocal introduction pleasingly shifts from 9/8 to 7/8 to common time in the space of a dozen words: "To lead a better life, / I need my love to be here." The song also offers an example of the Beatles' penchant for varispeed recording during this period and beyond. As with ADT, varispeed allowed them to manipulate their sound in an innovative fashion. As with several other instances on *Revolver*, "Here, There, and Everywhere" finds Martin and Emerick recording the track at a slower speed. During playback, varispeed recording results in a higher pitch—in this case, with the rendering of Paul's lead vocal at a higher frequency. As its title professes, "Here, There, and Everywhere" is explicitly about living in the here and know, about fully experiencing the conscious moment. With Paul on his Epiphone Texan and George on his Rickenbacker twelve-string, the composition assumes the texture of a smooth romantic ballad, and while "Love You To" is overtly libidinous in its intent, "Here, There, and Everywhere" tenders a ritualistic pledge of everlasting affection. In tandem, both songs offer corresponding examinations of the human experience of physical and romantic love.

And then there's "Yellow Submarine." A children's song? A drug-induced rave? Or a simple tune about the joys of carefree living and good clean fun? Mark Lewisohn provides an even more circumscribed interpretation: "It's either a weak Salvation Army band style sing-along or a clever and contagious piece of pop music guaranteed to please the kids, the grannies, and plenty others besides" (*The Complete Beatles Recording Sessions* 80). "Yellow Submarine" was written expressly as a vehicle for Ringo to sing. As Paul later remembered,

"I wrote that in bed one night. As a kid's story." In John's recollections, "Paul wrote the catchy chorus. I helped with the blunderbuss" (qtd. in Dowlding 138). And would he ever! After recording a basic rhythm track on May 26th featuring Ringo on drums, John strumming his Jumbo, Paul on bass, and George on tambourine, Emerick overdubbed Ringo's lead vocals and John, Paul, and George's backing vocals at a slightly reduced speed in order to achieve a brighter quality during playback. A tape-to-tape reduction of take four left the Beatles with ample room for the later addition of the numerous sound effects that afford the song with its distinctively playful demeanor.

On June 1st, the Beatles reconvened in Studio Two, where they were joined by a host of guests, including Rolling Stones' front men Brian Jones (who played the ocarina) and Mick Jagger, Jagger's girlfriend Marianne Faithfull, the Beatles' chauffeur Alf Bicknell, and Pattie Harrison. The group was rounded out by the band's ever-faithful roadies, Mal Evans and Neil Aspinall. The evening began with John recording his famous superimposed voices in the studio's echo chamber: "Full speed ahead, Mr. Boatswain. Full speed ahead." Were Lennon's ad-lib voices a forgotten vestige of a Liverpudlian, seafaring past that he never really knew? As Emerick recalled:

> The whole marijuana-influenced scene that evening was completely zany, straight out of a Marx Brothers movie. The entire EMI collection of percussion instruments and sound effects boxes were strewn all over the studio, with people grabbing bells and whistles and gongs at random. To simulate the sound of a submarine submerging, John grabbed a straw and began blowing bubbles into a glass—fortunately, I was able to move a mic nearby in time to record it for posterity. Inspired, Lennon wanted to take things to the next level and have me record him actually *singing* underwater. First, he tried singing while gargling. When that failed (he nearly choked), he began lobbying for a tank to be brought in so that he could be submerged! (120)

With Lennon's inspired voice work in the can, the glitterati in the studio assembled, conga-style, behind Mal Evans, who led the bizarre proceedings with a bass drum strapped to his chest. The already peculiar evening concluded on an even stranger note, with the recording of a thirty-one-second monologue by Ringo, accompanied by the sound of stomping feet, which they achieved by shifting coal around in a cardboard box. The monologue, which was later discarded, was an apparent effort to pay homage to a recent and well-publicized charity walk by physician Barbara Moore: "And we will march to free the day to see them gathered there, / from Land O'Groats to John O'Green, from Stepney to Utrecht, / to see a Yellow Submarine / We love it" (Lewisohn, *The Complete Beatles Recording Sessions* 81).[10] As a sing-along for children of all ages, the final product must have exceeded McCartney's dreams when "Yellow Submarine" soared to the top of the British charts in the summer of 1966.

While "Yellow Submarine" celebrates the sweet pleasures of youth, "She Said She Said" threatens to refute the reality of childhood bliss altogether. The composition finds its roots in an August 1965 party that the Beatles attended in Benedict Canyon, Los Angeles. It was a wild affair in which the group's rented house was surrounded by thousands of fans held back by a cadre of LA's finest. At one point, a pair of particularly motivated fans attempted, unsuccessfully, to land a helicopter in the house's garden. It was the kind of party that only the overwhelming tremors of Beatlemania could produce. Inside the house, John, Paul, George, and Ringo were joined by Roger McGuinn and David Crosby of the Byrds, as well as by actor Peter Fonda, with whom John and George shared a hit of acid. In the ensuing drug-addled malaise, Fonda famously claimed, "I know what it's like to be dead," to which Lennon angrily responded, "You're making me feel like I've never been born. Who put all that shit in your head?" before having Fonda expelled from the premises.[11] Inspired by the actor's strange remark, John decided to compose a song around the idea of being dead. On June 21st, "She Said She Said" emerged as the final track to be recorded for the album. "John brought it in pretty much finished," Paul remembered. Apparently, McCartney was angered when his suggestions for the recording were rebuffed. "I think we had a barney or something," Paul recalled, "and I said, 'Oh, fuck you!'" and left the studio in a huff (qtd. in Miles 287–88). "She Said She Said" is one of the few Beatles songs in which McCartney didn't participate, with George overdubbing the bass part on Paul's Höfner 500/1.

As with "And Your Bird Can Sing" and "Doctor Robert," "She Said She Said" enjoys a bright, metallic sheen accomplished by John and George's capoed Epiphone Casinos and a healthy dose of ADT. "She Said She Said" provides one of the Beatles' most disparaging portraits of contemporary life. In the song, Lennon's speaker reacts to a woman who claims to "know what it's like to be dead" by rejecting her observations, which leave him feeling negated: "You're making me feel like I've never been born." In short, her breadth of experience counters his inferior knowledge, which, in a moment of Blakean contrast, equates the innocence of birth—or, in the speaker's case, *pre*-birth. "When I was a boy," the speaker waxes nostalgically in the middle-eight, "everything was right." The woman's experiences with death ultimately imbue the speaker with a sense of overarching sadness, realizing, as he does, that he is engaged in the act of living a life whose resolution has already been foretold, whose experiences will be less than extraordinary, probably even trite. For Jacqueline Warwick, "She Said She Said" provides an intriguing illustration of binary, male-female relationships from a stereotypically masculine vantage point. "Note that Lennon counters the woman's creepy tale by invoking the homosocial universe of his boyhood days at school, when 'everything was right,'" she observes. "The song presents heterosexual relations negatively, depicting a woman who will not stop talking and a man who doesn't want to listen (but has difficulty tearing himself away)" (61). In their inability to remove themselves from each other's harmful orbit, the man and woman seem to inflict greater damage upon their warring selves. In Lennon's depiction, the male and female characters linger for all eternity in an absurdist play of their own making, like Didi and Gogo in Samuel Beckett's *Waiting for Godot* (1952).

The shrill circularity evoked by the song's accelerated fadeout gives way, in an intentionally discordant fashion, to the verdant, sun-drenched meadows of McCartney's "Good Day Sunshine." Inspired by the Lovin' Spoonful's smash-hit "Daydream," "Good Day Sunshine" involves an intricate time-signature in which the song's musical components shift among common, 5/4, and 3/4 time, producing a bouncing, galloping effect in the process. With Martin playing honky-tonk piano, "Good Day Sunshine" eschews balladry in favor—as with "I've Just Seen a Face" and, more recently, "Rain"—of a pure, imagistic portrait: "I need to laugh and when the sun is out / I've got something I can laugh about," Paul sings in shameless delight. "I feel good in a special way / I'm in love and it's a sunny day." The blissfully functional romantic love in "Good Day Sunshine" transitions into the dysfunctional tableau of "And Your Bird Can Sing," which found its origins in a gift that Cynthia Lennon presented to her husband. As Cynthia remembered: "I bought a clockwork bird in a gilded cage which I wrapped up carefully, just leaving the winding mechanism at the base exposed. Before handing it to John I wound it up. The imitation bird warbled loud and clear from its perch as John unwrapped the strange looking gift with an expression of sheer disbelief on his face" (*A Twist of Lennon* 128). For John, the bird in the gilded cage offered increasing testimony about their ineffectual marriage, as well as regarding what he perceived to be her utter failure to understand him: "You tell me that you've got everything you want, / And your bird can sing / But you don't get me, / You don't get me." The vitriol in Lennon's voice is matched by Paul and George's furious guitar work. The song's introductory riff pits George and Paul on their dueling Casinos: "We wrote [the guitar duet] at the session and learned it on the spot" McCartney recalled (qtd. in Everett, *Revolver through the Anthology* 46).

Inspired by the Merseys' "Sorrow," "And Your Bird Can Sing" witnesses Lennon at his acerbic best—reacting, with devastating honesty and venom, to his marital failures. Paul's "For No One" exists at some distant point on the romantic horizon beyond "And Your Bird Can Sing," taking place much later, after the lovers have irrevocably gone their separate ways. As with so many other McCartney tunes for which nostalgia performs a central function, "For No One" concerns the aftermath of lost love. Complemented by a hauntingly beautiful solo played by Alan Civil, the principal horn player for the London Philharmonic Orchestra, the song's lyrics rather intriguingly consider the transformation that such loss engenders in the former lovers: "And in her eyes you see nothing / No sign of love behind the tears / Cried for no one / A love that should have lasted years." Originally entitled "Why Did It Die?" the lyrics of "For No One" examine the ways in which the erstwhile lovers' change in status defines their feelings toward each other—the warmth of their romantic connection has been replaced with the coldness of post-romantic distance; the meaning of their relationship has become transfixed by the present and dispersed among an impenetrable sense of pastness. Possibly inspired by the Rolling Stones' "Lady Jane," "For No One" features Paul on a rented Clavichord, the keyboard instrument whose fragile tonality underscores the speaker's own brittleness and uncertainty. Interestingly, during the recording session on May 19th in Studio Three, Civil blanched at Martin's arrangement for the solo, which required him to play beyond his instrument's normal range. As Paul remembered, "On the session, Alan Civil said, 'George?' and looked at us both. He said, 'George, you've written a D,' and George and I just looked at him and held our nerve and said, 'Yes?' And he gave us a crafty look and went, 'Okay'" (qtd. in Miles 289).

With "Doctor Robert," the Beatles present their first overt reference to the drug usage that had been altering their lives and their songwriting aesthetic appreciably since their fateful meeting with Dylan some twenty months earlier. The song makes specific mention of New York physician Robert Freymann, who was well-known for prescribing a range of hallucinogenic drugs—specifically vitamin shots mixed with amphetamines—to his celebrity clientele.[12] In addition to Freymann, "Doctor Robert" may have been a veiled reference to John Riley, the dentist who, without their knowledge, had sent John and George on their first acid trip in early April 1965. At first, Riley attempted to keep his guests from leaving, given their onrushing hallucinogenic condition. Fearing that their host was attempting to detain the Beatles and their wives for an orgy, the two couples drove off in George's Mini Cooper to the Ad Lib Club. They eventually made their way to Kinfauns, the Harrisons' Esher bungalow, where John imagined himself to be captaining a giant submarine. For George, the experience was a revelation: "It was like I had never tasted, smelled, or heard anything before. For me, it was like a flash. It just opened up something inside of me, and I realized a lot of very heavy things. From that moment on, I wanted to have that depth and clarity of perception" (qtd. in

Badman 147). To Lennon's mind, the acid trip served as validation for the surrealistic imagery that he had been experiencing his entire life:

> Surrealism had a great effect on me because then I realized that the imagery in my mind wasn't insanity—that if it was insane, then I belonged to an exclusive club that sees the world in those terms. Surrealism to me is reality. Psychedelic vision to me is reality and always was. When I looked at myself in the mirror at 12, 13, I used to, literally, trance out into alpha. I didn't know what it was called then. I only found out years later that there is a name for those conditions. But I would find myself seeing these hallucinatory images of my face changing, becoming cosmic and complete. (*All We Are Saying* 158)

John later observed that "*Rubber Soul* was the pot album, and *Revolver* was the acid," yet "Doctor Robert" evinces an archly satirical tone—especially in terms of Lennon's characterization of the errant physician (*Anthology* 194). The middle-eight's depiction of the good doctor's patient enjoying an hallucinatory experience—"Well, well, well, you're feeling fine"—is tempered by the speaker's disapproving attitude toward his subject: "He helps you to understand / He does everything he can, Doctor Robert." While Lennon clearly had little problem ingesting the doctor's wares, he couldn't help feeling suspicious about anyone—particularly a shameless huckster such as Doctor Robert—who blithely promises to transform his clients into "new and better" people, and for a price, no less.[13]

In contrast with *Rubber Soul*, which ended rather poorly after registering such an auspicious beginning, *Revolver*'s closing trio of compositions finds the Beatles plowing an assortment of musical terrain—and doing so with the same skill and panache with which the album began. Affixed by Emerick with the working title "Laxton's Superb" (after yet another variety of apples), Harrison's "I Want to Tell You" inaugurates the sort of existential philosophy that will characterize his finest Beatles recordings from "Within You Without You" and "The Inner Light" to "While My Guitar Gently Weeps" and "I Me Mine." Clearly written with Eastern notions of karma in mind, "I Want to Tell You" addresses the individual as the result of a set of totalizing, lived experiences. George makes a point in the song of underscoring the significance of personal responsibility and the self-negating ills of ego-consciousness: "But if I seem to act unkind / It's only me, it's not my mind / That is confusing things." With its innovative and arresting guitar fade-in, "I Want to Tell You" is Harrison's most fully realized composition to date. Amazingly, George later asserted that there wasn't "much difference between *Rubber Soul* and *Revolver*. To me," he admitted, "they could be Volume 1 and Volume 2" (*Anthology* 212). Yet with three pioneering compositions of his own on *Revolver*, his remarks seem positively disingenuous in hindsight.

With "Got to Get You into My Life," McCartney presents yet another valentine to the Beatles' American influences. In this instance, he brilliantly captures the sound of Motown, especially the flavor of such Supremes hits as "Where Did Our Love Go?" and "Baby Love." A spirited composition about the speaker's desire to embrace life, as well as the irresistible charms of another human being, "Got to Get You into My Life" features a crisp musical attack courtesy of a quintet of studio musicians—three trumpets and two tenor saxophones. In order to achieve a more robust and all-encompassing sound, Emerick later double-tracked the brass. As the song closes in on the two-minute mark, George's inventive guitar solo on his Sonic Blue Fender Strat blows the proceedings wide open, and suddenly the worlds of R&B and guitar rock are united in perfect pop-music harmony.

While *Rubber Soul* concludes with a derivative throwaway in "Run for Your Life," *Revolver* reaches its zenith with "Tomorrow Never Knows," a psychedelic tapestry that ushered in new ways of thinking about the concept of "recording artists," not to mention rock and roll as a musical genre. As the first song recorded for the album on April 6th, "Tomorrow Never Knows" sported the working titles of "Mark I" and "The Void," clear indications, in and of themselves, about the composition's *avant-garde* nature. As a Ringo-inspired malapropism, "Tomorrow Never Knows" came into being as the result of the confluence of two events in John and Paul's lives. Only scant days before the first recording session for "Tomorrow Never Knows," John had purchased a copy of Timothy Leary's *The Psychedelic Experience: A Manual Based on the Tibetan Book of the Dead* (1964) at the trendy Indica Bookshop. In Leary's introduction to his reading of the *Tibetan Book of the Dead*, the American counterculture guru offers a morsel of advice that seized Lennon's attention: "Whenever in doubt, turn off your mind, relax, float downstream" (14). Meanwhile, Paul had immersed himself in London's diverse worlds of high and *avant-garde* culture. In the mid-1960s, he had embarked on a stringent personal program of reading the classics and theatergoing in order to broaden his literary and artistic intellect. "I vaguely mind anyone knowing anything I don't know," McCartney reported. "I'm trying to crowd everything in, all the things that I've missed" (qtd. in Schaffner 65). In terms of music, Paul had become especially enamored with the electronic, experimental works associated with *musique concrète*—and with Karlheinz Stockhausen's *Gesang der Jünglinge* [*Song of the Youths*] in particular. Paul was equally fond of the work of composer John Cage, the most famous pupil of the expressionist composer Arnold Schönberg. McCartney delighted in the concept behind Cage's experimental silent piano piece *4'33"*—a composition whose beginning and ending were indicated solely by the opening and closing of the piano lid. By the early

1960s, Cage had taken on a protégée of his own, a fledgling Japanese perform-ance artist named Yoko Ono.

When John debuted "Tomorrow Never Knows" for his mates in the studio, the composition's psychedelic underpinnings were already firmly in place. At this juncture, the only elements lacking in the production were the musical accompaniment and sound effects that would blast Lennon's ideas into the consciousness of a waiting world. During the first session, John and Ringo fashioned some rudimentary tape loops in a "'weird sound' contest," according to Emerick. Meanwhile, the engineer improved the sound of Ringo's percus-sion by moving the microphones closer to his drum kit and by stuffing an old woolen sweater inside his bass drum in order to deepen its resonance (111). And then there was the matter of John's lead vocal. At EMI Studios, Lennon had become famous for disliking the sound of his own voice, and he was con-stantly entreating Martin to alter his vocals during the recording process. For "Tomorrow Never Knows," he challenged the producer to make his "voice sound like the Dalai Lama chanting from a mountaintop, miles away." In an effort to satisfy Lennon's request, Emerick turned to the studio's Hammond organ and, in particular, the instrument's Leslie speaker system, which was essentially a wooden cabinet containing two sets of speakers with rotating sound baffles. After Emerick and Ken Townshend rewired the system, they were able to project John's voice through the Leslie cabinet, in front of which they had positioned a pair of microphones. The sound of Lennon's vocal was trans-fixing—"eerily disconnected, distant yet compelling," in Emerick's words (10). After listening to the playback, George suggested that he play the tamboura on "Tomorrow Never Knows": "It's perfect for this track, John," he explained. "It's just kind of a droning sound, and I think it will make the whole thing quite Eastern" (qtd. in Emerick 11). With the principal elements in place, the Beatles took their first pass at "Mark I"—a slower, pulsating version of the eventual "Tomorrow Never Knows"—and, after three takes, they called it a night.

The next evening, Paul—having been inspired by John and Ringo's initial efforts—showed up with a plastic bag filled with tape loops that he had made at home on his Brenell reel-to-reel tape recorder. As McCartney recalled:

> I would do them [tape loops] over a few days. I had a little bottle of EMI glue that I would stick them with and wait till they dried. It was a pretty decent join. I'd be trying to avoid the click as it went through, but I never actually avoided it. If you made them very well you could just about do it but I made 'em a bit ham-fisted and I ended up using the clicks as part of the rhythm. (qtd. in Miles 219)

After reviewing Paul's collection of sound effects, the group selected five tape loops for "Tomorrow Never Knows," the most recognizable of which sounds like a seagull. As it turned out, recording the tape loops was a chore in itself. Given that Studio Two had only one extra tape machine available that night, the complex's army of white-coated employees was forced to assemble the other machines at EMI Studios and run the various tape loops through them, all the while steadying pencils in their hands in order to provide the necessary tension. In addition to the seagull sound, the tape loops afforded the track with industrial, machinelike noises.[14] As the backdrop for an ostensible pop-music recording, they were a revelation. As Nick Bromell writes, "The unearthly sounds that *Revolver* released into the world were at once the antithesis of the human and a provocative indication of the *mysterium tremendum*. They allowed the imagination to traverse the netscape of the future in which biology and technology would come full circle and touch" (98). A few weeks later, Emerick grafted George's tamboura drone onto the beginning of "Tomorrow Never Knows" and, at Paul's suggestion, concluded the track by splicing in the recording of a spontaneous piano riff that the band had concocted on that very first evening.

Lyrically and thematically, the song explores the role of consciousness as a transformative phenomenon, as a way of simultaneously imagining one's place in the present, past, and future—ultimately, in an afterlife of sorts, like "death's other kingdom" in T. S. Eliot's "The Hollow Men" (80). "Tomorrow Never Knows" reminds us that the act of living implies that the past never really dies. When you "turn off your mind, relax, and float downstream"— when you truly "surrender to the void," the lyrics tell us—the self comes to recognize that the past, present, and future exist in perpetuity, that death is merely another state of being. This concept is illustrated by Emily Dickinson's "I Heard a Fly Buzz When I Died," when the speaker's eyes cease to function at the moment of death: the "windows failed, and then / I could not see to see" (224). In Dickinson's poem, as with Lennon's song, the speaker's existence continues unabated, merely having shifted from one state of being to another. After urging his pupils to "listen to the color of your dreams" in "Tomorrow Never Knows," John begins an extended circular coda—"Of the beginning / Of the beginning / Of the beginning"—that slowly vanishes into the fadeout, where the madcap piano riff suddenly wrests control of the track, plunging it into a nether world of oblivion and noise. As with the spontaneous studio clamor out of which "Taxman" had been born, the album eventually returns to the unruly din of its creation.

With the placement of "Tomorrow Never Knows" on *Revolver*, the Beatles developed the "sense of an ending" that marked their shift from mere rock-and-rollers into *narrateurs*, storytellers who recognize the significant role of beginnings and endings to the literary unity and effectiveness of their storylines. In *Revolver*'s case, the storyline involves an album-length song cycle in which the narrative is truly the sum of its parts. Beginnings and endings—births and deaths—are biological realities; they exist as archetypal life-cycle moments, yet they also function as key structural devices in terms of narrative. As Frank Kermode points out, "we look for a fullness of time" in our stories, "for beginning, middle, and end in concord." The human urge to foist order onto time, to stave off the chaos, is a primal aspect of storytelling. "It is not that we are connoisseurs of chaos," Kermode writes, "but that we are surrounded by it, and equipped for co-existence with it only by our fictive powers" (58, 69). For the Beatles, *Revolver* acts as a comforting mechanism just as the wheel of life, like a record on a turntable, spins around and around—*revolving* on its metaphorical axis—leading us from one life experience to another: from birth and death, to love and loss, to joy and pain, and back again. In the starkest terms of our transient human lives, *Revolver* illuminates the fleeting nature of our existence, shedding light on our mortality in nearly the same instant in which it challenges us to live deeply and embrace our worldly chaos. As e. e. cummings observes in "stand with your lover on the ending earth—":

> —how fortunate are you and i, whose home
> is timelessness:we who have wandered down
> from fragrant mountains of eternal now
>
> to frolic in such mysteries as birth
> and death a day(or maybe even less). (743)

In many ways, *Revolver* is about frolicking in cummings's "fragrant mountains of eternal now," about living in the moment even as we become ever conscious of the death-drive's inevitable role amongst our own beginnings and endings.

～

When the Beatles embarked on June 23rd for the first leg of their impending world tour—which began, as had their career as professional musicians not so many years ago, in West Germany—the album remained untitled. Before settling on *Revolver*, they considered naming the album *Abracadabra*, or, at Paul's suggestion, *Magic Circle*. John jokingly proposed that they call it *The Beatles on Safari*. Eventually, Paul floated the idea of calling it *Revolver*, the title stuck, and there was no turning back. *Revolver* it would be. Pete Shotton remembered rifling through newspapers and magazines with John and Paul at the Lennons' Weybridge estate. After selecting various pictures of the Beatles, they cut out the faces and glued them together in a "surrealistic montage," which was then superimposed on a line drawing by the band's old friend from Hamburg, artist and bass player Klaus Voormann (122). With its monochromatic imagery and intriguing assortment of photographs that seem to flower from Voormann's drawings of John, Paul, George, and Ringo, the result was the Beatles' most imaginative cover to date, a provocative sleeve design befitting a groundbreaking album such as *Revolver*. Not surprisingly, in March 1967, the album cover received "Best Album Cover/Graphic Arts" honors during the ninth-annual Grammy Awards.

Tim Riley astutely argues that "*Revolver* single-handedly made Beatlemania irrelevant" (176). But Beatlemania certainly wasn't *dead*—and not by a long shot. But in June 1966, its seamy underbelly began to emerge, and in short order, the group's reputation, not to mention their collective sanity, suffered from a series of unfortunate events and controversies that would shatter the image of the four lovable Mop Tops forever. Even more significantly, it would find the Beatles themselves running for cover to escape from a deluge of their own making. First, there was the attendant disaster associated with the so-called "Butcher" cover. Released on June 15th, Capitol Records' American LP *Yesterday . . . and Today* became the only Beatles album to actually *lose* money for the music juggernaut. Robert Whitaker's gory cover photograph featured the Beatles dressed in white laboratory coats, clutching decapitated baby dolls, and surrounded by raw meat. When numerous record retailers refused to stock the album, given its offensive cover art, Capitol hastily withdrew the LP from stores and re-released the album five days later with a benign photograph of the group playfully posing around a steamer trunk.[15]

And then things began steadily to get worse. In late June, the Beatles started their world tour in West Germany, and on June 25th, they played the Gruga-halle in Essen. During the concert, the venue's bouncers began taking overzeal-ous fans outside of the concert hall and beating them senseless. As the situation deteriorated, a pack of Luger-carrying police officers was dispatched to quell the very thugs who had been hired to provide security for the band in the first place. The next day, the Beatles were reunited in Hamburg with Astrid Kirchherr, who was engaged to marry Gibson Kemp, the young drummer who replaced Ringo in the ranks of Rory Storm and the Hurricanes back in 1962. The Beatles, especially John, were overjoyed to see her. For the group, it must have seemed like a lifetime ago that they had played the Reeperbahn with Stu amongst their number. The tour continued in Japan, where the Beatles began a series of five concerts in Tokyo on June 30th. A succession of death threats ensued after it was revealed that the band would be playing the city's celebrated Budokan, the octagon-shaped arena that had been reserved for traditional Japanese martial arts. Many Japanese felt that it was a sacred venue that shouldn't be desecrated by Western rock and roll music. Afraid that the world's most famous musicians might be injured—or, worse yet, perish—on their soil, the Japanese government overreacted in spectacular fashion, dispatching some thirty-five thousand police officers to protect the Beatles during their brief visit. The bandmates were held as virtual prisoners in the Tokyo Hilton, and the concerts themselves were sterile affairs in which some three thousand police had been distributed among the venue's ten thousand spectators in order to maintain control. With such an overwhelming police presence, the Japanese fans were reluctant to go berserk in the same fashion as their Western counterparts. Gone were the screams and tumult to which the band had become accustomed, and suddenly, without the comforting veil of teenage chaos and clamor, the Beatles could be heard, loudly and clearly, as an unhappy quartet of sloppy, out-of-tune musicians. As a surviving television broadcast of the first concert plainly demonstrates, their stage act by this juncture was simply awful (Lewisohn, *The Beatles Live!* 192).

On July 3rd, the tour pressed on, with the Beatles bringing their show to the Philippines for the first time. After landing in Manila, the bandmates were inexplicably whisked away to a yacht that was owned by a local media mogul. After some two hours, Epstein demanded that the group be removed from the vessel and provided with hotel accommodations in the city. When they finally checked into the Manila Hotel, the Beatles were blissfully unaware of an invitation from President Ferdinand Marcos and First Lady Imelda Marcos—the "Imeldific" one herself—requesting their appearance at Malacañang Palace at 11 o'clock the following morning. But "since the British embassy fiasco," the group's assistant Peter Brown recalled, "the policy was never to go to those things" (qtd. in Spitz 620). The next morning, the Beatles' entourage ignored further demands from Filipino officials that they go to the Palace, where the First Lady and some two hundred children were now anxiously awaiting their appearance. After playing an afternoon concert for some thirty-five thousand fans and an evening performance for another fifty thousand spectators at José Rizal Memorial Stadium, the band started to realize that they were in dire straits when news reports began detailing their snubbing of the royal family. Later that night, a genuinely contrite Brian Epstein attempted to ameliorate the situation by expressing his regrets to the First Family on the Channel 5 News, but a burst of suspicious static rendered his apology all but unintelligible. The next day, the Beatles were suddenly ordered to pay income tax on concert receipts that they still hadn't received from Filipino promoter Ramon Ramos. Worse yet, their governmental security detail had been suspended, given their allegedly rude treatment of the First Lady, and the group and their entourage were left to their own devices as they rushed to the Manila International Airport in order to make their KLM flight to New Delhi. But their ordeal wasn't over yet. They were jostled by an angry mob as they made their way to immigration, and things became even more dicey on the tarmac, when Mal Evans and press officer Tony Barrow were removed from the plane shortly before takeoff. The Beatles had been declared "illegal immigrants" by the Filipino government, and Mal and Tony spent some forty minutes negotiating the band's way out of the country. Stultified by what they considered to be their near-death experience in the South Pacific, the group roundly blamed Epstein for the disastrous turn of events. When the Beatles finally arrived back in London on July 8th, George Harrison joked to a reporter that "we're going to have a couple of weeks to recuperate before we go and get beaten up by the Americans" (qtd. in Lewisohn, *The Beatles Live!* 195).

By the time that the Beatles arrived in Boston on August 11th, George's words had taken on an eerie truth. Back in March, the *London Evening Standard* had published Maureen Cleave's latest interview with John. Having recently read Hugh J. Schonfield's bestseller *The Passover Plot* (1965), he was anxious to share his views regarding the plight of contemporary religion. During their discussion, Lennon remarked that "Christianity will go. It will vanish and shrink. . . . We're more popular than Jesus now; I don't know which will go first—rock and roll or Christianity. Jesus was all right, but his disciples were thick and ordinary. It's them twisting it that ruins it for me" (*Anthology* 223). John's comments passed without notice in the British press, but on July 31st, the American magazine *Datebook* republished the interview. Within days, radio stations across the nation's Bible Belt were sponsoring "Beatle-burnings" in which they invited the public to torch their Beatles records. As the group prepared to travel to the United States, John took to calling their upcoming spate of American concerts the "Jesus Christ Tour." He had no idea how accurate his words would prove to be. By the time that the Beatles alighted on American shores, Lennon's remarks to Cleave had set off a public-relations controversy that Epstein and the Beatles could scarcely have imagined. At a press conference in Chicago, John attempted to quell the storm: "I wasn't saying whatever they're saying I was saying," he told the media. "I'm sorry I said it really. I never meant it to be a lousy anti-religious thing. I apologize if that will make you happy. I still don't know quite what I've done. I've tried to tell you what I did do, but if you want me to apologize, if that will make you happy, then okay, I'm sorry." But the controversy didn't ebb so easily, and neither did the group's distaste for the relentless circus of Beatlemania. On August 19th, the band played a concert at the Mid-South Coliseum in Memphis, Tennessee, where the Ku Klux Klan staged a protest and a firecracker exploded on the stage. For a split second, they thought that they were under attack, that one of them had been assassinated. As Lennon remembered, "There had been threats to shoot us, the Klan were burning Beatle records outside, and a lot of the crew-cut kids were joining in with them. Somebody let off a firecracker and every one of us—I think it's on film—look at each other, because each thought it was the other that had been shot. It was that bad" (*Anthology* 227).

For the Beatles, enough was enough. On Monday, August 29th, 1966, the group performed at San Francisco's Candlestick Park before some twenty-five thousand fans, with the Ronettes, the Remains, and the Cyrkle as their trio of opening acts. As with numerous other venues on the calamitous "Jesus Christ Tour," Candlestick Park hadn't sold out—in fact, there were some ten thousand conspicuously empty seats that day. Having privately decided that Candlestick Park would be the scene of their last concert, the Beatles good-naturedly photographed themselves in order to commemorate the occasion. Meanwhile, Paul instructed Tony Barrow to make a cassette recording of their final set. It was a blustery evening—complete with a full moon, no less—and the Beatles took the stage at 9:27 p.m., having been escorted onto the baseball diamond in an armored car with a security detail of some two hundred police officers in tow. The stage itself was five feet tall, with a six-foot-high wire fence around the perimeter as an extra precautionary measure. The Beatles opened the concert with a searing rendition of "Rock and Roll Music," and, as Bob Molyneux had done in St. Peter's Church Hall way back in July 1957, Barrow held his cassette player's tiny microphone aloft in front of the stage and recorded the show for posterity. Barrow's tape of the Beatles' thirty-three-minute performance ran out of space less than a minute into "Long Tall Sally," the group's final number before a paying audience. After some 1,400 concerts, their lives as working rock-and-rollers were suddenly over. As the band prepared to leave the stage that evening, John loitered for just a moment, furtively strumming the opening chords of "In My Life," one of his most heartfelt and personal of compositions. And with that, they were gone.

Notes

1. In May 1966, the Beatles virtually invented the music video when they shot promotional films for "Paperback Writer" and "Rain." The production, which took half a day to complete, was supervised by American director Michael Lindsay-Hogg. For the band, promotional videos of this sort were preferable to gearing up for live performances on music-oriented shows such as *Top of the Pops* or variety programs like the *Ed Sullivan Show*.

2. In McCartney's hands, the bass guitar evolved into a lead instrument in its own right, as evinced by the majestic bass runs that undergird later Beatles compositions

such as "With a Little Help from My Friends," "Hello Goodbye," and "Something," among a host of others. With Wings, Paul's bass would drive the melody itself in compositions such as "Silly Love Songs" and "Goodnight Tonight" (see McCartney's *Wingspan: Hits and History* [2001]).

3. "Paperback Writer" was one of the very few *Rubber Soul-* and *Revolver*-era songs, along with "Day Tripper" and "Nowhere Man," that the band even bothered to attempt in live performance.

4. While Harrison's sardonic tale about the trials and tribulations of taxation results in a number of genuinely humorous moments—especially during the song's punchline, "Now my advice for those who die: / Declare the pennies on your eyes"— one cannot help but register the irony of an extraordinarily rich young man lecturing the populace about his financial troubles. In "The Other Side of Summer," Elvis Costello pokes fun at the irony of John Lennon's peace anthem "Imagine," in which the wealthy former Beatle bemoans the ills of materialism: "Was it a millionaire," Costello sings, "who said 'imagine no possessions'?"

5. While Lennon and McCartney disputed the authorship of "In My Life" and "Eleanor Rigby," Paul later pointed out that "I find it very gratifying that out of everything we wrote, we only appear to disagree over two songs" (qtd. in Miles 278).

6. Yet as Kevin Ryan and Brian Kehew observe, it is difficult to believe that *Fahrenheit 451* served as Martin's primary influence, given that it "was not released until November of 1966, seven months after the recording of 'Eleanor Rigby'; indeed, Herrmann reportedly only wrote the score in June of that year. The more obvious source of inspiration was Herrmann's 1960 score for Alfred Hitchcock's *Psycho*, which prominently featured the same scraping staccato string effect Martin employed here in 1966" (422).

7. As a songwriter, McCartney is particularly drawn to the plight of loneliness, as evidenced by "The Fool on the Hill," "Lady Madonna," "Rocky Raccoon," and, most recently, *Chaos and Creation in the Backyard*'s "Jenny Wren," who was based on the character of the same name from Charles Dickens's *Our Mutual Friend* (1864–1865).

8. Lennon continues this theme in 1968 with *The White Album*'s "I'm So Tired" and in 1980 with *Double Fantasy*'s "Watching the Wheels."

9. As Walter Everett points out, "Love You To" wasn't George Martin's first recording of Indian instrumentation. In addition to the previous year's "Norwegian Wood," Martin had worked with musicians playing the sitar and tabla for a 1959 track by Peter Sellers and the Goons in which they parodied *My Fair Lady*'s "Wouldn't It Be Loverly" (*Revolver through the Anthology* 42).

10. In July 1960, Moore concluded a 3,200-mile charity walk from Los Angeles to New York City.

11. As Peter Fonda later recalled, "I remember sitting on the deck with George, who was telling me that he thought he was dying. I told him that there was nothing to be afraid of and that all he needed to do was to relax. I said that I knew what it was like to be dead because when I was 10 years old, I'd accidentally shot myself in the stomach

and my heart stopped beating three times because I lost so much blood. John was passing at the time and heard me say, 'I know what it's like to be dead'" (qtd. in Cross 436).

12. Freymann lost his license in 1968 and was formally dismissed from the New York Medical Society in 1975. In 1983, he published a book entitled *What's So Bad about Feeling Good?* The inspiration for "Doctor Robert" is often incorrectly ascribed to Charles Roberts, the alias for the New York physician who provided celebrities—including film star Edie Sedgwick—with shots of vitamins mixed with methedrine. Robert Freeman, the photographer whose work graced five Beatles album covers, is also frequently misattributed as the song's inspiration.

13. Although the Beatles' creative accomplishments during this period are often attributed to the influence of illicit drugs—and there is little doubt that they consumed considerable amounts of hallucinogens, especially John—the bandmates were intensely focused and painstaking in the studio. "We were really hard workers," Ringo recalled, and "we worked like dogs to get it right" (qtd. in Spitz 606). While their hallucinogenic activities surely contributed to the band's evolving consciousness and creativity, the group required, as with most artists, to maintain their wits in their working environment. "The Beatles said they preferred not to work high," Mark Lewisohn adds, but "they took their high experiences into the studio" ("High Times" 182).

14. As Kevin Ryan and Brian Kehew point out, the five tape loops include "1) a 'laughing' male voice, played double-speed (the 'seagull' sound); 2) a B-flat major chord played by an orchestra (likely copied from a classical record); 3) a sitar phrase, reversed and played double-speed; 4) a phrase performed on what appears to be a mandolin (or possibly acoustic guitar with tape echo), played double-speed; 5) a scalar sitar line, reversed and played double-speed" (412).

15. Ironically, the company ultimately failed in its effort to eradicate the offending cover. During the long weekend in which Capitol employees were busy removing *Yesterday . . . and Today*'s cover artwork—at a reported cost of more than $200,000— many fatigued workers resorted to pasting the new photograph over the "Butcher" cover. As a result, numerous fans discovered that they could carefully extricate the original photograph. The butcher cover has since become a much-desired item of Beatles memorabilia among serious collectors (Schaffner 56-58). John later attributed the cover's origins to the band's "boredom and resentment at having to do *another* photo session and *another* Beatles thing. We were sick to death of it," he recalled, and "the photographer was into Dali and making surreal pictures" (*All We Are Saying* 219).

Chapter 9

The Act You've Known
for All These Years

How many more times will you remember a certain
afternoon of your childhood, some afternoon that's
so deeply a part of your being that you can't even
conceive of your life without it? Perhaps four or five
times more. Perhaps not even that. How many more
times will you watch the full moon rise? Perhaps
twenty. And yet it all seems limitless.

—PAUL BOWLES, *THE SHELTERING SKY*

How paradoxical it is to seek in reality for
the pictures that are stored in one's memory,
which must inevitably lose the charm that comes
to them from memory itself and from their not
being apprehended by the senses.

—MARCEL PROUST, *DU CÔTÉ DE CHEZ SWANN*

As the group's plane took off from San Francisco International Airport after their final concert, George settled into the seat next to Tony Barrow and announced, "Right—that's it. I'm not a Beatle anymore" (qtd. in Spitz 640). George's relief was palpable. After nearly four years of nonstop madness, Beatlemania's unremitting treadmill seemed finally to be slowing down, and for the next several months, the bandmates did something that they hadn't done in years, and certainly not for such a lengthy duration: they went their separate ways.

While Ringo settled in for an extended family vacation with his wife, Maureen, and one-year-old son Zak, George trundled off with Pattie to Bombay, where he indulged in a rigorous six-week sitar course. Practicing the difficult instrument up to eight hours a day, George took lessons from Ravi Shankar's disciple Shambu Das. Meanwhile, he studied Hindu culture with Shankar himself, visiting temples, reading Eastern philosophy, and listening to Hindustani music. For George, visiting India began to fulfill his life's great quest for spiritual connection. Meanwhile, Paul went on a two-week safari with Mal Evans in Kenya. Back in England, McCartney agreed to compose the soundtrack for Roy Boulting's *The Family Way*, a vehicle for screen star Hayley Mills. With George Martin serving as his arranger, Paul turned in a tenderhearted, evocative score. Much of his soundtrack for the movie features a series of nostalgic variations on a composition entitled "Love in the Open Air." As with McCartney, Lennon's future—at least in the short term—involved the world of film. John had recently accepted a part in Richard Lester's absurdist comedy *How I Won the War* as Private Gripweed—a wisecracking fascist trapped in a war against the evils of fascism. Donning the National Health "granny" glasses for which he would forever be associated, the Beatle went on location in Almería, Spain.[1] In no time, John discovered that a movie set—especially for an actor in a supporting role—was a decidedly boring place to be. Relaxing in the beach house that he shared with Michael Crawford, the star of *How I Won the War*, John gathered up his acoustic guitar and began picking out his first new composition in months. "Living is easy with eyes closed," the lyrics for the tune went. "Misunderstanding all you see."

For Brian Epstein, the post-touring world made for a bitter, unfulfilling life. As the architect of Beatlemania, he had been on a high-octane entertainment carousel for nearly five years, and toiling in its shadow was too much for him to bear. In late September 1966, Brian had dinner at his posh Chapel Street home with Peter Brown, who had recently moved into the manager's house in order to look after him in his desultory state. Later that evening, Peter discovered that his roommate had fallen unconscious in his bedroom. Unable to rouse Brian, Peter took him to a private hospital in Richmond, where the medical staff pumped his stomach and saved his life. While Brian described the event as a "foolish accident," Peter knew better. The next morning, he found an empty bottle of Nembutal and the manager's would-be suicide note: "I can't deal with this anymore," Brian had written. "It's beyond me, and I just can't go on" (qtd. in Spitz 647). Meanwhile, John was going through an ordeal of his own. Having returned from Spain, he descended back into the domestic doldrums of life with Cynthia in the suburbs. The couple barely spoke by this juncture, and John whiled away the hours in his music room, mindlessly watching television, tripping incessantly, and slowly losing his sanity. On the evening of November 9th—after staying up for three days in a protracted hallucinogenic haze—an unkempt and disheveled Lennon traveled into the city in his chauffeur-driven Mini Cooper. He had accepted an invitation from curator John Dunbar to preview an exhibition at the trendy Indica Gallery, which Paul had underwritten in 1965 to the tune of some £5,000. The exhibition, entitled *Unfinished Paintings and Objects*, was being presented by Yoko Ono, a performance artist who had recently made a splash on the *avant-garde* art scene by enclosing herself in a black bag and thrashing around in front of scores of bewildered spectators—tourists, mostly—in stately Trafalgar Square.

~

Born on February 18th, 1933, in Saitama, Japan, Yoko enjoyed a privileged upbringing as the oldest child of Isoko Yasuda, a wealthy heiress, and Eisuke Ono, a banker who, in his younger days, had pursued a career as a classically trained pianist. Yoko, whose name translates as "Ocean Child," attended Tokyo's elite Gakushuin academy. Her early years at the institution found her rebelling against her conventional education, as well as her disciplinarian-mother: "I was like a domesticated animal being fed information," she later remarked. "I hated it. And particularly music. I used to faint before my music lessons—literally. I suppose it was my way of escape" (qtd. in Goldman 211). During the Second World War, Yoko's family—including her brother Keisuke and sister Setsuko—fled the city for the countryside, where their well-heeled existence clashed with the harsh poverty of the nation's peasantry.

After the war, Yoko's family emigrated to Scarsdale, New York, where Yoko continued her education at Sarah Lawrence College. During this period, Yoko fell in with a bohemian crowd of artists and writers, dropping out of college during her junior year. In 1956, she married Japanese experimental composer Toshi Ichiyanagi, whose inferior class status enraged her mother to no end. The couple became estranged in the early 1960s, and Yoko engaged in a succession of sexual affairs, including a lengthy liaison with radical American composer La Monte Young, who introduced her to the New York art world, including composer John Cage and a host of other influential figures. In 1962, emissaries of Yoko's family escorted her back to Japan, where she became suicidal and was briefly institutionalized. During her stay in the mental hospital, Yoko met American jazz musician and film producer Tony Cox, who had sailed to the Orient after hearing tales from Young about a Japanese artist who had left New York City under mysterious circumstances. In November 1962, Yoko married Cox—but without first having bothered to divorce Toshi. In order to untangle the ensuing legal mess, her lawyers advised her in March 1963 to annul her marriage with Tony. They remarried in June 1963, and their daughter Kyoko was born on August 8th of that year. Tony and Yoko's marriage deteriorated rapidly in the wake of Kyoko's birth. At one point, their growing animus led to a knife fight that was broken up in the nick of time by Al Wunderlich, a visiting friend from the United States. Yet despite their tempestuous relationship, the couple remained together in order to nurture their respective careers.

In September 1964, Yoko returned to New York, where she attempted to res- urrect her artistic standing among the city's growing *avant-garde* community. Although it was slow going at first, she eventually found her place amongst the Dadaesque group of artists known as Fluxus (from the Latin word "to flow"), whose founder, George Maciunas, promoted Yoko's growing interest in per- formance art. Maciunas's whimsical approach to the genre was a driving force in Yoko's aesthetic, which explored, often playfully, the ironic interrelationships that exist between the natural and industrial worlds. Maciunas also influenced Yoko's creation of imaginary objects and works of interactive art. Under Cage's tutelage, Yoko added a variety of natural and mechanized sounds to her creative repertoire. As a performance artist, Yoko appreciated the power of shock value, often realized through nudity, as a means of conceptualizing her aesthetic. In her work entitled *Cut Piece*, for example, Yoko reclined onstage, while audience members cut off her clothing with a pair of scissors until she was naked. Her desire to provoke her audience continued with her film *No. 4*, known colloqui- ally as *Bottoms*, which exhibited a series of human buttocks as the subjects walked upon a treadmill accompanied by their own words in candid voiceover.[2] By the summer of 1966, Yoko had left New York in order to attend the *Destruc- tion in Art Symposium*, an international congress that Fluxus was hosting in London. Before long, she and Tony took to hanging out with the gaggle of other hipsters who frequented the Indica Gallery. At one point, she even met Paul, whom she regaled with tales about her work with Cage. Without missing a beat, she invited him to contribute to *Notations* (1969), Cage's forthcoming anthology of musical scores by contemporary composers. But the Beatle balked at her offer, suggesting that she consider sharing her ideas with his songwriting partner instead. After all, with the recent triumph of "Tomorrow Never Knows," John had been developing his own interest in the *avant-garde* of late.

~

After summoning up the necessary resolve to walk into the Indica Gallery on that fateful November evening, John came face to face with Yoko Ono, the Ocean Child herself. As a way of introducing her exhibition, which would be opened to the public the next evening, Yoko handed him a white card embossed with the word BREATHE. "You mean, like this?" John responded, before breaking into a pant. Almost immediately, Lennon found himself enjoying the humor behind her art. Following the diminutive Japanese woman around the gallery, John happened upon a ladder, above which hung Yoko's *Ceiling Painting.* "It looked like a black canvas with a chain with a spyglass hanging on the end of it," John remembered. At the top of the ladder, John peered through the magnifying glass at the canvas, which sported a single word: YES. The Beatle couldn't help but smile to himself. One of the final works in the exhibition encouraged visitors to hammer a nail into a piece of white plasterboard. But Yoko would have none of it. It was alright for John to preview the exhibit, but the plasterboard should remain unspoiled for the opening. Dunbar pulled the artist aside: "I argued strongly in favor of Lennon's hammering in the first nail," the curator later remarked. "He had a lot of loot—chances are, he would buy the damn thing." An angry Yoko finally relented, given the wealth and stature of her distinguished guest. "Okay, you can hammer a nail in for five shillings," she told him. "I'll give you an imaginary five shillings, if you let me hammer in an imaginary nail," John retorted, a sly grin growing across his face. It was the defining moment of the artist's life. "My God," Yoko thought to herself. "He's playing the same game I'm playing" (qtd. in Spitz 652–53).

Over the next several months, Yoko embarked upon a spirited campaign to win Lennon's patronage for her aspiring art. In addition to showering him with notes and letters, she presented him with a copy of her book *Grapefruit* (1964), which was half-autobiography, half-artistic statement. As Cynthia Lennon later recalled, "I didn't know then that Yoko was beginning a deter-mined pursuit of John. She wrote him many letters and cards over the next few months, but I knew nothing about them at the time, or that she had even come to our house looking for him several times" (*John* 257). John was impressed with Yoko's Zen-like directives, particularly *Cloud Piece,* in which she entreated her readers to "Imagine the clouds dripping. Dig a hole in your garden to put them in." And then there was *Snow Piece,* which instructed read-ers to "Think that snow is falling. Think that snow is falling everywhere all the time. When you talk with a person, think that snow is falling between you and on the person. Stop conversing when you think the person is covered by snow." Her art was imaginative, it was provocative, it was enticing. In short, it was Yoko, and Lennon's mind was intrigued in ways that it hadn't been for years—if ever.

As a group, the Beatles were poised for a renaissance of their own. John continued to listen avidly to Dylan's music during this period, while he and

Paul were both staggered by the guitar pyrotechnics of American musician Jimi Hendrix, who had exploded onto the London club scene in the autumn of 1966. Meanwhile, Paul had fallen in love with the natural ambience of the Incredible String Band, a Scottish quintet whose folk melodies, exotic instrumentation, and natural ambience had won the hearts of the city's budding counterculture. Although George listened almost exclusively to North Indian classical music, all of the Beatles had been inspired by the artistic heights of the Beach Boys' *Pet Sounds*, which had been directly influenced by *Rubber Soul*. Brian Wilson, the Beach Boys' founding member and principal songwriter, recalled the wonder that he experienced when he first encountered the album: "When I first heard [*Rubber Soul*], I flipped! I said, 'I want to make an album like that.' The entire album seemed to be like a collection of folk songs" (qtd. in Badman 194). Released in May 1966, *Pet Sounds* was the Beach Boys' crowning artistic achievement. With its magical array of sound effects, unconventional instrumentation, and ethereal ambience, *Pet Sounds* transformed the Beach Boys' innovative harmonies and lush California sound into pure pop-music majesty. The Beatles were thunderstruck by tracks like "Sloop John B," with its quirky nostalgia for the innocent shores of a windswept past, as well as the beautiful balladry inherent in "I Know There's an Answer," "Don't Talk (Put Your Head on My Shoulder)," and "You Still Believe in Me," McCartney's personal favorite among the album's assortment of gems. John and Paul were similarly overwhelmed by the emotional mindscapes of "Wouldn't It Be Nice" and "God Only Knows," the hit songs that soared about the airwaves during the summer of 1966. As Paul recalled, "The big influence was *Pet Sounds* by the Beach Boys. That was the album that flipped me. The musical invention on that album was, like, 'Wow!' That was the big time for me. I just thought, 'Oh, dear me. This is *the* album of all time. What the hell are we going to do?'" (qtd. in Badman 256). It was a question that the Beatles would answer—and quite emphatically—in fairly short order.[3]

But the big story in the fall of 1966 was no longer *Pet Sounds*, but rather, the Beach Boy's "Good Vibrations," the pioneering multipart sound collage whose composition had been influenced, at least in part, by *Revolver*. With its dreamy melodies, radiant harmonies, and inspired deployment of the Theremin, "Good Vibrations" emerged as the most influential pop single of all time—at least, that is, until the Beatles, sporting identical moustaches, reconvened after an absence of more than five months at EMI Studios. On November 24th, 1966, John unveiled "Strawberry Fields Forever," the composition that he had begun back in Spain. When he first heard the song in the studio that day, Martin couldn't believe his ears. "It was absolutely lovely," he recalled. "I was spellbound. I was in love" (qtd. in Spitz 654). The composition was recorded over several sessions during a series of organic moments in which the song evolved from its folkish origins into the full-flower of psychedelia. The first session was marked by the introduction of the Mellotron Mark II into the studio. Played by Paul on "Strawberry Fields Forever," the Mellotron is an electromechanical keyboard instrument that creates sound when its keys activate a bank of magnetic, forty-two-foot tape strips. The instrument's prerecorded tapes produce a wide variety of sounds, including string, woodwind, and brass instruments. John had first seen a prototype of the Mellotron back in the summer of 1965. "I must have one of these!" he exclaimed (qtd. in Babiuk 165). "It was a new instrument then," Emerick remembered. "John had one of the first ones, in a polished wooden cabinet. In the end, the Musicians' Union tried to stop manufacture because of the way it reproduced the sounds of other instruments" (qtd. in Lewisohn, *The Complete Beatles Recording Sessions* 87). The first take of "Strawberry Fields Forever" featured John's nasally lead vocal, Paul playing the Mellotron with the instrument's flute setting toggled, and George's twangy slide guitar. A few days later, the group added a rhythm track before treating Lennon's vocals with ADT and overdubbing Paul's Rickenbacker bass part onto the composition. But as far as "Strawberry Fields Forever" was concerned, they were only just beginning.

On December 8th, the Beatles continued shaping the track under the supervision of technical engineer Dave Harries, while Martin and Emerick attended the world premiere of Cliff Richards' film *Finders Keepers*. In their absence, the group recorded Ringo's cymbals, which were replayed backward, Paul and George flailing away on the tympani, and Mal Evans on the tambourine. Neil Aspinall provided additional percussion on the Güiro, a hollow gourd played by rubbing a wooden stick across the instrument's series of parallel notches. After numerous iterations that evening, the Beatles chose takes fifteen and twenty-four for the next phase of the recording life of "Strawberry Fields Forever." That same evening, Paul continued working on "When I'm Sixty-Four," a track that the band had started working on two nights earlier. One of McCartney's earliest compositions from the group's Cavern-era days, "When I'm Sixty-Four" was nothing short of a vaudevillian throwback. On December 9th, George added the sound of a swordmandel, or Indian harp, to "Strawberry Fields Forever," and four trumpets and three cellos were superimposed on tracks three and four of the burgeoning recording, whose two versions now included the original, breezier take of the song and the later, heavily orchestrated rendition. A few days before Christmas, John came up with a solution for addressing the composition's competing versions, both of which met with his authorial approval. Why not splice the two takes together into a single, magnificent whole? "Well, there are only two things against it," Martin told him. "One is that they're in different keys. The other is that they're in different tempos." But for Lennon, there were no limits to the imagination, only temporary obstacles. "Yeah, but you can do something," John told the producer. "You can fix it, George" (qtd. in Everett, *Revolver through the Anthology* 79). Martin and Emerick reasoned that if they sped up the remix of the original version, which was take seven, and then slowed down the remix of the latter version, which was take twenty-six, they could align both recordings in terms of key and tempo. "We gradually decreased the pitch of the first version at the join to make them weld together," Emerick recalled (qtd. in Lewisohn, *The Complete Beatles Recording Sessions* 91). After Martin and Emerick edited the two halves together—the join can be heard at 0:59—"Strawberry Fields Forever" was finally finished, complete with the "free-form coda," in Walter Everett's words, that brings the track to its revolutionary conclusion (*Revolver through the Anthology* 80).[4]

At the end of December, the Beatles began working on "Penny Lane," McCartney's latest composition, which, as with "Strawberry Fields Forever," explores the bandmates' Liverpudlian past. At this juncture, both songs were recorded as part of the group's planned follow-up album to *Revolver*, but by early the next year, they were allocated as the band's next single under pressure from both Epstein and the EMI Group, who were clamoring for new product. As Martin recalled, "Brian Epstein wanted a single and he was genuinely frightened that the Beatles were slipping. He wanted another single out that was going to be a blockbuster, and so I put together 'Strawberry Fields Forever' and 'Penny Lane' and said to him, 'If this isn't going to be a blockbuster, then nothing is!'" (qtd. in Badman 263). Fearing that too much time had elapsed since the last Beatles release, Parlophone released the band's first greatest hits compilation, *A Collection of Beatles Oldies*, in Great Britain in early December 1966. During a December 29th session, Paul devoted several takes to playing the central piano figure that drives "Penny Lane," while adding a supplemental piano part that was played through a Vox guitar amplifier. The next evening, Paul recorded his lead vocal, while John provided a backing vocal, both of which were recorded at a slightly slower speed in order to sound faster—and, hence, brighter—during playback. The Beatles revisited "Penny Lane" during the new year, although work on the song was halted on January 5th, while John and Paul attended to "Carnival of Light," an *avant-garde* recording that had been invited for presentation by the organizers of *The Million Volt Light and Sound Rave*, an art festival comprised of electronic music and light shows that would debut on January 28th at London's Roundhouse Theatre. By turns hypnotic, surreal, and frightening, "Carnival of Light" consists of nearly fourteen minutes' worth of electronic noise, prefiguring the experimental soundscapes of *The White Album*'s "Revolution 9" in the process. With assistance from Ringo—

along with bemused looks from Martin and Harrison, who were decidedly unimpressed with the recording—the duo superimposed a host of distorted drum and organ sounds onto the track, as well as tape echo and random interjections by John and Paul, including "Are you alright?" and "Barcelona!"[5]

On January 6th, the Beatles continued working on "Penny Lane," with John, Paul, and George providing a guide vocal by scat singing during the bars where additional musical accompaniment—including four flutes, two piccolos, two trumpets, and a flügelhorn—would be overdubbed later. The next evening, a set of orchestral chimes was added to the mix, with a tubular bell being rung whenever the song referenced the fireman or his fire-engine—his "clean machine." Studio musicians complemented the accompaniment from the January 6th session with two trumpets, two oboes, two *cor anglais* (English horns), and a double-bass. The Beatles finally completed "Penny Lane" during a whirlwind session on January 19th. A few days earlier, Paul had seen musician David Mason playing the trumpet on Bach's *Brandenburg Concerto No. 2 in F Major* for the BBC program *Masterworks*. A member of the New Philharmonia Orchestra, Mason was summarily recruited to play the piccolo trumpet solo on "Penny Lane." In its quaint magnificence, Mason's solo afforded the song with the perfect note of tradition befitting the composition's highly imaginative and nostalgic study of the past.

As with "Strawberry Fields Forever," "Penny Lane" offers a dreamlike veneration of youth and the power of memory. John wanted "Strawberry Fields Forever" to sound "like a conversation" among the song's various selves, but ultimately, "Strawberry Fields Forever" engages in conversation with "Penny Lane" about the telling discrepancies between illusion and reality (qtd. in Everett, *Revolver through the Anthology* 75). Both songs are the logical result of *Rubber Soul* and *Revolver*, given the former album's nostalgic search for wholeness and the latter's journey toward consciousness—the natural progression of humanity as we move from different states of living toward the death-drive itself. Having explored those vistas of meaning rather fully on the last two Beatles albums, John and Paul gazed inwardly and toward the past in "Strawberry Fields Forever" and "Penny Lane" in order to resurrect childhood memories and establish a sense of connectedness and transcendence. In this sense, a nostalgic return seems rather appropriate at this juncture of their career. By calling such considerable attention to the notion of innocence, "Strawberry Fields Forever" and "Penny Lane" underscore its increasing absence from their lives—and from our own.[6]

For Lennon and McCartney, the past functions as a living, breathing thing. "Strawberry Fields Forever" and "Penny Lane" merge a pair of realistic settings with the brash sentimentality of memory. In this manner, both songs establish a sense of pastness upon which they reflect the quotidian life of a fictive universe that brims with the spurious whimsy of nostalgia. As place names with actual Liverpudlian antecedents, "Penny Lane" and "Strawberry Fields" reflect each songwriter's interest in demonstrating nostalgia's time-bending and reality-skewing powers. As W. Edson Richmond observes, "The place names of any land reflect not only its topography but its history, its heroes (and villains), its cultural and intellectual development, and the peculiarities of its language as well" (23). In many ways, the Beatles capitalize on the dreamlike spirit of their childhood memories of Liverpool in "Penny Lane" and "Strawberry Fields Forever"—songs that establish, quite literally, the unspoken topography of *Rubber Soul*'s "In My Life."

Not surprisingly, Paul's inspiration for "Penny Lane" finds its origins in "Fern Hill," Dylan Thomas's beloved poem about the halcyon days of childhood: "Now as I was young and easy under the apple boughs / About the lilting house and happy as the grass was green, / The night above the dingle starry," Thomas writes. "Time let me hail and climb / Golden in the heyday of his eyes" (178). Named after a Liverpool bus roundabout, "Penny Lane" offers a shrewd reading of the manner in which we frequently reconceive the past in our memories, as with Thomas's poem, in order to imbue it with idyllic hues.[7] "Memory," Nancy Martha West observes, "depends on a personalized narrative; nostalgia transforms that narrative (including the possible stresses and uncertainties of events in progress) into fullness, innocence, simplicity" (175). Semantically, "Penny Lane" connotes a negligible amount of money, the elevation of life's simple pleasures over the pursuit of wealth (*OED*); for McCartney, this is a crucial sentiment, given the song's surface reverie about carefree life in a city center. Indeed, with its overarching "blue suburban skies" and perpetually convivial environs, "Penny Lane" effects a utopian neighborhood where life borders on perfection and even the banker eschews a raincoat despite the "pouring rain." In "Penny Lane," McCartney's dreamlike refrain— "very strange"—suggests the ways in which the stuff of memory might be all too easily manipulated in order to conform with our most fervent desires for impeding the past's irrevocable course. In "Penny Lane," a "pretty nurse is selling poppies from a tray"—an overt reference to Armistice Day (November 11th), when the veterans of world wars are honored through the act of collectively remembering the past. In the song's most ironic instance, Paul identifies the nurse's discrepant awareness of her real and illusory lives: "And though she feels as if she's in a play, / She is anyway." Lennon investigates similar terrain in "Strawberry Fields Forever," a song that takes its name from a Liverpool Salvation Army home called Strawberry Field. A place where "nothing is real" and where there is "nothing to get hung about," the Strawberry Fields of Lennon's composition invoke the pulpy, pungent fragrance of wild strawberries. In so doing, the lyrics and music create a peaceful, liberating space where "living is easy with eyes closed," a sea of tranquility in dramatic contrast with the invariably more complicated reality of the present. As with the multicolored ambience inherent in the "Marmalade skies" of the forthcoming "Lucy in the Sky with Diamonds," "Strawberry Fields" connotes blithe and liberating possibilities for reflecting upon the past through nostalgia's sentimentalized lens. The song also invites us to delight in the dreamstates of childhood in spite of the stultifying distance of maturity and middle-age.

In his description of "Penny Lane," Wilfred Mellers underscores the manner in which both sides of the Beatles' latest single address the enduring role of our childhoods well into our adult lives: "For both musical and verbal reasons the song comes out as childishly merry yet dreamily wild at the same time," Mellers writes. "The hallucinatory feeling concerns problems of identity rather than drugs specifically, asking what, among our childhood memories, is reality and what is illusion" (83). In itself, this question encapsulates the latter years of the Beatles' musical journey. How, indeed, are our identities shaped by our childhoods, our periods of loneliness and triumph, our unquenchable nostalgia for the past and a deep yearning and optimism for an unknown but no less hopeful future? The "Strawberry Fields Forever"/"Penny Lane" single pointedly begins with an invitation—"Let me take you down"—and concludes with the sensory imagery of the "blue suburban skies" of youth. The coda for "Strawberry Fields Forever," which effectively exists as the textual conduit between the two sides of the single, provides listeners with a deceptive fadeout, a false ending in which the music effects a return, in the circular fashion of Joyce's *Finnegans Wake*, only to undercut the seeming finality of the past, which comes alive yet again with the sweet whimsy of "Penny Lane." Released on February 17th, 1967, the single stalled in second place behind Englebert Humperdinck's massive hit "Release Me." After twelve straight number-one singles on the UK charts, the Beatles had come up short with number thirteen. But no matter—the band's latest single was a pure work of art, and any variation in commercial success was meaningless in terms of its larger creative significance. "In my estimation," Martin later remarked, "it was the best record we ever made" (qtd. in Everett, *Revolver through the Anthology* 87).

~

With the completion of the "Strawberry Fields Forever"/"Penny Lane" single in mid-January 1967, the Beatles were left with "When I'm Sixty-Four" as the only composition that they had recorded for their unnamed album-length project. Although the single was obviously a high-water mark for the band, they had been drifting along somewhat aimlessly in the months following their retirement from life on the road. In fact, George Martin argues that the recording of the album through this juncture had been "out of control." As Allan F. Moore observes, the Beatles had been "virtually incommunicado" during their latest recording sessions, and, with the exception of "Carnival of Light," they had severed themselves almost entirely from the external world (25). Yet in mid-January, the album began to gather steam with the initial session for an exciting new Lennon composition that sported the working title of "In the Life of. . . ." On February 1st, the album gained even more coherence with the recording of a new McCartney song about a fictitious, Edwardian military-style band. Flying back from the United States with Mal Evans, who had been working as his housekeeper on Cavendish Avenue for the past several months, Paul came up with the idea of establishing alter-egos for the band:

> We were fed up with being the Beatles. We really hated that fucking four little Mop-Top boys approach. We were not boys, we were men. It was all gone, all that boy shit, all that screaming, we didn't want any more, plus, we'd now got turned on to pot and thought of ourselves as artists rather than just performers. . . . Then suddenly on the plane I got this idea. I thought, "Let's not be ourselves. Let's develop alter-egos so we're not having to project an image which we know." (qtd. in Miles 303)

After Paul imagined the album's overarching concept, Mal Evans coined the *faux* band's name—Sgt. Pepper's Lonely Hearts Club Band—in the tradition of the contemporary San Francisco-area groups with longwinded handles such as Big Brother and the Holding Company or the Quicksilver Messenger Service.

With a title track in hand, the Beatles' follow-up album to *Revolver* took shape in a hurry. Picking up where *Revolver* left off, *Sgt. Pepper* continues the Beatles' exploration of consciousness (and the sociocultural lack thereof) by depicting various degrees of interrelational distance, as well as the human cost of communal detachment, on a macro level, and unchecked loneliness, from an individual perspective. "Sgt. Pepper's Lonely Hearts Club Band" stages the Beatles' transformation from the familiar Fab Four of yore into Sgt. Pepper's band, a strange admixture of traditional brass instrumentation and sizzling hard-rock—decidedly harder rock, in fact, than any previous Beatles track. As the song commences, the ambient noise of an orchestra warming up can be heard. And that's when the misdirection begins: rather than the anticipated sounds of classical music, the listener is confounded by the ecstatic blare of hard-driving guitar rock. Surely, this isn't the Beatles? And then the lead vocalist interrupts the din, singing—or, perhaps more accurately, *shrieking*—his introduction:

It was twenty years ago today,
Sgt. Pepper taught the band to play.
They've been going in and out of style,
But they're guaranteed to raise a smile.
So may I introduce to you
The act you've known for all these years?
Sgt. Pepper's Lonely Hearts Club Band.

The lyrics, in themselves, are a revolutionary moment in the creative life of the Beatles, given their explicit penetration of the so-called Fourth Wall that divides artists from their audiences. As if to provide palpable reassurance for the group's understandably bewildered fans, McCartney reminds us that they're "the act you've know for all these years." Sure, they may sound a bit more raucous, but they're still the Mop Tops, only they're now sporting epaulets, moustaches, and multicolored attire. As if by magic, the guitars in the title track transmogrify into a regal quartet of French horns, and the audience—as they begin to realize the song's humorous undertones—erupts in a giddy fusillade of laughter that borders on condescension. Are they laughing along with the proceedings—or *at* them?

As the vocalists reenter the mix—singing, "We're Sgt. Pepper's Lonely Hearts Club Band"—the brass ensemble gives way to a dirty undercurrent of electric guitars, courtesy of John's Casino, Paul's Fender Esquire, and George's Gibson SG Standard.[8] It's an element of organic rock fusion that we've never heard before from the Beatles, and its intentionally unsettling quality is mirrored by the song's lyrical overtures to the group's horde of anxious fans:

It's wonderful to be here,
It's certainly a thrill.
You're such a lovely audience,
We'd like to take you home with us,
We'd love to take you home.

On the one hand, the lyrics exemplify the mindless rhetoric of rock concert banter; yet on the other, they mock the very notion of a pop album's capacity for engendering authentic interconnection between artist and audience in the first place. By simultaneously gesturing toward their audience and yet keeping them at arm's length, are the Beatles shrinking or increasing the textual distance between themselves and their massive international audience? Or, paradoxically, are they doing *both*?

The ironic authorial distance is the song's most salient feature. As Virginia Woolf famously observed, "So much depends upon distance" (191). With "Sgt.

Pepper's Lonely Hearts Club Band," the Beatles manufacture an artificial textual space in which to stage their art. In so doing, they call their media-generated personae into question, revising and repackaging themselves in the
process in order to create new spaces of possibility. "The 'Pepper' idea," Walter
Everett points out, "allowed the Beatles to remove themselves from the public
by an extra layer—they were now giving a performance of a performance"
(*Revolver through the Anthology* 99). As the title track continues, the master-
vocalist of ceremonies unveils yet another surprise: "So let me introduce to
you / The one and only Billy Shears." / And Sgt. Pepper's Lonely Hearts Club
Band." As if their revamped musical identity weren't enough to fathom
already, the bandmates dare to confront their listeners with a new member
altogether. The beauty of being a studio production in their entirety, of course,
is that the Beatles can assume total control of their representation beyond the
confines of the recording complex. As Mark Hertsgaard remarks: "By pretend-
ing to be somebody else (and a somewhat hapless bunch at that), they both
escaped and deflated their media image while laughing at both themselves and
the public. They punctured the absurdity of stardom by stepping outside of it"
(213). But the Beatles' psychedelic masquerade had only just started.

The album's title track offered the first hint of the band's evolving creative
promise. Musically, "Sgt. Pepper's Lonely Hearts Club Band" was bolstered by
direct injection, the technique devised by Ken Townshend in which electric
guitars are plugged directly into the mixing desk, thus mitigating the need for
amplifiers in the studio. "One of the most difficult instruments to record was
the bass guitar," Townshend recalled. "The problem was that no matter which
type of high quality microphone we placed in front of the bass speaker it never
sounded back in the control room as good as in the studio" (qtd. in Ryan and
Kehew 156). In the case of "Sgt. Pepper," Paul had availed himself of direct
injection during the song's initial recording session on February 1st. It was the
first usage of this technology on a Beatles track, and it afforded McCartney's
bass with richer textures and tonal clarity. Meanwhile, the track was chockfull
of special effects, with the canned laughter and audience applause courtesy of
the satirical British stage revue *Beyond the Fringe*, which had been borrowed
from the EMI tape library's *Volume 6: Applause and Laughter* (Moore 27). The
sound of the orchestra warming up was recorded on February 10th during the
orchestral overdubs for "A Day in the Life," the album's climactic number. Perhaps even more intriguingly, *Sgt. Pepper's Lonely Hearts Club Band* was the
first Beatles LP—indeed, the first pop recording—to be mastered without rills,
eschewing any formal breaks between songs because Martin had explicitly
instructed the engineers not to band the album into individual tracks. By
doing away with the rills—the silent spaces of demarcation between songs on

long-playing records—the Beatles succeeded in using every available creative space at their disposal, transitioning from one number into another without bothering to slow the pace of their art, while employing the ending of one song as the introduction to another.

As *Sgt. Pepper*'s title track segues into "With a Little Help from My Friends"—with Martin shrewdly masking the edit between the songs in a warm bath of screaming fans that he had recorded during one of the group's concerts at the Hollywood Bowl—the Beatles' elaborate stage play moves ever forward. As the raw power of "Sgt. Pepper" disappears behind the tumult, Billy Shears emerges as none other than the comforting baritone voice of Ringo, the most universally beloved member of the Beatles, and all is right with the world once more, if only briefly. Written at Paul's home on Cavendish Avenue with Paul on piano and John on guitar, "With a Little Help from My Friends" went under the working title of "Bad Finger Boogie."[9] Direct-injected on his Rickenbacker, Paul's splendid, melodic bass lines imbue the composition with a heartfelt air, and the lyrics resonate with the charming sincerity of Ringo's lead vocal, which affords the entire production with a sense of earnestness in sharp contrast with the ironic distance of the title track. In "With a Little Help from My Friends," John, Paul, and George's call-and-response backing vocals interrogate Ringo—or, within the context of the album, Billy Shears—about the essence of true love and unerring friendship:

> (Would you believe in a love at first sight?)
> Yes, I'm certain that it happens all the time.
> (What do you see when you turn out the light?)
> I can't tell you, but I know it's mine.

The wonderful internal ambiguity inherent in the speaker's ultimate response to his tribunal—"I can't tell you, but I know it's mine"—demonstrates his understanding of the tentative and fleeting nature of romance. Whomever he is within the margins of *Sgt. Pepper's Lonely Hearts Club Band*, Billy Shears certainly isn't a man who kisses and tells about it later. The song's larger, unblanched message about the necessity of community—the idea of getting by, of getting high in a natural sense, of trying to engage life on its own terms—is the central ethical tenet of "With a Little Help from My friends," as well as of the album as a whole. To embrace lived experiences, as opposed to turning away and becoming emotionally vacant, emerges as the dominant Lennon-McCartney philosophy in the wake of *Revolver*'s rallying call on behalf of human consciousness.

The concept of imagined experience is the thematic focus of "Lucy in the Sky with Diamonds," the colorful, Lewis Carroll-inspired musical adventure that found its origins in three-year-old Julian Lennon's painting of a classmate named Lucy: "It's Lucy, in the sky, with diamonds," he told his father.[10] In the composition's phantasmagoria, the Beatles achieve their most vivid instance of musical timbre by merging the nonsensicality and visual imagery of John's lyrics with the ADT-treated sounds of Paul's unforgettable Lowrey organ intro-duction, George's hypnotic tamboura, and John's dreamy lead vocal. The sense of mystery and adventure is heightened by shifts in both key and time signa-ture. The verses float along merrily in 3/4 time, while common time establishes a more insistent mood for the chorus. According to Lennon, the song's princi-pal images hail from *Through the Looking-Glass, and What Alice Found There* (1871), the sequel to Carroll's *Alice's Adventures in Wonderland* (1865):

> It was Alice in the boat. She is buying an egg and it turns into Humpty Dumpty. The woman serving in the shop turns into a sheep and the next minute they are rowing in a rowing boat somewhere and I was visualizing that. There was also the image of the female who would someday come save me—a "girl with kalei-doscope eyes" who would come out of the sky. (*All We Are Saying* 181)

In this way, "Lucy in the Sky with Diamonds" invokes the momentous scene in *Through the Looking-Glass* as Alice glides down the river—"A boat beneath a sunny sky, / Lingering onward dreamily"—setting her magical journey into motion. As with "Strawberry Fields Forever," "Lucy in the Sky with Diamonds" greets its listeners with an invitation in the form of an imperative: "Picture yourself in a boat on a river." The dreamstate continues with the inventive imagery of "cellophane flowers," "rocking horse people," "newspaper taxis," and "looking glass ties," as well as the alliterative "tangerine trees" and "plas-ticine porters." By channeling nonsensicality into narrative reality, Lennon succeeds in espousing the power of textual experience—of enticing the Beat-les' listeners to join Lucy at the turnstile of surreal life.

While "Lucy in the Sky with Diamonds" acts as the gateway number into the group's imaginative explorations of musical timbre during their psychedelic era, "Getting Better" challenges the band's audience to usurp the past by living well and flourishing in the present. With John taking his Rickenbacker 325 out of mothballs to join Paul's pulsing Fender Esquire and George's droning tam-boura, "Getting Better" offers a driving rock sound in contrast with its multi-colored counterparts on *Sgt. Pepper*. The song's title finds its roots in the words of Jimmy Nicol, who employed "getting better" as his stock-phrase during his brief stint as Ringo's replacement in the early summer of 1964. Recorded on March 1st, the session for "Getting Better" was truncated by an untimely Lennon acid trip. Concerned about his colleague's anxious demeanor and unaware of his recent ingestion of LSD, Martin took John on the roof of EMI

Studios to get some fresh air. Realizing that Lennon could easily fall off of the roof in his altered state, the other Beatles rushed upstairs in the nick of time (Badman 271). It was one of the few occasions, interestingly enough, when the band's legendary drug usage interrupted their work in the studio. As a true collaboration between John and Paul "Getting Better" posits Lennon's ironic "couldn't get much worse" as a sarcastic rejoinder to McCartney's hopeful chorus, "It's getting better all the time." Paul later described John's riposte as "against the spirit of the song, which was all super-optimistic—then there's that lovely little sardonic line. Typical John" (qtd. in Everett, *Revolver through the Anthology* 106). The song also features Lennon's confessional lyrics about his violent treatment of women in the past. "I used to be cruel to my woman," John recalled, "and physically—any woman. I was a hitter. I couldn't express myself, and I hit" (qtd. in Dowlding 168). After admitting to his days as an "angry young man"—an intriguing (and hardly accidental) invocation by Lennon and McCartney of the culture of alienation represented in such 1950s-era literary works as Kingsley Amis's *Lucky Jim* (1954) and John Osborne's *Look Back in Anger* (1956)—the speaker enjoins his listeners to live by his example and alter their own angst-ridden ways: "Man, I was mean but I'm changing my scene, / And I'm doing the best that I can."

With "Fixing a Hole," Paul advocates a similar ethical stance about the reification of personal identity. Other than their recordings at Paris's Pathé Marconi Studios in January 1964, the Beatles' production of "Fixing a Hole" on February 9th at Regent Sound marked a rare session that had occurred beyond the confines of EMI Studios, which was unavailable that evening. With Paul effecting a sprightly harpsichord and George playing a quirky distorted solo on his Sonic Blue Strat, "Fixing a Hole" offers a study in musical timbre. Inspired by repairs that McCartney needed to make on his Scottish farmhouse, "Fixing a Hole" finds Paul refashioning a line—"Well, there's a hole in the roof where the rain pours in"—from Elvis Presley's "We're Gonna Move" (Everett, *Revolver through the Anthology* 107). In "Fixing a Hole," the speaker reveals a deep need to clear his mind and recapture a sense of selfhood in the face of the workaday world: "I'm taking my time for a number of things / That weren't important yesterday." In the larger tableau of *Sgt. Pepper*, "Fixing a Hole" addresses the speaker's search for identity among the crowd, particularly the individual quests for consciousness and connection that distinguish him from the vacuousness of the mass culture in which he finds himself. The song also features an interesting redaction, on Paul's part, of the one-sided power dynamics that he had earlier expressed in "We Can Work It Out." In "Fixing a Hole," Paul pointedly adopts a more pacific worldview: "And it really doesn't matter if I'm wrong / I'm right where I belong / I'm right where I belong."

Notions of belonging, and the pointed lack thereof, exist at the forefront of "She's Leaving Home," a song, in Bill Martin's words, "where growing up, 'liberation' if you will, and sorrow are inextricably intertwined" (17). Paul discovered his inspiration for the composition in the newspaper headlines—specifically, in the found object, the *objet trouvé*, of a *Daily Mail* article about the increasing phenomenon of teenage runaways. McCartney had been drawn to the case of seventeen-year-old Melanie Coe, who had run away from home to join a man whom she had met at a gambling casino. "My mother didn't like any of my friends," the troubled teen remarked after rejoining her distraught family. "I wasn't allowed to bring anyone home. She didn't like me going out. She didn't like the way I dressed." Melanie's father was confused by his daughter's decision to leave the family home, particularly in light of the many material comforts that Melanie enjoyed: "I can't imagine why she'd run away. She has everything here. She is very keen on clothes, but she left it all, even her fur coat" (qtd. in Cross 438).[11] When an enthusiastic McCartney arrived at EMI Studios in March 1967 to begin work on his latest composition, he learned that George Martin was otherwise indisposed with a Cilla Black session. Caught up in the excitement of the song, Paul simply didn't want to wait, enlisting the services of Mike Leander as the arranger for "She's Leaving Home": "I had one of those 'I've got to go, I've got to go!' feelings and when you get those, you don't want anything to stop you," Paul recollected. "You feel like if you lose the impetus, you'll lose something valuable" (qtd. in Cross 438). Although he later conducted the studio musicians with his usual professionalism during the March 17th orchestral overdub, Martin was bothered by Paul's impatience. "I minded like hell," the producer later recalled about Paul's employment of a different arranger (qtd. in O'Gorman 242).

As it turns out, Leander's arrangement coaxed a memorable harp performance from Sheila Bromberg, while it also provided a moving palette for Paul's quaint study of a young woman's need to discover a sense of identity and become a conscious participant in the world.[12] As with "You've Got to Hide Your Love Away" and "Eleanor Rigby," the composition examines the human cost of inveterate loneliness, and in the case of "She's Leaving Home," the young woman's parents emerge as her insular, albeit loving, subjugators. After "leaving the note that she hoped would say more," the song's protagonist escapes into the waiting world: "Stepping outside, she is free." In its pure simplicity, the track's chorus provides one of John and Paul's most beautiful vocal duets:

> She (We gave her most of our lives)
> Is leaving (Sacrificed most of our lives)
> Home (We gave her everything money could buy)

In keeping with the article in the *Daily Mail*, "She's Leaving Home" eschews objectivity and passes judgment on the parents for neglecting their daughter's emotional needs in favor of what they perceive to be her overarching consumeristic desires.[13] Their daughter begins her new life by "meeting a man from the motor trade," and a spiccato violin flourish underscores the good tidings of this event in McCartney's miniature fable. Meanwhile, her parents come to the terrible recognition that they had given her everything but simple human pleasure: "Fun is the one thing that money can't buy," John sings. "Something inside that was always denied / For so many years," Paul adds in resplendent narration. As with much of the rest of the album, "She's Leaving Home" is about embracing consciousness—in this instance, for both the parents and their estranged daughter. "We didn't know it was wrong," the parents lament in the song's dénouement. Is the conclusion hopeful, or is the family's separation permanent?

Sgt. Pepper's Lonely Hearts Club Band reaches its halfway point with "Being for the Benefit of Mr. Kite!" Lennon transcribed the lyrics verbatim from a circus poster that he had purchased during the filming of the "Strawberry Fields Forever" promotional video in Sevenoaks, Kent. The poster advertised a circus near Rochdale, Lancashire, in February 1843, and John later described his musical interpretation of this found object—the found "poetry" of the circus poster—as "pure, like a painting, a pure watercolor" (qtd. in Dowlding 173). By taking the existing language of the circus poster and setting it to music in an entirely different venue, Lennon creates a mixed-media production in "Being for the Benefit of Mr. Kite!" In this case, the poster acts as the Ur-text, and, when combined with the Beatles' music, it becomes reinterpreted. "The key question about musical meaning," Lawrence Kramer points out, "is not whether it can be ascribed; it is ascribed all the time" (164). With "Being for the Benefit of Mr. Kite!" John succeeds, then, in textually reinscribing the circus poster, which, within the context of the revivified track on *Sgt. Pepper*, experiences new layers of meaning. "What interpretation carries over from the mixed-media application is the productive power of the ascriptive process, by which the music both absorbs meaning and returns it in new or heightened form," Kramer adds. "The musical details produce meaning precisely by exemplifying a meaning that exceeds them" (165). In terms of "Being for the Benefit of Mr. Kite!" the interpretive power of the mixed-media application accrues its meaning through the musical production with which the group imbues the Ur-text of the poster. With John playing the Hammond organ and Martin working the countermelody on a carnivalesque Wurlitzer, the track's instrumentation finds Paul concocting a lively, imaginative bass part on his Rickenbacker and George, Ringo, Mal, and Neil on a quartet of harmonicas. On

February 20th, Emerick diced up small sections of old calliope tapes of Sousa marches, tossed them in the air, and then randomly reassembled them during the song's pair of middle-eight musical interludes. The more conventional, circus atmosphere of the first passage is counterpoised by the madcap, at times insidious, music of the second, in which the circus train has figuratively fallen off of its tracks. It's a masterpiece of aural effect that casts the rest of the song into spellbinding question. By merging the Beatles' psychedelic music with the Edwardian circus motif inherent in the Ur-text, "Being for the Benefit of Mr. Kite!" takes on a multiplicity of meanings that ultimately serve to disrupt both musical and temporal contexts in the same instant—and thus becoming a transhistorical work of art in the process.

In "Within You Without You," Harrison grapples with transhistorical issues of another sort altogether—in this case, the world of Eastern philosophy and its relevance to Western value systems, which exist at variance with the former ontology's dicta about the reality of being human. "Within You Without You" was the final composition recorded for the album. Written by Harrison on the harmonium at Klaus Voormann's Hampstead home, the song went under the working title of "Not Known," yet another clever nontitle from George. The basic track was realized at a March 15th session, which featured George on sitar with a gauzy ADT-treated vocal, Neil Aspinall on tamboura, and session musicians from London's Asian Music Circle on dilruba, tamboura, tabla, and swordmandel. Martin later overdubbed eight violins and three cellos onto the composition, which features a tempo rubato—unique among the Beatles' corpus—which involves a flexible or fluctuating tempo that maximizes the song's capacity for expressiveness. "The best part of it for me," Harrison recalled in *I Me Mine* (1980), "is the instrumental solo in the middle which is in 5/4 time—the first of the strange rhythm cycles that I caught on to—one-two; one-two-three; one-two-one-two-three" (112). George's earlier contribution to the album, "Only a Northern Song," was recorded in February and rejected by his bandmates, especially Lennon, who felt that the composition's dour dismissiveness conflicted with the egalitarian spirit of *Sgt. Pepper*. By contrast, "Within You Without You" represents, quite arguably, the album's ethical soul. Harrison based his composition on the Hindustani philosophy of *Maya*, which contends that the idea of humanity is the only genuine notion of reality, that mortals generally believe in false realities—"walls of illusion"—well beyond the scope of their corporeal selves. In "Within You Without You," George sings "about the space between us all / And the people who hide themselves behind a wall of illusion." Harrison's *Mayan* discourse establishes the firmament for the Beatles' utopian sentiments that ultimately propel the Summer of Love into being: "With our love we could save the world," George sings. Chosen by the songwriter in an effort to sustain the album's convivial mood in spite of the song's weighty contents, the laughter overdubbed at the conclusion of the song was selected from *Volume 6: Applause and Laughter* in the EMI tape library.

Demure in contrast with the disdainful laughter depicted in the title track, the woman's disarming giggle of amusement at the end of "Within You Without You" effects a subtle transition into the Vaudevillian past where "When I'm Sixty-Four" resides.[14] With Ringo working the chimes and studio musicians on a trio of clarinets, Paul takes the Beatles' study of consciousness into the existential uncertainty of the sunset years: "When I get older losing my hair, / Many years from now," McCartney sings. "Will you still be sending me a valentine, / Birthday greetings, bottle of wine?" The recording was undoubtedly inspired by Paul's father, Jim, who turned sixty-four in July 1966. The musical roots of "When I'm Sixty-Four" actually run much deeper, to 1958, when Paul composed the rudiments of the song on the family piano at Forthlin Road, and the Beatles included an earlier version of the number in their stage repertoire during their Hamburg days. The generic differences between "When I'm Sixty-Four" and "Lovely Rita," *Sgt. Pepper*'s next cut, couldn't be greater. One moment, the Beatles are swinging to the sounds of yesteryear before sashaying into full-tilt psychedelia in the very next instant. In many ways, "Lovely Rita" is the album's only genuine trifle, presaging the band's less-effectual composition's during the post-*Pepper* months of 1967. Famously featuring all four bandmates forcing swathes of toilet paper through metal combs, "Lovely Rita" offers another example of McCartney's yen for creating imagistic musical portraiture—inspired, in this case, by traffic warden Meta Davis, who had recently issued a parking ticket to an unsuspecting Paul. While the song accomplishes little in the way of advancing the album's journey toward a more expansive human consciousness, the music is irresistibly charming, with Martin playing a nifty barrelhouse piano (courtesy of his trademark wound-up piano effect) and George reaping all manner of irreverent musical color on his slide-driven Fender Strat.

Sgt. Pepper's final act begins with the sound of a rooster crowing the introduction to John's "Good Morning, Good Morning." Although in later years the songwriter would dismiss the composition as a "throwaway, a piece of garbage," "Good Morning, Good Morning" offers a note-perfect overture for the Beatles' final assault on human consciousness (qtd. in Dowlding 179). Lennon found his inspiration, rather appropriately, in a television commercial for Kellogg's Corn Flakes: "Good morning, good morning, / The best to you each morning, / Sunshine breakfast, Kellogg's Corn Flakes, / Crisp and full of fun." Shifting wildly amongst 5/4, 3/4, and 4/4 time signatures, the song is a masterpiece of electrical energy, with John's kinetic vocal—heavily treated with ADT and with the singer's inner boredom at the very thought of enduring yet another day of unchecked tedium—as well as with Paul's blistering guitar solo on his Fender Esquire. The beefy brass and saxophone stylings of Sounds Incorporated underscore the speaker's perfunctory worldview and his utter inability to express himself, to connect with other people in any meaningful fashion whatsoever. He conceals his interior vacancy behind a breezy façade of urban-cool: "I've got nothing to say, but it's okay," he repeats to himself like a mantra. The song's middle-eight proves to be his release, the only moment in which his mounting desperation and anxiety truly come alive:

> Everybody knows there's nothing doing,
> Everything is closed, it's like a ruin,
> Everyone you see is half-asleep.
> And you're on your own, you're in the street.

For the speaker, there is literally no hope in sight, only a lifetime of interminable sameness. As the song devolves into a sea of gleeful, albeit no less empty, salutations—"Good morning, good morning, good!"—the mix is overwhelmed by, of all things, a barnyard menagerie.[15]

It is, without question, one of the Beatles' most cinematic moments on record. In the ensuing chaos of animalia, an English fox hunt runs well adrift of its brushy covert and into the sweeping pastures of a family farm. As a wayward lion's roar echoes in the distance, the sound of a clucking hen transforms into the cold-steel pluck of an Epiphone Casino. And Sgt. Pepper's band begins to play once more, fuelled by the thunder and growl of a hard-rocking combo, the stately brass quartet evidently having called it quits for the evening.[16] Having reached its conclusion, the reprise of "Sgt. Pepper's Lonely Hearts Club Band" crashes into an oblivion of cheers and applause, the audience settling in gamely for "A Day in the Life," the album's (if not the Beatles') most stunning, luminous achievement. As with McCartney's "She's Leaving Home," Lennon discovered his muse in the found objects of newspaper headlines. A December 19th, 1966, issue of the *Daily Sketch* published a photo of Tara Browne's grisly car crash. The twenty-one-year-old heir to the Guinness fortune had blown his mind out in a car after speeding through the streets of South Kensington in his sleek Lotus Elan with his girlfriend, runway model Suki Potier, in tow. Blazing through a traffic light at more than 100 mph, he smashed the sports car into a truck that was parked across the intersection. Browne was killed instantly. Amazingly, Potier survived the collision and was relatively unscathed. Lennon brought his composition to fruition with imagery from a January 17th, 1967, article in the *Daily Mail* on "The Holes in

Our Roads." As John later recalled, it "was a story about 4,000 potholes in Blackburn, Lancashire, that needed to be filled." After hearing John's original verses for "A Day in the Life," Paul shared the song that would eventually comprise the middle-eight for Lennon's original text. Paul had borrowed the passage's opening phrase from the first line of Dorothy Fields's 1930 hit "On the Sunny Side of the Street." McCartney was also responsible for crafting "I'd love to turn you on" into the song's one-line chorus, which Lennon described as a "damn good piece of work" (*All We Are Saying* 184).

The Beatles began recording "A Day in the Life" on January 19th, with John counting off the first take by muttering "sugar plum fairy, sugar plum fairy" in rhythm with the ensuing acoustic guitar part that he strummed on his Jumbo. In addition to John's echo-laden lead vocal, the instrumentation included Paul on piano, George on maracas, and Ringo on the bongos. Take four featured Mal Evans counting out twenty-four bars in order to afford space for future musical adornment before setting off an alarm clock (at 2:18) to mark Paul's entrance during the middle-eight.[17] The next evening, Paul overdubbed a bass track on his Rickenbacker and recorded a rough version of his lead vocal. During the February 3rd session, Paul re-recorded his vocal, with the alarm clock appropriately sounding a split second before he sings, "Woke up, fell out of bed." That same day, Ringo came up with one of his most inventive drum parts on record. Despite the drummer's words of protests—"Come on, Paul, you know how much I hate flashy drumming"—McCartney talked Ringo into trying out the fantastic, innovative tom-tom fills that punctuate the lyrics of "A Day in the Life" (qtd. in Emerick 149).[18] Emerick punched up the sound of Ringo's drums by removing the bottom heads from his tom-toms and placing microphones directly beneath them.

On February 10th, the Beatles made history during one of their most chaotic sessions to date. With seven movie cameras running, Paul directed a forty-piece orchestra, its membership having been culled from the London Philharmonic and the Royal Philharmonic. Their mission? To fill in Mal Evans's twenty-four empty bars with the sound of pure apocalypse. Instead of asking Martin to provide the musicians with a score, Paul distributed written instructions to the players, as opposed to musical notation: "We just wrote it down like a cooking recipe," McCartney recalled. "Twenty-four bars, on the ninth bar the orchestra will take off and it will go from its lowest note to its highest note." In an effort to establish the appropriately zany atmosphere in cavernous Studio One, the Beatles asked the guest musicians, whose number included Alan Civil and David Mason, to dress the part. As Ian Peel points out, McCartney was evoking the "outlandish performance art of Stockhausen" by requesting that the orchestra members attend the session in formal evening dress, while wearing funny masks, false teeth, and bulbous noses (39). For his own part, Paul donned a kitchen apron for the occasion. A variety of rock and roll personalities were present, including Mick Jagger, Marianne Faithful, Keith Richards, Donovan (born Donovan Philips Leitch), and Michael Nesmith. Meanwhile, John—with a bald wig perched awkwardly on his head—wore an outrageous blue-velvet coat (Winn, *That Magic Feeling* 97).

In spite of the convivial mood, the classically trained musicians were not very keen on performing in such an unscripted fashion. The orchestral passages for "A Day in the Life" required them to create a massive crescendo in the space of two dozen measures. According to Martin, both composers had suggested the orchestral passages, with McCartney hoping for a "freak-out" and Lennon desiring a "tremendous build-up, from nothing up to something absolutely like the end of the world" (qtd. in Everett, *Revolver through the Anthology* 118). Emerick recorded the musicians on two separate tape machines in order to delay the signal at varying intervals. This tactic was supplemented by the pioneering use of ambiophonics on the track. The process of creating "ambiophony" involved the placement of one hundred loudspeakers along all four walls of Studio One. A forerunner of contemporary surround-sound, ambiophonics assisted Emerick in capturing the orchestra's powerful crescendos. With the work of the studio musicians complete, the Beatles turned to the conclusion of "A Day in the Life," a composition that demanded the appropriate punctuation mark for the most evocative rallying call to consciousness in the Lennon-McCartney songbook. The initial ending for the track was going to be a "choir of voices" singing a long "hummm-mmm," an effect that they attempted during the February 10th session (Lewisohn, *The Complete Beatles Chronicle* 244). But within a few weeks, they had scrapped the hummmmmm idea altogether in favor of the famous fifty-three-second piano chord—an E major—played by John, Paul, Ringo, and Mal Evans on a trio of pianos. Martin supplemented the awe-inspiring sound on the studio's harmonium. Not surprisingly, it took nine takes before they all succeeded in pounding the chord simultaneously. In order to enhance the sound of the chord, Emerick allowed for a forty-five-second sustain. "I reached full volume," he recalled, "and the gain was so high that you could literally hear the quiet swoosh of the studio's air conditioners" (161). It may not have been the end of the world, but it certainly sounded like it.

In itself, "A Day in the Life" virtually re-imagined the *avant-garde*—and this from the band that had only just recorded the groundbreaking "Tomorrow Never Knows." "A Day in the Life" contrasts Lennon's impassive stories of disappointment and remorse with McCartney's deceptively buoyant interlude about the numbing effects of the workaday world. The song's luminous, open-ended refrain—"I'd love to turn you on"—insinuates a sense of salvation on a universal scale. Yet John and Paul's detached lyrics seem to suggest, via their nuances of resignation and unacknowledged guilt, that such a form of emotional release will always remain an unrealized dream:

> I saw a film today, oh boy.
> The English Army had just won the war.
> A crowd of people turned away.
> But I just had to look,
> Having read the book.
> I'd love to turn you on.

With his nonchalant mien, the speaker pointedly narrates our cultural malaise from a position of consciousness, while the desensitized crowd turns away in unconscious vacancy. Living, as they do, behind the "walls of illusion" of which Harrison speaks in "Within You Without You," the crowd exists at a conspicuous distance from any semblance of an emotional, human reality. In the ensuing middle-eight, Paul's internal parable for "A Day in the Life" brings the interpersonal trauma vividly to life. With yet another working day in the offing, the speaker awakens to the mind-numbing reality of an indifferent world:

> Woke up, fell out of bed,
> Dragged a comb across my head,
> Found my way downstairs and drank a cup,
> And looking up I noticed I was late.
> Found my coat and grabbed my hat,
> Made the bus in seconds flat,
> Found my way upstairs and had a smoke,
> Somebody spoke and I went into a dream.

With the flick of a match, the speaker lights up a cigarette, a coworker snaps into verbal action, and the world is set firmly into its nightmarishly endless motion.[19] As Lennon's voice soars in the background, the orchestra begins its slow burn, culminating in the song's—indeed, the album's—most decisive moment: a sarcastic brass retort that acts as an irreverent corrective for an insensate Western world. As the music of the Beatles and the studio orchestra spirals out of control and into oblivion, a massive piano chord punctuates the song's melancholic ambiance. And the illusion of infinitude is made real.

The chord's metaphorical open-endedness suggests—in dramatic contrast with the self-contained love songs of the Beatles' musical youth—the proffering of a larger philosophical question for which there is no immediate answer.

"A song not of disillusionment with life itself but of disenchantment with the limits of mundane perception," MacDonald observes, "'A Day in the Life' depicts the 'real' world as an unenlightened construct that reduces, depresses, and ultimately destroys" (181). In "A Day in the Life," the songwriters revisit the vexing relationship that invariably exists between the self and the outside world. They consider the distressing double-bind inherent in our interhuman bond, an interrelationship that possesses the power for engendering genuine love and connection, on the one hand, while creating untold loneliness and neglect, on the other. By trumpeting "I'd love to turn you on" to the anxious ears of a waiting world—and ensuring that the song was ultimately banned by the BBC in the process—the Beatles dared their audience to embrace self-awareness and mind-consciousness in spite of the harrowing headlines that seem to foretell humanity's doom on a daily basis. Modernists to a fault, the Beatles never stop experimenting with their art, they never cease exploiting ironies of distance and situation, and they refuse to silence their narrative without first reminding us that there is an ethical center out there some-where—we simply have to keep questing for it, no matter what the cost. As Walter Everett astutely writes, "'A Day in the Life' represents the Beatles' wake-up call for whomever might be listening. The song is not merely a warning of an ashy apocalypse, as it has often been taken, but suggests that there is yet hope for the phoenix" (*Revolver through the Anthology* 116). As if to under-mine the finality of the colossal chord that brings "A Day in the Life"—and the album—to a close, the Beatles concocted the unlisted "Sgt. Pepper's Inner Groove," which had been inserted during the mastering process into the record's concentric run-out groove. In so doing, they succeeded in detonating the silent afterglow of "A Day in the Life" with a sudden onslaught of sound effects, ambient noise, and gibberish that Emerick had chopped up and reassembled in random and backward fashion. To conclude the experiment, John suggested that they record a high-pitched 15-kilocycle whistle to rouse the family dog—as they had presumably just accomplished with their human listeners via "A Day in the Life."

If nothing else, *Sgt. Pepper's Lonely Hearts Club Band* effects an emphatic line of demarcation between the Mop Tops of days gone by and the studio-ori-ented band of the present. It is difficult to imagine that scarcely four years had passed since the heady days of "She Loves You," "I Want to Hold Your Hand," and unbridled Beatlemania. Indeed, it is almost impossible to believe that they're even the same band. Perhaps the most poignant example of this trans-formation is evidenced by Peter Blake's cover art for *Sgt. Pepper*, which depicts the competing narratives of the paradigmatic Fab Four with the incarnation of the Summer of Love-era Beatles, decked out, as they are, in psychedelic military regalia as Sgt. Pepper's fabled troupe. The album cover depicts the group's former mythological selves standing stage right of their remythologized contemporary counterparts, themselves surrounded by similarly mythologized figures from the annals of history, religion, Hollywood, music, sports, and literature. While the album's cover art prefigures the newly remythologized identities that the group would bring to life in *Magical Mystery Tour* and *Yellow Submarine* over the next twelve months, it also finds the Beatles implicitly recognizing the constraints inherent in the mythologizing process itself. In addition to the high literary presence of Lewis Carroll, Edgar Allan Poe, and Oscar Wilde, the cover montage ranges from Marlon Brando's steely visage in *On the Waterfront* (1954) and Bob Dylan in thoughtful repose to the stereotypically one-dimensional portrait of boxer Sonny Liston and the lost, penetrating gaze of Stu Sutcliffe. With its motley representation of cultural iconography, *Sgt. Pepper's* cover reminds us that nuance and complexity have relatively little to do with the act of myth-making. Although remythology ostensibly provides the Beatles with avenues for exploring new artistic spaces, their culturally inscribed identities insisted that they adhere to many of their narrowly defined character traits as prescribed by the mythos of Beatlemania. With the album cover sporting obvious evidence of the band's forays into counterculture—*Sgt. Pepper* finds them replete with moustaches and sideburns while standing amidst a garden of flower power and *faux* cannabis—they were determined to undermine the fan-consoling notion of being four mild-mannered lads from Liverpool. It is little wonder that Brian Epstein wanted to release the album in a plain-brown wrapper.[20]

As it turns out, the very notion of being the "act you've known for all these years" was McCartney's meager attempt at affording the group's listeners with the solace of sameness and reassurance. The monumental June 1967 release of *Sgt. Pepper's Lonely Hearts Club Band* found the Beatles, and especially their principal songwriters, attempting to establish a more concrete narrative structure in their work. Perhaps even more significantly, *Sgt. Pepper* saw the Beatles erasing the boundaries that they had been challenging since *Rubber Soul* and *Revolver*. "Until this album, we'd never thought of taking the freedom to do something like *Sgt. Pepper*," McCartney recalled. "We started to realize there weren't as many barriers as we'd thought, we could break through with things like album covers, or invent another persona for the band" (qtd. in Dowlding 161). Fans and critics alike refer to *Sgt. Pepper* as popular music's first "concept" album. But in truth, the Beatles' notion of a fictitious ensemble peters out after "With a Little Help from My Friends," the album's second track. The concept "doesn't go anywhere," Lennon later remarked. "But it works 'cause we *said* it works" (qtd. in Dowlding, 160).[21] Yet the reason that it doesn't go anywhere is because the album's *real* concept involves a rallying call to consciousness, as opposed to a cohesive storyline about the trials and tribulations of Sgt. Pepper and his band of lonely hearts. As with the enduringly prescient words of E. M. Forster—"Only connect!"—the album's ultimate theme invokes the signal import of self-awareness, and the awareness of others, at nearly every turn. In the end, *Sgt. Pepper* embodies the Beatles' long-playing conception of love and community—a dramatic *re*-conception of themselves and their art for the ages.

Notes

1. A film still from *How I Won the War* featuring Lennon as Private Gripweed graced the cover of the inaugural issue of *Rolling Stone* magazine on November 9th, 1967.

2. In his review of Yoko's film in the *Sunday Times* on February 12th, 1967, Hunter Davies famously dismissed *Bottoms*, writing, "Oh no, Ono" (qtd. in Cross 196).

3. The Beatles would respond to *Pet Sounds*, of course, with *Sgt. Pepper's Lonely Hearts Club Band*. The production of *Smile*, the Beach Boys' much-ballyhooed answer to *Sgt. Pepper*, would result in Wilson's drug-addled nervous breakdown, as well as a disastrous shift in the critical and commercial fortunes of the band. While the Beach Boys would release the inferior *Smiley Smile* in 1967, it took some thirty-seven years for Wilson to bring his vision for the long-awaited sound collage to fruition with *Smile*, which he released as a solo project in 2004.

4. During the coda, Lennon famously mutters "cranberry sauce," a remark that was misinterpreted as being "I buried Paul" during the "Paul is dead" craze. In October 1969, a DJ in Dearborn, Michigan, announced that McCartney had been dead since 1966. Over the ensuing months—indeed, years—overzealous fans dissected a variety of "clues" regarding Paul's death (and subsequent replacement by a look-alike) that the surviving Beatles had ostensibly secreted amongst the lyrics and artwork for *Sgt. Pepper's Lonely Hearts Club Band* (1967), *Magical Mystery Tour* (1967), *The White Album* (1968), *Abbey Road* (1969), and *Let It Be* (1970). See Andru J. Reeve's *Turn Me On, Dead Man: The Beatles and the "Paul Is Dead" Hoax* (2004).

5. "Carnival of Light" has never been officially released by the Beatles, although a one-minute excerpt of the track circulates on bootleg releases and among collectors on the Internet. According to Craig Cross, McCartney wanted to include the experimental song on *Anthology 2* (1996), but his suggestion was ultimately vetoed by Harrison, who didn't care for the track (193).

6. In classic Beatles fashion, Lennon and McCartney simply cannot refrain from undercutting their principal thematics, counterpoising the song's seemingly innocent bliss with the tawdry comedy of human experience. As Paul later remarked: "We put in a joke or two: 'Four of fish and finger pie.' The women would never dare say that, except to themselves. Most people wouldn't hear it, but 'finger pie' is just a nice little joke for the Liverpool lads who like a bit of smut" (qtd. in Dowlding 148).

7. In July 2006, the City of Liverpool briefly considered renaming Penny Lane because of its historical associations with the slave trade. The street had been named in honor of James Penny, an eighteenth-century slave ship owner and vehement anti-abolitionist.

8. The raw power of the Beatles' guitar work likely found its inspiration in the high-wattage musicianship of Jimi Hendrix, whom McCartney had seen in concert on multiple occasions in recent months in various Soho nightclubs (see Cross 433).

9. The title would resurface in 1969, when the Iveys changed their name to Badfinger at the suggestion of Neil Aspinall. Badfinger made their recording debut with the single "Come and Get It," their rendition of a Paul McCartney composition that was included on the soundtrack for *The Magic Christian* (1969).

10. "I don't know why I called it that or why it stood out from all my other drawings," Julian later remarked, "but I obviously had an affection for Lucy at that age. I used to show Dad everything I'd built or painted at school, and this one sparked off the idea for a song about 'Lucy in the Sky with Diamonds.'" Julian sat next to Lucy O'Donnell, the subject of his painting, at Heath House School. The title's acrostic is often erroneously believed to be a not-so-subtle reference to the frequent acid trips that the Beatles had been taking during this period.

11. The Beatles had actually met Coe in person in October 1963, when they made their inaugural performance on *Ready Steady Go!* Having won the show's lip-sync competition, Coe was presented with the top prize by the group themselves (Cross 438).

12. The feminist undertones of "She's Leaving Home" are echoed in a number of Lennon and McCartney post-Beatles compositions, including McCartney's "Another Day" and "Daytime Nighttime Suffering," as well as Lennon's "Woman Is the Nigger of the World" and "Woman."

13. Although a number of Beatles songs offer explicit critiques regarding the ills of consumerism, Lennon and McCartney never went so far as to deny the obvious commercial motives behind their efforts as hit-makers. As Paul later remarked, the idea that the Beatles were antimaterialistic was "a huge myth. John and I literally used to sit down and say, 'Now, let's write a swimming pool'" ("Sir James Paul McCartney, MBE").

14. As a songwriter, McCartney has made numerous forays into music's jazz age, including such Wings throwback tunes as "You Gave Me the Answer" and "Baby's Request" from *Venus and Mars* (1975) and *Back to the Egg* (1979), respectively, as well as "A Room with a View," which McCartney contributed to *Twentieth-Century Blues: The Songs of Noël Coward* (1999). Such recordings, as with the Beatles' "Martha My Dear," "Oh! Darling," and "Honey Pie," underscore McCartney's penchant for speaking about the past and nostalgia in purely musical terms.

15. The sound effects were courtesy of the EMI tape library's *Volume 35: Animals and Bees* and *Volume 57: Fox-Hunt.* As Geoff Emerick recalled, "John said to me during one of the breaks that he wanted to have the sound of animals escaping and that each successive animal should be capable of frightening or devouring its predecessor. So those are not just random effects. There was actually a lot of thought put into all that" (qtd. in Dowlding 178). On April 19th, Martin came up with the notion of using the

final cluck of the hen as the innovative transitional device into "Sgt. Pepper's Lonely Hearts Club Band (Reprise)."

16. Created in nine takes on April 1st as Paul prepared to leave for an extended break in the United States—where Jane Asher had been traveling since mid-January with a touring company from the Old Vic—"Sgt. Pepper's Lonely Hearts Club Band (Reprise)" brought the album's formal recording process to a close. Neil Aspinall is credited with the idea for the Reprise, which was recorded in the relative largesse of EMI's Studio One, complete with ambient arena and audience sounds.

17. John had originally brought the wind-up alarm clock into Studio Two as a joke, according to Emerick, "saying that it would come in handy for waking up Ringo when he was needed to do an overdub" during the lengthy sessions for *Sgt. Pepper* (147). In later years, Ringo grew fond of saying that *Sgt. Pepper* was the album during which he learned to play chess. As for the sound of the alarm clock itself, Emerick spent a significant amount of time attempting to delete it from the recording, eventually giving up when he realized it was impossible to separate it from the mix.

18. The band's producer remembered things differently: "That was entirely [Ringo's] own idea," Martin recollected. "Ringo has a tremendous feel for a song, and he always helped us hit the right tempo the first time. He was rock solid, and this made the recording of all the Beatles' songs so much easier" (qtd. in Lewisohn, *The Complete Beatles Recording Sessions* 95).

19. While it has become a critical commonplace to interpret Paul's lyric "Found my way upstairs and had a smoke" as an explicit reference to marijuana usage, the middle-eight's workplace context suggests that the speaker will not be zoning out in any hallucinogenic sense, but rather, because of the monotonous tedium inherent in contemporary life.

20. For Epstein, the album cover proved to be a complicated legal tangle. The original art work had been designed by the Fool, an *avant-garde* Dutch art collective, before their crude phantasmagoria was rejected in favor of the work of pop artist Peter Blake and photographer Michael Cooper, who assembled *Sgt. Pepper*'s renowned cover on a budget of some £2,800, at Cooper's Chelsea studio. With so many public personalities on display—many of whom were still among the living—NEMS was forced to undergo the laborious task of securing permissions. At one point, Mae West famously remarked, "What would *I* be doing in a lonely hearts club?" In the end, only the Bowery Boys' Leo Gorcey demanded a fee, and he was subsequently deleted (Spitz 681).

21. Allan F. Moore traces the emergence of the mythology regarding the album's ostensible conceptual harmony to a preview of the record in the May 6, 1967, issue of the *New Musical Express*. "So begins the myth of the unity of *Sgt. Pepper*," Moore writes (58).

Chapter 10

Roll Up for the Mystery Tour

"The time has come," the Walrus said,
"To talk of many things:
Of shoes–and ships–and sealing-wax–
Of cabbages–and kings–
And why the sea is boiling hot–
And whether pigs have wings."

—Lewis Carroll, "The Walrus and the Carpenter"

Is there any terrestrial paradise where, amidst
the whispering of the olive-leaves, people can be
with whom they like and have what they like and
take their ease in shadows and in coolness?

—Ford Madox Ford, *The Good Soldier*

There is little question that the Beatles' decision to stop touring in August 1966 represents the signal moment of their career as recording artists. In so doing, they enacted a self-conscious choice to become a studio band and to create their art almost exclusively within the confines of the recording complex. The logical result of this decision was the album *Sgt. Pepper's Lonely Hearts Club Band*, of course, and it is at this point, quite arguably, that the Beatles emerge as an "idea," displacing their long-standing identity as a working rock combo. By functioning as a self-conceived idea, the Beatles operated in the express service of crafting their tracks to be as artistically effective and as unified as possible. And by no longer functioning as a band, *per se*, but as an idea, their songs didn't require (as indeed they hadn't since *Revolver*) that vocal and instrumental parts be apportioned to each of the group members in an egalitarian fashion. As a band, the Beatles necessarily concentrated on the aesthetics of performance and re-performance, as well as on issues related to the portability of their repertoire. But as recording artists—as the high-concept notion of the Beatles as a shared, pliable idea—their aesthetic ideals shifted considerably from the hallmarks of live performance to the comparatively liberating world of studio creativity. As George Martin later observed:

> When I first started in the music business, the ultimate aim for everybody was to try and recreate, on record, a live performance as accurately as possible. But then, we realized that we could do something other than that. In other words, the film doesn't just recreate the stage play. So, without being too pompous, we decided to go into another kind of art form, where we are devising something that couldn't be done any other way. We were putting something down on tape that could only be done on tape. (qtd. in Badman 256)

Obviously, multitrack recording had already made it possible for the Beatles—and especially for John and Paul, as the group's most prolific songwriters—to move beyond issues of musical allocation in which they ensured that each member had a particular role to play in a given composition and, hence, to shift toward a new model in which creativity, musicianship, and technical mastery were the presumptive forces of artistic control. Determined to capture the essence of their vision on tape—as opposed to reproducing it via the act of live performance in front of an audience—the Beatles' creative imperatives shifted from the construction of songs to the creation of tracks. And if the goal is not only to reproduce but to perfect the songwriter's vision in the recording studio, then the issue of musical personnel becomes decidedly contingent upon the individual's ability to reciprocate the composer's textual desires. It is hardly surprising, then, that this transition toward the Beatles as an idea would act as the impetus behind their artistic achievements in the latter half of the 1960s, while also playing a powerful role in their undoing, causing internal political fissures in their group chemistry that would dramatically recast their future in the process.[1]

    Scant days before the global release of *Sgt. Pepper*—and in advance of the attendant, blinding euphoria that ensued before morphing into that free-spirited summer of 1960s mythology—the Beatles made themselves available for journalistic inspection. For the first time since the press junkets devoted to the "Jesus Christ Tour" some nine months earlier, the Beatles broke their media silence on May 19th, 1967, for the occasion of the *Sgt. Pepper* launch party at Brian Epstein's Chapel Street townhouse. The bandmates strode into the celebration in full Carnaby Street garb. Moustached and done up in their psychedelic finery, their entrance was met with stunned silence from the gaggle of reporters and photographers. The Beatles had remade themselves alright, and rock culture would never be the same again. The Summer of Love had once and truly begun. Brian's guests included *Town and Country* magazine's Linda Eastman, a twenty-five-year-old American photographer with a yen for rock journalism and an alluring demeanor to match her considerable skills behind the lens. The daughter of affluent New York attorney Lee Eastman, Linda was in London to take a series of photographs for a forthcoming book, *Rock and Other Four-Letter Words*, on which she was collaborating with J. Marks.[2] As fate would have it, Paul had met Linda four days earlier at the trendy Bag O'Nails, where she was taking in the jazzy sounds of Georgie Fame and the Blue Flames in the company of the Animals (Badman 275). As Paul prepared to leave the club that evening, he made his move—"my big pulling line!" he recalled—and Linda accompanied him to the Speakeasy, where Paul first heard Procol Harum's "A Whiter Shade of Pale"—the nostalgic anthem that left him mesmerized. "God, what an incredible record," Paul later remarked. "It was a benchmark." John himself had become so infatuated with the song that he would play it over and over again, while being chauffeured around the city for hours at a time in his psychedelically ornamented Rolls Royce Phantom, which had been outfitted with a custom turntable (Barrow, *John, Paul, George, Ringo, and Me* 223). After leaving the Speakeasy in the wee hours of the morning, Linda joined Paul back at his home on Cavendish Avenue, where she admired his art collection. "I was impressed to see his Magrittes," she slyly remembered (qtd. in Miles 432–33). For her part, Jane Asher was conveniently out of town, still touring the United States in the company of the Old Vic.

 Sgt. Pepper was released to nearly universal praise on June 1st, and the album's influence and acclaim have hardly ebbed in the interim. In the ensuing decades, British critic Kenneth Tynan lauded *Sgt. Pepper* as "a decisive moment in the history of Western civilization," while composer Leonard Bernstein once remarked that "three bars of 'A Day in the Life' still sustain me, rejuvenate me, inflame my senses and sensibilities" (qtd. in Dowlding 161, 184). Having taken more than seven hundred hours to record, *Sgt. Pepper* was a watershed moment in the history of popular music. With its *avant-garde* cover art, its cardboard cut-outs—including a do-it-yourself moustache—its gatefold design, and the printed lyrics on the back cover, *Sgt. Pepper* wasn't just an LP. It was an event— and one that still resounds, year in and year out, as the album continues to snake its way through world culture. Yet for all of the album's accolades and time-warping renown, McCartney was most gratified by Jimi Hendrix's myth-making performance of the title track only scant days after its release at the Saville Theatre. Hendrix's rendition of the song was "the single biggest tribute" to *Sgt. Pepper*, Paul stated at the time (qtd. in Badman 289). As Noel Redding, the bassist for Jimi Hendrix and the Experience, remembered: "*Pepper* came out on a Thursday, and we were playing on the Sunday, June 4th, at the Saville Theatre, which was owned by Brian Epstein. We always used to meet at [manager] Chas Chandler's flat before the gig and get a taxi around there, or we'd meet in a pub near the theatre. Hendrix said, 'Let's play "Sgt. Pepper."'" So there in the dressing room we learned the intro, which is A, C, and G. We didn't do the middle part, because we didn't know it. . . . I found out later that all the Beatles were in the audience and it freaked them out" (qtd. in Babiuk 205–06). In truth, only Paul and George were in attendance that evening. Although the Experience hadn't bothered—nor had the time—to learn the middle-eight, it hardly mattered to McCartney. As Hendrix began the set with his raw and thunderous rendition of "Sgt. Pepper's Lonely Hearts Club Band," it became abundantly clear that the guitarist understood the song's mettle implicitly, having reduced Paul's splendid mergence of pop majesty and electric gusto into rock and roll gutturality. Condensed into its most primitive ingredients—guitar, bass, drums, vocals—the song came alive with Hendrix's veritable tremble and roar.[3] What if the Beatles allowed themselves to enjoy such abandon, to release their own pop inhibitions and fully loose their primordial selves upon the world?

In itself, *Sgt. Pepper* exists as the thematic nexus for the group's final, lengthy artistic thrust. Although issues of authorship and the Beatles' modernity will continue to increase in significance during this period, we can understand the band's creative movements via three principal areas of existential inquiry associated with nostalgia, spirituality, and loneliness. In the first regard, the Beatles' nostalgic search for a comforting sense of home begins in earnest. This form of loss is prefigured by "She's Leaving Home," although the Beatles' nostalgic soundings range across their career from such compositions as "There's a Place," "I'll Be Back," and "In My Life" to more bracing narratives like "Yesterday" and "She Said She Said." The carefree charm of "Strawberry Fields Forever" and "Penny Lane" foreshadows Lennon and McCartney's more nuanced explorations of nostalgia on *The White Album* and beyond. This period also finds the Beatles, led by Harrison, on a larger search for spiritual oneness. With songs such as "Love You To" and "Within You Without You," he engages in extended cultural critique with a keen sense of Eastern philosophy, while the works of Lennon and McCartney witness their adolescent and post-adolescent effusions about romantic love commutating into more complex readings of adult relationships. Finally, the Beatles' analyses of loneliness continue the examinations begun in "Nowhere Man" and "Eleanor Rigby," anticipating much darker tales about desolation and loss. For the quartet's primary songwriters, loneliness shifts from the product of romantic separation or dissolution into a more broadly rendered aspect of human experience that can devastate the soul of the individual and, through its microcosmic corruption, threaten to destroy the spiritual essence of the larger human community. As Colin Campbell and Allan Murphy remark, the Beatles' "concern with the intense personal loneliness of the abandoned or rejected lover becomes, in turn, the model for the later treatment of loneliness in general. The principal difference therefore between the lyrical content of the earlier and later songs is that the sentiments and attitudes contained in the earlier ones are taken out of the restrictive context of romantic love and extrapolated in a self-conscious fashion to life itself" (xxviii). In this way, the notion of an evolving self-consciousness will define the Beatles' work—as it had done since at least the advent of *Revolver*—for as long and as far as their partnership would take them.

∿

But first there was *Magical Mystery Tour*. The idea for the Beatles' next project found its roots in Paul's April 11th return flight to London from the United States, where he had squired the touring Jane Asher around Los Angeles and Denver. With Mal Evans in tow, Paul hastily concocted lyrics for "Magical Mystery Tour," the title track for his proposed made-for-television movie about the popular British seaside tours that he remembered from his youth. As Paul recalled:

> The *Mystery* show was conceived way back in Los Angeles. On the plane. You know they give you those big menus, and I had a pen and everything and started drawing on this menu and I had this idea. In England, they have these things called mystery tours. And you go on them and you pay so much and you don't know where you're going. So the idea was to have this little thing advertised in the shop windows somewhere called *Magical Mystery Tours*. (qtd. in Gambaccini 47–48)

Alive in Paul's imagination before *Sgt. Pepper* even hit the stores, *Magical Mystery Tour* also offered an affectionate nod to Ken Kesey's Merry Pranksters, who conducted "Acid Tests" while trolling America's highways in a multicolored school bus. The Beatles convened at EMI Studios in late April, where they began working on "Magical Mystery Tour," the title track for their latest fantasia. During the first session, sound effects—including the *vroom* of a tour bus panning from the left to right sound channels—were drawn from the EMI tape library's *Volume 36: Traffic Noise Stereo*. After preparing the song's basic rhythm track with his trusty Rickenbacker, John on his Jumbo, and George on "Rocky," the nickname for his treasured Fender Strat, Paul tasked Mal with the job of canvassing bus stations in order to raid authentic mystery tour posters for lyric ideas, à la John's found object for "Being for the Benefit of Mr. Kite!" In addition to a glockenspiel, the Beatles added vocal tracks—including John ad-libbing "Step right this way!"—before overdubbing a quartet of trumpets, led by the ubiquitous David Mason, who delivered a spirited barrage of high-velocity sixteenth notes. For all its gusto and gumption, "Magical Mystery Tour" is little more than *Sgt. Pepper* lite. It masquerades as an intriguing invitation—where satisfaction is guaranteed indubitably—yet as with the eventual film, it doesn't really go anywhere, and in spite of all the commotion, no less. Although the music offers a panoply of styles and instrumentation—including a furtive "mock *misterioso*" section, in Tim Riley's words—the repetitive, directionless lyrics devolve into the kind of banality that few Beatles tracks ever know (237).

But their post-*Pepper* creative stupor had only just begun. With *Sgt. Pepper* on the cusp of making cultural history, the Beatles were mired in a streak of inconsistency—at least in terms of their own lofty standards. In mid-May, the band turned to "Baby, You're a Rich Man" at Olympic Sound Studios, the Rolling Stones' favorite recording haunt. With John playing the studio's handy Clavioline and sharing keyboard duties with Paul on a Knight upright piano, "Baby, You're a Rich Man" offers up a psychedelic miasma, an aspect of the song that is heightened by John's peripatetic Clavioline lines, Paul's staccato bass riffs on his Rickenbacker, and a vibraphone part courtesy of tape operator Eddie Kramer. Lyrically, "Baby, You're a Rich Man" merges John's verses with Paul's chorus, much like the collaborative format that spawned "A Day in the Life," although that's where the comparison comes to a crashing halt. With an alleged backing vocal by Mick Jagger, who observed the proceedings at Olympic that evening, the song begins with an intriguing, modish question—"How does it feel to be one of the beautiful people?"—before faltering in its own lyrical and musical circularity.[4] During the fadeout for "Baby, You're a Rich Man," Lennon is rumored to have sung "Baby, you're a rich fag Jew" as a sardonic barb aimed at the Beatles' manager, of whom John was growing increasingly suspicious during their post-touring months, particularly regarding the group's complex and bewildering financial picture.[5] The next evening, the Beatles recorded "All Together Now," an upbeat children's song written by Paul, with John's genial assistance on the middle-eight, in the same merry vein as "Yellow Submarine." With John strumming his Jumbo and playing harmonica on a Beatles track for the first time in two years, the instrumentation is rounded out by Paul's rhythmic Epiphone Texan, Ringo on finger cymbals, and all four Beatles engaging in a lighthearted sing-along that gathers momentum before galloping into a sudden climax. The song is a trifle, to be sure, but it marks some of their best work since finishing *Sgt. Pepper*.

The Beatles' May 1967 efforts concluded with two of the strangest entries in their corpus. The first composition originates from, of all things, the 1967 London metropolitan telephone directory, which Lennon spotted during a visit to McCartney's Cavendish home. "You know their NAME?" the telephone directory's cover intoned, "look up their NUMBER." With another quirky found object on his hands, John began imagining a doo-wop number in the style of the Four Tops as he walked the short distance to EMI Studios with Paul. By the time they set down to work on the track, it had been transformed, at Paul's suggestion, into a zany, screwball comedy tune in the tradition of the Goons, or, more recently, the Bonzo Dog Doo-Dah Band.[6] The song first came into being as an instrumental, complete with Rolling Stones guitarist Brian Jones wailing away on an alto saxophone. The original track clocked in at more than six minutes and was comprised of five discrete sections. With the assistance of the unwavering Mal Evans, John and Paul finally overdubbed a series of uproariously funny vocals on April 30th, 1969—nearly two years after the track's genesis. "You Know My Name (Look Up the Number)" begins with an intentionally overwrought, soulful introduction before cascading into "Slaggers," a smoke-filled cocktail lounge where Paul adopts the smooth jazz stylings—as well as the breathy lower register—of nightclub singer Denis O'Bell, whose name was fashioned after Beatles assistant Denis O'Dell. As Slaggers fades-out into obscurity, O'Bell surrenders the stage to none other than John Lennon, who, adopting a pseudo-grandmotherly voice for the occasion, absurdly counts out loud, while singing the song's title, mantralike, amidst a sea of pennywhistles and percussion. The song's penultimate segment showcases McCartney's piano and Jones's alto sax before coalescing—with a trademark Beatles false ending—into Lennon's *a cappella* gibberish. The song's inherent comedy owes little, if anything, to the repetition of its title, no matter how clever its origins. Instead, the track's humor develops out of the Beatles' effusive wit and obvious willingness to rush headlong into absurdity. Their sheer delight in producing the composition is made palpable at every turn. And their delight, as with the finest of Beatles efforts, becomes our own.[7]

In late May, the band assembled at London's De Lane Lea Recording Studios to begin crafting a new Harrison composition that went under the working title of "Too Much." Conspicuously absent that evening was producer George Martin, who had skipped a number of sessions of late, having become exasperated with the Beatles' aimless demeanor. "Sometimes," the producer recalled, "they would jam for hours in the studio, and we would be expected to tape it all, recognizing the moment of great genius when it came through. The only trouble was, it never did come through" (*With a Little Help from My Friends* 138). During the chaotic first session, the Beatles created a basic rhythm track for "Too Much," which included the recording of a twenty-five-minute jam session based on the rather convoluted composition. With the assistance of the De Lane Lea personnel, the song was eventually mixed down to a more reasonable eight minutes, which featured John and George on heavily distorted Casinos and Paul turning in an uninspired bass part on his Rickenbacker. The "Too Much" chant that concludes the song morphed, at various instances, into "tuba" and "Cuba," as John and Paul's backing vocals devolved into further chaos (Lewisohn, *The Complete Beatles Recording Sessions* 112; *The Complete Beatles Chronicle* 256). Lennon and McCartney's flippancy in the studio underscores their inherent disdain for what they perceived, at least at the time, to be the youngest Beatle's lesser compositions.

The June 1st session for "Too Much"—occurring on the very day of the much-heralded release of *Sgt. Pepper*—found the group at De Lane Lea yet again, where their work on "Too Much" produced hour after hour of mindless instrumental jam sessions, with little real progress being made on the song. Martin rejoined the proceedings the next evening, and in spite of the chaos of additional instrumental jamming, managed to assemble a parcel of studio musicians, including David Mason, in order to bring the rambling song to an end. Although "It's All Too Much" ultimately exists as a rather minor track in the Beatles' canon, it features a variety of intriguing elements, including trumpet quotations from Jeremiah Clarke's "Prince of Denmark's March" (often incorrectly identified as the "Trumpet Voluntary"), as well as Harrison's borrowing of a lyric from the Merseys' 1966 hit single "Sorrow": "With your long blonde hair and your eyes of blue." Even more interesting is the arresting prefatory guitar work. Described by Tim Riley as "the resplendent surge of a Hendrix electric fireball," George's introduction, played on the hollow-bodied Casino, finds the guitarist engaging the instrument's Bigsby bar in searing, full vibrato force (243). Yet for the most part, "It's All Too Much" witnesses the band squeezing the life out of a two-chord guitar figure before settling in for a seemingly interminable coda. Inspired by the overwhelming aesthetic experience of acid trips and meditation, Harrison's lyrics, coupled with the Beatles' psychedelic musical stew, attempt to capture the essence of hallucinogenic and spiritual overload. In that sense, the song is a stark-raving success, confronting listeners with wave after wave of sound and vision. But in the end, the track provides "too much" textual anarchy and not enough artistic drive. As Mark Lewisohn shrewdly observes, "The single-minded channeling of their great talent so evident on *Sgt. Pepper* did seem, for the moment at least, to have disappeared" (*The Complete Beatles Chronicle* 256).

The same band that once eschewed chaos and disorganization in favor of workmanlike precision and efficiency was now firmly lost in a sea of free-form improvisation—both in their music, it turns out, as well as in their lives. The group's years on the road had forced them to approach their work in the studio with a sense of economy; but now, without the benefit of structure or boundaries, the Beatles had been left to their own devices, which were served poorly by their intense usage of hallucinogens during this period. With *Sgt. Pepper* spinning continuously on the world's turntables, the Beatles' notorious drug-induced experiences came to a head, with Paul admitting in the June 16th, 1967, issue of *Life* magazine to ingesting acid. In addition to being "deeply committed to the possibilities of LSD as a universal cure-all," he championed it as the catalyst for sociopolitical awakening: "After I took it, it opened my eyes," he reported. "We only use one-tenth of our brain. Just think what all we could accomplish if we could only tap that hidden part. It would mean a whole new world. If politicians would use LSD, there would be no more war, or poverty, or famine" (qtd. in Thompson 105). Paul's remarks flummoxed the other Beatles—especially John and George, who felt that he was grandstanding, given his comparatively infrequent usage of the drug: "It seemed strange to me," Harrison later recalled, "because we'd been trying to get him to take LSD for about 18 months—and then one day he's on the television talking all about it" (*Anthology* 255). And while Paul's admission might have engendered delight among some segments of the population, it was met with scorn and derision by the establishment, whom the Beatles had been courting with great success in recent years via such classics as "Yesterday," "Michelle," "In My Life," and "Eleanor Rigby."

The band's revitalization, if only temporarily, came virtually out of the blue, as they made preparations to represent Great Britain on the international *Our World* telecast, slated for broadcast on June 25th. Negotiated by Epstein some months back and made public in mid-May, the Beatles' appearance on the satellite telecast required the proffering of a new song. With their internal rites of composition in full swing, John and Paul vied for the opportunity of displaying their wares on this most international of stages. While Paul allegedly offered up "Your Mother Should Know" for consideration, John suggested his latest composition, entitled "All You Need Is Love," a rather obvious selection, given its universal theme.[8] "It was an inspired song and they really wanted to give the world a message," Epstein remarked. "The nice thing about it is that it cannot be misinterpreted. It is a clear message saying that love is everything." For his part, George later described "All You Need Is Love" as a "subtle bit of PR for God" (*Anthology* documentary). The group recorded thirty-three takes of the song in mid-June at Olympic, with John on harpsichord, Paul playing a double bass, complete with bow, Ringo on his Ludwigs, and George plucking a violin, guitarlike, with mixed results. A few days later, Martin added a barrelhouse piano, while Lennon strummed a banjo, his lost mother Julia's instrument of choice. Given free rein to compose an orchestral score, the producer imagined an elaborate sound collage that begins with an intentionally stilted version of "La Marseillaise," in a barefaced attempt to conjure up stereotypical notions of the French as the world's greatest lovers, and concludes with a pastiche of musical quotations.[9] Martin's sly misquote of the "Marseillaise" is pure parody, in many ways, of the French themselves, whom the British love to poke fun at anyway, as well as a caricature of the idea of love itself. In addition to the French national anthem, Martin concludes the song with an instrumental montage that features "Greensleeves"—a rather appropriate choice, given the sixteenth-century tune's despairing phrases about a heart that remains forever in captivity—as well as a fragment from Glenn Miller's "In the Mood," which would subsequently result in an out-of-court settlement for copyright infringement. Martin also adorned the pastiche with a recurring phrase from Bach's *Two-Part Invention in F Major*, featuring the ever-faithful David Mason in a trumpet duet with Stanley Woods.

In itself, the *Our World* broadcast was the high-water mark for the Beatles' much-vaunted dreams for universal hope and tranquility. Leaving almost nothing to chance, Martin arranged for the group to accompany their pre-recorded track, with a gum-chewing John on lead vocals, Paul on his Rickenbacker, George playing his Casino on a four-bar solo, and Ringo behind the drums. McCartney and Harrison's guitars were decked out in newly painted psychedelia for the occasion. Their clothes were even more flamboyant, with Paul dressed in a white sport coat and a garish, hand-colored shirt; John paradoxically wearing a conventional pin-striped suit; George adorned in an orange paisley jacket; and Ringo enveloped by a heavy, beaded getup consisting of suede, satin, and pseudo-fur (Spitz 702). Clearly, the days of coordinated suits and Beatle boots had been irrevocably lost among the staves of time. With a studio audience of friends and family belting out the chorus—including such rock and roll glitterati as Mick Jagger, Keith Richards, Eric Clapton, Keith Moon, and Graham Nash, among others—EMI's Studio One enjoyed a festive atmosphere for the seven-minute broadcast, with a thirteen-piece orchestra, placard-toting extras, and a flourish of streamers, confetti, and balloons on global display.[10] With an estimated audience of some 350 million people on five continents, it was flower power's finest moment. Martin's post-production efforts for the upcoming single's release—which featured "Baby, You're a Rich Man" as its B-side—included the addition of Ringo's introductory snare roll and some subtle tidying up of John's vocals. Rather fittingly, "All You Need Is Love" witnesses the Beatles bidding farewell, in a manner of speaking, to their early years, as well as to the naïve, idealistic visions of love that brought them world fame in the first place. As the song begins its protracted fadeout, Martin's arrangement of Bach's *Two-Part Invention* kicks into gear, with "Greensleeves" and "In the Mood" swirling joyfully in the background. Meanwhile, John delivers a non sequitur reference to "Yesterday," followed closely on the heels by his buoyant duet with Paul, as they provide a brief refrain from "She Loves You." As Alan W. Pollack astutely remarks, "To my ears, their quote from 'She Loves You' goes beyond the merely clever literary association of the lyrics to become the more profound musical equivalent of the wax models [of the Beatlemania-era bandmates] on the cover of *Sgt. Pepper.*" In so doing, the group offers a telling salute to the past as "All You Need Is Love" disappears into oblivion.

While it may reference "Yesterday" and "She Loves You," "All You Need Is Love" eschews the egocentric bliss of romantic love to extol the anticupidity of *caritas*—a divine and spiritually minded love for all humanity. But alas, the Beatles' utopian mirage would sour rather precipitously after the *Our World* triumph. First, there was the Beatles' misguided effort to buy a parcel of Greek islands. By the end of July, *Sgt. Pepper* had already sold some 2.5 million copies and "All You Need Is Love" had shot to the number-one position on the charts. And that's when John floated the idea of the Beatles building an island retreat where they could live in peace with their friends and families. They could even construct a state-of-the-art recording studio, Lennon added. Yet McCartney remained unconvinced, attributing his partner's scheme to "a drug-induced ambition" (qtd. in Hunt 263). Unfortunately, John had recently fallen under the spell of Alexis Mardas, a self-styled inventor whom John rechristened as "Magic Alex" because of his penchant for imagining new forms of electronic gadgetry. Magic Alex helpfully suggested that the Beatles consider purchasing an island off the coast of his native Greece. Not missing a beat, the group dispatched Magic Alex and Alistair Taylor, Brian Epstein's loyal assistant, to the eastern reaches of the Mediterranean Sea. On July 21st, John and Paul flew to the island of Leslo, where they joined George, Ringo, and their families. Epstein missed the trip because of the recent death of his father, Harry, for whom the manager was sitting *Shiva*. During the trip, the Beatles were swarmed by fans and media at nearly every stop. Apparently, Magic Alex had struck a deal with the Ministry of Tourism in which he would share details of the band's every move if the government promised not to search their luggage at the airport. By the time that the group encountered the pristine beaches of Leslo, their enthusiasm for island living had dissipated and the entourage returned to England empty-handed. "We were great at going on holiday with big ideas, but we never carried them out," Ringo later remembered. "It was safer making records, because once they let us out we went barmy" (qtd. in Hunt 263).

And then there was George's early August visit to San Francisco's Haight Ashbury district, ground zero for American hippiedom. Home to such as acts as

Jefferson Airplane, the Grateful Dead, and Janis Joplin, the Haight transformed in the mid-1960s into an impromptu bohemian village, where hallucinogens, free love, and communal living abounded. While Scott McKenzie's hit single "San Francisco (Be Sure to Wear Some Flowers in Your Hair)" rather sentimentally commemorated the city as a "love-in," where "gentle people" adorn their locks with flowers, Harrison found something altogether different in the Haight:

> I went there expecting it to be a brilliant place, with groovy gypsy people making works of art and paintings and carvings in little workshops. But it was full of horrible spotty drop-out kids on drugs, and it turned me right off the whole scene. I could only describe it as being like the Bowery: a lot of bums and drop-outs; many of them very young kids who'd dropped acid and come from all over America to this mecca of LSD. (*Anthology* 259)

For George, it was an instance of intense cataleptic impression—a moment of epiphany from which he simply couldn't turn back—and the Beatle ceased taking LSD on the spot. As George later recalled, "That was the turning point for me—that's when I went right off the whole drug cult and stopped taking the dreaded lysergic acid. I had some in a little bottle (it was liquid). I put it under a microscope and it looked like bits of old rope. I thought that I couldn't put that into my brain anymore" (*Anthology* 259). Having sworn off LSD, Harrison sought a new form of awakening, and his spiritual discovery would change the course of the Beatles in the process.

But things began to go seriously wrong as August—and the Summer of Love itself—was coming to a close. For Brian Epstein, the summer of 1967 had been one long nightmare. In addition to his father's sudden death in July, he had suffered from a deep depression since the Beatles ceased touring a year earlier. On May 17th, his psychiatrist, John Flood, encouraged Brian to admit himself to the Priory Hospital in Roehampton. On May 19th, he left the sanitarium for the *Sgt. Pepper* launch party, only to return to the mental health facility immediately afterward. As if his psychiatric problems weren't enough, Brian had spent much of the summer in turmoil over his business relationship with the band. On May 25th, the Beatles created Apple Music, Ltd., and Brian assumed that the company's formation effectively concluded their association. "He'd decided this was the Beatles' first real step toward ending their relationship with him," Peter Brown remarked (qtd. in Spitz 693). But nothing was further from the truth. The group had established Apple Music expressly as a tax dodge—and they had done so at Brian's urging, no less.[11]

Meanwhile, Brian had become frightened to death of a notorious American accountant named Allen Klein, who had recently strong-armed Decca Records into rewarding the Rolling Stones with a $1.25 million signing bonus.

Known for his crude mannerisms and tough-guy demeanor, he had similarly approached Brian about restructuring the Beatles' EMI contract. Epstein had become deathly afraid of the American interloper, particularly after Paul inquired about Klein's recent success on the Rolling Stones' behalf. "What about us?" he asked Brian. For months, the manager had been attempting to convince the Beatles to tour again, but to no avail. Even after he successfully negotiated a contract extension with EMI, he felt that his days with the group were numbered—a situation that he did nothing to improve by offering a controlling interest in NEMS to Robert Stigwood, a British rock promoter with ambitions of becoming the next Brian Epstein. Stigwood had recently begun grooming an Australian group known as the Bee Gees for the big time. When Brian balked at signing them, Stigwood inked them to a contract with Atlantic Records. With his keen eye for talent and the smooth verbal gifts to match, he set his sights on the Beatles. For a paltry £500,000—considerably undervaluing the company in the process—he bought his way into NEMS, with the option of obtaining a controlling interest in the corporation after six months (Spitz 667–68). By the time that summer rolled around, Stigwood had begun handling the daily operations of NEMS, although Brian had already decided, if only in his mind, to decline Stigwood's option. Yet as the days wore on, the manager became ever more paranoid about his progressively tenuous relationship with the Beatles.[12] With his psyche in disarray, he increasingly turned to drugs and alcohol to salve his aching heart.

But the Beatles had fallen under the spell of an entirely different sort. After his epiphany in California, George had determined to restore his inner soul. With John and Paul in tow, he attended a lecture given by the Maharishi Mahesh Yogi at the Hyde Park Hilton on August 24th. The bandmates were on a quest for meaning—an effort that had failed them throughout the summer, whether in Greece or the United States—and the Maharishi, with his knowledge of Eastern philosophy and his concern for inner peace, seemed like the perfect solution. At fifty-years-old, the Maharishi had been on a journey of spiritual regeneration for much of his life. In 1945, he began a personal program of solitary meditation in the Himalayas that lasted for more than a decade. When he literally came down from the mountain, the Maharishi devoted himself to spreading traditional Indian teachings to the masses, a project that he started in 1957 with the founding of the Spiritual Regeneration Movement, the crusade that would eventually bring him to London during the Summer of Love. His timing couldn't have been better. Of particular interest to the Beatles was the Maharishi's development of an increasingly popular technique known as Transcendental Meditation. The Maharishi urged his followers to engage in a pair of twenty-minute daily sessions in which they focus on their mantra, the simple phrase whose repetition promises to open new vistas of spirituality, inner calm, and human consciousness. Increasingly bemused by the prison-house of their celebrity, the Beatles gravitated rather naturally to the tiny, charismatic man in the lotus position, whose life and message were devoted to individual contentment and communal peace.

Swept up in their latest euphoria, the Beatles trundled off to Euston Station on August 25th, where they boarded the train for University College in Bangor, Wales, the site of the Maharishi's upcoming Transcendental Meditation seminar. The Beatles' entourage included their significant others, save for Ringo's wife Maureen, who had given birth to their son Jason six days earlier. The usual rock retinue was in tow, including Mick Jagger, Marianne Faithfull, and Donovan. Brian Epstein had been invited to attend the seminar by John, but the manager refused, having already decided to go out on the town with Peter Brown. In the wake of Harry Epstein's death, Brian's mother, Queenie, had moved in with him at his Chapel Street home ten days earlier, and he was desperate to rejoin the London nightlife that had once been the staple of his existence. When the Beatles' train departed Euston Station that afternoon, it not only left without Brian, but also without Cynthia Lennon, who had been struggling with the luggage back on the platform. Calling to his wife from the train, John urged her to hitch a ride with Neil Aspinall, who intended to drive to Bangor later that day. Yet for Cynthia, missing the train was an omen that she would never shake: "I was crying because the incident seemed symbolic of what was happening to my marriage," she later wrote. "John was on the train, speeding into the future, and I was left behind" (*John* 264).

But the Beatles' spiritual excursion to Wales would be short-lived, their exhilaration replaced by shock when they learned of Brian's death, at the relatively tender age of thirty-two, on August 27th. In one of his last interviews, Brian expressed his all-consuming fear of loneliness: "I hope I'll never be lonely, although, actually, one inflicts loneliness on oneself to a certain extent" (qtd. in Badman 299). When the London nightlife failed to rouse his aching soul that weekend, he drove home in his beloved Bentley, dying alone in his bedroom. "At that time," Alistair Taylor remembered, "Brian was taking all sorts of medication. He lived on pills—pills to wake him up, pills to send him to sleep, pills to keep him lively, pills to quieten him down, pills to cure his indigestion" (187). While the shadow of suicide lingered over Brian's sudden death, his passing was officially ruled as an accidental overdose of barbiturates mixed with alcohol. As George later recalled, "In those days everybody was topping themselves accidentally" (qtd. in Spitz 718). But nothing could have prepared the Beatles for life without Brian. They loved him, to be sure, and they were thunderstruck with grief. But they also intuitively understood his role as the architect of Beatlemania and their attendant superstardom. The tragedy of his untimely death notwithstanding, Brian also existed—for better or worse—at the center of their financial vortex. He had been the keeper of their business affairs, and his sudden absence from their world had left a power vacuum in his place. And it was a void that they were in absolutely no way prepared to fill. "I knew that we were in trouble then," John later remarked. "I didn't really have any misconceptions about our ability to do anything other than play music. And I was scared. I thought, 'We've fucking' had it'" (*Lennon Remembers* 25).

〰

For all of their sorrow and confusion, the Beatles wasted little time in returning to EMI Studios, where they gathered during the first week of September to begin recording Lennon's "I Am the Walrus." Four days earlier, the group had convened at Paul's house on Cavendish Avenue, where he unveiled his *Magical Mystery Tour* schema. His outline for the movie consisted solely of a circle representing sixty minutes, with eight pie-shaped segments apportioned into sketches and musical numbers:

1. Commercial introduction. Get on the coach. Courier introduces.
2. Coach people meet each other / (Song, Fool on the Hill)
3. marathon—laboratory sequence.
4. smiling face. LUNCH. Mangoes, tropical (magician)
5. and 6: Dreams.
7. Stripper & band.
8. Song.
END. (qtd. in Spitz 720–21)

Postponing their plans to join the Maharishi in India for a lengthy retreat, the group decided to begin principal photography for their holiday-inspired lark during the week of September 11th. Although he had begun working on the idea of filming a mystery tour since April, Paul now had a far different motive in mind, given the leadership vacuum that had emerged within the band after Brian's death, "If the others clear off to India again now on another meditation trip," he confided in Tony Barrow, "I think there's a very real danger that we'll never come back together again as a working group. On the other hand, if I can persuade them today that we should go straight into shooting this film, it could save the Beatles" (qtd. in *The Making of the Beatles' Magical Mystery Tour* [6]). It is easy to read Paul's desires as power-driven, as many biographers have done; yet it is essential that we also recognize how central the Beatles were in the construction of his identity. As the express vehicle for his rich, creative life, the band's survival must have been understandably dear to him.

Although the idea behind "I Am the Walrus" originated from Lennon's hallucinogenic experiences, the composition's inspirational elements included Lewis Carroll's nonsensical poem "The Walrus and the Carpenter" from *Through the Looking-Glass*, as well as the verbal and textual convolutions of Bob Dylan's "Desolation Row," the lyrical *tour-de-force* that acts as the climax for *Highway 61 Revisited* (1965).[13] John ultimately trumps his antecedents' penchant for verbal esoterica with a series of disjunctive, acid-soaked images—word pictures that, by virtue of their tightly packed visual imagery, defy easy interpretation. "I Am the Walrus" features a profundity of textual absurdities, ranging from "stupid bloody Tuesday," "crabalocker fishwife," and "pornographic priestess" through "expert textpert choking smokers" and "elementary penguin." As with Carroll's nonsensical poem "Jabberwocky," phrases like "crabalocker" and "fishwife" find Lennon utilizing portmanteaux, in which single words are laden with a multiplicity of possible meanings (Sauceda 14). On September 5th, the Beatles recorded sixteen takes of the song's basic rhythm track in which the shaping of "I Am the Walrus" can be plainly heard. With John on electric piano, Paul on his Rickenbacker, George on his Fender Strat, and Ringo behind the drums, the session begins with the Beatles lumbering rather tentatively around the song's chord patterns and rhythmic foundations before slowly gaining confidence and shifting more deftly among the number's complex of structural elements. In spite of their musical finesse, the lingering sadness over Brian's death remained palpable. "I distinctly remember the look of emptiness on all their faces while they were playing 'I Am the Walrus,'" Geoff Emerick later recalled. "It's one of the saddest memories I have of my time with the Beatles" (214).

With a basic track in place, the group began adorning "I Am the Walrus" with one layer after another of words and music, timbre and sound. With the addition of each new textual stratum, the song's levels of meaning become even more oblique. With his ADT-treated vocal, John's chorus of "goo goo g'joob" provides a kind of doo-wop infused jabberwocky, while the recurrent "I am the eggman" seems positively creepy, if not downright frightening in Lennon's hyperkinetic performance.[14] Although he disliked the chaotic nature of "I Am the Walrus" from the start, George Martin created a stirring string arrangement, with sixteen musicians participating in the orchestral overdub in Studio One. Meanwhile, the Mike Sammes Singers plied their craft on that very same evening in Studio Three, where the eight male and eight female singers gathered to record some of the most outrageous backing vocals in Beatledom. At Lennon's behest, the choral group recorded the positively devilish "ho-ho-ho, hee-hee-hee, ha-ha-ha!" After shouting "oompah, oompah, stick it up your jumper!" the singers chanted "got one, got one, everybody's got one" before devolving into a spate of high-pitched whooping sounds (qtd. in Lewisohn, *The Complete Beatles Chronicle* 268). A few days later, John was fumbling with the radio in Studio Two's control room, where he aimlessly dialed up a BBC production of Shakespeare's *The Tragedy of King Lear*. Featuring a selection from Act IV, Scene VI— which Emerick fed directly onto the master tape—the passages from *King Lear* include audible lines from Oswald ("O, untimely death!") and Edgar ("Sit you down, father; rest you—"). With the found object of *King Lear* in place, the multifaceted sound college of "I Am the Walrus" had reached its fruition.

As the last burst of the Beatles' self-conscious psychedelia, "I Am the Walrus" functions—on both a lyrical and musical level—as a brilliant tirade against the ills of enforced institutionalism and runaway consumerism. Teeming with stunning wordplay and linguistic imagery—"obscurity for obscurity's sake," in the words of Michael Roos (26)—"I Am the Walrus" pits Lennon's bitter vocals against a surrealistic musical tableau comprised of McCartney's hypnotic bass, Harrison and Starr's playful percussion, and Martin's exhilarating string arrangements. "I Am the Walrus" opens with Lennon's Mellotron-intoned phrasings designed to replicate the monotonous cry of a police siren. As the song's spectacular lyrics unfold—"I am he as you are he and you are me and we are altogether"—Starr's wayward snare interrupts the proceedings and sets Lennon's intentionally absurd, Whitmanesque catalogue of images into motion. While an assortment of cryptic voices and diabolical laughter weave in and out of the mix, Lennon's pungent lyrics encounter an array of ridiculous characters, including that madman of literary effrontery himself, Edgar Allan Poe. When "I Am the Walrus" finally recedes amongst its ubiquitous mantra of "goo goo g'joob," the song dissolves into the scene from *King Lear*, and the whole production suddenly dies by its own hand in a symbolic meta-suicide denoting the spiritual death of the individual in a Western world beset by corporate monoliths and identity politics. As with "A Day in the Life," "I Am the Walrus" prods its listeners into consciousness through brute force. In the former song, the Beatles harness the thunder of a symphony orchestra run amok; for "I Am the Walrus," they muster the noise of discordant sound and language in order to rock our worlds. Described by Ian MacDonald as "the most idiosyncratic protest song ever written" (216), "I Am the Walrus" features Lennon's most inspired verbal and aural textures, as well as the Beatles' supreme moment of narrative paradox: in one sense, "I Am the Walrus" seems utterly devoid of meaning, yet at the same time its songwriter's rants about prevailing social strictures absolutely beg for interpretation, its layers of meaning fecundating and expanding with every listening. In "I Am the Walrus," Lennon looms large, containing multitudes.[15]

On August 22nd, the Beatles gathered at London's Chappell Recording Studios to work on Paul's "Your Mother Should Know," with its echo-laden pianos, somber lower register, and subterranean nostalgia. During the next evening's session, the Beatles had been joined at Chappell Studios by Brian Epstein for what turned out to be his very last meeting with the group. The song had already been chosen as the dancehall number to grace the conclusion of the *Magical Mystery Tour* movie, with the Beatles swaying in unison down a staircase and across a glitzy soundstage brimming with costumed, sashaying extras. Even in its final state, "Your Mother Should Know" seems oddly unfinished, with an aura of untapped nostalgia gurgling beneath its wistful surface. While the song's lyrics never progress beyond its basic thematics—"Let's all get up and dance to a song / That was a hit before your mother was born"—the instrumental bridge, with John's contemplative organ phrases arrayed against the composition's wistful empty spaces, is an unrealized treasure. In early September, the group had begun working on George's "Blue Jay Way," a composition inspired by a *cul-de-sac* in the Hollywood Hills that Harrison had visited during his recent trip to California. Although the lyrics trace the rather one-dimensional story of a speaker whose friends have become lost on their way to meet him, the music proves to be the composition's most interesting feature, with Harrison and Lennon playing hypnotic passages in a psychedelic duet of dueling Hammond organs. The track sports a pointedly hazy texture created through the use of phasing, which had been deployed to great effect on the Small Faces' recent hit "Itchycoo Park." A recording technique in which slight changes in the interaction of related audio signals result in a flanging effect, phasing was the most salient feature of "Blue Jay Way," imbuing the speaker's words of concern with an eerie (yet oddly welcome) sense of paranoia. Without phasing, the song would be a somewhat empty gesture, like "Your Mother Should Know," that walks in place, both lyrically and musically, without ever moving forward. The Beatles rounded out the *Magical Mystery Tour* soundtrack with two additional numbers, the instrumental "Flying" and Paul's "The Fool on the Hill." The first track to be credited to all four Beatles as composers, "Flying" had gone under the working title of "Aerial Tour Instrumental" in reference to its role in the movie's psychedelic interlude. With the Mellotron's trumpet setting toggled, the group sang along, doubling the *faux* brass sounds in wordless "la la" style, before concluding with a prerecorded Mellotron tape of a Dixieland band in full swing (Winn, *That Magic Feeling* 134). John later added flute sounds on the Mellotron, while also concocting tape loops comprised of electronic effusions, organ melodies, and chimes. When played in reverse, the tape loops were substituted for the Dixieland ending (now deleted), imbuing "Flying" with its mysterious, otherworldly terminus.

Along with "I Am the Walrus," Paul's "The Fool on the Hill" finds the Beatles at their creative peak during the *Magical Mystery Tour* project. Begun in earnest on September 25th, "The Fool on the Hill" was assembled, as with "I Am the Walrus," in several increasingly elaborate layers. The early takes feature Paul on Studio Two's upright piano, a concord of flutes and recorders, and Ringo on the finger cymbals. In addition to double-tracking his vocal, Paul added a plaintive recorder solo, while John and George played harmonicas in downbeat accompaniment. In addition to scoring an arrangement for a trio of flutes, Martin inserted an unusual tape effect at 2:40—an intensely fluid, meandering sound that hearkens back to the birdlike noises that adorn "Tomorrow Never Knows" (Everett, *Revolver through the Anthology* 138). Lyrically, "The Fool on the Hill" concludes the Beatles' midcareer analyses of loneliness as an alienating, albeit heroic stance in relation to an emotionally anesthetized society—indeed, much like the crowd who stand idly by as "A Day in the Life" descends into chaos and destruction. As with John's "Nowhere Man," the solitary figure in "The Fool on the Hill" contends with his unforgiving universe by remaining steadfast on his perch, never giving an answer while the world spins 'round and 'round beyond his grasp. Although he's a "man of a thousand voices talking perfectly loud," the Fool buries his emotions in a private oblivion that the crowd neither bothers, nor cares, to apprehend. In contrast with the cynical jesters of Shakespearean fame, McCartney's Fool retains a sunny optimism in spite of his disconnection with the world, remaining blissfully unaffected by the potential, long-range effects of his detachment from human interaction. The song's gentle musical accompaniment seems to situate the protagonist in a sanguine oasis, a weigh station in advance of the Beatles' more tragic narratives, in 1968 and beyond, about what happens when alienation becomes the norm and the alienated themselves begin to realize the awful, dehumanizing consequences of their disaffection.

With their film music firmly underway, the Beatles spent five days in mid-September 1967 on location in Surrey, Devonshire, Cornwall, and Somerset. Mal Evans and Neil Aspinall rounded up thirty-three actors—including such British comic personalities as Jessie Robbins, Derek Royle, Ivor Cutler, and Victor Spinetti—along with four cameramen, a soundman, and a technical advisor. Amazingly, one Richard Starkey was credited as the director of photography, adding yet another layer of mythology to the drummer's ever-growing legend, while the Beatles were acknowledged collectively as the project's directors. Having rented a sixty-two-seat bus as their mobile prop, the troupe patrolled the English countryside, hampered much of the time by a growing phalanx of media and fans who trailed their every move. Eventually, the production settled for another five days in the large empty hangars of Kent's West Malling Air Station, which doubled as their soundstage. At the end of October, Paul traveled to Nice with a cameraman to film a daydream sequence, effectively bringing the movie's principal photography to a close. During the first week of *Magical Mystery Tour*'s production, Robert Stigwood made his anticipated pitch to captain the Beatles' fiscal future—a move that, in hindsight, given their growing financial straits, might have changed their fortunes: "Now that Brian isn't here," he told the group over lunch, "I'm the natural successor, and I want to take over the operation" (qtd. in Spitz 725). Undaunted and suspiciously overconfident in their current spate of advisors during the post-Epstein era, the Beatles politely rebuffed Stigwood's offer, paying him a buyout of £25,000 for his trouble.

As they readied *Magical Mystery Tour* for its television debut, the group turned to another McCartney composition, "Hello Goodbye," as their next single. Although Lennon championed "I Am the Walrus" for the A-side, McCartney and Martin lobbied in favor of "Hello Goodbye," given its more readily obvious commercial possibilities. As a kind of pop-musical update of George and Ira Gershwin's "Let's Call the Whole Thing Off," "Hello Goodbye" had been written by Paul in the company of Alistair Taylor, who sat at the harmonium with the Beatle and improvised a series of antonyms: "You say yes, I say no / You say stop, and I say go go go." Initially rehearsed under the working title of "Hello Hello," "Hello Goodbye" benefited from one of the group's most inspired moments of creative caprice when they concocted the song's impromptu "hela heba-hello-a" finale in the studio. In its finished state, the recording of "Hello Goodbye" is something of a misnomer in the Beatles' corpus, evincing acute instrumental separation with piano and drums on the extreme left channel, while the backing vocals, strings, and electric guitars occupy the far right. In contrast with its B-side's eccentric social commentary, "Hello Goodbye" revels in good-natured fun and games, qualities that found the single racking up sales of some three hundred thousand copies within a day of its late-November release in the United Kingdom, where, as in the American marketplace, it easily attained the number-one spot.[16] Yet for all of the record's considerable success, John's ego had been indelibly wounded with the relegation of "I Am the Walrus" to the single's B-side. As Walter Everett observes, "Hello Goodbye" is undeniably "well crafted and fun, but putting 'I Am the Walrus' on the A-side would probably have encouraged Lennon to lead the Beatles to new heights in the 1970s; as it is, 'Hello Goodbye' was one more nail in the Beatles' coffin" (*Revolver through the Anthology* 144). It may have been a dear price to pay indeed.

The release of the *Magical Mystery Tour* EP in early December met with similar runaway success throughout the holiday season, as did the LP release in the United States. Yet 1967 would end with a shudder for the Beatles—and most particularly for Paul, who expected the television movie to validate the band's multiplicity of talents in art forms well beyond the strictures of pop music. *Magical Mystery Tour* seemed like an appropriate opportunity, given Epstein's death and their 1967-era identity reconstruction, to reinvent themselves. For the Beatles, the act of remythology allowed them to account for their evolving artistic interests and continue to stoke the fires of global celebrity at the same time. Their concomitant desires for wealth and artistic freedom were at loggerheads with one another, as they had realized during their first brush with the Maharishi's teachings, yet remythology—the process of reconfiguring one's own mythos in an effort to approximate more closely the nuances of our projected identities—afforded them with a narrative bridge connecting the story of who they were (the four Mop Tops of 1964 and 1965) with who they were becoming (the recording artists and cultural figures who would emerge as equally unknowable legends for the tailor-made consumption of future generations). And they could only accomplish this end, as history shows us, by grafting signs of their earnest explorations of new musical and hallucinogenic vistas, the spiritual possibilities of Transcendental Meditation, and the ethics of pacifism onto the more innocent and wholesome images of *A Hard Day's Night* and *Help!* Hence, the lads continue to perform certain character traits in *Magical Mystery Tour* that reaffirm the mythologized aspects of their former selves. In this reified world, Lennon still winks for the camera, Starr bumbles for comic relief, McCartney effects a benign Adonis, and Harrison remains ever so quiet.

But with Epstein's untimely death and a renewed desire to consolidate their popularity and become the masters of their own economic and artistic destiny—the Kleins and Stigwoods of the world be damned—the band shrewdly attempted to remythologize their media personalities in *Magical Mystery Tour*. But it was a gamble, however well-intentioned, that failed miserably. As perhaps their single greatest artistic failure, the film version of *Magical Mystery Tour* showcases the band members in a beguiling series of burlesques that is memorable solely for its utter disarray. The film's chaotic narrative features musical iterations from Beatles films past, including a marching band's intentionally cloying version of "She Loves You" and a string arrangement of "All My Loving" during a romantic interlude involving Ringo's wanton Aunt Jessie (Robbins) and staid courier Buster Bloodvessel (Cutler). In the movie's finest moments, it offers quasi-music videos for "The Fool on the Hill," "I Am the Walrus," and "Blue Jay Way." The film reaches its ridiculous nadir in a variety of nonsensical skits—set in, of all places, an army recruiter's office and a strip club—that attempt to recall the zany vignettes inherent in *A Hard Day's Night* and *Help!* Their efforts at remythologizing their public personalities especially fail when they attempt to merge their early Beatles' identities with their post-1965 profiles as spiritually and psychotropically inclined artists. By the advent of *Magical Mystery Tour*, there is simply no avenue for going back to the heady (or, in retrospect, perhaps not so heady) days of *A Hard Day's Night* and *Help!*

The poor reviews that *Magical Mystery Tour* received after its debut on Boxing Day (December 26th) on the BBC—which premiered the film in black and white, thus mitigating its multicolored virtues—revealed the awful reality of its failure.[17] ABC television, which owned the rights to broadcast *Magical Mystery Tour* in the United States, opted not to air the film at all.

The reviews were swift and merciless. "The bigger they are, the harder they fall. And what a fall it was," James Thomas wrote in the *Daily Express*. "The whole boring saga confirmed a long held suspicion of mine that the Beatles are four pleasant young men who have made so much money that they can apparently afford to be contemptuous of the public." Meanwhile, the *Daily Sketch* couldn't help poking fun at the Beatles' recent forays into Eastern mysticism: "Whoever authorized the showing of the film on BBC1 should be condemned to a year squatting at the feet of the Maharishi Mahesh Yogi." For its part, the *Daily Mirror* condemned *Magical Mystery Tour* as "Rubbish . . . Piffle . . . Nonsense!" (qtd. in Badman 332–33).[18] For the Beatles, it was a critical drubbing that proved difficult to stomach—especially after enjoying the artistic heights of *Sgt. Pepper*. The balance of 1967 had found the group drifting rather aimlessly, bringing their ideas to fruition—from songwriting to rehearsal to performance to multitrack enhancement—almost entirely within the studio. There were moments of sheer greatness ("I Am the Walrus" and "The Fool on the Hill") tempered by meandering self-indulgence ("It's All Too Much" and "Your Mother Should Know"). But allowing psychedelia to course through their creative faculties was a necessary phase for the Beatles, providing them with a fresh palette—along with an empty, white canvas— upon which to re-inscribe their art.

Notes

1. As early as January 1967, Neil Aspinall presciently remarked upon the band's shifting calculus: "You might say they're not even the Beatles anymore. They only come together now to record as sort of hobby, a very, very deep hobby, if you accept the definition of hobby as something you don't have to do for money. The Beatles are now four very different, four incredibly wealthy men, who have lives of their own to lead" (qtd. in Thompson 104–05).

2. Given her surname, Linda is often incorrectly assumed to be related to George Eastman, the founder of Eastman Kodak.

3. A live recording of Jimi Hendrix and the Experience performing "Sgt. Pepper's Lonely Hearts Club Band" on September 5th, 1967, in Stockholm, Sweden, is included on the four-disc compilation entitled *The Jimi Hendrix Experience* (2000).

4. While the song seems to address issues of wealth and celebrity, the concept of "beautiful people" references the burgeoning hippie generation in the parlance of 1960s counterculture.

5. According to Bob Spitz, several of the aborted takes featured improvisational lyrics in which John also "took some wicked shots at Paul, Ringo, and Mick" (686). In this way, "Baby, You're a Rich Man" prefigures Lennon's infamous 1971 solo track "How Do You Sleep?" in which he launches a searing diatribe against his former partner: "The only thing you done was 'Yesterday,' / And since you've gone you're just 'Another Day,'" referring to McCartney's recent solo hit. Lennon's vitriol likely emanated from his anger at being called out publicly by Paul in such tunes as "Too Many People" from *Ram* (1971) and "Dear Friend" on *Wild Life* (1971), the inaugural Wings album. McCartney effectively buried the hatchet with *Band on the Run*'s (1973) "Let Me Roll It," in which he sings, "My heart is like a wheel / Let me roll it to you." In March 1974, John and Paul reunited in a studiolike setting for the last time, recording sloppy cover versions of "Lucille," "Stand by Me," and "Working on the Chain Gang," with the assistance of fellow musicians Stevie Wonder, Harry Nilsson, Jesse Ed Davis, and Bobby Keys. The session is commemorated on the bootleg CD entitled *A Toot and a Snort in '74* (1992) in direct reference to Lennon's "Lost Weekend" of unchecked drug and alcohol indulgence during his lengthy, eighteen-month separation from Yoko Ono.

6. The Beatles' comedic efforts on "You Know My Name (Look Up the Number)" reveal the same zany brand of humor that they employed in the production of their annual fan-club Christmas records. Featuring a series of jokes, holiday music, and seasonal greetings, seven Beatles Christmas records saw release between 1963 and 1969, culminating in a special December 1970 compilation album. The Beatles' most recognizable holiday number, entitled "Christmas Time (Is Here Again)," was written by all four Beatles and released in December 1967.

7. "You Know My Name" was finally mixed for commercial release in November 1969 as the A-side, rather amazingly, of a potential Plastic Ono Band single slated to feature "What's the New Mary Jane?" as its flip side. Having been edited down to a more economical 4:19 in length, "You Know My Name" eventually saw release as the B-side of "Let It Be" in March 1970.

8. Spitz claims that the McCartney entry was the recently penned "Hello Goodbye," as opposed to "Your Mother Should Know" (700).

9. Ironically, the French national anthem's lyrics—while certainly nostalgic in their own right—revel in bloody images of war and carnage: "*Entendez-vous, dans la compagnes / Mugir ces farouches soldats? / Ils viennent jusque dans nos bras / Egorger vos fils, vos compagnes* [Do you hear in the countryside / The roar of these savage soldiers? / They come right into our arms / To cut the throats of your sons, your country]." Rather fittingly, the anthem was originally entitled "*Chant de guerre de l'armeé du Rhin* [War Song of the Army of the Rhine]," which certainly connotes the song's militaristic roots. Interestingly, Pollack contends that Martin's arrangement "intentionally misquoted" the anthem in an effort both to reference "La Marseillaise" and to subvert its power as an enduring cultural cliché.

10. The placards included "All You Need Is Love" translated in four languages, as well as the mysterious "COME BACK MILLY! ALL IS FORGIVEN!" in reference to Paul's aunt, who had fled Liverpool for Australia. Fearing that Milly might never return, Paul's cousin Anne Danher hastily prepared the placard before the broadcast (Spitz 703).

11. According to Paul, the company's simple name found its origins in the introductory words of English schoolbook primers everywhere: "A is for Apple."

12. Brian's fears were entirely unwarranted, according to Nat Weiss, the Beatles' American attorney and Epstein's business partner: "At worst, they might have renegotiated his commission, reducing it from 25 percent to perhaps 15," he recalled, "and I told Brian this whenever he wrestled with the subject" (qtd. in Spitz 687).

13. It later dawned on Lennon that he had misread Carroll's poem: "I realized that the walrus was the bad guy in the story, and the carpenter was the good guy. I thought, 'Oh, shit, I picked the wrong guy. I should have said, 'I am the carpenter.' But that wouldn't have been the same, would it?" (qtd. in Dowlding 198).

14. The phrase "I am the eggman" finds its origins in the erotic practices of the Animals' Eric Burdon, who enjoyed cracking open raw eggs on the bodies of his female companions during sex (Spitz 721).

15. With "Sowing the Seeds of Love," Tears for Fears channel "I Am the Walrus" in their buoyant valentine to the Beatles in specific and the Summer of Love in general. With its mergence of "I love a sunflower" and "love power," "Sowing the Seeds of Love" evokes the mythos of "flower power" and that fabled summer, as does the song's introductory call-to-arms—its ode to the timeless urgency of social change: "High time we made a stand and shook up the views of the common man."

16. The song's inherent sense of delight was translated into an exultant music video, which the Beatles filmed at the Saville Theatre—still under the ownership of NEMS—on November 10th. The most famous of the three promotional clips recorded that day features the Beatles clad in their *Sgt. Pepper* uniforms, culminating in the lively "Maori finale" in which the bandmates, now in street-clothes, gyrate deliriously in the company of delectable dancing girls in grass skirts. Lennon is particularly ebullient, striking an Elvis Presley pose during the song proper, while breaking into a spirited Chubby Checker-style twist during the coda.

17. For several months, the Beatles had also considered making a television movie based on *Sgt. Pepper's Lonely Hearts Club Band*. The principal photography for the would-be production was scheduled for October and November 1967, with a screenplay by Ian Dallas under the direction of Keith Green. In addition to a mammoth "A Day in the Life" segment, the film was slated to feature 115 extras—including a troupe of motorcycle-riding "rockers" and a dozen "Model Rita Maids" (Lewisohn, *The Complete Beatles Chronicle* 245). In 1978, Robert Stigwood produced a movie musical of *Sgt. Pepper's Lonely Hearts Club Band*, starring Peter Frampton and the Bee Gees, that was met with widespread critical disdain.

18. Having seen the finished product and sensing imminent disaster, Peter Brown recommended that the Beatles mothball the *Magical Mystery Tour* movie for the foreseeable future: "I tried to suggest writing off the £40,000 [in production expenses] and moving on. But Paul didn't know it was a mess and insisted on making the deal [with the BBC]" (qtd. in Spitz 734).

Chapter 11

Whiter Shades of Pale

We tell ourselves stories in order to live. . . . We look for the sermon in the suicide, for the social or moral lesson in the murder of five. We interpret what we see, select the most workable of the multiple choices. We live entirely, especially if we are writers, by the imposition of a narrative line upon disparate images, by the "ideas" with which we have learned to freeze the phantasmagoria which is our actual universe.
—JOAN DIDION, *THE WHITE ALBUM*

Wherever we are, what we hear is mostly noise. When we ignore it, it disturbs us. When we listen to it, we find it fascinating. The sound of a truck at 50 mph. Static between the stations. Rain. We want to capture and control these sounds, to use them, not as sound effects, but as musical instruments.
—JOHN CAGE, "THE FUTURE OF MUSIC: CREDO"

All those who live in the past live with us now. Surely none of us would be an ungracious host.
—KAHLIL GIBRAN, *SAND AND FOAM*

On January 25th, 1968, the Beatles reunited at Twickenham Film Studios to shoot a cameo for the *Yellow Submarine* animated feature. As with the intervening months after the "Jesus Christ Tour" had concluded in August 1966, the bandmates had gone their separate ways yet again. Ringo had taken a supporting role in the movie *Candy*, based upon Terry Southern's 1958 novel and

211

directed by Christian Marquand. The film, which parodies Voltaire's *Candide*, stars Ewa Aulin as Candy, a beautiful ingénue who embarks upon a sexual odyssey that brings her into the orbit of a randy Mexican gardener named Emmanuel, played by Ringo to hilarious effect. Meanwhile, George had traveled to India, where he conducted recording sessions for the soundtrack of *Wonderwall*, an art film being directed by Joe Massot. The movie traces the life and work of an introverted scientist named Oscar Collins (Jack MacGowran), who becomes obsessed with his neighbors, especially the aptly named Penny Lane (Jane Birkin), a delectable model. The "wonderwall" of the film's title refers to a shaft of light that streams through a hole in the wall that separates their apartments, illuminating Penny while she poses during a photo session. As time passes, Oscar's obsession begins to overwhelm him, and soon he drills even more holes in order to observe Penny's every move. At EMI's Bombay facility, George recorded a series of *ragas* for the *Wonderwall Music* soundtrack, while also preparing the instrumental track for a new composition entitled "The Inner Light." Back in London, Paul served as producer for his brother Michael's latest album with Roger McGough. The highlight of the January 1968 recording sessions was an appearance by Jimi Hendrix, who lent his talents to the proceedings. Over the Christmas holidays, Paul had become engaged to Jane Asher, although without having set a date for the nuptials. In contrast with his bandmates, John's world had been threatening to implode for months. For the life of him, he simply couldn't get Yoko out of his mind. Way back in April 1967, John had attended the *14 Hour Technicolor Dream*, a benefit sponsored by the *International Times* at the Alexandra Palace and Pavilion, where Yoko was one of the featured performers. Her *Half-a-Wind Show*, subtitled as *Yoko Plus Me*, opened that October under John's patronage at London's Lisson Gallery. Inspired by Yoko's work with Fluxus, the exhibition featured everyday furniture and appliances that had been cut in half and embossed in white paint. Before long, John confessed his fascination with the diminutive Japanese artist to an incredulous Pete Shotton. In actuality, John and Yoko had spent very little time together since their November 1966 meeting at the Indica Gallery. But it hardly mattered to John. He was already hooked.

The shadowy presence of Yoko Ono notwithstanding, the elements of historical conjuncture in the Beatles' lives in early 1968 are almost too numerous and varied to ascertain. Yet even with the benefit of hindsight, it is difficult to fathom the complex of events that was swirling about them during the five, mostly frenetic months that preceded the production of their next album. As the *Magical Mystery Tour* saga had so clearly demonstrated, the single-mindedness that allowed the band to launch *Revolver* and *Sgt. Pepper* into being was now the stuff of memory. And without Brian Epstein to guide them through the storm, the

Beatles' personal, creative, and financial lives had been set on a collision course that they were virtually powerless to avert. The only saving grace, as always, was their music. In contrast with the inconsistent nature of their collective muse during the latter half of 1967, the new year's recordings had begun with a flurry of top-drawer compositions. And while the Beatles were still operating as a studio-conceived idea, they did so with a renewed sense of purpose and vigor.

On February 3rd, the Beatles convened in Studio Three, where they began working on Paul's superb "Lady Madonna." He had been inspired to write the song after seeing a magazine photograph of an African woman holding a baby. Paul was especially intrigued by the caption, which described the woman as a "Mountain Madonna" (Everett, *Revolver through the Anthology* 153). In addition to concocting a driving bass part on his Rickenbacker, Paul liberally borrowed his piano arrangement for "Lady Madonna" from "Bad Penny Blues," a 1956 hit produced by George Martin for jazz musician Humphrey Lyttelton. With his "Elvis voice" in full flower—and well-supported by a zesty tenor sax solo by the legendary Ronnie Scott—Paul tells the heartrending story of a woman desperately attempting to provide sustenance for her growing brood. As with "Eleanor Rigby," "Lady Madonna" posits the image of a lonely heroine whom society has neglected—and, even more significantly, for whom organized religion remains conspicuously silent:

> Lady Madonna, children at your feet.
> Wonder how you manage to make ends meet.
> Who finds the money, when you pay the rent?
> Did you think that money was heaven sent?

McCartney employs the days of the week as the song's structure, pointedly excluding Saturday—there is no Sabbath, no day of rest for Lady Madonna, whose children grow up in spite of her.[1] "See how they run," the narrator laments, while the unwed mother sells her soul—not to mention her body—in order to make ends meet by any means necessary: "Lady Madonna, lying on the bed, / Listen to the music playing in your head." As she plies her loveless trade, the music washes across her being, transporting Lady Madonna to another world beyond the stale bedroom, beyond her hopelessly expanding ménage. With its explicitly holy antecedent, Lady Madonna's name paradoxically elevates the status of McCartney's heroine, while calling the church's capacity for engendering charity into question at the same time. As with "Eleanor Rigby," "Lady Madonna" portrays a world in which, time and time again, an insensate society turns a blind eye to the suffering. No one is saved.

Released as the B-side of "Lady Madonna," George's "The Inner Light" offers similar observations about humankind's vexing inability to reap wisdom from the past. At the suggestion of Cambridge Sanskrit scholar Juan Mascaró, George composed "The Inner Light" based on the professor's translation of a poem by Lao Tzu from *Tao Te Ching*, the seminal sixth-century work of Chinese scripture (Everett, *Revolver through the Anthology* 152). In the narrative of "The Inner Light," transcendent knowledge is a rare thing indeed: "The farther one travels, / The less one knows," George sings.[2] To achieve genuine self-awareness and perceive one's inner light, the song suggests that humankind must embrace consciousness and "Arrive without traveling / See all without looking / Do all without doing." In George's evolving Eastern-oriented philosophy, epiphanies abound in the simplicity of human language and experience. Not to be outdone, John's "Across the Universe" harnesses the pure beauty of poetry in an effort to sate the weary soul. Influenced by the Beatles' recent experiences with Transcendental Meditation, "Across the Universe" came to John, its lyrics fully formed, as he lay in bed one evening with Cynthia: "Words are flowing out like endless rain into a paper cup, / They slither while they pass, they slip away across the universe." Recorded in early February with John on his Martin D-28 and George on tamboura, the composition captures Lennon in one of his most earnest, lyrical, and hopeful performances. With "Across the Universe," Tim Riley remarks, "the free-floating imagery determines the musical flexibility— the words evoke the creative process as much as a creative state of mind" (296). As a work of metapoetry, "Across the Universe" captures both the aesthetic intensity of creative expression and the artist's struggle to rend language into meaning. As Yeats observes in "Adam's Curse," the act of articulating "sweet sounds together" is difficult work indeed—and no different, in its own way, from the backbreaking toil of the "old pauper" who must "break stones" in "all kinds of weather" (29). In Lennon's composition, inspiration comes calling— literally from across the universe—with seeming ease before just as mysteriously slipping away into the writerly void. In those exquisite moments, when the artist's creative faculties blossom and pour forth, the writer achieves a sense of tranquility and oneness akin to Transcendental Meditation's cosmic consciousness, a state of immutable peace. Consider the calming refrain of "Across the Universe" in which John invokes the Sanskrit phrase "Jai guru deva om," which we might loosely translate as follows:[3]

Jai	Live Forever
Guru	Teacher
Deva	Heavenly One
Om	The Vibration of the Universe

By espousing ideas of optimism and community in response to the malaise and fragmentation of the crowd, the Beatles' ineluctable modernism shines ever brightly. "Nothing's going to change my world," Lennon sings. As the closest thing to stream-of-consciousness narration among the group's wide-ranging corpus, "Across the Universe" is arguably the most authentic and heartfelt representation of their art.[4]

The Beatles wrapped up their invigorating February 1968 sessions with John's "Hey Bulldog," a playful rock and roll tune, originally entitled "Hey Bullfrog," that finds the bandmates, particularly Lennon and McCartney, enjoying the simple pleasures of fun and frivolity that had earned them a global audience in the first place. With John on piano, Paul on his Rickenbacker, George on his Gibson SG Standard, and Ringo flailing away on the drums, the song features a deftly constructed terraced effect in which the instrumentation slowly builds in advance of a lead vocal that witnesses John at his fiery, throat-searing best: "If you're lonely, you can talk to me!" he screams. John matches the intensity of his singing with a razor-edged guitar solo that he plays with a Vox Wah-Wah pedal engaged, likely having borrowed George's Gibson SG. The entire session finds the Beatles in top form, loosing their artistic inhibitions to create one of their most energetic and appealing performances on record. The proceedings come to a fantastic close as John and Paul howl, bulldog-like, into the fadeout.[5] When the mix was complete, George Martin hastily dispatched "Hey Bulldog" to King Features Syndicate, the conglomerate that was preparing the *Yellow Submarine* animated film for release in July.[6] Brian Epstein had originally negotiated the production of *Yellow Submarine* in order to fulfill the band's contractual obligations to United Artists, and, in retrospect, it turned out to be one of the late manager's sharpest of moves.

Released to widespread critical acclaim—and to the sheer delight of children of all ages—*Yellow Submarine* succeeded in putting the Beatles back on the cinematic map with an original and, for the time period at least, significant artistic accomplishment. It was a far cry from *Magical Mystery Tour*, to say the least. Directed by Canadian animator George Dunning, *Yellow Submarine* was produced by Al Brodax, one of the creative forces behind the Beatles cartoons. Co-written by Brodax, Lee Minoff, and Erich Seagal—who would later author the screenplay for *Love Story* (1970)—*Yellow Submarine* featured little actual input from the band. Initially skeptical about the value of making another film, the Beatles only contributed four new songs, a few script alterations, and a brief appearance at the end of the movie. Yet the finished product clearly exceeded their expectations. As Tony Barrow notes, the Beatles were "so pleased with the way the whole production had been put together that they were only too happy to associate themselves with it more closely from then on" (*"Yellow Submarine"* 13). And indeed they should be: in addition to contributing yet again to the promulgation of their constructed celluloid personalities, *Yellow Submarine* added another layer to their remythology by portraying their genuine interests in pacifism and universalism. In the film's climactic scene, Lennon's character battles an insidious flying Glove by hurling the word *Love* at the accessory while singing "All You Need Is Love." Although John would interrogate his own pacifist ideology on *The White Album*'s "Revolution 1," *Yellow Submarine*'s cartoonish vision of the Beatles living a near-utopian existence in Pepperland coheres rather easily with their earlier, equally carefree narratives about life as members of the Fab Four. The Beatles' tacit (and, ultimately, enthusiastic) approval of *Yellow Submarine* reminds us that myth-making is an inherently collaborative process in which intentionality plays a comparatively minor role in relation to the star turn of celebrity culture.[7]

In February, the band would engage in a myth-making turn of an entirely different sort. During the February 11th recording session for "Hey Bulldog," Tony Bramwell captured the band performing the song on film, later editing the footage into a promotional video for the "Lady Madonna" single, which was released by Parlophone in March. By that time, the Beatles were literally thousands of miles away, having rejoined the Maharishi in Rishikesh, the holy city that rests on the banks of the Ganges. The group had been planning to travel to India for several months. Initially delayed by Brian Epstein's death, the Beatles finally agreed upon a mid-February departure for their journey to the Maharishi's ashram, which was nestled in the foothills of the Himalayas. "A few days before our departure," Cynthia recalled, "we had a meeting with the Maharishi's assistant at a house in London to finalize details of the trip. As we entered the main room I saw, seated in a corner armchair, dressed in black, a small Japanese woman. I guessed immediately that this was Yoko Ono, but what on earth was she doing there?" (*John* 274). In spite of her alarm over Yoko's sudden manifestation in her life, Cynthia enjoyed the peaceful extended break that life in the Valley of the Saints afforded the band and their entourage, which included the Beatles' significant others, Pattie Harrison's sister Jenny Boyd, Donovan, the Beach Boys' Mike Love, jazz flautist Paul Horn, and the ever-present Magic Alex.

Despite its remote location, the Maharishi's six-acre compound was replete with creature comforts, including a swimming pool, a laundry, a post office, and a lecture hall from which the holy man would deliver his teachings to his assembled guests. At one point, the Maharishi arranged for a pair of helicopters to fly his distinguished visitors on a sightseeing tour up and down the Ganges. Each of the Beatles responded to their experience in the ashram in radically different ways. Complaining about the spicy cuisine, Ringo left after only ten days, having exhausted his secret supply of Heinz Baked Beans.[8] For Paul, life in Rishikesh offered a sublime opportunity to cleanse his mind and replenish his writerly muse. When he and Jane left after six weeks in the compound, he graciously thanked their host: "Maharishi, you will never fathom what these days have meant to us. To have the unbroken peace and quiet and all your loving attention—only a Beatle could know the value of this" (qtd. in Herrera 237). For George, it was one of life's great privileges to ponder the Maharishi's lectures and practice Transcendental Meditation in the ashram. But of all the Beatles' reactions to the experience, John's ended up being the most peculiar. At one point, he announced, with uncharacteristic ebullience, that "we're going to build a transmitter powerful enough to broadcast Maharishi's wisdom to all parts of the globe—right here in Rishikesh" (qtd. in Herrera 238). He went so far as to fantasize about a new life for himself in the Maharishi's orbit, suggesting to the holy man that he and Cynthia retrieve young Julian from England and join the Maharishi in order to continue their spiritual training in Kashmir. Yet as John gravitated ever closer to the Maharishi, Magic Alex grew increasingly suspicious of their host. Within a few days, John's mood abruptly shifted from exultance to gloom without explanation. To everyone's astonishment, John gruffly declared that he and George were leaving the compound immediately. When questioned by one of the Maharishi's followers about his sudden change of heart, Lennon angrily replied: "If you want to know why, ask your fuckin' precious guru" (qtd. in Herrera 244). Quite suddenly, eight weeks of serenity had evaporated into thin air by mid-April, and the Harrisons and the Lennons began making their way back to London, where the merry month of May would take them on the ride of their lives.

First, there was Apple. The tax dodge that the Beatles had concocted a year earlier had transmogrified into a full-fledged enterprise. Reflecting a pun devised by Paul, Apple Music was rechristened as Apple Corps in an explicit effort by the Beatles to wrest hold of their business affairs and control their own destiny after months of uncertainty in the wake of Brian's death. "We're just going to do—everything!" John announced to Pete Shotton. "We'll have electronics, we'll have clothes, we'll have publishing, we'll have music. We're going to be talent spotters and have new talent" (qtd. in Spitz 727–28). But the corporation had gone awry almost from the very start. Back in December 1967, they had opened the Apple Boutique at 94 Baker Street. To mark the occasion, the Fool created a brilliantly arrayed psychedelic mural that enveloped the building—that is, until legal entanglements from the City of Westminster led to its removal after only a few weeks (Spitz 731). By midsummer, the bandmates had lost interest, not very surprisingly, in operating the boutique, famously giving away its wares to an eager public after first ransacking its racks and aisles for themselves. On May 11th, John and Paul traveled to the United States in an effort to promote Apple's musical interests on an international stage. In New York City, they taped a surreal appearance on NBC's long-running *Tonight Show*, where they were interviewed by Major League Baseball's Joe Garagiola, who was sitting in for regular host Johnny Carson. It made for an odd combination, to say the least, with an obviously bemused Lennon and McCartney fielding glib questions from the star-struck former catcher. At a press party later that evening, Paul recognized Linda Eastman among the throng of photographers, dutifully acquiring her telephone number. The Beatle's transformation in her presence wasn't lost on Nat Weiss: "Paul's whole demeanor—that cocky defensive shield he wore like armor— melted away, and, for a moment, he seemed fairly human" (qtd. in Spitz 761).

Back in England, life took yet another bizarre turn when John announced that he was none other than Jesus Christ. With Cynthia away on vacation in Greece, he was anxious to share his good news with the world. On May 18th, the self-proclaimed Messiah called a meeting with the other Beatles in order to acquaint them with his new identity, which they attributed to his latest bout with hallucinogens. It was in this manic state that John decided to invite Yoko out to Weybridge. Unbeknownst to Cynthia at the time, Yoko had been bombarding John on a daily basis with postcards, which he eagerly retrieved at the Maharishi's post office back in Rishikesh. Shortly before midnight on May 19th, Yoko took a taxi to John's estate. They stayed up all night improvising recordings, with John manipulating his pair of Brenell reel-to-reel tape recorders while Yoko shrieked a series of wordless, discordant vocals into the growing cacophony. At dawn, they made love, consummating the relationship between their artistic and corporeal selves. A few days later, Cynthia returned from her Grecian holiday just in time to experience the great shock of her life. Kenwood was eerily silent, its front door strangely unlocked. As she prepared to open the sunroom door, Cynthia "felt a sudden frisson of fear":

> John and Yoko were sitting on the floor, cross-legged and facing each other, beside a table covered with dirty dishes. They were wearing the toweling robes we kept in the poolhouse, so I imagined they had been for a swim. John was facing me. He looked at me, expressionless, and said, "Oh, hi." Yoko didn't turn around. (*John* 284)

John's indifference spoke volumes, and Cynthia understandably fled the scene, finding temporary shelter in the house that Jenny Boyd shared with Magic Alex. Legend has it that Cynthia expelled her grief in the eager arms of Magic Alex, that she exacted her vengeance by sleeping with one of her husband's closest friends. It's a rumor that the self-styled wizard did nothing to quell. "Alex crept into the bed and was attempting to kiss and fondle me, whispering that we should be together," Cynthia recalled. "I pushed him away, sickened"

(*John* 289). The tackiness of Alex's advances was a minor footnote in the final act of John and Cynthia. She could only contemplate the remains of her marriage, which lay in tatters back in the Kenwood sunroom.

In spite of the turmoil in the Beatles' lives, May 1968 concluded with a spurt of creative activity that rivals, if not supersedes, some of the most prolific moments of their career. "The entire *White Album* was written in India," John later remarked. "We got our mantra, we sat in the mountains eating lousy vegetarian food, and writing all these songs. We wrote *tons* of songs in India" (qtd. in Badman 388). During the last week of May, the bandmates gathered at Kinfauns, where George had fashioned a home recording studio, complete with an Ampex four-track reel-to-reel tape recorder. While it has become *de rigueur* among Beatles biographers to characterize *The White Album* as one of the group's more disconnected recording ventures—ground zero for their eventual disbandment—the reality of the work's production suggests otherwise. At Kinfauns, they created twenty-three demos in preparation for recording the songs that would eventually comprise *The White Album*.[9] In contrast with their painstaking efforts in the studio, the Esher Tapes witness the Beatles working in unison and exalting in the pure joy of their music. With its splendid acoustic introduction, the demo for "Revolution" offers a perfect case in point. The band had rarely, if ever, sounded more uninhibited and free. With its enthusiastic handclaps, ad-libs, and lighthearted harmonies, it makes for one of the Beatles' most convivial recordings. Yet for all of their geniality, the Esher Tapes were calculated rough drafts—coherent blueprints for the upcoming project. The group had seldom exhibited such a self-conscious and highly organized approach to their art. One way or another, their new record would be different.

~

A work of astonishing fecundity and brain-wracking convolution, *The White Album* takes us almost everywhere that music can possibly go. It's an endurance test of the senses, as the Beatles inflict aural whiplash upon their audience by galloping through an array of competing musical styles. In a self-consciously constructed song cycle that guides the listener from the Cold War-inspired "Back in the USSR" through the psychosexual "Happiness Is a Warm Gun," the somber realities of "Blackbird," and the sheer terror of "Helter Skelter," *The White Album* pits our yearnings for love, hope, and peace in sharp contrast with an increasingly fragmented postmodern void.[10] Through parody, hyperbole, and bitter irony, *The White Album* tells the story, in dissonant and highly metaphorical fashion, of the sociocultural calamity that the world experienced in 1968. From assassination and racial unrest to political disjunction and the growing shadows of the Vietnam War, 1968 displaced the optimism of 1967's Summer of Love with equal doses of alienation and uncertainty. As Ian Marshall astutely remarks, "A Beatles song offers not the pontificating of a sermon, but the open-endedness of dialogue where the next word is the reader's" (24). And *The White Album*—with the blank, empty space of its glossy pearl cover— dares us to re-inscribe the Beatles' art with our own passion, our own reality, our own terror.

Recorded in January 1969, the coda from "I've Got a Feeling" finds John lamenting that "everybody had a hard year." And it was a hard year indeed. In April 1968, Dr. Martin Luther King, Jr., was gunned down in Memphis, Tennessee, by sniper James Earl Ray. The assassination of the American civil rights leader spawned riots in more than sixty American cities, resulting in the deaths of thirty-nine people. In contrast with the previous year's Summer of Love, the summer of 1968 replaced the decade's growing senses of hope and optimism with bloody despair. Two months later, surging Democratic presidential candidate Robert F. Kennedy was felled by Sirhan Sirhan, a Palestinian who opposed the Senator's support of Israel. Kennedy's murder led to a power vacuum that effectively destabilized the antiwar faction of the Democratic party. The summer's awful events reached their nadir in August at Chicago's Democratic National Convention, where thousands of people, including members of Students for a Democratic Society and the Youth International Party (the "Yippies"), gathered to protest the Vietnam War and the policies of President Lyndon B. Johnson. After violent confrontations erupted between the demonstrators and the Chicago police, Mayor Richard J. Daley ordered some twelve thousand officers to attack the protesters with clubs, dogs, and tear gas for nearly three days. Broadcast to a horrified American television viewing audience, the convention's tragic turn of events weakened support for Democratic candidate Hubert Humphrey, who lost the November 1968 election to Richard Nixon. If you're the Beatles—for whom *Sgt. Pepper* served as the soundtrack for the Summer of Love—how do you go about textualizing the Summer of Disillusion and Hate?

In many ways, *Sgt. Pepper* and *Magical Mystery Tour* exist as mere warm-ups—psychedelic diversions, if you will—in advance of *The White Album*'s more considerable achievement as a compelling act of extended storytelling. In contrast with its predecessors, *The White Album* eschews the micro-narratives of individual songs in favor of a long-playing song cycle in which the record's discrete elements come together, as with an impressionistic painting, in order to form a magisterial, seamless whole. Released on November 22nd, 1968— exactly five years after *With the Beatles*—*The White Album* affords its listeners with a host of literary figures, from Dear Prudence, Bungalow Bill, and Rocky Raccoon to Sexy Sadie, a sty of political Piggies, the ghostlike Julia, and a pensive Blackbird "singing in the dead of night." Conceived when albums existed as the self-consciously imagined "sides" of long-playing records, *The White Album*'s first side is a mind-bending suite characterized by moments of arch parody, simple romantic pleasures, and bitter drama.

The album begins with Paul's "Back in the USSR," complete with its tongue-in-check pastiche of Chucky Berry's "Back in the USA" and the Beach Boys' fun-in-the-sun, bikini-clad "California Girls." The song finds its roots in India, when Paul and Mike Love took to singing "I'm Backing the USSR" as a parody of the recent "I'm Backing Britain" campaign spearheaded by the government to lower the national debt (Everett, *Revolver through the Anthology* 187). The Beatles rehearsed the song during an August 22nd session that went horribly awry when Ringo—frustrated by his inability to play the requisite drum part and fed up with Paul's increasingly proscriptive attitude—announced that he was leaving the band. "I'm sure it pissed Ringo off when he couldn't quite get the drums to 'Back in the USSR,' and I sat in," McCartney remarked. "It's very weird to know that you can do a thing someone else is having trouble with" (qtd. in Dowlding 222–23). Trundling on without their misplaced drummer, the other three Beatles agreed to keep his defection a secret from the wide world beyond the studio. "Back in the USSR" is a masterpiece of multitrack recording, with John on his Jumbo and six-string Fender bass; George on his Fender Telecaster and Fender Jazz Bass; and Paul on his Rickenbacker, his Casino, and playing Ringo's vacant Ludwigs. With McCartney adopting his "Jerry Lee Lewis voice," Lennon and Harrison supply fantastic, soaring Beach Boys-like harmonies (qtd. in Spizer 103). In an effort to imbue the track with an appropriately international feel, Ken Scott created a tape loop of Viscount jet sounds from the EMI tape library's *Volume 17: Jet and Piston Engine Airplane*. The result is a brilliant send-up of life behind the Iron Curtain, a world of ostensible mystery and danger—particularly from a Western ideological perspective nursed on *Sputnik* and James Bond—where "Moscow girls make me sing and shout," while the speaker entreats his listeners to "come and keep your comrade warm." In the song's most outrageous of its many puns, Paul transposes the American South of Ray Charles's "Georgia on My Mind" with the comparatively icy clime of the Soviet Republic of Georgia.

With its jet engines disappearing beyond the horizon, "Back in the USSR" crossfades into "Dear Prudence," drawing a warm bath of guitar balladry in place of its precursor's perplexing, albeit playful, attempts at achieving sociopolitical dislocation. With Paul once again behind the drums, John's composition commemorates the Beatles' days in the Maharishi's compound, where the group was joined by actress Mia Farrow and her reclusive younger sister Prudence, who refused to leave her room, prompting various members of the compound to alight outside her door, speaking and singing to her in an effort to draw her forth. "Won't you come out to play?" the song's speaker beckons. "Dear Prudence" makes for one of the album's most pleasing interludes, with its daisy chains and carefree romantic disposition, both of which are brought vividly to life by John and George's intricate, highly textured guitar work. "Dear Prudence" ultimately reveals itself to be transitory—as with the album's other oases of comfort and solitude—as a pair of staccato drumbeats usher in John's "Glass Onion," the Beatles' most self-referential and self-conscious track. Recording sessions for the song commenced on September 11th, and the composition features Paul's double-tracked recorder solo, as well as a piano part on which he plays a nifty glissando at the conclusion of the song's instrumental bridge. To the great relief of his bandmates, Ringo plays the drums on "Glass Onion," having returned to the fold a week earlier, his drum kit smothered in flowers, courtesy of Mal Evans. As balance engineer Ken Scott later observed: "The classic for me is in the song 'Glass Onion.' There's a drum thing that goes *blat blat*. It happens three times in the song. Well, with that drum part, even though it was on the basic track, we double- and triple-tracked the snare drum onto one separate track," imbuing Ringo's drum work with its impudent, highly layered thud (40). Tea towels were used to dampen Ringo's drums, particularly his snare, which was fortified with a pack of Everest cigarettes—Geoff Emerick's favorite brand—sitting on the drum head in order to enhance the effect. Searching for an innovative means for bringing the composition to a close, John supervised a bizarre late-September session in which he overdubbed the sound of broken glass, a ringing telephone, and BBC soccer commentator Kenneth Wolstenholme exclaiming "It's a goal!" over a roaring football crowd (Spizer 104).[11] When George Martin returned shortly thereafter from an extended holiday, he was suitably unimpressed with John's inexplicably arcane epilogue. By superimposing an arrangement for four violins, two violas, and two cellos onto the track, Martin afforded "Glass Onion" with an eerie string coda that serves to enhance the song's textually subversive contents, rather than shrouding them behind a veneer of disconnected sound effects.

In his post-Beatles years, John characterized "Glass Onion" as a trifle, as yet another puzzle designed to occupy the band's legion of overzealous fans. But that would be selling the song decidedly short, given its rich sense of people and place. "Glass Onion" encounters a wide range of Beatles characters and songs—from "Lady Madonna" and "The Fool on the Hill" to "Fixing a Hole" and "Strawberry Fields Forever"—and it takes place, the speaker reports, on

Liverpool's "cast-iron" shore, a paradoxical universe in which the notion of comely beach terrain is undercut by the rust and decay of a dying shipbuilding town.[12] As with the embedded layers of meaning in a composition, peeling back the glass onion's diaphanous skin reveals a narrative that constantly turns inward upon itself until meaning becomes diffuse, even meaningless. The song's impetus becomes resoundingly clear in its waning moments, when John barks his vocal: "Trying to make a dove-tail joint." In its pointed reference to the woodworking process known for improving tensile strength, Lennon's composition effects a carpentry metaphor about the inherent complexity in creating art. A work of metapoetry, "Glass Onion" functions as a parable about the act of storytelling itself, about the difficulty of plying a writerly trade. As with Wallace Stevens's "motive for metaphor"—where "everything is half dead" with "an obscure moon lighting an obscure world," where the "wind moves like a cripple among the leaves / And repeats word without meaning"— "Glass Onion" revels in the brute power of language (288).

As the string coda for "Glass Onion" drifts into the ether, the album doubles back on itself yet again. The parody thickens in "Ob-La-Di, Ob-La-Da," with its white reggae pretensions, the hippie nonchalance of "Wild Honey Pie," and "The Continuing Story of Bungalow Bill," which camouflages the cold-blooded, thrill-killing of a tiger with the cheerful air of a children's song. The elaborate recording sessions for Paul's "Ob-La-Di, Ob-La-Da" began on July 3rd, with Paul on Fender Jazz Bass and piano, John on maracas and providing backing vocals, George on his Gibson J-200 acoustic, and Ringo on the drums. The song found its inspiration in the words of Jimmy Scott, a Nigerian Conga player who was fond of repeating the Yoruban expression "*ob-la-di, ob-la-da, life goes on.*" In an early rendition of the song, the Beatles fashioned a south-of-the-border reading of "Ob-La-Di, Ob-La-Da," complete with John's enthusiastic preface: "Yes, sir! Take one, and the Magic Jumbo Band!" Over the next several nights, the composition underwent numerous takes as the group attempted different versions of the song and Paul continuously tinkered with his vocal, testing his colleagues' patience in the process. Things finally came to head on July 9th, when John contrived the tune's jangly piano introduction. "I AM FUCKING STONED!" he announced upon entering the studio that evening. "And this is how the fucking song should go," he said, before pounding out the famous piano opening (qtd. in Emerick 247). In its finished state, "Ob-La-Di, Ob-La-Da" finds the Beatles turning in an admirable ska-inflected version of the song, with ambient studio voices in the style of February's "Hey Bulldog." John and George engage in playful banter throughout the track—at one point, Lennon spells out "H-O-M-E" in jocular response to Paul's lead vocal, which traces the simple story of Desmond and Molly, a pair of lovers who succeed in living happily ever after by evoking the homespun wisdom inherent in Scott's Yoruban adage.[13]

The strife associated with "Ob-La-Di, Ob-La-Da" was not limited to the Beatles themselves. During a July 15th session, Emerick witnessed Martin shouting at McCartney about his lead vocal, and the balance engineer decided that he had to escape the tension-filled atmosphere. Having become increasingly depressed over the summer, Emerick resigned as the group's balance engineer the very next day. But as far as Emerick was concerned, the band's growing stress and strain had relatively little to do with their personal strife. The Beatles "were virtual prisoners of their fame," he later remarked. EMI Studios "had no relaxation facilities at all; for them, it was more like working in a prison. Sure, there was a canteen downstairs, but they couldn't go there for fear of being mobbed. Neither could they go out for a breath of fresh air, thanks to the ever-present legions of fans waiting outside" (257). Emerick had also grown weary of newcomer Chris Thomas, George Martin's protégé from AIR who had been fulfilling the elder producer's duties when he was away from the studio. "Though he would tread carefully at times," Emerick recalled about Thomas, "he began developing an attitude, an arrogance, that I just didn't like. I felt that he had no business being there; he had no background or training, so why should we value his opinion? George Martin and I had been doing these sessions for years, with great success, and all of a sudden Chris had infiltrated the inner sanctum, without having ever paid any dues" (238). But the inner sanctum clearly wasn't what it used to be, and between the Beatles' sour demeanor and the presence of Chris Thomas, Golden Ears could simply no longer stomach the turmoil.

And Emerick was by no means alone in his melancholy. On July 19th, Harrison and Martin quarreled, with the guitarist chiding the producer for being "very negative!" (qtd. in Winn, *That Magic Feeling* 207). In spite of Emerick's criticisms, Chris Thomas had emerged as the emollient that the band sorely needed—if only during the difficult days of *The White Album*. As tape operator John Smith observed, "I do seem to remember that with Chris being there, it was just a different vibe. I think they thought Martin was like a schoolteacher, sort of out of place, and with Chris, I think there was a much cooler vibe." With Martin increasingly absent from the console, the Beatles often operated without benefit of a producer at all. "I remember a lot of sessions where there was *no one* there producing," Ken Scott recalled. "The Beatles were very much in control" (qtd. in Ryan and Kehew 476, 477). During Martin's extended vacation in August and September 1968, Thomas had taken over the production duties in their entirety, with Ken Scott sitting in as balance engineer.[14] As far as Thomas was concerned, working with the Beatles was the opportunity of a lifetime: "The thing I always remember about them, and where they were different to all the other bands, was that they were very playful—in the way that kids are. You know, a bit mischievous like that," he later remarked. "And that's where a lot of the mad ideas came from. They'd just try anything, really, to see what it was like: 'What happens if you do this, what happens if you do that?' They were very different from anybody else in that way" (qtd. in Ryan and Kehew 496).

If *The White Album* indeed contains a trifle among its contents, then McCartney's "Wild Honey Pie" surely qualifies. With Paul on vocals and strumming his Martin D-28, the bouncing, bubbly "Wild Honey Pie" acts as an appropriately whimsical overture for John's "The Continuing Story of Bungalow Bill," a lighthearted parody about American conquest and colonialism. The song finds its origins back in the ashram, where John had become acquainted with Nancy Cooke de Herrera, one of the Maharishi's devoted followers. During the Beatles' stay in India, Herrera's eldest son, Rik Cooke, had shot and killed a tiger during a hunt with his mother in the Sitabani Forest, providing perfect fodder for Lennon's simple tale about an "all American bullet-headed Saxon mother's son." The Beatles recorded the song between midnight and dawn on October 9th—Lennon's twenty-eighth birthday. "The Continuing Story of Bungalow Bill" featured Chris Thomas on the Mellotron, playing with the mandolin stop engaged during the verses and using the bassoon stop during the coda. The song's sophisticated flamenco guitar introduction was actually a preset track on the Mellotron. Having based the composition's melody on Mack Gordon and Henry Revel's "Stay as Sweet as You Are," John assembled a chorus that included Ringo's wife, Maureen, and Yoko, who turned in a vocal cameo, singing "not when he looked so fierce" as the voice of Bungalow Bill's mother. By this time, Yoko had become a mainstay in the recording studio, trailing John's nearly every move to the point of exasperating his befuddled bandmates. By mid-June, John and Yoko had made their first public appearance, planting acorns for peace at Coventry Cathedral. While the other Beatles may have harbored their own illusions about the couple's future, she wasn't going anywhere. Having finally found her way into John's heart, she was there to stay.

In contrast with the playfulness of "The Continuing Story of Bungalow Bill," George's "While My Guitar Gently Weeps" offers a sobering indictment of the crowd in the same vein as "A Day in the Life." During his composition of the song, George had been thinking about the Chinese *I Ching*—specifically "The Book of Changes." As a powerful redaction of Western individualism and vacuous materialism, the song's maudlin lyrics and pessimistic orchestration reek of unrequited love and wasted life. In so doing, they underscore the discrepant existential philosophies inherent in the East and the West, where the life of the mind takes on entirely different connotations. But the real story behind "While My Guitar Gently Weeps" involves the composition's searing guitar work, as well as its surging, dirgelike firmament. After George recorded a solo acoustic version in late July, the band remade the song in mid-August, with George on lead vocals and his Gibson J-200, John on his Casino, Paul on his Fender Jazz Bass and the track's distinctive piano introduction, and Ringo on the drums. In an explicit attempt to improve the band's flagging attitude during *The White Album* sessions, George invited Eric Clapton to record the song's guitar solo on September 6th: "Just bringing in a stranger among us made everybody cool out," George later remarked (*Anthology* 306). Clapton played his magnificent, driving solo on a Gibson Les Paul Standard.[15] At Clapton's request, the solo was heavily treated with ADT in order to achieve a more "Beatley" sound. "I was given the grand job of waggling the oscillator on the 'Gently Weeps' mixes," Chris Thomas recalled. "We did this flanging thing, really wobbling the oscillator in the mix. I did that for hours" (qtd. in Babiuk 229). Thomas's efforts more than paid off, as "While My Guitar Gently Weeps" not only elevated Harrison's songwriting stock considerably, but echoed across the decades, especially during the heyday of 1970s-era guitar rock.[16]

During the song's lengthy fadeout, a guitar can be heard moaning in the distance. The sound makes for a fitting preface for "Happiness Is a Warm Gun," the album's lewd philosophical centerpiece. With its continuous, non-repetitive structure, "Happiness Is a Warm Gun" offers a rare example of a "through-composed" entry in the Lennon-McCartney songbook. John had been inspired to write the song after George Martin showed him a magazine cover with the phrase "Happiness Is a Warm Gun." As John later remarked. "I just thought it was a fantastic, insane thing to say. A warm gun means you just shot something" (*Lennon Remembers* 115). The article in the gun magazine was no doubt alluding to Charles Schultz's well-known early 1960s *Peanuts* cartoon. With the caption "Happiness is a warm puppy," the cartoon depicts beloved beagle Snoopy locked in the brawny embrace of Lucy Van Pelt (Spizer 108). Intrigued perhaps by the bizarre pop-cultural convergence of guns and *Peanuts*, John had located the perfect vehicle for exploring society's lunatic fringe, with its cynical lechers, its drug addicts, and its madmen. Recording sessions for the song began on September 23rd, with the Beatles struggling through a mind-numbing seventy takes before completing the track. In addition to portraying "Happiness Is a Warm Gun" as a miniature "history of rock and roll," Lennon described the composition's three principal sections as "the Dirty Old Man," "the Junkie," and "the Gunman" (*Anthology* 307). In a feast of competing time signatures, John vocalizes the introduction over a gurgling hot stew of arpeggiated electric guitars. The song's female lead, the speaker informs us, is "not a girl who misses much." In short, she's become jaded by her very own shrewdness, by the breadth of her own experience. John's description of the character's prurient eroticism—"She's well-acquainted with the touch of the velvet hand / Like a lizard on a window pane"—finds his poetry at its salacious best. She likes a soft touch alright, but only when it's well-tempered by the scaly raw urgency of human sexuality. Her sleazy voyeuristic counterpart is "the man in the crowd with the multicolored mirrors / On his hobnail boots." He masturbates publicly—"Lying with his eyes while his hands are busy / Working overtime"—before Lennon's psychosexual nether world dissolves before our very ears.

As the second section ensues, a soaring bass line tumbles out of the stratosphere to ignite a lumbering guitar section, played by George in lugubrious 9/8 time on his Les Paul: "I need a fix 'cause I'm going down," John drawls, "Down to the bits that I left uptown." The quartet kicks into higher gear as one iteration after another of "Mother Superior, jump the gun" reminds us that nobody, not even a nun, will be saved in the stark, Godless world of Lennon's composition. The third section, which acts as the song's extended coda, transforms John's sordid ruminations on base animal instinct into a contemptuous paean to 1950s-era notions of *faux* innocence and veiled sexuality. The composition's thematics effect a coherent sense of musical unity by finishing the song, Alan W. Pollack notes, in "a mid-fifties cliché-saturated dialect of C major." In the Esher demo for "I'm So Tired," John sings, "When I hold you in my arms, / When you show me each one of your charms, / I wonder should I get up and go to the funny farm." Astutely revising and transplanting this passage into "Happiness Is a Warm Gun," he turns the entire song inside out. As the music slows perceptibly, we shift from the mean streets of the heroin addict into the lily-white world of "Earth Angel" and the Stroll. But then the sock-hop comes to a premature close, the school gym's makeshift spotlight seeking out the lead singer, hair slicked back and gripping the silvery microphone with all his might: "When I hold you in my arms, / and I feel my finger on your trigger," John sings in jaw-dropping 12/8 time. "I know nobody can do me no harm, because / Happiness is a warm gun." With Paul and George singing "bang-bang, shoot-shoot" in perfect harmony, the song teeters between earnestness and kitsch. In the end, "Happiness Is a Warm Gun" is a revolution unto itself: on the one hand, it basks in the seamy residue of unfettered lust, while on the other, it whitewashes our sins with a doo-whop chorus lost amidst its own restless insincerity. Either way, it's a hall of mirrors, and the only way out, it seems, is through an Id-cleansing time-warp.

Perhaps more so than any other Beatles album, *The White Album*'s rollicking second side reveals the ways in which the band's musicality contributes to the lyricism of their narratives. With their dizzying array of musical styles, the nine tracks from "Martha My Dear" through "Julia" loom as masterworks of artistic virtuosity. They also illustrate *The White Album*'s stunning eclecticism—the true measure of the album's resilience. Recorded in early October at Trident Studios, Paul's Baroque-sounding "Martha My Dear," with its crisp brass accompaniment, introduces the sequence, which meanders, rather lazily, into John's bluesy "I'm So Tired," which its author later described as "one of my favorite tracks. I just like the sound of it, and I sing it well" (qtd. in Dowlding 232). As a valentine to Paul's wooly sheepdog Martha, the former composition functions almost entirely as a work of style, displacing the razor-sharp guitar work and aberrant sexuality of "Happiness Is a Warm Gun" with the rich ambience of the music hall. Recorded in mid-June, McCartney's folksy "Blackbird" imagines a contemplative metaphor for the United States's civil rights struggles during the 1960s. As Paul later observed: "I had in my mind a black woman rather than a bird. Those were the days of the civil rights movement, which all of us cared passionately about. So this way really a song from me to a black woman experiencing these problems in the States: 'Let me encourage you to keep trying, to keep your faith, there is hope'" (qtd. in Ryan and Kehew 484). Based on Bach's *Bourée for Lute in E Minor*, which Paul and George had learnt in their youth, Paul's distinctive acoustic guitar melody for "Blackbird," played on his Martin D-28, alternates among 3/4, 4/4, and 2/4 time signatures. The tapping sound throughout the song is not a metronome, as one might reasonably conclude, but rather, the sound of Paul's feet gently rapping on the floor of EMI's Studio Two. Emerick had helpfully placed a microphone nearby to capture the moment. Having been culled from the EMI tape library's *Volume 7: Birds of Feather*, the sweet sound of a chirping blackbird—a European *Turdus Merula*, to be exact—eventually segues into George's acerbic political satire "Piggies" (Ryan and Kehew 484). With Chris Thomas playing the harpsichord, "Piggies" specializes in brazen "social comment," its songwriter later remarked, weaving slovenly images of politicians supping at the trough of their unsuspecting constituencies. George's mother, Louise, had composed the tune's signature lyric—a punishment suitable for misanthropic politicians everywhere: "What they need's a damned good whacking!"[17]

    The White Album's song cycle continues with McCartney's countrified "Rocky Raccoon," a track that shifts, rather astonishingly, from the disquieting universe of cowboys, gunplay, and hoedowns into a surprisingly moving tale about the nature of nostalgia and loss. Written under the working title of "Rocky Sassoon," "Rocky Raccoon" was recorded in mid-August, with Paul on his Martin D-28, John on harmonica and the Fender Bass VI, and George strumming his Gibson J-200. The sound effects abound, with Ringo signaling the loud report of a gun with a rim-shot and Martin establishing a saloonlike ambience on the Challen "jangle box" piano, which he played at half-speed, honky-tonk style, and created using his wound-up piano technique. For the lyrics and storyline of "Rocky Raccoon," Paul drew on yet another found object, Robert Service's poem entitled "The Shooting of Dan McGrew":

> A bunch of the boys were whooping it up in the Malamute saloon;
> The kid that handles the music-box was hitting a jag-time tune;
> Back of the bar, in a solo game, sat Dangerous Dan McGrew,
> And watching his luck was his light-o'-love, the lady that's known as Lou. (29)

"The Shooting of Dan McGrew" afforded Paul with an inspiring canvas for animating his nostalgia-tinged story about love and loss in the Wild West. Having ventured into the "black mountain hills of Dakota," Rocky Raccoon is dead, quite literally, before the song even starts. Future commutates into present when Rocky, with only Gideon's Bible to nurture his aching heart, pledges to avenge the loss of his beloved—in a masterstroke of ambiguous identity, "Her name was Magil, and she called herself Lil / But everyone knew her as Nancy"—who has left him, it seems, for another man. As her new paramour, Danny Boy is the narrative's most symbolically rendered character, with his name invoking the unvarnished nostalgia of a funeral wake. The expected showdown between Rocky and Danny Boy is intentionally anticlimactic, resulting, as it does, in Rocky's fatal shooting. As he teeters toward death on the drunken physician's table, Rocky optimistically plots his revival: "Doc, it's only a scratch / And I'll be better, I'll be better, Doc, as soon as I am able." With precious little time remaining, Rocky returns to his hotel room, where Gideon has already "checked out," leaving the gunslinger to die alone. In contrast with the Biblical Gideon's theophanic mission to inspire the Israelites, Rocky's spiritual savior sees scant value in rescuing yet another relic from the Old West. With no place in the future and a desolate present spread out before him, Rocky fades away into a quickly receding past. As with the lover's waning romantic aspirations in *Revolver*'s "For No One," Rocky can only contemplate the inevitable measure of his loss in an alien world in which nostalgia engenders nothing but sadness and death, spiritual or otherwise.

Starr's "Don't Pass Me By," with its barrelhouse piano chorus, steers the sequence abruptly into the sudsy world of the beer hall. Originally entitled "Ringo's Tune (Untitled)," and later, "Some Kind of Friendly," the song became a number-one hit, rather fittingly, in Scandinavia. Other than his contribution to "Flying," "Don't Pass Me By" marks Ringo's first original composition. Recorded in early June, the song features Paul on Studio Three's jangly piano and studio musician Jack Fallon tearing it up on the fiddle. In one of the album's most jarring of its many discordant transitions, Fallon's violin trails off into the sunset, all but erased by the hard-driving rock of "Why Don't We Do It in the Road." As one of McCartney's finest blues effusions, "Why Don't We Do It in the Road" sets the stage for the side's final two numbers, "I Will" and "Julia." Recorded on October 9th, "Why Don't We Do It in the Road" caused a minor rift in the band when Paul—accompanied only by Ringo on the drums—overdubbed all of the instruments himself. Having been inspired to write the composition by the sight of monkeys copulating in the Maharishi's compound, Paul dominated the track, playing his Rickenbacker, Martin D-28, Casino, and piano.[18] With a throat-gnashing vocal commonly assumed to belong to John, Paul presents an intriguing contradiction about the nature of human modesty: on the one hand, the speaker beckons his mate to join him in an uninhibited bout of sexual exhibitionism, while on the other, he sees fit to reassure her (and perhaps even himself) that "no one will be watching us / Why don't we do it in the road?" *The White Album*'s first half concludes with the delicate balladry of Lennon and McCartney, beginning with Paul's "I Will," which was recorded over sixty-seven takes in mid-September, with Paul on his Martin D-28 and scatting his bass part, John on shakers, and Ringo plying the cymbals, bongos, and maracas in a veritable feast of percussion. In a nostalgic backward glance toward the music of his youth, Paul adorns the spaces between the verses with the unmistakable sound of Buddy Holly-styled guitar phrasings. A soothing melody about the tenuous interplay between romance and commitment, "I Will" remains one of McCartney's most memorable experiments in brash sentimentality.

Arguably his most powerful and fully realized composition, Lennon's "Julia" memorializes the songwriter's late mother while simultaneously addressing his spiritual deliverance at the hands of his new-found soul mate, the "ocean child" Yoko Ono. With John playing his capoed Jumbo, "Julia" witnesses the Beatle trying his hand at the highly arpeggiated finger-picking style—the distinctive "claw hammer"—that he had picked up from Donovan back in Rishikesh. John had borrowed two of the song's key phrases from Lebanese poet Kahlil Gibran's *Sand and Foam: A Book of Aphorisms* (1926), including "Half of what I say is meaningless, but I say it so that the other half may reach you"; and "When Life does not find a singer to sing her heart she produces a philosopher to speak her mind" (14). Musically, John effects a dreamlike feel through the mergence of his gentle acoustic guitar with the natural wonder of his voice. As a work of poetry, the song revels in the skillful word pictures that John realizes through a pair of imagistic dyads—"seashell eyes, windy smile" and "sleeping sand, silent cloud." The middle-eight is simply breathtaking—perhaps the finest among the songwriter's multitudinous compositions: "Her hair of floating sky is shimmering, glimmering, / In the sun." By double-tracking his voice in crucial instances, John allows different aspects of his self to emerge, particularly when he draws upon his imagination in order to establish a sense of connection with his lost mother.[19] At the same time, the composition finds him examining the nature and beauty of his new relationship with Yoko through the auspices of Julia's memory. It's an astounding achievement that Lennon never equals, especially given the song's remarkable personal and musical significance in his life. Through its placement on the album, the somber quietude of "Julia" acts as an ironic counterpoint to side two's rampant animalia, its mock seriousness, and its whimsy. And as with the rest of the album, it finds the Beatles seeking to undermine the act of meaning-making at every turn. Just as we're about to bring our interpretations to fruition, the group draws the curtain on the scene before raising it above an entirely different setting. And the resonances shift yet again.

Side three begins with "Birthday"—a spontaneous guitar-bash that the Beatles conjured up on the spot in the studio in September. As Lennon later observed, "I think Paul wanted to write a song like 'Happy Birthday, Baby,' the old '50s hit" (qtd. in Dowlding 238). Ted Goranson has suggested that McCartney was thinking about the Tuneweavers' 1957 hit "Happy, Happy Birthday" when he devised the song's central guitar riff. As one of the group's rare moments of improvisation, "Birthday" features John and Paul on lead vocals, each playing their Casinos to the hilt. Meanwhile, Pattie and Yoko share the backup vocals. As with several other compositions on *The White Album*, the song finds the band indulging in yet another moment of parody, with the group reconceiving the act of birthday celebration in their own image. The album shifts gears rather precipitously into "Yer Blues," a razor-edged musing about all-out desolation and suicide. Written by John in India while he was "up there trying to reach God and feeling suicidal," the composition features a complex structure, as the song transitions among 12/8, 6/8, and 4/4 time signatures (qtd. in Spizer 111). "Yer Blues" was recorded in mid-August in Studio Two's closet-sized Annex, a relatively tiny room in which all four Beatles huddled with their instruments. Initially written as a tongue-in-cheek response to the British blues boom during the latter half of the 1960s, "Yer Blues" begins to take on more serious connotations when Lennon explores the gravest aspects of loneliness, going so far as to read suicide as the logical result of protracted isolation. "Yes, I'm lonely / Wanna die," Lennon sings, before invoking Bob Dylan's Mister Jones, the aloof everyman from "Ballad of a Thin Man" on *Highway 61 Revisited*: "Something is happening here / But you don't know what it is," Dylan sings. "Do you, Mister Jones?" While the song takes on obvious intertextual overtones—as with the self-referential "Glass Onion"—John's allusion to Mister Jones in "Yer Blues" offers a crucial misreading of Dylan's composition. Given his considerable detachment from his community, Mister Jones isn't suicidal in the slightest—in fact, he's either too distant or too self-absorbed (or both) to register such tendencies in the first place. If anything, "Ballad of a Thin Man" posits an indictment of our own self-involved humanity. Dylan's contemptuous laugh at the song's onset suggests that the real target of his satire is none other than his very own listening audience. The enemy, in short, is us. Despite misreading "Ballad of a Thin Man," John's ruminations about suicide and despair signal a new direction in Lennon and McCartney's ongoing study of loneliness as a corruptive force. In contrast with the spiritually vacant Mister Jones, John's speaker knows better, realizing, as he does, that his society has given up on him, that his existence has become devoid of meaning.

Ever-mindful of the dislocating power of textual disparity, the Beatles take yet another musical right turn—in this instance, into the folkways of McCartney's "Mother Nature's Son," which pursues a starkly different line of inquiry from "Yer Blues." Recorded over two sessions in August, "Mother Nature's Son" finds Paul playing his Martin D-28, the tympani, and the bass drum. Studio musicians supply the song's brass accompaniment, an aspect that George Martin had originally desired for "Blackbird" until the songwriter politely declined his suggestion. With the warm embrace of the trumpets and trombones in the background, Paul can be heard tapping a copy of Henry Wadsworth Longfellow's *Songs of Hiawatha* during the latter half of the song, with Ken Scott thoughtfully positioning a mic over the book in order to capture its sound. With "Mother Nature's Son," Paul imagines a pastoral environment in which his speaker lives in an interminably idyllic present: "Born a poor young country boy, Mother Nature's son / All day long I'm sitting singing songs for everyone." Rather than blithely memorializing the past in the vein of *Magical Mystery Tour*'s "Your Mother Should Know," "Mother Nature's Son" establishes an artificial present in which the speaker's yearnings for transcendence have seemingly already been satisfied. Yet as surely as the sun goes down, Paul's "swaying daisies [that] sing a lazy song beneath the sun" will die. The song rather pointedly avoids discussion of life's cyclical maneuvers between birth and death, even though the recording's very fleeting subject matter necessarily prefigures a nostalgic experience in some distant (or perhaps not so distant) future.[20] As with "In My Life," "Penny Lane," and "Strawberry Fields Forever," "Mother Nature's Son" depicts life as a generally benevolent experience with scant regard for its corporeal limits.

With the sound of a fire bell acting as its strident introduction, "Everybody's Got Something to Hide Except for Me and My Monkey" explodes its precursor's sweetness with all of the subtlety of an atomic bomb. "It was about me and Yoko," John later remarked. "Everybody seemed to be paranoid except for us two, who were in the glow of love" (qtd. in Dowlding 241). Recorded in late June under the working title of "Come On, Come On," the song's first line—"Come on is such a joy"—was a favorite saying of the Maharishi's (Spizer 112). Once again connoting the album's larger themes of chaos and uncertainty—"Your inside is out and your outside is in"—the song offers a manic interpretation of love's capacity for effecting disruption and dis-ease beyond the relative safety afforded by the lovers' romantic cocoon. A moment of pure excitement and adrenaline, the guitar riff at the conclusion of "Everybody's Got Something to Hide Except for Me and My Monkey" evokes the inexplicable exuberance of love with the bruising panache of rock and roll. It's a rhythmic burst of high-octane modulation that is intentionally undermined by the clanging, midbar introduction of Paul's piano preamble to "Sexy Sadie." As Lennon's acidic footnote to the Beatles' experiences under the Maharishi's tutelage, "Sexy Sadie" displaces the previous song's hyper-realized sincerity with pure salaciousness: "We gave you everything we owned just to sit at your table / Just a smile would lighten everything." John had written the song as a caustic critique of the Maharishi, the ostensibly celibate holy man who had, according to a rumor floating around the ashram courtesy of Magic Alex, made sexual advances upon a young woman staying at the compound. Having discovered what he believed to be an unforgivable hypocrisy, John insisted that the Beatles' entourage depart the ashram immediately. When the incredulous Maharishi inquired about his guest's sudden impulse to leave, John offered a bitter riposte: "Well, if you're so cosmic, you'll know why." John had intended to entitle the song "Maharishi," although at George's urging, he changed "Maharishi" to "Sexy Sadie" in advance of recording the Esher demos (Spizer 112). While the lyrics understandably devolve into a rant, the song's musical structure remains particularly interesting. As Paul's tinkling piano phrases spar with Harrison's bristling guitar, "Sexy Sadie" maneuvers effortlessly through chord changes and one harmonic shift after another. When the song finally ascends to its closing musical interchange, the Beatles' instrumentation and John's vocal coalesce in a magnificent instance of blissful resolution.[21]

For the first instance since the plaintive brass accompaniment to "Mother Nature's Son," the album seems to achieve a sense of wholeness with "Sexy Sadie." It's a fleeting sensation, of course, that is annihilated by the electric horror of "Helter Skelter." Paul had been inspired to write the song after learning that the Who's latest single, "I Can See for Miles," was being described by Pete Townshend in *Melody Maker* as "the raunchiest, loudest, most ridiculous rock and roll record you've ever heard" (*Anthology* 311). With the explicit goal of one-upping the Who, Paul composed "Helter Skelter," a slower, twenty-seven-minute version of which was recorded by the band during a drug-addled session in mid-July. A remake was recorded in September, with Paul playing his Casino and turning in a larynx-searing lead vocal, John on his Fender Jazz Bass, and George on his Gibson Les Paul Standard—nicknamed "Lucy," it was his guitar of choice during the making of *The White Album*. Meanwhile, Mal Evans played a dyspeptic trumpet, while Ringo pounded away on the drums through some eighteen versions of the song during rehearsal (Spizer 113). The phrase "Helter Skelter" refers to the spiral slides on the English playgrounds of the Beatles' youth, although in Paul's composition, the childhood thrill ride takes on very different, highly sexualized connotations:

> Do you, don't you want me to love you?
> I'm coming down fast but I'm miles above you.
> Tell me, tell me, tell me, come on tell me the answer.
> You may be a lover but you ain't no dancer.

But the song's latent eroticism is merely a surface feature. If nothing else, "Helter Skelter" witnesses the Beatles in the act of evoking the sound and mettle of pure unadulterated terror.[22] With its shouts and its screams and its scorching guitar work, "Helter Skelter" heightens our sense of trauma through a series of false endings, punctuated by Starr's most notorious moment on record: "I've got blisters on my fingers!" It's a breathless effusion that puts our nightmares to bed, if only temporarily, with Harrison's overtly somber "Long Long Long." Recorded over three days in early October, "Long Long Long" went under the working title of "It's Been a Long, Long, Long Time," featuring George on his capoed Gibson J-200, John on his Martin D-28, and Paul on the Hammond organ. George borrowed the song's chord structure, while alternating the time signature between 6/8 and 3/8, from Dylan's "Sad-Eyed Lady of the Lowlands," the haunting, epic track that brings *Blonde on Blonde* to a close. George had become infatuated with the acoustic- and organ-oriented sound that Dylan achieved with the Band, and, as a result of his adulation, "Long Long Long" "was as close as the Beatles ever came to plagiarism," Walter Everett writes (*Revolver through the Anthology* 204). Harrison's version of the song dispenses with the vague romantic imagery of its precursor in order to fashion a stirring religious paean. The distinctive sound at the end of the song materializes from a bottle of Blue Nun spontaneously rattling atop the Hammond organ's Leslie speaker cabinet. Ringo joins in with a tom-tom roll, while George begins wailing in impromptu accompaniment. In keeping with the restless spirit of the entire project, it makes for a truly spooky moment that undercuts the composition's prevailing gravity.

With side four, *The White Album*'s brilliant psychosocial palette reveals a number of instances in which the band presents intentionally contradictory canvases for our inspection, particularly in terms of the so-called "Revolution" series that helps drive the album to its cataclysmic conclusion. Recorded on May 30th, "Revolution 1" features John on his heavily distorted Fender Strat, while Paul and George offer an intentionally jarring series of "bam shoo-be-doo-wop" backing vocals. As if to compound the incongruous nature of the composition's mêlée of competing styles and instrumentation, George Martin scored an arrangement for two trumpets and a quartet of trombones. A sloppy edit at 0:02—intentionally retained in the mix at Lennon's request—witnesses Geoff Emerick muttering "take two" and adding an extra beat to the song's introduction. In an attempt to lend his voice a breathy quality, John recorded his vocal lying flat on his back in the control room, with a microphone, courtesy of Emerick, hovering over his head. In "Revolution 1," Lennon ponders the tempting qualities of revolution and revenge: "When you talk about destruction / Don't you know that you can count me out—in." As with "Happiness Is a Warm Gun," John delivers his polemic against the dislocating backdrop of a 1950s-era doo-wop refrain. With "Revolution 1," the composition's first iteration, John teeters between revolutionary and antirevolutionary stances: "I put in both because I wasn't sure," he later remarked (*Anthology* 298). In the up-tempo, even more distorted version of the song (entitled simply "Revolution" and released as the B-side of "Hey Jude"), John abandons his militant extremism, thus embracing the peace movement's pacifist outlook.[23] What renders the song even more compelling is its author's own uncertainty about battle and bloodshed as viable interpersonal solutions. As Everett points out, the song's "slow tempo, laid-back brass, restful lead vocal, and smooth backing vocals have the calming effect counseled in the lyrics, an effective counterpoise to the revolution sizzling in the distance with metric stabs and distorted electric guitars" (*Revolution through the Anthology* 174). John desperately wanted to release "Revolution 1" as a single—as the Beatles' explicit statement about the violence of their age. Yet as with "I Am the Walrus," his bandmates wouldn't have it. They said "it wasn't fast enough," John later recalled. "But the Beatles could have afforded to put out the slow, understandable version of 'Revolution' as a single, whether it was a gold record or a wooden record. But because they were so upset over the Yoko thing and the fact that I was again becoming as creative and dominating as I had been in the early days, after lying fallow for a couple of years, it upset the applecart" (*All We Are Saying* 187).

And then there's "Honey Pie," a McCartney non sequitur that defuses the inner tension wrought by its predecessor with the white noise of a phonograph needle alighting a 78-RPM record. The guitar rock of "Revolution 1" is suddenly exploded by the big-band sounds of yesteryear. Recorded in early October at Trident Studios, "Honey Pie" finds Paul at his schmaltzy, parodic best, with John turning in a terrific retro guitar solo on his Casino. "Honey pie," McCartney sings, "You are making me crazy / I'm in love but I'm lazy / So won't you please come home?" The Beatles intend to take us home alright, but not before traversing the dessert fare of Harrison's "Savoy Truffle," with its sax-driven melodies and, as with the allusion to "Lucy in the sky" in Lennon's "I Am the Walrus," a benign intertextual reference—"We all know Obla-Di-Bla-Da"—that affords the group's wider musical narrative with a sense of coherence and continuity. "Savoy Truffle" had been inspired by Eric Clapton's notorious sweet tooth. The legendary guitarist simply couldn't get enough of Mackintosh's Good News Double Centre Chocolates, a candy assortment that featured such delectables as Creme Tangerine, Ginger Sling, and Coffee Dessert. A quartet of studio musicians established the track's "beefy" sound with an ensemble of tenor and baritone saxophones.

Despite a clever middle-eight in which George sings "You know that what you eat you are," courtesy of the wit of Derek Taylor, "Savoy Truffle" doesn't really go anywhere, in contrast with "Not Guilty," the Harrison track that didn't make the final cut.[24] Recorded in early August, it required an astounding 110 takes to perfect. Intensely autobiographical, the composition makes explicit reference to the Beatles' complex of creative and, with increasing frequency, extra-creative responsibilities. In 1967, they had tried their hand (and failed) at filmmaking, only to attempt to manage their own multimillion dollar business, with its myriad financial strands, the following year. As if by premonition, George alludes to the inevitable self-interest that comes with such enterprises: "I won't upset the applecart / I only want what I can get." In "Savoy Truffle," the songwriter concocts a sweet-tasting novelty, while "Not Guilty" brews up a bitter dose of reality. In the wake of "Savoy Truffle," John's "Cry Baby Cry" distorts the album's momentum yet again. Based on the children's nursery rhyme "Sing a Song of Sixpence," "Cry Baby Cry" offers a series of nonsensical tales about being "old enough to know better," while positing an implicit reminder that human beings so rarely take their lessons from the past—in spite of the wisdom that it contains. In many ways, it is precisely these sorts of backhanded motifs that set the Beatles apart from the other practitioners of their genre—songwriters who, more often than not, substitute bombast for subtlety.[25]

The Beatles conclude the album with what amounts to their most purposefully disconcerting trio of recordings: the unlisted outtake "Can You Take Me Back"; the fiercely chaotic "Revolution 9," a jarring montage of indiscriminate noise, tape loops, and sound effects; and "Good Night," the lushly over-sentimentalized lullaby that brings *The White Album* to a close. As the coda for "Cry Baby Cry," Paul's haunting fragment literally pleads for a transcendent return to a simpler past: "Can you take me back where I came from? / Can you take me back?"—a question that will be revisited with dramatically different results in *Abbey Road*'s "Golden Slumbers." The speaker's answer arrives in the menacing form of the Stockhausen-inspired "Revolution 9," some eight minutes of nightmarish surreality. Recorded on a series of Brenell tape recorders by John and Yoko, "Revolution 9" presents a sound collage comprised of tape loops, backward recordings, and all manner of reconfigured noise. The track's eerily antiseptic spoken refrain, "number nine, number nine," was lifted from an examination recording for the Royal Academy of Music in the EMI tape library, while the tape loops include portions of Schumann's *Symphonic Etudes*, Vaughan Williams's "O Clap Your Hands," Sibelius's *Symphony No. 7*, and even a violin trill from "A Day in the Life" (Everett, *Revolver through the Anthology* 174–77). Non sequiturs abound, with a multitude of verbal fragments courtesy of John, including the triumphant bequeathing of a sword, a weapon of honor in a dishonorable world: "Take this, brother, may it serve you well." In addition to the ambient noise of gunfire and crackling flame, the sound of a gurgling baby is oddly counterpoised by Yoko's erotic nonchalance—"If you become naked"—while the entire sonic morass concludes with the welcome resolve and determination afforded by a football cheer: "Hold that line. Block that kick." As the last desperate gasps of a dying civilization, the disconnected voices portend an oblivion that they cannot possibly stay.

As John later observed, "Revolution 9" was "just abstract, *musique concrète*, [tape] loops, people screaming." But the track is also striking for its author's self-described misreading of his own creation: "I thought I was painting in sound a picture of revolution—but I made a mistake, you know. The mistake was that it was anti-revolution" (*Anthology* 307). The "Revolution" series finds Lennon vacillating, in "Revolution 1" and the up-tempo "Revolution," between revolutionary and antirevolutionary postures. As the logical conclusion of the series, "Revolution 9" witnesses Lennon in the act of devising an aural representation of this conundrum. Alan W. Pollack rightly describes the recording as a "random anti-narrative effect," which indeed it is. Yet by accruing disruptive layer upon layer throughout that same antinarrative's stultifying vision, the track succeeds in establishing one of popular music's most disturbing listening experiences. With its intense sonic violence and sociocultural destruction, "Revolution 9" would seem, at least at face value, to be positively revolutionary. What ultimately persuaded John, then, to explain "Revolution 9" as a portrayal of "anti-revolution"—especially given its deliberately unsettling and lacerating nature?

Devin McKinney astutely interprets "Revolution 9" as a "picture of psychosocial breakdown which is every bit as merciless, grotesque, and anti-ideological as the rigors of art require that it be; in which the dullest familiars of ordinary life beat a constant pulse beneath the most appalling noises of a world collapsing upon itself" (244). In McKinney's reasoning, the track's anti-revolutionary quality has absolutely nothing to do with the act of revolution itself—with governmental overthrow or political violence. Rather, the anti-revolutionary aspects of "Revolution 9" are inherent in its depiction, in McKinney's words, "of a world collapsing upon itself." As the textual representation of a culture spiraling out of control and stumbling toward its irremediable doom, "Revolution 9" illustrates a desensitized world in which self-destruction has become inexorable, in which humanity has become vanquished. It's a world in which the answer to Paul's desperate appeal for a return to innocence—"Can you take me back?"—is nothing short of a resounding negative.

But as the haunting soundscape of "Revolution 9" recedes from earshot, a distant harp ushers in the sounds of comfort and solace inherent in "Good Night," complete with Ringo's warm farewell to the band's understandably disoriented listeners: "Good night, everybody / Everybody everywhere."[26] In this way, *The White Album* pointedly concludes with the intentionally syrupy mawkishness of "Good Night," the band's explicit attempt to console their audience, to provide palpable reassurance in the cataclysmic wake of "Revolution 9." As Allan Kozinn shrewdly observes, "The juxtaposition is brilliant in its incongruity" (178). Through the act of liberating their audience from the oblivion of "Revolution 9," the Beatles' poetics of apocalypse finds them tempering their larger sense of cultural despair with the lingering images of peace and resilience afforded by "Good Night." In so doing, they opt to mute the chaos and horror, if only temporarily, with an overtly hopeful gesture.

~

As the Beatles whiled away the summer of 1968 recording *The White Album*, they briefly interrupted the proceedings to record their landmark single "Hey Jude" b/w "Revolution." It was a watershed moment in many respects. In addition to being the first 45-RPM release by Apple Records—with its familiar Granny Smith logo—the single's A-side clocked in at more than seven minutes in length, exploding the dimensions of the conventional pop song in the process. "Hey Jude" finds its origins in Paul's mid-1968 visit to Weybridge in an effort to console Cynthia and five-year-old Julian after John's defection for Yoko. While driving out to the suburbs in his Aston Martin, Paul started "coming up with these words in my own mind. I was talking to Julian: 'Hey Jules, don't take it bad. Take a sad song and make it better.'" Realizing that "Hey Jules" was a "bit of a mouthful," Paul changed the name to "Jude" (*Anthology* documentary). Paul drew his musical inspiration from the Drifters' "Save the Last Dance for Me." Thrilled with his new composition, he played it for John and Yoko. "These words won't be on the finished version," he told them in reference to the cryptic lyric "the movement you need is on your shoulder." As Paul later recalled, "John was saying, 'It's great!' I'm saying, 'It's crazy. It doesn't make any sense at all.' He's saying, 'Sure it does, it's great'" (qtd. in Dowlding 203). Sagely heeding his partner's advice, Paul allowed the lyric to survive.

On Monday, July 29th, the Beatles gathered at EMI Studios to rehearse the song. At one point, George wanted to play a guitar riff that echoed the melody, an idea that Paul sternly rebuffed. "It was a bit of a number for me to dare to tell George Harrison—one of the greatest, I think—to not play," he later remarked. "It was like an insult, almost" (qtd. in Babiuk 224). In spite of Paul's squabble with George, the initial session was jovial, with John ad-libbing "goo goo g'Jude" and Paul adopting his "Elvis voice" and singing "Here come the Jude!" (qtd. in Winn, *That Magic Feeling* 213). On Wednesday, July 31st, they moved to Trident Studios, with its state-of-the-art eight-track recording facilities and its exquisite Bechstein Concert Grand piano. According to Paul, Ringo was in the bathroom at the beginning of the final take: "He heard me starting," Paul remembered. "He does up his fly, leaps back into the studio, and I suddenly see him tiptoeing past my back, rather quickly, trying to get to his drums. And, just as he got to his drums, boom boom boom—his timing was absolutely impeccable." On Thursday evening, George Martin recorded a forty-piece orchestra to accompany the song's lengthy coda, "a wordless four-minute mantra," according to Walter Everett, that includes an extended sing-along and fadeout (*Revolution through the Anthology* 192). Legend has it that a member of the orchestra left the session in a huff, stating that "I'm not going to clap my hands and sing Paul McCartney's bloody song!" (qtd. in Cross 368). But it didn't matter in the slightest to the Beatles, who were pleased with the relative alacrity of their creative pace in comparison with *The White Album* sessions. By Friday, "Hey Jude" was finished, with the Beatles receiving their customary acetate copies in advance of the single's release.[27]

Paul's vocal performance on "Hey Jude" gestures toward the sublime. Rich and buoyant, his voice has rarely sounded better. John and George's harmony vocals are equally superb—particularly Lennon's doubling of McCartney's lead vocal during the final verse. Lyrically, the song begins with a much-needed bout of commiseration and reassurance from its author—"don't make it bad," "don't be afraid," "don't carry the world upon your shoulders"—and slowly transforms into a tender caution about the ways in which loneliness begets even more loneliness: "For well you know that it's a fool who plays it cool / By making his world a little colder." Ultimately, "Hey Jude" ponders the notion—idealistic perhaps, during that jaded summer of 1968—that individual healing is rendered possible through a renewed relationship with the human community that exists beyond the self. "Remember to let her into your heart," Paul counsels his protagonist (and possibly even himself), "Then you can start to make it better." The composition's lyrics are made manifest by its music, which slowly builds from a solitary voice and explodes, finally, with the joyful sounds of Jude rejoining the wider world from whence he had lost his way. As if to illustrate the character's triumph, the track's terraced effect offers a study in musical subtlety and finesse. Beginning with voice and piano, the song accrues a gentle layer of acoustic guitar and tambourine before appending harmony vocals, drums, and bass to the mix. Eventually, an electric guitar emerges during the first pass at the "na-na-na" interlude that telegraphs the coda, where Martin's orchestra provides the firmament for the euphoric sing-along. Lost in his own isolation at the beginning of the song, Jude, like the vocalist, is no longer alone. He's a man of a thousand voices, like the Fool on the Hill, and, with a little goodwill and encouragement—not to mention a healthy dose of self-confidence—he'll soon be talking perfectly loud. The song's fadeout performs an essential role in demonstrating the character's movement from isolation to reinvigoration—but only to a point. As Sean Cubitt observes, the prolonged fadeout at the end of "Hey Jude" is a conscious evocation of its infinite replicability. Quoting Aristotle—"A whole is that which has a beginning, a middle, and an end"—Cubitt argues that "we have in this case an aesthetic object which is not whole, not complete in itself, and therefore not aesthetic in Aristotelian terms" (210). By intentionally deferring the long-term consequences of Jude's interpersonal shift—by eschewing an absolute sense of an ending in "Hey Jude"—the Beatles remind us of life's inevitable uncertainties and contingencies. Jude has taken a sad song and made it better alright, but his future remains appropriately blurry and indistinct.

As the B-side of "Hey Jude," "Revolution" finds the Beatles complementing the warm, communal hopefulness of its partner with the blistering, infectious sound of unvarnished rock and roll. With ace session man Nicky Hopkins contributing a lightning-hot electric piano solo, the song sports a highly distorted sound that Geoff Emerick achieved by overloading the pre-amps and direct-injecting John's Casino into the mixing desk.[28] As an explicit rejoinder to the bloody activities of the Communist Left, "Revolution" acts as John's gritty response to the Cultural Revolution in the People's Republic of China. Incensed by the Maoist exploitation of millions of youth militia forces in an express attempt to crush the Chairman's enemies, John authored his fearsome screed in order to denounce the violence and destruction. While "Revolution" clearly adopts an antirevolutionary stance, John offers a pointed critique of the insensate and dehumanizing behavior of unchecked political institutions. For Lennon at least, the Beatles' initial effort at social protest had been long overdue.

With a landmark single's release on their hands, the group was determined to give it an appropriate launch. Directed by Michael Lindsay-Hogg on September 4th at Twickenham Film Studios, the promotional films for "Revolution" and "Hey Jude" were recorded for rebroadcast on David Frost's popular British talk show, *Frost on Sunday*, and on the American variety show *The Smothers Brothers Comedy Hour*. Although the Beatles mimed much of the instrumentation, save for the vocals, the footage affords viewers with some of the last moving images of the group—even if only in quasi-performance. With his long hair and familiar granny glasses, John can be seen playing his Casino, which had been sanded down to its natural finish, its psychedelic paint stripped away after its owner's return from India. Meanwhile, George worked his Gibson SG, with Ringo playing his oyster-black pearl Ludwigs, his bass drum still adorned with its burnt orange head from the *Magical Mystery Tour* production. For the film shoot, Paul dispensed with his Rickenbacker, having selecting his lightweight Höfner, with the set list for the "Jesus Christ Tour" still taped to its upper body. In addition to the Beatles' guests, the audience at Twickenham that day had been recruited and bused in from the city by Mal Evans, who invited a group of lucky fans who had been hanging around EMI Studios to join the proceedings.

With a blood-curdling scream, Paul launched the band into "Revolution," for which John effected a series of increasingly hideous faces during the electric piano solo by an absent Nicky Hopkins. Having been introduced by their host as "the greatest tea-room orchestra in the world" after trying their hand at playing "By George! It's the David Frost Theme," a jazzy composition written by none other than George Martin, the tightly arrayed quartet began miming "Hey Jude" for the cameras. During the famous coda, the spectators mobbed the bandmates on stage for a spirited sing-along. It was a bravura moment indeed, and the excellent vibe on stage didn't escape the notice of the Beatles, who were thrilled to be playing in front of audience. The entire presentation was the work of artifice, to be sure—with the group simulating their performance and the studio audience undoubtedly reacting on cue—but the promotional films for "Revolution" and "Hey Jude" couldn't help taking on an enduring poignancy, given their relatively late date in the life of the Beatles. Perhaps even more remarkably, the videos witness the bandmates in the simple act of having fun.

The Beatles' appearance on *Frost on Sunday* would be one of their last public triumphs. Within a month, John and Yoko would be busted in Ringo's Montagu Square flat for possession of marijuana by Detective-Sergeant Norman Pilcher, the crusading leader of Scotland Yard's drug enforcement unit, which had recently nabbed Donovan and Keith Richards on similar charges. As the narcotics squad searched the premises, John telephoned Neil Aspinall: "Imagine your worst paranoia," he told Apple's Managing Director, "because it's here" (qtd. in Doggett 5). John blamed the drug raid for Yoko's mid-November miscarriage. "We were in real pain," he later remarked, and their understandable misery in the wake of the loss of their baby, whom they had named John Ono Lennon II, led to the couple's protracted heroin abuse—the overpowering drug habit that left them debilitated for the balance of 1968 and the early months of 1969, if not longer.[29] "The two of them were on heroin," said Paul, "and this was a fairly big shocker for us because we all thought we were far-out boys but we kind of understood that we'd never get quite that far out" (qtd. in Miles 567). But at the time, John and Yoko created a much wider stir on November 11th, when they released their first album, *Unfinished Music No. 1: Two Virgins*, whose controversial cover photograph portrayed the couple in all their naked glory. Parlophone patently refused to distribute the album in the UK, paving the way for its release on England's Track label and by fledgling Tetragrammaton in the United States.[30] Meanwhile, Paul's five-year relationship with Jane Asher had come to a crashing end that summer when his fiancée learned of his affair with Francie Schwartz, an American who had immigrated to London, like so many others, in hopes of landing a job with Apple Corps. Francie attended a number of recording sessions that summer—even getting the opportunity to join the famous chorus on the coda for "Hey Jude."[31] Yet by autumn, Paul had left Francie for the lovely Linda Eastman, who, with daughter Heather in tow, was poised to join her favorite Beatle for good.

The promotional films aired in Great Britain on September 8th, and within a month, the Beatles began fervently preparing *The White Album* for release. On October 16th, John and Paul conducted a twenty-four-hour session at EMI Studios in which they organized the songs in an effort to establish thematic unity. As John later recalled, "Paul and I sat up putting *The White Album* in order until we were going crazy" (*All We Are Saying* 55). Their strategy distributed the heavier rock and roll tracks on side three, with the animal-oriented songs relegated to side two. In order to create a sense of balance, they apportioned George's songs across all four sides. With George Martin, Ken Scott, and

John Smith in tow, they crossfaded and edited the tracks, ensuring that the album, like *Sgt. Pepper*, would be mastered without rills. The daylong session made for one of the most self-conscious moments in the history of the Beatles' artistry. Some eight months earlier, *The White Album* had found its origins in the Maharishi's ashram, only to be rehearsed and recorded at Kinfauns, reborn at EMI and Trident Studios, and transformed for the ages by John and Paul in the control room.[32] And then there was the matter of the cover art. For several months, the group considered entitling the album *A Doll's House* at the suggestion of John, who wanted to pay homage to Norwegian playwright Henrik Ibsen. But with the July release of Family's *Music in a Doll's House*, the Beatles were forced to go back to the drawing board. At the suggestion of Robert Fraser, Paul met with Pop Art designer Richard Hamilton, who proposed that the cover effect a dramatic contrast with the colorful albums of their recent psychedelic past. Hamilton recommended a plain white cover imprinted with individual numbers in order to assume the exclusive quality of a limited edition—although in this case, it would be a limited edition comprised, quite ironically, of some five million copies. At Hamilton's urging, the bandmates decided to name the album *The Beatles*, a deliberately simple title in relation to *Sgt. Pepper's Lonely Hearts Club Band*. But as the album's title, *The Beatles* never really stood a chance. With its stark white cover art, the two-record set became known as *The White Album* within scant days of its release.

In the ensuing years, there has been unremitting conjecture about the Beatles' motives in producing a double album in the first place. Some argue that they were trying to hasten the completion of their latest EMI contract. Perhaps they were attempting to sate their seemingly relentless creative impulses with the expansive artistic spaces of four long-playing sides? Yet others have suggested that the Beatles, competitive to the end, were trying to match, if not exceed, the critical success of Dylan's two-record masterwork *Blonde on Blonde*. In spite of all the speculation, George Martin has never minced words regarding his feelings about *The White Album*'s sprawl: "I thought we should probably have made a very, very good single album, rather than a double." In retrospect, Ringo has argued that it should have been released as two separate LPs—"the *White* and the *Whiter* albums" (*Anthology* 305)—while George felt that thirty songs was "a bit heavy" (qtd. in Spitz 794). For Paul, the question was moot. Self-reflexively withdrawing from himself and the band's art, he made no bones about the indisputable quality of their achievement: "It's great. It sold. It's the bloody Beatles' *White Album*. Shut up!" (*Anthology* documentary).

Regardless of the record's impetus, *The White Album*'s rough magic succeeded, if only briefly, in restoring the Beatles' earlier unity and cohesiveness—

so much so, in fact, that they returned to the studio less than two months later, eager and energized to commence their next project. As George later recalled, *The White Album* "felt more like a band recording together. There were a lot of tracks where we just played live." Meanwhile, Ringo saw the record as a sign of the Beatles' artistic renaissance: "As a band member, I've always felt *The White Album* was better than *Sgt. Pepper* because by the end it was more like a real group again. There weren't so many overdubs like on *Pepper*. With all those orchestras and whatnot, we were virtually a session group on our own album" (qtd. in Ryan and Kehew 476). Although he later described *The White Album* as the "tension album," Paul appreciated the opportunity to simplify and re-consolidate the group's sound, to retreat from the highly orchestrated production of their 1966- and 1967-era recordings. Perhaps even more so than Paul, John was absolutely delighted to dispense with their previously elaborate production efforts in favor of a spare and more conventional rock and roll sound. And while he later portrayed *The White Album* as a series of solo recordings by each of the individual Beatles, with the others acting as each other's session men, he was quick to point out that, in reality, their demeanor in the studio hadn't changed all that much since the early days: "We were no more openly critical of each other's music in 1968, or later, than we had always been" (qtd. in Dowlding 219). For John, *The White Album* represented a spectacular return to form. His musicianship was back with a fury, his songwriting was by turns breathtakingly intricate and refreshingly simple, his lyrics as imaginative and enthralling as ever. The album was a signal moment in his recording career—and, along with *John Lennon/Plastic Ono Band* (1970), it is arguably his last gasp of sustained greatness and originality. As with Yeats's epic rediscovery of his poetic muse in "The Circus Animals' Desertion," John had found his way back to the "foul rag and bone shop of the heart" (472). And so, too, had the Beatles.

With *The White Album*, the group reconciled the encroaching postmodern void on their own terms. By dramatizing it with all of its narrative detachment and terror before euthanizing it with a lullaby of their own making, the band dared to trump the fragmentation of their age in hopes of achieving something larger and more lasting. *The White Album* is a work of stylistic excess, to be sure, but it also represents the Beatles' most brazen attempt at staying the chaos of an increasingly convoluted and ethically dubious world by hurtling one narrative after another into the darkness. In all its discordant splendor, their act of hyperkinetic storytelling succeeds in positing art instead of apathy, noise instead of silence, life instead of death. By seeking wholeness in the midst of humanity's manifold contradictions, conflicts, and absurdities, *The White Album* suggests that self-awareness and pure human resilience continue to matter in a world beset by violence and turmoil. *The White Album* pointedly reminds us that we can take our broken wings and fly, that we can still say "good night" after the revolution, that we will always find a way to endure. Is there any grander narrative than that?

Notes

1. In his characterization of Lady Madonna's brood, Paul explicitly invokes "Monday's Child," the time-honored nursery rhyme about childhood destiny that was originally published in a September 1887 issue of *Harper's Weekly*: "Monday's child is fair of face. / Tuesday's child is full of grace. / Wednesday's child is loving and giving. / Thursday's child works hard for a living, / Friday's child is full of woe. / Saturday's child has far to go. / But the child that is born on Sabbath-day / Is bonny and happy and wise and gay."

2. Harrison explores similar terrain on "Any Road," a track on his final studio album, *Brainwashed* (2002). "If you don't know where you're going," George sings, "any road will take you there."

3. I am indebted to Sheila Hardie for this translation. See <www.proz.com> for additional details.

4. "Across the Universe" would undergo several different iterations, including the initial rendition, with a pair of acoustic guitars, a table harp, and George's tamboura. During the second session, John added his celestial vocal, while Ringo provided tom-tom accompaniment. Later that same evening, the Beatles invited a pair of Apple Scruffs—the Beatles' nickname for the horde of fans who trailed their every move—to sing harmony on "Across the Universe." Having been handpicked outside EMI Studios by Paul, an ecstatic Lizzie Bravo and Gayleen Pease provided backup vocals. Meanwhile, John agreed to share the recording—complete with Apple Scruffs and the sound of birds on the wing—with Spike Mulligan, who was organizing a charity LP for the World Wildlife Fund. The album was entitled *No One's Gonna Change Our World*, invoking Lennon's hopeful words as the rallying call for the animal rights movement. While the song would experience even more drastic changes in different hands in 1970, the original, ethereal version of the song (sans Scruffs, sans birds) can be heard in all of its majesty on the Beatles' posthumous LP *Let It Be . . . Naked* (2003).

5. In John's memory, the February 11th recording of "Hey Bulldog" marked the occasion of Yoko Ono's first appearance at a Beatles session. He remembered being startled by her unvarnished critique of his work: "Why do you always use that beat all the time? The same beat," she reportedly remarked. "Why don't you do something a bit more complex?" (*Lennon Remembers* 77).

6. The Beatles released their soundtrack for *Yellow Submarine*—including incidental music scored by George Martin and performed by the George Martin Orchestra—in January 1969. The remastered *Yellow Submarine Songtrack* was released in 1999.

7. While much of the biographical and autobiographical material related to the Beatles suggests their genuine endorsement of *Yellow Submarine*, Lennon characteristically

remembers things differently. The filmmakers behind the project, he contends, "were gross animals apart from the guy who drew the paintings for the movie. They lifted all the ideas for the movie out of our heads and didn't give us any credit. We had nothing to do with that movie, and we sort of resented them. It was the third movie that we owed United Artists. Brian had set it up and we had nothing to do with it. But I liked the movie, the artwork," he nevertheless concedes (qtd. in *All We Are Saying* 204). Robert R. Hieronimus's *Inside the Yellow Submarine: The Making of the Beatles' Animated Classic* (2002) offers a useful rejoinder to Lennon's claims, particularly his feelings of resentment about the Beatles' ostensible role—or lack thereof—in the film's production (50–51).

8. As Nancy Cooke de Herrera points out in her memoirs, Ringo's claims were largely unfounded: "Maharishi eliminated spicy foods from our diet," she writes. "Evidently, they stimulate the senses, which would have been counterproductive for meditation" (185).

9. The Esher demos include "Cry Baby Cry"; "Child of Nature"; "The Continuing Story of Bungalow Bill"; "I'm So Tired"; "Yer Blues"; "Everybody's Got Something to Hide Except for Me and My Monkey"; "What's the New Mary Jane"; "Revolution"; "While My Guitar Gently Weeps"; "Circles"; "Sour Milk Sea"; "Not Guilty"; "Piggies"; "Julia"; "Blackbird"; "Rocky Raccoon"; "Back in the USSR"; "Honey Pie"; "Mother Nature's Son"; "Ob-La-Di, Ob-La-Da"; "Junk"; "Dear Prudence"; and "Sexy Sadie." John had earlier recorded four additional acoustic demos at Kenwood, including "Happiness Is a Warm Gun"; "Mean Mr. Mustard"; "Polythene Pam"; and "Glass Onion."

10. The Beatles' alleged postmodernist tendencies are a matter of ongoing critical debate. While it is possible to argue—as Kenneth Womack has done in "The Beatles as Modernists"—that the Beatles work from a modernist position that posits a unified moral center, there is a growing certainty among Beatles scholars that frames the band as innovative postmodern visionaries. In such works as Henry W. Sullivan's *The Beatles with Lacan: Rock 'n' Roll as Requiem for the Modern Age* (1995), David Quantick's *Revolution: The Making of the Beatles' White Album* (2002), Ed Whitley's "The Postmodern White Album," and Jeffrey Roessner's "We All Want to Change the World: Postmodern Politics and the Beatles' White Album," the Beatles are essentially—indeed, *unflinchingly*—categorized in terms of an increasingly popular reading of *The White Album* as a series of arch parodies that emphasizes their postmodernity.

11. The September 26th version of "Glass Onion" is included, broken glass and all, on *Anthology 3* (1996).

12. In sharp contrast with John Haines's nostalgic musings about the "cast-iron" shore in "The Skipper's Lament," the Beatles' Liverpool in "Glass Onion" exists as a downtrodden home for Lennon and McCartney's restless, corrosive urbanites—the characters who act as the songwriting duo's stock-in-trade. Like cast-iron, they're a hard people, "insensible to fatigue; rigid, stern, unyielding" (*OED*).

13. The character of Desmond is a reference to Desmond Dekker, a renowned Jamaican ska musician who befriended Paul during the 1960s.

14. Thomas produced six songs during Martin's absence, including "Helter Skelter"; "Glass Onion"; "I Will"; "Birthday"; "Piggies"; and "Happiness Is a Warm Gun."

15. Clapton was credited in the album's liner notes as "Orlando Furioso."

16. Harrison paid homage to "While My Guitar Gently Weeps" with his 1975 composition "This Guitar (Can't Keep from Crying)," which turned out to be the final singles release on the Apple label.

17. The sounds of the pigs grunting in the barnyard were selected from *Volume 35: Animals and Bees.*

18. "Why Don't We Do It in the Road" offers a clear precursor to Paul's solo work on *McCartney* (1970), *McCartney II* (1980), and *Chaos and Creation in the Backyard* (2005), albums on which he played most of the instrumentation himself.

19. Through his experiences with Arthur Janov's controversial primal-scream therapy, Lennon addressed key issues related to his childhood trauma and his residual adult anger. On *John Lennon/Plastic Ono Band*, his celebrated 1970 solo album, he made further gestures toward Julia's untimely loss in such songs as "Mother" and "My Mummy's Dead."

20. McCartney's nostalgic contentment in "Mother Nature's Son" is brought into bold relief on the *Grey Album* (2003), DJ Danger Mouse's controversial "mash-up" of the Beatles' *White Album* with Jay-Z's hip-hop *Black Album* (2003). In spite of its notorious (and, quite frankly, illegal) origins, Danger Mouse's revisioning of "Mother Nature's Son" makes for one of the *Grey Album*'s finest tracks. By combining McCartney's sanguine acoustic guitar in "Mother Nature's Son" with Jay-Z's heartbreaking lyrics in "December 4th" about growing up in a world fraught with poverty and drugs, Danger Mouse succeeds in brilliantly contrasting McCartney's idyllic childhood memories with Jay-Z's difficult youth—especially in terms of the hip-hop star's disquieting relationship with his mother, Gloria Carter, whose strained memories are featured in a moving pair of narrative interludes. Danger Mouse's coalescence of "Mother Nature's Son" and "December 4th" posits an implicit commentary about the harshly divergent sociohistorical experiences among various segments of white and black culture, as well as a meaningful analysis of the ways in which we think and feel about the past. Boston's DJ BC offers a similar, humor-oriented reading of "Mother Nature's Son" in a mash-up of the Beatles and the Beastie Boys, entitled "Mother Nature's Rump."

21. As it turns out, the rumors about the Maharishi's behavior may have been fallacious—and perhaps even the vitriolic work of Magic Alex (see Herrera 276; Cynthia Lennon, *John* 279–80). According to Nancy Cooke de Herrera, the impetus for John's sudden change of heart had relatively little to do with Magic Alex's act of character assassination, but rather with a competing movie deal in which the Maharishi had agreed to allow Four Star Productions to film his life story instead of Apple Corps (245). In 1993, George asked the Maharishi for forgiveness for the events of 1968, claiming he had confirmed that the allegations were false. According to Deepak Chopra, the Maharishi told George that "there's nothing to forgive—you're angels in disguise."

22. The song would achieve infamy of a far different sort following the August 1969 Tate-LaBianca murders by Charles Manson and his followers in Southern California.

With *The White Album* as the Manson Family's Ur-text for destruction, their leader reportedly interpreted "Helter Skelter" as the rallying cry for a race war.

23. In order to distinguish between the two versions of "Revolution," the studio personnel took to calling "Revolution 1" the "Glenn Miller version," according to tape operator John Smith (qtd. in Ryan and Kehew 485).

24. George remade "Not Guilty" and later included the track on his eponymous 1979 solo album, *George Harrison*. A number of other songs were recorded and discarded during the production of *The White Album*, including several of the Esher demos: "Child of Nature" (the working title of "Jealous Guy" on Lennon's *Imagine*); "Circles" (later remade and released by George on *Gone Troppo*); "Junk" (which went under the working title of "Jubilee" and was eventually released on *McCartney*); "Sour Milk Sea" (which George produced for Apple recording artist Jackie Lomax); and "What's the New Mary Jane" (an aborted B-side for the Plastic Ono Band). The most mysterious of the unused *White Album* tracks is a McCartney composition entitled "Etcetera," which the Beatles recorded on August 20th, 1968. It left EMI Studios with Paul that day, never to be heard from again.

25. Fredric Jameson interprets the Beatles and the Rolling Stones as the "high-modernist moment" of punk and new wave rock. In the same breath, he locates the Beatles somewhere just beyond modernism's steady decline, yet nevertheless appears to acknowledge their incongruity with postmodernism's "inverted millenarianism" (1).

26. Having been tasked by John to arrange the song in an intentionally "corny" style, Martin ornamented "Good Night" with a harp, a thirty-piece orchestra, and a choir of four boys and four girls. An early version of the song includes Ringo's spoken introduction: "Come along, children, it's time to toddle off to bed" (qtd. in Dowlding 250).

27. In the final version of the song, an undeleted expletive occurs at 2:58. After missing a chord during an earlier take, John shouted, "Fucking hell." As balance engineer Ken Scott remarked: "I was told about it at the time but could never hear it. But once I had it pointed out I can't miss it now. I have a sneaking suspicion they knew all along" (qtd. in Cross 368). Were they providing a bit more smut, as with "Penny Lane," for the lads back in Liverpool?

28. In addition to his work on "Revolution," Hopkins enjoyed a celebrated career as a guest artist on such classic songs as the Who's "The Song Is Over" and "Getting in Tune"; the Rolling Stones' "She's a Rainbow," "Gimme Shelter," and "Moonlight Mile"; Rod Stewart's "You're in My Heart"; and Joe Cocker's "You Are So Beautiful," among a host of others.

29. John also claimed that he and Yoko began snorting heroin "because of what the Beatles and their pals did to us" (qtd. in Winn, *That Magic Feeling* 344).

30. EMI Chairman Joseph Lockwood was thunderstruck by the cover photograph. "If you must have a naked man on the cover," he reportedly asked Lennon, "why didn't you use Paul instead?" (qtd. in Doggett 6). McCartney had given the project his own imprimatur, famously remarking on the album sleeve that "when two great saints meet, it is a humbling experience."

31. Jane Asher announced the end of her engagement with Paul during an appearance on Simon Dee's BBC talk show in late July. While it has been widely rumored that Jane discovered Paul in bed with Francie at his Cavendish Avenue home, Schwartz denies this version of events in her memoir *Body Count* (1972), alleging that the couple had already broken up by that time.

32. Although he didn't participate in the October 16th session at EMI Studios, George ended up making a belated and very significant contribution to the album's production. While visiting the Capitol Tower in Los Angeles, he listened to test pressings for *The White Album*. Aghast at their subpar quality, George insisted that he be allowed to work with Capitol's engineers during the mastering process. Capitol's production team had employed a limiter to compress the volume range, and the results were disastrous (Spizer 118). "If George had not heard it in time and taken the tape away to work on it himself and returned it the way it should be," Mal Evans later remarked, "the American LP might have been a bit of a mess! It was a lot of work for George but worthwhile" (qtd. in Ryan and Kehew 494).

Chapter 12

Getting Back

Children picking up our bones
Will never know that these were once
As quick as foxes on the hill.
—WALLACE STEVENS, "A POSTCARD FROM THE VOLCANO"

It's very difficult to keep the line between the past
and the present. You know what I mean?
—EDITH BOUVIER BEALE, *GREY GARDENS*

The idea for the so-called *Get Back* project finds its origins in the wee hours of September 5th, 1968. Having recorded the promotional films for "Hey Jude" and "Revolution" the previous evening, the Beatles had stayed up much of the night with Denis O'Dell and director Michael Lindsay-Hogg. As they downed one convivial Scotch-and-Coke after another, the group reminisced about performing in front of the studio audience that Mal Evans had assembled. As the newly appointed director of Apple Films recalled, "Collectively, they said, 'Denis, this was a great evening. Now we must talk about doing a big show together.'" The group had been exhilarated by their performance—not only because of their interaction with the audience, but more importantly in terms of the simple joy that they experienced in playing together as a band. "They were jamming and having a good time and having a better time than they thought they were going to have," Lindsay-Hogg remembered. "So they sort of thought maybe there is some way they can do something again in some sort of performance way" (qtd. in Matteo 18). And with that, the *Get Back* project was born. Over the years, the sessions have come to be associated with the group's notion—particularly evinced by John—of "getting back" to their musical

251

roots, of recapturing the live sound and sense of spontaneity that characterized their earlier work. While this was certainly true, given the sparse approach
that the Beatles took regarding the project's instrumentation and its overall
lack of elaborate studio production, the group had something entirely different, even unexpected, in mind. Buoyed by the audience response to "Hey Jude"
and "Revolution," they intended to rehearse a new live act and unveil it in the
new year. It would be their triumphant return to the stage.

In order to document their preparation for the concert, the Beatles tasked
Lindsay-Hogg with the job of filming their rehearsals at Twickenham Film
Studios, the very same soundstage where they had shot *A Hard Day's Night*
five years earlier. As the group honed their plans for the project, which at one
point included the possibility of a television special, Lindsay-Hogg devised a
scheme of his own. In December, he had directed the Rolling Stones' *Rock and
Roll Circus*, a production originally slated to debut as a television program in
which performances by the Stones, the Who, Jethro Tull, and Eric Clapton,
among others, were introduced by playful banter among the assembled glitterati, which included John and Yoko in an inspired cameo. After performing
"Yer Blues," John turned the spotlight over to Yoko, who offered a wailing rendition of the improvisational "Her Blues." Filmed underneath the replica of a
big top on a British soundstage with acrobats and clowns performing before a
live studio audience, the production literally took on the connotations of a cir-
cuslike atmosphere.[1] But for the Beatles, Lindsay-Hogg had something very
different in mind. He would dispense with the plasticine veneer of big-top
spectacle and strive instead for the brute, gritty truth of authenticity. Using a
pair of Nagra tape recorders and two cameramen, Lindsay-Hogg intended to
shoot the documentary in *audio vérité* style. As with *cinéma vérité*—which
roughly translates as the "cinema of truth"—the idea behind *audio vérité* is to
seize upon the essential human truth inherent in the text. As an unscripted
documentary production, *audio vérité* necessitates an unmediated presentation of the subject. With reels of tape at the ready, Lindsay-Hogg hoped to capture the Beatles' music and conversations in excruciating detail. Lindsay-Hogg
would act as a shameless participant in the proceedings, provoking the group
into a series of exchanges about their plans for live performance, the evolving
nature of the songs being rehearsed, and their shifting internal politics. In so
doing, Lindsay-Hogg's *audio vérité* approach managed to record the Beatles at
a critical crossroads in the twilight of their career.

The *Get Back* project began at Twickenham during the late morning of
Thursday, January 2nd, 1969.[2] As with nearly all of the rehearsals during the
Beatles' fortnight at the soundstage, the first day's proceedings were determined by the sporadic arrival of the bandmates, especially Lennon, who, along
with Yoko, would often be the last member to arrive on the scene. In addition

to the film crew, the Beatles were joined by George Martin and Glyn Johns, who had been hired to supervise the sound recording for the television broadcast.[3] As the project progressed, he began to assume the role of sound engineer, overseeing the recording and playback of their rehearsals. After the complexities of *The White Album*, Martin was excited about what he perceived to be the "brilliant" concept behind the band's latest project: "The original idea was that we should record an album of new material and rehearse it, then perform it before a live audience for the first time—on record and film. In other words, make a live album of new material, which no one had ever done before." For his part, Lennon wanted the resulting LP to be an "honest album"; in John's mind that meant no editing or overdubbing: "We just record a song and that's it," he told the producer (qtd. in Ryan and Kehew 504). In spite of his initial enthusiasm, Martin only made himself available sporadically throughout the *Get Back* sessions, growing increasingly bewildered as the band went through one fragmented rehearsal after another trying to knock their new material into shape. With the hazy lens of historical hindsight, John derided Twickenham's sterile atmosphere and the experience of working under the watchful eyes and ears of Lindsay-Hogg's production unit: "We couldn't get into it. It was just a dreadful, dreadful feeling in Twickenham Studio, being filmed all the time. I just wanted them [the film crew] to go away. You couldn't make music at eight in the morning or ten or whatever it was, in a strange place with people filming you and colored lights" (qtd. in Doggett 10). The group had become used to working evening sessions at EMI Studios, and the sudden shift to daylight must have been understandably jarring. In striking contrast with Lennon's memories, Glyn Johns recalled the *Get Back* sessions with fondness: "The whole mood was wonderful," he later remarked. "There was all this nonsense going on at the time about the problems surrounding the group. . . . In fact, they were having a wonderful time and being incredibly funny. I didn't stop laughing for six weeks" (qtd. in Doggett 78).

During the first rehearsal, the Beatles worked through rudimentary versions of John's bluesy new composition "Don't Let Me Down," George's meditative "All Things Must Pass," and a pair of up-tempo rock and roll tunes by Paul, "I've Got a Feeling" and "Two of Us." As the sessions continued, conversation was dominated by discussion about the location for the upcoming live performance, which they planned to undertake, impractical as it may seem, by mid-January. They initially considered a lavish concert at the Royal Albert Hall, with Apple recording artists Mary Hopkin and James Taylor on the bill, before settling, for a short while, on the comparatively intimate Roundhouse, the unofficial headquarters for the London underground music scene. Other ideas included performing in a Roman amphitheatre in North Africa, or perhaps onboard a ship at sea, or even by torchlight in the middle of the Sahara desert. At one point, Lennon suggested, half-jokingly, that a concert in an insane asylum might be more appropriate, given the band's recent spate of interpersonal problems. Ringo made it known on several occasions that he refused to go abroad, prompting Paul to tease the drummer that they would be forced to replace him with Jimmy Nicol. While Denis O'Dell suggested that they film the concert with the band performing in the middle of one of London's renowned art museums, Yoko had become particularly intrigued by the *avant-garde* concept of the Beatles playing a concert before twenty thousand empty seats in order to signify "the invisible nameless everybody in the world" (qtd. in Doggett 20). In one instance, she even suggested that they re-orient the documentary so as to film the Beatles' personal activities, reality-television style, from dusk to dawn in their private homes. The group's outlandish concert ideas began to wane rather precipitously, however, when Yoko pointed out that "after 100,000 people in Shea Stadium, everything else sucks" (qtd. in Matteo 48). How, indeed, could they ever hope to top their already mind-boggling roster of accolades and accomplishments?

In addition to rehearsing new material, the *Get Back* sessions found the Beatles manically improvising one song after another, including a wide range of classic rock and roll numbers like "Shake, Rattle, and Roll," "Johnny B. Goode," "Lawdy Miss Clawdy," "Lucille," "You Really Got a Hold on Me," "Mailman, Bring Me No More Blues," "Little Queenie," "Rock and Roll Music," "Blue Suede Shoes," and "Be-Bop-a-Lula," among a host of others. Surprisingly, they improvised very few original songs, with the exception of a risqué tune entitled "Suzy's Parlor." With John taking lead vocals and George and Paul singing backup, the song borrows key elements from the Everly Brothers' "Wake Up Little Susie" and Ritchie Valens's "That's My Little Suzie." As a sardonic homage to Suzy Parker (born Cecilia Ann Renee Parker), the sophisticated, fresh-faced American supermodel for Coco Chanel, Lennon's innuendo-laden lyrics re-imagine her as a one-woman brothel from whom no one departs dissatisfied:

> Well, come on Suzy's Parlor, everybody's welcome to come.
> (Suzy Parker, come on, Suzy Parker)
> Said come on Suzy's Parlor, everybody's welcome to come.
> (Suzy Parker, come on, Suzy Parker)
> When you come to Suzy's Parlor, everybody gets well done.

Although it occupies a relatively minor place in the band's canon, "Suzy's Parlor" continues Lennon and McCartney's uneasiness with their pre-Beatles past. In advance of *The White Album*, the songwriters' modernism had begun to reflect increasingly their anxiety of influence over their formative, 1950s-era youth.[4] Insouciant and fun-loving in the Beatles' early years, this dis-ease with their musical precursors had become positively venomous with "Happiness Is a Warm Gun" and, to a certain extent, "Revolution 1." As with "Suzy's Parlor," such songs find the group indulging this proclivity yet again, as the songwriters reveal their veneration for the decade of their youth, on the one hand, while seeking to redact it, on the other.

As the *Get Back* sessions proceeded, John and Paul slowly began to surmount this tendency, delving deeper and deeper into their writerly heritage. At one juncture, the songwriters revisited "Just Fun," one of their first compositions together back in the late 1950s, later attempting versions of such juvenilia as "Thinking of Linking" and "I Lost My Little Girl," the latter of which found John taking lead vocals on Paul's early composition about his mother Mary's untimely demise. Yet as January rolled along, the Beatles seemed increasingly unable to concentrate on the project at hand, with John and Paul persistently "playing riffs and half-snatches of melodies on their guitars." This "aimless noodling," in the words of Doug Sulpy and Ray Schweighardt, finally began to irritate Paul in spite of his own culpability in distracting his mates (85). Fed up with being the band's solitary cheerleader, the normally well-mannered Beatle became unhinged during the January 7th session: "We've been very negative since Mr. Epstein passed away," he remarked. "I don't see why any of you, if you're not interested, get yourselves into this. What's it for? It can't be for the money. Why are you here?" (qtd. in Doggett 24–25). Worse yet, he attributed the band's inability to move forward creatively as the ruinous work of their own suffocating nostalgia: "When we do get together, we just talk about the fucking past. We're like OAPs [old-age pensioners], saying, 'Do you remember the days when we used to rock?' Well, we're here now, we can still do it" (qtd. in Doggett 27). If nothing else, Paul's angry words of wisdom served to revive his flagging partner, who seemed to be unable to rouse the necessary creative energy to generate new material. When Paul finally confronted him about his inability to produce new compositions beyond "Don't Let Me Down," John responded with his classic defensive posture, a combination of sarcasm and petulance:

Paul: "Haven't you written anything?"
John: "No."
Paul: "We're going to be facing a crisis."
John: "When I'm up against the wall, Paul, you'll find that I'm at my best."
Paul: "I wish you'd come up with the goods."
John: "I think I've got Sunday off."
Paul: "I hope you can deliver."
John: "I'm hoping for a little rock-and-roller." (qtd. in Doggett 29)

Lennon's lethargy was understandable, given the band's considerable output and activity during the previous year, not to mention his escapades with Yoko and the personal tragedy of her miscarriage. John and Yoko's protracted heroin abuse may have been taking its toll—at one juncture during the Twickenham sessions, Yoko joked about shooting heroin as the couple's form of exercise (Doggett 34).

Whatever the cause for his malaise, for his lack of productivity, John began increasingly to focus his wrath upon George. The annals of Beatles history tend to blame Paul's controlling behavior for the group's interrelational dilemmas during the *Get Back* sessions, a conclusion that seems to be buttressed by a January 6th quarrel in which Paul and George resumed their rancor from the previous summer involving "Hey Jude." Apparently still smarting over Paul's rebuke of his creative suggestion, Harrison reacted to McCartney's patronizing attitude about his guitar arrangement for "Two of Us": "I'll play whatever you want me to play or I won't play at all if you don't want me to play," he told Paul. "Whatever it is that will please you, I'll do it." There is no denying McCartney's increasingly proscriptive songwriterly behavior, although Sulpy and Schweighardt contend that "the common portrayal of Paul as an excessively bossy, egocentric bully during this period is simply erroneous and unfair. It's the moribund behavior of the other Beatles that makes Paul's assertiveness stand out" (2). If nothing else, the *Get Back* project demonstrated Harrison's—not to mention Ringo's—second-class citizenship in the band, an aspect of their communal makeup that had been growing in intensity in recent years as the guitarist's songwriting abilities began to improve radically. "The problem for me was that John and Paul had been writing the songs for so long," George pointed out. "It was difficult. They had such a lot of tunes, and they automatically thought that theirs should be the priority, so I'd always have to wait through 10 of their songs before they'd even listen to one of mine. It was silly. It was very selfish, actually" (qtd. in Doggett 11). As a means of blowing off steam, George took to singing impromptu Dylan tunes during the rehearsals, including the symbolic "I Shall Be Released" and "All Along the Watchtower," with its prophetic opening lyric, "There must be some way out of here." George Martin, for one, was sympathetic to Harrison's plight, although he ascribed the guitarist's lower artistic stratum in the Beatles to a kind of natural creative order: "He'd been awfully poor up to then. Some of the stuff he'd written was very boring. The impression is sometimes given that we put him down," Martin recalled. "I don't think we ever did that, but possibly we didn't encourage him enough. He'd write, but we wouldn't say, 'What've you got then, George?' We'd say, 'Oh, you've got some more, have you?' I must say that looking back, it was a bit hard on him. It was always slightly condescending. But it was natural, because the others were so talented" (qtd. in Doggett 12).

George had spent the past few months producing an album by Apple recording artist Jackie Lomax, as well as hanging out with Dylan and the Band, who had developed enormous respect for Harrison's musicianship. It must have been understandably difficult to return to his largely subordinate role in the Beatles after his post-*White Album* bout of creative energy. But in spite of the increased tension, George attempted to appease his elder bandmates during the *Get Back* sessions, at one point tenderly observing that "there's so much material for us to get out, and there's no one better to get it out with than us, for me, really. Heart of hearts" (qtd. in Doggett 19). Despite such gestures, Lennon had trouble taking his younger mate seriously. Was the difference in age that had disturbed John back in 1958 still at work as far as George was concerned?[5] As Sulpy and Schweighardt note, "It's interesting to observe that John will entertain any number of musical suggestions from Paul, but not allow George to present his view as to how the song should be played. When working within the framework of the Lennon-McCartney partnership, George is viewed as a sideman" (64). As the sessions trudged onward, John even seemed to be baiting George. During a rehearsal of George's new composition "I Me Mine," John "jokes that a collection of freaks can dance along with George's waltz," before telling the guitarist "to get lost—that the Beatles only play rock and roll and there's no place in the group's playlist for a Spanish waltz" (qtd. in Sulpy and Schweighardt 124). As if on cue, Paul later took to singing "I Me Mine" while feigning a Spanish accent. The trio's behavior tellingly reminds us that the stakes of authorship—and the divisions that it creates—had never really ebbed. They had merely been redistributed among three Beatles instead of two.

Although John may have been equally annoyed by George's obvious profundity of new material, there is little question that their growing feud involved Harrison's exasperation with Yoko's constant presence in the studio, particularly when she spoke up for John, while her silent boyfriend nervously plucked at his guitar. For his part, John had been distressed over his bandmates' refusal to embrace the love of his life, to understand his fervent need to be in Yoko's company during his every waking moment. In 1968, he composed a pseudo-Joycean narrative that vents his obvious frustration about the callous behavior of his "beast friends":

WONSAPONATIME there was two Balloons called Jock and Yono. They were strictly in love-bound to happen in a million years. They were together man. Unfortunatimetable they both seemed to have previous experience—which kept calling them one way oranother (you know howitis). But they battled on against overwhelming oddities, includo some of there beast friends. Being in love they cloong even more together man—but some of the poisonessmonster of outrated buslodedshithrowers did stick slightly and they occasionally had to resort to the drycleaners. Luckily this did not kill them and they werent banned from the olympic games. They lived hopefully every after, and who could blame them. (*Skywriting by Word of Mouth* 39)[6]

But George made little effort to hide his vexation with Yoko's unremitting presence, and on Friday, January 10th—after enduring a morning session in which Paul goaded him about how to perform his guitar part—Harrison abruptly quit the group. After a heated argument with Lennon during lunch, George made a hasty exit, uttering, "See you 'round the clubs" as he left the soundstage.

Either out of spite or ennui—or both—John began improvising the Who's "A Quick One While He's Away" within minutes of Harrison's departure. At one point, he sarcastically called for an absent George to play the guitar solo (Sulpy and Schweighardt 170). Back at Kinfauns, George burned off his anger with a bout of songwriting that produced "Wah-Wah." As a pun on the name of the popular guitar effects pedal, "Wah-Wah" became George's euphemism for a pounding headache: "Wah-wah / You've given me a wah-wah." The song's autobiographical elements are undeniable, and they speak, in particular, to the complex nature of his uneasy relationship with John, the older, more experienced boy whom he had looked up to during his early teen years: "And I'm thinking of you / And all the things that we used to do," George sings. The composition makes specific reference to his indebtedness to John: "You made me such a big star / Being there at the right time." Not long after George's departure, John began calling for the group to replace him with Eric Clapton, a caustic suggestion, given Harrison's close friendship with the renowned guitarist: "The point is: if George leaves, do we want to carry on the Beatles? I do," John told Paul and Ringo. "We should just get other members and carry on" (qtd. in Doggett 33). The day's session ended with a spate of improvised jamming, including a rendition of "Martha My Dear" in which Yoko provided a screeching solo, screaming John's name over and over. Meanwhile, Paul played on, seemingly unfazed by the chaos around him (Sulpy and Schweighardt 176).

On Sunday, the Beatles gathered at Brookfields, Ringo's Surrey estate, and the rift between John and George grew even wider when the guitarist refused to return to Twickenham. The next day, John, Paul, and Ringo ran through sloppy versions of McCartney's "Get Back," and by Wednesday, the sessions had ground to a halt. That afternoon, the group met yet again, this time settling their differences to everyone's apparent satisfaction. The truce involved at least two considerations: first, that they would abandon Twickenham's dour atmosphere immediately in favor of Apple's newfangled basement studio; and second, that they would dispense with the concept of a live performance, staging instead a concert for Lindsay-Hogg's cameras without benefit of an audience. The shift from Twickenham to Apple effectively spelled the end for the television production, with the Beatles now setting their sights on recording a new album and a concomitant documentary. Although their fantasy of making a spectacular return to the stage had perished, the idea for a new studio album had been born—and if the Beatles knew nothing else, they understood implicitly how to make an LP.

The sessions would have begun on the following Monday, were it not for Magic Alex, who had promised to build a seventy-two-track recording studio for the group in the basement of the Apple building at 3 Savile Row in Soho. Magic Alex also dreamt of devising an invisible force field to serve as the sound screen for Ringo's drums. When George Martin arrived at the studio, he was shocked to discover sixteen speakers arrayed along the basement walls, with Magic Alex's multitrack system nowhere in evidence. As Harrison later recalled, "Alex's recording studio was the biggest disaster of all time. He was walking around with a white coat on like some sort of chemist, but he didn't have a clue what he was doing. It was a 16-track system, and he had 16 tiny little speakers all around the walls. You only need two speakers for stereo sound. It was awful. The whole thing was a disaster, and it had to be ripped out" (qtd. in Miles 532–33). To make matters worse, Magic Alex's ostensibly state-of-the-art mixing desk "looked like it had been built with a hammer and chisel," second engineer Alan Parsons remarked.[7] "None of the switches fitted properly, and you could almost see the metal filings. It was rough, all right, and it was all very embarrassing, because it just didn't do anything" (qtd. in Babiuk 236). Consequently, Martin and Johns spent the next two days turning Apple's basement into a respectable recording studio by bringing in two mobile four-track mixing consoles from EMI, overhauling the basement's amateurish soundproofing, and attempting to quiet the building's noisy heating system. "I'm a rock gardener," Magic Alex said in his own defense, "and now I'm doing electronics. Maybe next year, I make films or poems. I have no formal training in any of these, but this is irrelevant. Man is just a small glass, very, very clear, with many faces, like a diamond," he rambled. "You just have to find the way, the small door to each face" (qtd. in Badman 415). For Magic Alex, the small door was slowly transforming into an exit.

On Wednesday, January 22nd, George officially returned to the fold, performing a duet of "You Are My Sunshine" with John in order to signify their renewed camaraderie. Later that day, George decided to alter the band's chemistry, as he had done so successfully back in September 1968 with Clapton, by inviting ace keyboard player Billy Preston to lend his talents to the Beatles. As luck would have it, Harrison and Clapton had seen Preston performing in Ray Charles's band on January 19th. The Beatles had first met Preston back in Hamburg in 1962 when he was a member of Little Richard's backup band. "I pulled in Billy Preston," George later recalled. "It helped because the others would have to control themselves a bit more. John and Paul mainly, because they had to, you know, act more handsomely," he continued. "It's interesting to see how people behave nicely when you bring a guest in because they don't want everyone to know that they're so bitchy" (qtd. in Ryan and Kehew 506; *Anthology* documentary). Harrison's gambit worked its magic, with John lobbying hard for Billy to become a permanent member of the group, although Paul demurred at the thought of five Beatles: "It's bad enough with four!" he exclaimed (Sulpy and Schweighardt 232; qtd. in Doggett 38). For the next several days, the five bandmates rehearsed with a vengeance. Time was clearly of the essence, as Ringo was due to star in *The Magic Christian* with Peter Sellers in early February. Meanwhile, Glyn Johns was scheduled to record an album with the Steve Miller Band in the United States, and Preston was about to embark upon a concert tour back in his native Texas. If the Beatles were going to salvage the *Get Back* project, something had to happen—and soon.

~

On January 24th, the *Get Back* recording sessions finally ensued, although they began somewhat inauspiciously, with the Beatles concocting a hasty rendition of the traditional nineteenth-century Liverpool ditty "Maggie Mae." After a couple of false starts, they managed to play the song for some forty seconds before it fell into total collapse. But therein lies the entire project's lingering charm: in spite of all of the obvious tension, there were genuine moments of grandeur hidden amidst the nooks and crannies of that crazy month. After yet more rehearsal, the band began to pick up some much-needed steam during the recording session devoted to George's "For You Blue." Originally entitled "George's Blues," the song shares much in common with Elmore James's "Madison Blues," an aspect that Harrison does absolute nothing to conceal, at one point ad-libbing, "Elmore James got nothing on this baby." With Paul playing a nifty honky-tonk piano, this twelve-bar blues effusion is noteworthy for John's slide-guitar solo—played with a Höfner 5140 Hawaiian Standard resting on his knees. Technically, it's a bit of a mess, but John's obvious delight in playing the solo more than makes up for any blemishes. Buoyed by yet another ad-lib from George—"Go, Johnny, go!"—Lennon seems to lose himself in the moment, perhaps for the first time since the *Get Back* sessions had begun. The next day, the Beatles recorded John's "Dig It," a free-form, improvisational rant of some twelve minutes that at one point featured Lennon in an unlikely duet with six-year-old Heather Eastman, the daughter of Paul's fiancée, Linda. Essentially a "slice of late '60s hippie slang," in the words of Peter Doggett, "Dig It" finds the band in the act of ridding themselves of the considerable demons that they had amassed over the past three weeks (82).

Their symbolic musical purging had come just in the nick of time, enabling the Beatles to achieve the most amazing, improbable result that one might imagine, given the emotional traumas of their recent experience. Over the next five days, they would commit no less than four classic songs to tape, as well as at least three near-classics to boot. Riding on an incredible burst of energy—no doubt assisted by the good vibes and superb musicianship of Billy Preston—they transformed their own hostility into the stuff of rock music history. Over the course of seventeen days, they had rehearsed some fifty-nine iterations of Paul's "Get Back." In so doing, they slogged through a seemingly endless parade of false starts and bouts of sloppy instrumentation on the way to perfecting the distinctive galloping groove of "Get Back." The song had been born way back on January 7th, when Paul toyed with the bass riff that drives Lulu's "I'm a Tiger" before happening upon the melody of his latest composition. He had borrowed a portion of the song's lyrics from Harrison's "Sour Milk Sea," one of May 1968's Esher demos in which George sings, "Get back to the place you should be." An earlier version of "Get Back" witnessed McCartney indulging in a comparatively rare moment of political satire. On January 9th, John and Paul had improvised a number entitled "Commonwealth" in which they derided the Conservative party's repatriation movement to limit the sudden influx of thousands of Indian and Pakistani immigrants who had been denied the right to work in Kenya. Things had come to a head in April 1968, when British politician Enoch Powell delivered his controversial "Rivers of Blood" speech in response to the Labour Government's introduction of anti-discrimination legislation. According to Powell, the pending race relations bill "would make colored people a privileged class" (qtd. in Sulpy and Schweighardt 157–58). As "Get Back" began to emerge from the Beatles' chaotic mid-January sessions, Paul's lyrics satirized Powell's anti-immigration position: "Don't dig no Pakistanis taking all the people's jobs / Get back to where you once belonged." But within a few days, the song took a decidedly different, more playful turn. Originally known as Joe and Teresa, Paul's quirky "Get Back" characters eventually morphed into pot-smoking Jo-Jo and Sweet Loretta Martin, an enigmatic drag queen. But the real story of "Get Back" involves the song's music, rather than its eccentric, albeit one-dimensional storyline. With an infectious forward momentum provided by Ringo's relentless snare, "Get Back" finds Paul contributing an unforgettable, near-falsetto vocal, while John concocts a wonderfully funky guitar solo on his Casino. The 45-RPM single version of the song, which would become an international hit come April, features a classic false ending, Beatles-style, with Paul gleefully ad-libbing the coda: "Get back Loretta / Your mommy's waiting for you / Wearing her high-heel shoes / And her low-neck sweater / Get back home, Loretta."

Later described by McCartney as "a song to roller-coast by," "Get Back" was yet another in a long line of top-drawer Beatles singles releases in which the A- and B-sides comprise an exquisite whole. As a tribute to the keyboard player's buoyant effect upon the band's tenuous interpersonal atmosphere, the single was pointedly credited to "The Beatles with Billy Preston." The fun and frolic of "Get Back" is fiercely counterpoised by its B-side, "Don't Let Me Down," Lennon's most scathing and heartfelt love song. Musically, the composition is a wonder to behold—one of the finest ensemble performances in the band's career. John's raw, breathless vocal is complemented by George's evocative, bluesy riffs on his Rosewood Telecaster. And then there's Paul's harmony vocal, confident in its supporting role—bolstering John's voice of pain and fury, while never overwhelming it. In later years, Lennon would suggest that McCartney subconsciously sought to "sabotage" his partner's compositions.[8] There is no more forceful rebuttal to this charge than Paul's performance on "Don't Let Me Down." His unfailing commitment to John's emotional integrity is utterly palpable. Matching the ferocity of Lennon's lead vocal, McCartney's bass runs absolutely wild in its electric duet with Preston's Fender Rhodes electric piano. Meanwhile, Ringo's cymbal crashes afford John with the courage to bare his aching soul. The song reaches its fever pitch in the middle-eight, which is at once John's most vulnerable and authentic moment on record. His vocal is beautifully rendered against the sound of George's cascading guitar part, a descending figure that seems to respond to the singer's emotional confession, urging him to transcend his own misgivings, his own cynicism, and take the leap of faith that love demands:

> I'm in love for the first time.
> Don't you know it's gonna last.
> It's a love that lasts forever.
> It's a love that has no past.

The idea of erasing the past—of effecting a return to innocence through the sheer force of human will—is the song's most salient feature. With "I Saw Her Standing There," Lennon and McCartney embraced the pure beauty of innocence and true-blue love. It was a fanciful dream, of course, and one that they went on to reconsider, time and time again, as their music transformed into a more knowing critique of the divine comedy (and tragedy) of human desire. But with "Don't Let Me Down," John imagines a return, however impossible, from the jaded world of self-knowledge to the glow and wonder of unblemished love. The song never shies away from depicting the manic, far-flung urgency of desire—the "heat of a luxurious bed," in the words of William Shakespeare, another poet, like Lennon, who implicitly understood the unruly passions of the human heart.

On January 29th, Lindsay-Hogg evinced the understandable frustration of a filmmaker whose project had spiraled out of control. As a work of *audio vérité*, the *Get Back* project made sense as a documentary of the band's rehearsals for their grand return to the stage. But the group's shift from preparing for a concert to recording an album had left the director at cross-purposes. He had untold hours of material devoted to a planned live performance that his subjects had discussed *ad nauseum* for Lindsay-Hogg's furtive tape recorders, then scuttled. Where was his narrative thrust now? "At the moment, this documentary's like *No Exit*," Lindsay-Hogg complained. "There's a lot of good footage, but no pay-off" (qtd. in Doggett 40). Had the *auteur* and his celebrated *artistes* become like the characters in Jean-Paul Sartre's 1944 existentialist drama—a play in which they torture each other endlessly, residing in a kind of living hell from which they are free to leave, yet unable to escape? The answer to the director's woes had actually begun to percolate a few days earlier. On the previous Saturday, he had ventured up to the roof of the Apple building with Paul and Mal Evans in tow. After jumping up and down on the boards and looking around at the cityscape, they realized that the climax for Lindsay-Hogg's film was finally at hand. And with an invisible audience below and the rooftops and chimneys of the Mayfair district as their only spectators, the band would fulfill Yoko's *avant-garde* dream of playing to an empty house.

On Friday, January 30th, the group trundled up to the roof, where Mal Evans and Neil Aspinall acted as the Beatles' concert roadies for the last time. Their instruments were ready and waiting, the P.A. system and amplifiers prepared to blast their sound through the bitter winter winds blowing above the garment district. But the concert nearly didn't happen at all. As Lindsay-Hogg later recalled, "We planned to do it about 12:30 to get the lunchtime crowds. They didn't agree to do it as a group until about twenty to one. Paul wanted to do it and George didn't. Ringo would go either way. Then John said, 'Oh fuck, let's do it,' and they went up and did it" (qtd. in Matteo 83). While some eleven cameramen trained their lenses on the band, with a few of them dispatched to capture reaction shots from bystanders on the streetscape, Glyn Johns observed the performance on the roof, leaving George Martin to supervise the recording of the forty-two-minute concert with the converted eight-track equipment six floors below in the basement. In order to fend off the cold, John donned Yoko's fur coat, while Ringo wore his wife Maureen's orange raincoat. With his long hair whipping in the wind, John played his beloved Casino, a bearded Paul strapped on his Höfner for the occasion, and an elegantly moustached George adorned his Rosewood Telecaster. Ringo's new drum kit, a set of Ludwig Hollywoods with a maple finish, made its concert debut that day, with the drummer retaining his trusty oyster-black pearl snare from his old kit. In the midst of a series of false starts and aborted rehearsals, the Beatles performed five songs that day—"Get Back," "Don't Let Me Down," "I've Got a Feeling," "One after 909," and "Dig a Pony"—before concluding with a spirited reprise of "Get Back," followed by the band's famous farewell to the stage: "I'd like to say thank you on behalf of the group and ourselves," John remarked. "I hope we passed the audition." Was he making a reference to the Decca sessions of New Year's Day 1962? Or, perhaps more fittingly, was he alluding to the minor miracle of the Beatles pulling off the rooftop concert in the first place?

The proceedings had been briefly interrupted that day when a squad of London Bobbies was dispatched to quell the noise. As Ringo later remarked, "I always felt let down about the police. I was playing away and I thought, 'Oh, great! I hope they drag me off!' I *wanted* the cops to drag me off—'Get off those drums!'—because we were being filmed and it would have looked really great, kicking the cymbals and everything" (qtd. in Ryan and Kehew 506). But it was not to be. Although Beatles lore and Lindsay-Hogg's eventual documentary depict the police officers as being determined to end the concert prematurely, the truth was far less dramatic and eminently predictable. As technical engineer Dave Harries recalled, one of the Bobbies agreed to allow the concert to continue as long as they could watch: "When they found out who it was," said Harries, "they didn't want to stop it" (qtd. in Matteo 86). But the greatest story of the rooftop concert may be George Harrison himself. Tentative at first, hanging back, desperately playing his guitar with his fingers growing numb with cold, it must have been a truly surreal moment. Twenty days earlier he had quit the band, and here he was, standing on the loose boards on the roof of the group's office building, strumming away in the icy chill above Savile Row to an invisible audience he could barely hear, much less see. In his brown fur coat and Converse tennis shoes, he cut an unlikely figure. But then it happened. Something must have clicked for the guitarist during the second number of that most improbable of impromptu concerts. He stepped up to the microphone to join John and Paul on the chorus—"Don't let me down!" they belted out in unison—and suddenly his shoulders had relaxed, his grip had loosened ever so slightly around his Rosewood Telecaster, and John's most evocative composition had come alive in the guitarist's own hands. Less than an hour ago, George had bristled at the very idea of climbing the Apple stairs into the London air. But now he was back.

Over the years, three recordings from the rooftop concert have been featured in various releases of the *Get Back* project, including "I've Got a Feeling," "One after 909," and "Dig a Pony." As one of Paul's finest efforts at achieving hard-driving R&B, "I've Got a Feeling" is also his most visceral love song. With Preston on his Fender Rhodes and the band whipping up a groovy gruel of guitar rock, "I've Got a Feeling" begins with a deceptively simple tableau consisting of a catchy, distorted guitar riff and a buoyant McCartney lyric: "I've got a feeling, a feeling deep inside / Oh yeah," he sings. "I've got a feeling, a feeling I can't hide / Oh no." At face value, the composition appears to be a wide-eyed musing upon newfound love, a meditation on the serenity of his new life with Linda. But everything changes when the Beatle turns in his most primal, most inspired, and most explosive of middle-eights on record:

> All these years I've been wandering around,
> Wondering how come nobody told me
> All that I was looking for was somebody
> Who looked like you.

In a searing, gut-wrenching performance, Paul packs as much emotion and meaning into those nine measly seconds as he does in nearly any other song in his massive corpus. It's a bravura moment in which he lays himself bare. While it seems to be directed outward, the middle-eight is really an act of self-critique in which the songwriter castigates himself for his own inability to recognize that true love had been waiting on his doorstep—waiting for him to wake up and smell the proverbial coffee—for quite some time. The raw power of the middle-eight is underscored by George's elongated, subtly descending guitar figure that underlines the speaker's pent-up anger with a brooding musical afterword. "I've Got a Feeling" is shrewdly balanced by an unfinished Lennon composition entitled "Everybody Had a Hard Year." As with "A Day in the Life," "I've Got a Feeling" finds John and Paul merging a pair of relatively incomplete compositions into a seamless whole. As with "She's Leaving Home," the song finds Lennon and McCartney moving from the micro-narrative of the individuated early passages to collective, universal experience: "Everybody had a hard year. / Everybody had a good time," John sings. "Everybody had a wet dream. / Everybody saw the sunshine." After the first iteration of John's verses, Paul returns to the introductory stanza, joining his partner in a quodlibet structure in which their superimposed voices merge in a cathartic counterpoint.

The rooftop concert also witnessed the Beatles finally loosing "One after 909" into the public consciousness. One of the earliest Lennon-McCartney compositions, "One after 909" was John's obvious attempt to parrot skiffle's infatuation with life on the railroad in such tunes as Lonnie Donegan's "Rock Island Line," Johnny Duncan's "Last Train to San Fernando," and the Chas McDevitt Skiffle Group's "Freight Train." Both musically and lyrically, "One after 909" is nothing more than a rock and roll trifle, although it remains indispensable to the quality and feel of the *Get Back* sessions, if only for the sheer enjoyment that the Beatles evinced in performing a song with such deep connotations to the comparative innocence of their Liverpudlian youth. As John Mendelssohn astutely notes, "'C'mon, baby, don't be cold as ice' may be at once the most ridiculous and magnificent line Lennon-McCartney ever wrote" (qtd. in Doggett 127). The goodtime rock and roll of "One after 909" is continued with John's "Dig a Pony," a masterpiece of whimsical nonsensicality. Originally entitled "All I Want Is You," "Dig a Pony" features an arresting guitar preface in 3/4 time—an "aggressive ostinato riff," in Alan W. Pollack's words— that introduces the speaker's unabashed, free-form ruminations about falling in love. The speaker's attempt to express his passion with concrete words underscores the seeming impossibility of capturing the nature of romantic love with the precision of concise language. The speaker's verbal effusions range from the ecstatic—"you can celebrate anything you want" and "you can penetrate any place you go"—to the more profound "you can radiate every-thing you are" and the appealingly ludicrous "you can syndicate any boat you row." John's oblique reference to picking a "moondog"—an obvious allusion to the band's fleeting existence way back in November 1959 as Johnny and the Moondogs—demonstrates the manner in which the Beatles' nostalgia was clearly running vast and deep during the *Get Back* sessions.

On January 31st, the group effectively concluded the principal recording sessions for the project with a trio of first-rate McCartney compositions, including "Two of Us," "Let It Be," and "The Long and Winding Road." Back at Twickenham, the Beatles had struggled mightily with "Two of Us," especially during the song's early stages. Paul was determined to maintain its initial elec-tric guitar format, ignoring Glyn Johns' suggestion on the very first day that the composition might be more effectively rendered using acoustic guitars instead. In an early iteration of "Two of Us," Paul adopted his "Elvis voice" in an up-tempo version that features John on a lively rhythm guitar part. When the composer eventually acquiesced to Glyn Johns's acoustic arrangement, "Two of Us" fell into place rather quickly, with John and Paul sharing lead vocals. In spite of the song's roots in Paul and Linda's lengthy driving trips around the English countryside, the recording inevitably takes on the connotations of Lennon and McCartney's nostalgia for their more convivial early days together. Originally entitled "On Our Way Home," "Two of Us" juxtaposes the idea of literally returning home with the grand sweep of memories. With a gentle, vaguely country and western acoustic guitar part on Paul's Martin D-28, the song's recurring lyrical image—"we're on our way home"—suggests that the speaker and his companion have come full circle, that they've arrived at some inevitable destination from whence life as they know it will be different. It's a bittersweet emotion that merits contemplation, if not acknowledgment, for its invariable place in the human life-cycle. This phenomenon is presciently captured in McCartney's superb middle-eight: "You and I have memories / Longer than the road that stretches out ahead." Intuitively recognizing that it was the song's most essential feature, Paul had led the group in a thirteen-minute rehearsal of the middle-eight on January 25th (Sulpy and Schweighardt 260). John's whistle solo during the coda tenderly punctuates the composition's layers of meaning, denoting the simple joys of friendship, on the one hand, while signaling a wistful farewell, on the other.

As history well knows, McCartney's "Let It Be" would emerge as the spiritual centerpiece for the *Get Back* project—not to mention as an international hit and a pop-music classic in nearly the same breath. With the Beatles experiencing the winter of their discontent, Paul had found comfort in a dream in which his lost mother Mary came to visit him to remind her son to release his worldly troubles, to let it all be. "It was such a sweet dream," Paul later recalled. "I woke up thinking, Oh, it was really great to visit with her again. I felt very blessed to have that dream. So that got me writing the song 'Let It Be.' I literally started off 'Mother Mary,' which was her name, 'When I find myself in times of trouble,' which I certainly found myself in. The song was based on that dream." Earlier versions of the song found Paul singing, "There will be no sorrow / Let it be," a lyric that he sagely revised as "There will be an answer," affording the recording with a more optimistic mien. Played on the exquisite Blüthner grand piano in Apple's basement studio, "Let It Be" enjoys obvious quasi-religious overtones for its invocation of "Mother Mary," an aspect that has never troubled McCartney in the slightest: "I don't mind. I'm quite happy if people want to use it to shore up their faith" (qtd. in Miles 538). Released in March 1970, the single version reveals a more overt sense of religiosity—with Billy Preston's Hammond organ and the choirlike backing vocals elevated in the mix, effecting the ambience of a hymn. In late April, George remade his guitar solo, playing a deliberately subdued rendition in comparison with the January 1969 performance, where it is considerably rougher around the edges. Played on Harrison's Rosewood Telecaster, the earlier solo's distortion shifts the song's mood considerably from a spiritualized sense of acceptance, an oasis of calm amidst the storm, to a dramatic triumph against the fearsome odds of surviving the storm itself.

For "The Long and Winding Road," Paul had been thinking during the song's composition of producing a soul-rending number in the style of Ray Charles. As for the circuitous road of the title, Paul was undoubtedly referring to the B842 in Scotland, which winds its way through the Mull of Kintyre peninsula near the songwriter's rustic Campbeltown farm. With Paul on the Blüthner grand, the January 1969 recording effects a somber quietude, a gentle musing on the vexing emotional difference between a sentimentalized past and an agonizing present. The song's inherent beauty is unnecessarily blemished by John's slipshod work on the Fender Bass VI, a guitar part that Paul had numerous opportunities to refine as the ensuing album went through its various iterations over the course of the spring, summer, and fall months of 1969.[9] While the Beatles offer several nostalgic forays during the *Get Back* project, Lennon and McCartney's bleak reflections about nostalgia's deceptive tendencies in recent years had clearly softened into a series of timely meditations on the heartbreaking power of regret. With songs like "Let It Be" and "The Long and Winding Road," McCartney crafts rueful tones about the manner in which the past continues to elude us despite our best efforts to memorialize it and render it into permanence through the auspices of music and language. "Let It Be" and "The Long and Winding Road" provide similarly minded excursions into nostalgia's death-defying limbo, a place in which disillusionment and anguish commingle *ad infinitum*. While "Let It Be" counsels us to contemplate "words of wisdom" during our hours of darkness and to embrace the gentle consolation of peace, "The Long and Winding Road," in many ways, knows better. For the speaker, nostalgia's tortuous road "will never disappear." And while it always leads us back to the memories of lost friends and loved ones, the long and winding road never quite gets us there. For the song's speaker, the panacea inherent in "Let It Be" merely produces "a pool of tears" in the harsher reality lost amidst the restless and unconvincing hopefulness of "The Long and Winding Road." Both songs might easily have become swept up in their composer's well-known penchant for sentimentality, yet McCartney—perhaps sensing the magnitude of this late moment in the life of the Beatles—succeeded in transforming would-be schmaltz into the stuff of poetry.

∿

What were the Beatles to do, then, with the accumulated material output from the *Get Back* sessions? Lindsay-Hogg's experiment in *audio vérité*—not to mention the *cinéma vérité* approach of his documentary—had resulted in the accrual of 223 rolls of audio and film, tallying up some sixty hours' worth of sound and footage from the group's ten days at Twickenham. A staggering 530 more rolls had been amassed after the project's relocation to Apple (Sulpy and Schweighardt 317). In early March, John and Paul turned the virtual mountain of audio tapes associated with the *Get Back* project over to Glyn Johns. In so doing, they set a series of events into motion that would spiral out of their control, resulting in the tortuous saga of the album's release more than a year later. As Johns later recalled: "They pointed to a big pile of tapes in the corner and said, 'Remember that idea you had about putting together an album? Well, there are the tapes. Go and do it'" (qtd. in Doggett 45). Johns would prepare at least two full-length versions of the *Get Back* album over the next nine months. Lennon and McCartney were confident enough in Johns's ability to whip the material into shape that they commissioned Angus McBean to shoot a cover photograph for an LP to be entitled *Get Back, Don't Let Me Down, and Twelve Other Songs*. On May 13th, the Beatles convened at EMI House, where McBean positioned the bandmates in the same fashion as they had appeared six years earlier for the cover of *Please Please Me*. In retrospect, it was a clever idea—a means of bookending their career, as well as underscoring their intent to return to the unadulterated rock and roll sound that brought them fame and fortune in the first place.

And it might have worked, too, were it not for the slipshod efforts of Glyn Johns, who, in historical hindsight, had probably taken John and Paul's notion of getting back to the basics far too literally. In May 1969, Johns debuted his preliminary mix of *Get Back* for the Beatles' inspection, and it was an ungodly mess. Brimming with studio banter and false starts, his version of the album was clearly designed to seem rough and spontaneous in contrast with their previous LPs. If nothing else, Johns succeeded in adhering to Lennon's dictum against the slick "jiggery-pokery" of professional studio production. But Johns didn't fail in his attempt to make the album appear impulsive and unstructured. Rather, Johns's presumptive mistake involved his textual choices for the LP's contents. In sober backcast, it's difficult to imagine what led him to select ineffectual versions of the songs for inclusion when he had so many different renditions, thanks to Lindsay-Hogg's no-holds barred recording effort, from which to choose. As it turns out, he made highly suspect decisions throughout the post-production process, selecting subpar recordings of key songs when much stronger versions were available—particularly in terms of the tracks that the Beatles had recorded during that last burst of creative energy in Apple's basement studio (as well as on its rooftop) at the end of January. His biggest sin, by far, involved his selection of a comparatively unfinished version of "Don't Let Me Down" from the January 22nd session when an extant rendition from the 28th was tighter and more polished in almost every possible respect. Even the rooftop version was superior, in spite of John's inability to remember the lyrics for the second verse, for which he resorted to conjuring up some gibberish on the spot as an impromptu guide vocal. Amazingly, Johns resorted to the same procedure for "Dig a Pony" and "I've Got a Feeling." The Beatles had performed far better versions of both songs on the roof, yet Johns had selected earlier and comparatively sloppier takes for inclusion on the album. In the case of "I've Got a Feeling," Johns opted for a rendition from the January 24th session that features a shoddy introduction, and, worse yet, that falls into utter collapse during its conclusion. Johns also selected a sluggish version of "Two of Us" recorded on the very same day as "I've Got a Feeling," once again choosing an inferior take when a significantly stronger version was available. Whether it had been done in haste or the producer had been overly concerned with preserving the immediacy of the sessions, Johns had missed a crucial opportunity to bring the project to fruition, allowing the tapes to remain in limbo—and just long enough to permit other hands to intervene.

As the months rolled by, it became increasingly apparent that the Beatles would scuttle Johns's version of the *Get Back* album altogether. Although Johns later substituted a comparatively more professional January 1970 mix for his May 1969 version of the album, by then it was much too late. While McCartney apparently approved of Johns's work—praising, in particular, the producer's attempt to preserve the album's spare sonic textures—Lennon despised *Get Back*, later claiming that it would succeed, for better or for worse, in breaking the Beatles' myth: "That's us, with no trousers on and no glossy paint over the cover and no sort of hope," he remarked. "This is what we are like with our trousers off, so would you please end the game now?" (*Anthology* 322). By the early spring of 1970, the tapes had fallen into the hands of renowned American producer Phil Spector—the esteemed progenitor of the "wall of sound." Lennon had recently worked with Spector on his hit solo single "Instant Karma," and he had been impressed enough with the producer's lightning-quick results to turn the *Get Back* tapes over to him with little concern—and, perhaps more significantly, without Paul's knowledge. In December, the Beatles' revolving management had sold the rights to Lindsay-Hogg's documentary to United Artists, who reincarnated the project as a feature film. The Beatles subsequently altered the title of their album from *Get Back* to *Let It Be* in order to synchronize the marketing of its release with the movie of the same name. McBean's EMI House photograph of the band was used in a March 1970 mockup for *Let It Be*'s cover art, although it was later replaced by Ethan Russell's January 1969 still photographs of the group in various states of rock and roll performance. In late March, Spector began his post-production activities, culminating in a massive overdubbing session in Studio One on April 1st, in which he edited and remixed the *Get Back* recordings in order to prepare the soundtrack album for release. With orchestral arrangements provided by Richard Hewson, Spector applied his wall of sound to "Across the Universe," "The Long and Winding Road," and "I Me Mine," which the Beatles had recently remade for the soundtrack, given the song's relatively conspicuous place in the movie.

In his autobiography of the same name, George described "I Me Mine" as the explicit result of his experiences with LSD, which forced him to reconceive his personal ego as the function of a larger, collective force: "The big I; i.e., Om, the complete whole," Harrison wrote, a "universal consciousness that is void of duality and ego" (158). In addition to its obvious critique of his bandmates' selfish behavior, the song also owes its genesis to the *Bhagavad Gita*, which states that "They are forever free who renounce all selfish desires and break away from the ego-cage of 'I,' 'me,' and 'mine' to be united with the Lord. This is the supreme state. Attain to this, and pass from death to immortality" (2:71–72). With the estranged John on a lengthy vacation with Yoko in Denmark, George, Paul, and Ringo remade the song on January 3rd at EMI Studios.[10] As they prepared to record "I Me Mine," George acknowledged Lennon's absence with a wry reference to the popular British band Dave Dee, Dozy, Beaky, Mick, & Tich: "You all will have read that Dave Dee [Lennon] is no longer with us, but Mickey and Tich and I [Paul, Ringo, and George] have decided to carry on the good work that's always gone down in [EMI Studios'] Number Two." With a potent dose of musical drama supplied by the songwriter's vocal and Paul's ominous Hammond organ work, Harrison's waltzing composition offers a knowing critique of humanity's penchant for elevating the desires of the self over the welfare of the community. Their rendition of the song clocked in at less than two minutes, a constraint that Spector remedied by repeating various portions of the track in order to make it seem more robust. The next evening, Paul, George, and Linda remade the harmony vocals for "Let It Be," for which George Martin crafted a brass accompaniment. And with that, the soundtrack album lay dormant until Spector's intervention.

In contrast with more coherent and unified albums such as *Sgt. Pepper* and *The White Album, Let It Be* (and, for that matter, the *Magical Mystery Tour* project) ultimately suffers for its lack, in Allan F. Moore's perceptive words, of "authorial control" (71). With three different producers at the helm and a filmmaker to boot, the project's overriding sense of creative incongruity should have been a foregone conclusion. In Phil Spector's hands, the LP retained much of the studio banter that had given Glyn Johns's version a sense of charm in comparison to its rough exterior. Yet the wall-of-sound overdubbing sessions succeeded in altogether mitigating the project's philosophy of getting back to the basics. McCartney, for one, was mortified by Spector's post-production efforts. While "In My Life" and "Eleanor Rigby" would pit Lennon and McCartney in a contest of memories about the songs' creation, Paul's "The Long and Winding Road" is, quite easily, the songwriter's most personally vexing recording amongst his entire *oeuvre*.[11] But in this case, his angst had almost nothing to do with Lennon and everything to do with the track's post-*Get Back* textual history. Although it is impossible to deny Paul's anger at not being consulted about the album's disposition, he directed much of his vitriol toward Spector's decision to imbue "The Long and Winding Road" with a thirty-three-piece orchestra, a fourteen-member choir, two studio musicians on guitar, and one drummer—ironically, Ringo, the last Beatle to join the band and the last member to play on a Beatles session. At one point, McCartney even attempted, albeit unsuccessfully, to block the album's release. "I'm not struck by the violins and ladies' voices on 'The Long and Winding Road,'" he complained (qtd. in Gambaccini 20). Although McCartney vehemently objected to the manner in which Spector recorded orchestral and choral tracks onto his songs from the *Get Back* sessions, Lennon later defended Spector's efforts on the disintegrating band's behalf: "He worked like a pig on it," Lennon recalled. "He'd always wanted to work with the Beatles, and he was given the *shittiest* load of badly recorded shit—and with a lousy feeling to it . . . and he made *something* out of it" (*Lennon Remembers* 101–02).

Quite obviously, McCartney couldn't have agreed less. His vision for one of his most personal of compositions had been shattered—and entirely without his permission. Tim Riley proves to be equally unforgiving in his analysis of the song: "All of the sudden," he writes, "it's as if we're in the showroom of a large casino, and Paul is cruising into a schmaltzy ballad" (301).[12] There is little question that Spector's orchestration works at variance with Martin's consistent efforts over the years to afford the Beatles' tracks with tasteful, fashion- and time-defying arrangements that contributed to the band's musical aspirations without overpowering them. Yet on the other hand, there is something to be said for Spector's full-blown rendering of the song in spite of its apparent divergence from the songwriter's intentions. Ian MacDonald, for instance, praises Spector's version as an elemental study of illusion and nostalgia. "'The Long and Winding Road' was so touching in its fatalistic regret, and so perfect as a downbeat finale to the Beatles' career," he writes, "that it couldn't fail, however badly dressed" (273). And while the Spectorized version obviously sacrifices the ethereal beauty inherent in the original January 31st recording, it pointedly affords the song with a markedly different bearing, shifting the gentle nostalgia of the Ur-text toward a more totalizing, overwhelming sense of loss and lament that seemed entirely warranted when "The Long and Winding Road" topped the American charts as the Beatles' final number-one single in the spring of 1970.[13]

As with its soundtrack, Lindsay-Hogg's documentary hardly fared any better. Where *A Hard Day's Night* and *Help!* had labored in the service of the Fab Four's media-friendly mythology, *Magical Mystery Tour* and *Yellow Submarine* had worked to concretize it for all time. But *Let It Be*, for all of its joy and spontaneity—and make no mistake about it, there is plenty of joy and spontaneity in the movie—could only hope to demythologize the band forever. While the earlier films established vast, fictive personae for the Mop Tops, *Let It Be* portrayed them as indelibly human—"The Beatles as Nature Intended," as the advertisements for the "Get Back" single had so proudly proclaimed. For all of the tension and disagreement at the documentary's unruly core, *Let It Be*'s famous conclusion couldn't help but take a sad song and make it better. The rooftop concert seems to energize the Beatles, all but erasing the earlier, comparatively dismal images of the group in the act of recording a lackluster album. In this way, the Beatles' myth seems to emerge intact even during their most self-conscious acts of demythology. The album sleeve for the soundtrack triumphantly announces that "this is a new phase Beatles album," and although this new phase would be decidedly short-lived, it offers a singular truth in its effort to preserve "the warmth and the freshness of a live performance." If nothing else, the lingering image of John, Paul, George, and Ringo on that legendary rooftop finds them reveling in the raw power of their musicianship. The motley group on that makeshift stage is really not so different from the Beatles of August 1962—the very same bandmates who thrilled the Cavern Club faithful with the breakneck adrenaline of rock and roll when fame and fortune were nothing but a glint in their collective eyes. In James Joyce's *Ulysses* (1922), Stephen Dedalus famously observes that "history is a nightmare from which I am trying to awake." With the *Get Back* project, the Beatles tried to conquer their own nightmares, to effect a new narrative for themselves and their increasingly vague future by reclaiming the past. Not surprisingly, the long reach of history has been unkind to *Let It Be*, both the album and the documentary alike. For many, the fleeting highs and soul-crushing lows of January 1969 are simply too much to take after the great triumphs of *Rubber Soul*, *Revolver*, and *Sgt. Pepper*. But one thing remains certain: in spite of everything—even their own darker angels—the Beatles had found a way, impossible as it may seem, to get back.

Notes

1. *Rock and Roll Circus* included the last footage of founding member Brian Jones performing with the Rolling Stones. He died the following July, having been found unconscious at the bottom of his swimming pool. Dissatisfied with their performance in the production, the Rolling Stones delayed the release of *Rock and Roll Circus* until 1996.

2. The *Get Back* sessions are documented in impressive detail in Doug Sulpy and Ray Schweighardt's monumental work of scholarship entitled *Get Back: The Unauthorized Chronicle of the Beatles' Let It Be Disaster* (1997), which provides a day-by-day, song-by-song analysis of the band's activities in January 1969.

3. Johns went on to produce such legendary albums as the Rolling Stones' *Get Yer Ya-Ya's Out!* (1970), as well as sharing production and engineering duties on several albums by the Who, including *Who's Next* (1971), *Quadrophenia* (1973), *The Who by Numbers* (1975), and *Who Are You* (1978).

4. This concept finds its roots in Harold Bloom's *The Anxiety of Influence: A Theory of Poetry* (1973). Bloom contends that artists—poets in particular—pursue their craft in uneasy relationship with their antecedents, whose work they must react to, and ultimately usurp, in order to create original art and achieve renown and posterity of their own making.

5. Lennon admitted as much in a September 1980 interview: "George's relationship with me was one of young follower and older guy. . . . I was already an art student when Paul and George were still in grammar school. There is a vast difference between being in high school and being in college, and I was already in college and already had sexual relationships, already drank and did a lot of things like that." In the same interview, John confessed to being hurt by George's 1980 autobiography *I Me Mine*, which scarcely mentions Lennon at all: "By glaring omission in the book, my influence on his life is absolutely zilch and nil. Not mentioned. In his book, which is purportedly this clarity of vision of each song he wrote and its influences, he remembers every two-bit sax player or guitarist he met in subsequent years. I'm not in the book" (*All We Are Saying* 148–49).

6. John was heartbroken by his bandmates' refusal to accept Yoko as his soulmate. "You sit through 60 sessions with the most big-headed, uptight people on earth and see what it's fuckin' like. And be insulted just because you love someone. George insulted her right to her face in the Apple office at the beginning, just being straightforward, that game of, 'Well, I'm going to be upfront because this is what I've heard and Dylan and a few people said you've got a lousy name in New York and you give off bad vibes.' That's what George said to her, and we both sat through it. And I didn't hit him, I don't know why. But I was always hoping that they'd come 'round. I couldn't believe it! They all sat there with their wives like a fucking jury and judged us. The only thing I did was write that piece about 'some of our beast friends'—in my usual way, 'cause I was never honest. I always had to write in that gobbledy-gook. And that's what they did to us" (*Lennon Remembers* 45).

7. Parsons would achieve renown as the engineer for Pink Floyd's *The Dark Side of the Moon* (1973), as well as for his work with the Alan Parsons Project.

8. John later accused Paul of "subconscious sabotage" during their Beatles years: "We'd spend hours doing little detailed cleaning-ups of Paul's songs; when it came to mine, especially if it was a great song like 'Strawberry Fields' or 'Across the Universe,' somehow this atmosphere of looseness and casualness and experimentation would creep in" (*All We Are Saying* 192).

9. In *Revolution in the Head*, Ian MacDonald catalogues key instances involving John's erratic bass playing on "The Long and Winding Road": "Recurring wrong notes at 0:28, 2:10, and 3:07; mis-strikes at 2:39 and 2:52; drop-outs at 2:59 and 3:14; a fumble at 0:19; a vague glissando at 1:03; a missed final push at 3:26. (One can hear McCartney grin at his partner's incompetence at 1:59)" (271).

10. Twenty-four years later, Paul, George, and Ringo would reunite to record two of John's 1970s-era demos, "Free as a Bird" and "Real Love," for the Beatles' *Anthology* project.

11. McCartney's disgust with Spector's alteration of "The Long and Winding Road" would resound for years to come. By 2002, no less than six additional versions of "The Long and Winding Road" had been made available on various McCartney projects, including four telling concert performances of the track. The first of these later versions of the Beatles' final American hit single surfaced during McCartney's celebrated return to the international stage, an event that was commemorated by the release of *Wings over America* (1976). The album features a somber rendering of the Beatles classic, complete with a plaintive trumpet accompaniment. Yet another version of "The Long and Winding Road" appeared on McCartney's 1990 concert album, *Tripping the Live Fantastic*. While this latest rendition of the song imitated the simple melody of the pre-orchestral version of "The Long and Winding Road," McCartney's backup band clearly attempts to replicate the violin solo created during Spector's postproduction work in 1970. Similar concert performances were included on *Back in the US* (2002) and the *Live 8* DVD (2005). Paul's various interpretations of the song reached their ridiculous nadir in yet another rendering of "The Long and Winding Road" on his 1984 album, *Give My Regards to Broad Street*. In an outrageous jazz reading of the song, McCartney offers an overproduced, saxophone-accompanied performance. The original, pre-Spector version of the song finally became available on *Anthology 3*. Reproduced without Spector's string and choral arrangement, "The Long and Winding Road" seems to have come full circle, ostensibly satisfying McCartney's artistic designs for the song for the first time.

12. Riley was only the latest in a long line of critical voices besieging Spector's work on "The Long and Winding Road." George Martin felt that the track's orchestral arrangement wreaked of the saccharine sounds of Mantovani and Muzak, while John Mendelsohn called the song "oppressive mush" and "virtually unlistenable with hideously cloying strings and a ridiculous choir." Nicholas Schaffner blamed Spector's orchestration for destroying the "sense of intimacy, informality, and honesty" that the song possessed in its original form (138).

13. *Let It Be*'s worldwide release in May 1970 would seem to have concluded the album's torturous post-production journey, but in November 2003, the band's unvarnished recordings from the *Get Back* sessions were released as *Let It Be . . . Naked*, demonstrating that the Beatles—both the estates and the survivors—have yet to make sense of the complex of interpersonal events that they experienced during the *Get Back* project's convoluted production all those years ago.

Chapter 13

The Dream Is Over

The past is a foreign country; they do things differently there.
—L. P. HARTLEY, *THE GO-BETWEEN*

I suppose all is reminiscence from womb to tomb.
—SAMUEL BECKETT

In order for the Beatles to truly get back—to genuinely reclaim themselves as artists and to find their way back homeward as a musical unit—it was imperative that they regain control over their misbegotten financial lives, which had run rampant during the post-Epstein era. And for all of his incoherency and disillusion during the *Get Back* sessions, Lennon understood the nature of their fiscal crisis implicitly. Within days of Brian's demise, John had recognized the implications of the manager's absence from their midst. When the *Magical Mystery Tour* movie tanked, John astutely chalked it up to their lack of experience, their inability to excel in any arena beyond the world of popular music that they had conquered, and continued to conquer, with veritable ease. And nowhere was this lack of inexperience more apparent than in the disposition of Apple Corps, the business conglomerate that was spiraling out of control. On January 13th, John had been interviewed during a break in the *Get Back* sessions by Ray Coleman, the editor for *Disc & Music Echo*, about the precarious state of Apple Records: "Apple's losing money every week because it needs closely running by a big businessman," Lennon confided. "We did it all wrong, you know, Paul and me running to New York, saying we'll do this and encourage this and that. It's got to be a business first. We realize that now. It needs a broom and a lot of people there will have to go. It needs streamlining. It doesn't need to make vast profits, but if it carries on like this, all of us will be broke in the next six months" (qtd. in Badman 413). While Paul and George had been critical of John's public revelations about their private business affairs, there is little question that his observations about Apple's impending insolvency were absolutely germane to solving their interpersonal woes. When George briefly quit the band back in January, John had been lucid enough to recognize how much he still needed the Beatles as his primary creative outlet, and he was determined to do something about it before it was too late.

Lennon had resolved to work with a "big businessman" alright. On January 28th, John and Yoko went to London's Dorchester Hotel, where they held an audience with Allen Klein, the American accountant who had instilled so much fear in Brian Epstein during his final days on earth. Lennon was roundly impressed with the no-nonsense, tough-talking New Yorker. John especially liked the accountant's earthy demeanor—"he had all the charm of a broken lavatory seat," in the words of Alistair Taylor—and Lennon believed that Klein had the necessary resolve to put the group's house in order, no matter what the cost (242). Not long afterward, the Beatles assigned Allen Klein and attorney Lee Eastman, Paul's future father-in-law, with the task of cleaning up their business and legal affairs, respectively. Their first order of business was to win back control of NEMS Enterprises, which was now under the management of Clive Epstein, who was considering a bid for control from Triumph Investments, to whom he sold 70 percent of NEMS. The saga of Northern Songs came to a head in March 1969, when Dick James threatened to sell his shares in Lennon and McCartney's publishing company to the UK's Associated Television (ATV). Lennon was incensed: "I'm not going to be fucked around by men in suits sitting on their fat arses in the City!" he remarked at the time (qtd. in Koskimäki 58). To make matters worse, Paul had been secretly buying shares of Northern Songs, which infuriated John, although to his great credit, he forgave Paul and resolved to work with his partner to effect a joint solution. In order to purchase Northern Songs outright, Lennon and McCartney needed to come up with £9.5 million, but they simply didn't have access to that kind of cash, with Apple's dire financial straits no doubt contributing to their weak financial position (Koskimäki 41). By the time that John and Paul marshaled their forces in order to purchase a controlling interest in their publishing company, it was too late. London's money men in suits had prevailed. When ATV successfully negotiated their buyout later that year, John and Paul were powerless to do anything about it, other than voice their opposition. The songs that had earned for them international songwriterly acclaim were now the property of a faceless corporate entity.[1] Klein countered by renegotiating the Beatles' contract with EMI and demanding that future royalties bypass NEMS—which had been collecting 25 percent of their royalty income while providing little, if any genuine service on their behalf—and go directly to Apple Corps, now under Klein's management.

By April, Klein was firmly in control—and in spite of heated opposition from Paul, who refused to sign the brutish New Yorker's management contract in May, further splintering the bandmates' relationship. On the evening of May 9th, Paul was scheduled to hold a recording session with Steve Miller at Olympic Studios. The other Beatles converged on the studio, claiming that Klein was outside and that they needed to sign his management contract, which called for a 20 percent fee, immediately. "He'll take 15 percent," McCartney countered. "You're just stalling," the other Beatles told him. "No, I'm working for us. We're a big act—the Beatles. He'll take 15 percent" (*Anthology* documentary). After John, George, and Ringo left the studio—without receiving Paul's signature— McCartney recorded the appropriately titled "My Dark Hour" with Steve Miller. The Beatle adopted "Paul Ramon" as his *nom de plume* for the recording session—an allusion to the stage name that he had assumed all those years ago on the Johnny Gentle tour. But that was then, and this was now. Paul's remonstrations had gone for naught. As McCartney himself was fond of saying, the Beatles had always operated as a democracy, albeit one in which each member had veto power. In this case, Paul was loath to find himself in a rare minority position— and he couldn't bring himself to accede to his bandmates' unwavering decision. The long-range fallout from McCartney's choice would be devastating indeed, but there is no arguing with the new manager's results in the short run. After losing millions of pounds over the past sixteen months, Apple Corps was now in the hands of someone—like him or not—who knew how to stop the bleeding with a vengeance. Klein's first order of business was to fire much of Apple's enormous staff, which had bloated to some two hundred employees by the spring of 1969. One of the first casualties of Klein's bloodletting was the not-so Magic Alex, his days as the Beatles' resident inventor and self-styled electronics expert having finally come to an end. Denis O'Dell would follow soon thereafter, as would Apple's General Manager Alistair Taylor, who had made the ironic suggestion, several months back, that the Beatles bring in a high-powered accountant to sort out the fiscal rot at the heart of Apple Corps. Perhaps even more significantly, it had been less than eight years since Taylor had descended the Cavern steps in the company of Brian Epstein, with whom he encountered a cellarful of noise and the future of popular music in the same instant.

In concert with their business lives, the Beatles' personal and professional lives were as harried as usual. While Ringo continued working on *The Magic Christian*, Paul had written and produced hit singles for a pair of Apple artists, including Mary Hopkin's "Goodbye" and Badfinger's "Come and Get It." Meanwhile, George wrestled with a serious bout of tonsillitis that left him hospitalized, and in March, he had been arrested—as with John and Yoko back in October—by Sgt. Pilcher. George claimed to have been framed, a charge that was validated by Pilcher's own arrest for perjury and obstruction of justice in November 1972. He eventually served four years in prison. On March 12th, the same day that George had been arrested, Paul married Linda at the Marylebone Registry office. On March 20th, John and Yoko held a wedding of their own near the Rock of Gibraltar, followed by their well-choreographed honeymoon, which included a weeklong "bed-in" for peace in Room 902 at the Amsterdam Hilton Hotel. As they had planned, their nonviolent protest of the Vietnam War enjoyed substantial media attention, especially given that John and his bride had conducted twelve-hour press conferences each day from their hotel room bed, their handwritten signs extolling "Hair Peace" and "Bed Peace" for global inspection. "Behaving as if they had personally invented peace," Ian MacDonald writes, the newly minted Lennons "jetted around the world in first-class seats selling it at second-rate media-events" (276–77). Anxious to capture his experiences in the limelight for posterity, John composed a song about their increasingly public escapades entitled "The Ballad of John and Yoko." Recorded under the working subtitle of "They're Gonna Crucify Me," the song witnesses its composer, as with "A Day in the Life," turning to the daily news for his inspiration—although in this case, John's *objet trouvé* finds Lennon sifting through his *own* newspaper clippings. In this sense, John avails himself of a found object of a very different sort, an act of self-inscription in which he textualizes his madcap life with Yoko for all time.

"The Ballad of John and Yoko" b/w "Old Brown Shoe" would be the last 45-RPM record that the group prepared specifically for release as a single. It also marked the return of Geoff Emerick to the Beatles' fold—and just in the nick of time. With an anxious Lennon determined to commit his latest creation to tape, the erstwhile Beatles engineer had been invited by Peter Brown to operate EMI Studios' newly installed eight-track recording console. With George traveling abroad in the United States and Ringo still toiling away on the set of *The Magic Christian*, the Beatles' personnel was limited to John and Paul, who recorded the song during a lengthy April 14th session. While Lennon handled the lead and rhythm guitar parts, McCartney provided a one-man rhythm section. In addition to his pounding bass lines and assorted piano flourishes, Paul kept a steady beat on Ringo's Ludwig Hollywoods. McCartney achieved a distinctive cracking drum sound courtesy of Emerick, who placed microphones both above and below the snare. Lennon and McCartney recorded the song in workmanlike fashion, clearly enjoying each other's company and the opportunity to revel in their musicianship. They couldn't resist good-naturedly acknowledging their conspicuously absent mates. "Go a bit faster, Ringo!"

John exclaimed to Paul. "Okay, George!" he replied from behind Ringo's kit. With Paul's tinkling piano and the lyrics' whimsical progress from the Southampton docks to the Amsterdam Hilton, "The Ballad of John and Yoko" evinces seriocomic overtones, with Lennon effecting a martyr complex for the chorus: "Christ you know it ain't easy, / You know how hard it can be," he sings. "The way things are going / They're gonna crucify me."

Given its unequivocal self-referentiality, the composition makes for a peculiar entry in the Beatles' canon—perhaps even more so than the reflective "Julia," which affords listeners with universal notions of self-awareness even amidst its highly personalized context. In this way, "The Ballad of John and Yoko" explodes the group's carefully embroidered shroud of literary distance. The Beatles' fictive world, having been populated by the likes of Nowhere Man and Lady Madonna, had been roundly displaced by the flesh-and-blood personae of John and Yoko, leaving the comparatively stolid text of an exacting, unambiguous autobiography in its stead. "So outrageously eccentric is this song," MacDonald writes, "that it's difficult to know whether to deplore its vanity or admire its *chutzpah* in so candidly promoting Self to artistic central place" (277). Yet the Beatles' excursion into the idiosyncratic realm of the personal would be decidedly short-lived. Recorded just two days later with all four members present and accounted for, George's "Old Brown Shoe" offers a hint of greater things to come from the Beatles' most underrated (and hitherto junior) songwriter. A rhythm and blues fusion with McCartney playing a deft series of triplets on his galloping bass, "Old Brown Shoe" features an ecstatic guitar solo from George, whose sizzling Rosewood Telecaster benefits from a heavy dose of ADT. As the last burst of the band's spirited effort to get back to their free-wheeling rock and roll roots, the song makes for one of the Beatles' most electrifying B-sides.

~

In the pivotal months leading up to the bittersweet summer of 1969, John, Paul, George, and Ringo had become lost in a dizzying dance of emotional extremes. Far too often, they would spend their days in mind-numbing business meetings devoted to unscrambling the sprawling financial empire that threatened to tear them asunder. But come evening, they would reassemble at EMI Studios, where they attempted to cast off their demons just long enough to pursue the music that they had loved since their youth—and that had brought them to love one another. And somehow, under these most trying and bewildering of circumstances, the Beatles recorded the album that came to be known as *Abbey Road*.

After taking off the month of June in order to amass more material, the group was set to begin working on their next project on July 2nd. For all of the rancor and trauma that they experienced in recent months, the band-mates were genuinely excited about recording the new album. Only George Martin, it seems, was uncertain about their potential for seeing the project through to fruition:

> Let It Be was such an unhappy record (even though there are some great songs on it) that I really believed that was the end of the Beatles, and I assumed that I would never work with them again. I thought, "What a shame to end like this." So I was quite surprised when Paul rang me up and said, "We're going to make another record—would you like to produce it?" My immediate response was: "Only if you let me produce it the way we used to." (*Anthology* 337)

With Martin back in the producer's chair, the Beatles were poised to record their tenth studio album. John was especially eager to begin working on the project: "If I could only get the time to myself, I think I could probably write about 30 songs a day," he observed in an interview with *Disc* magazine. "As it is, I probably average about 12 a night. Paul, too: he's mad on it. As soon as I leave here, I'm going 'round to Paul's place and we'll sit down and start work. The way we're writing at the moment," he added, "it's straightforward and there's nothing weird. The songs are like 'Get Back,' and a lot of that we did in one take" (qtd. in Doggett 48). The Beatles' manic energy to complete the album led to them working simultaneously in all three EMI studios, from which they communicated using walkie-talkies in order to coordinate the project's overall production. Meanwhile, Ringo was thrilled with the sound of his Ludwig Hollywoods. Recording the album "was tom-tom madness," he later remarked. "I had gotten this new kit made of wood, and calfskins, and the toms had so much depth. I went nuts on the toms. Talk about changes in my drum style—the kit made me change because I changed my kit" (qtd. in Everett, *Revolver through the Anthology* 245). In addition to Ringo's impassioned drumming, the album's sound would benefit from the studio's eight-track recording technology, particularly in terms of its solid-state electronics, as opposed to the vacuum tube-driven equipment that had served them throughout their career. Consequently, the album evinces a perceptibly different sound, a "mellower" flavor and tonality, according to Emerick, who resumed his role as the band's balance engineer and Martin's right-hand man on a full-time basis in late July (277).

With the recording team at the helm that had launched *Revolver* and *Sgt. Pepper* into the stratosphere before disappearing into the vortex of *The White Album*, the Beatles were poised for greatness yet again, although the as-of-yet untitled album project was not without its attendant stresses and strains. The

LP's defining moment occurred on July 1st, less than twenty-four hours before work on the album was formally set to begin. Some six hundred miles to the north of EMI Studios, John had been tooling around the narrow roads of Scotland with Yoko by his side and their children—six-year-old Julian and five-year-old Kyoko—in the rear of their Austin Maxi. The newly married couple had been visiting Lennon's relatives in the far north when John lost control of the car and drove off of a steep embankment near Golspie. Yoko crushed several vertebrae and received a concussion in the accident, while all four suffered cuts and bruises. In truth, they were lucky to have escaped with their lives. Recognizing this twist of fate, John and Yoko had the wreckage compressed and shipped to their estate at Tittenhurst Park, where they planted it as a work of sculpture outside their living room window. They were hospitalized for five days before making their way back to London, where John rejoined the band on July 9th. As EMI engineer Phil McDonald recalls: "We were all waiting for them to arrive, Paul, George, and Ringo downstairs and us upstairs. They didn't know what state he would be in. There was a definite 'vibe': they were almost afraid of Lennon before he arrived, because they didn't know what he would be like. I got the feeling that the three of them were a little bit scared of him. When he did come in it was a relief, and they got together fairly well. John was a powerful figure, especially with Yoko—a double strength" (qtd. in Doggett 59–60). Between his injuries, which required seventeen stitches in his face, and his renewed heroin abuse with Yoko in the accident's wake, John missed several July sessions. According to Emerick, Yoko took to wearing a tiara in order to hide the scar on her forehead from the car wreck. Given her high-risk pregnancy, Yoko was under her physician's orders for constant bed rest, so John had a double bed shipped into EMI Studios from Harrods and a microphone positioned within easy reach so as to allow her to be in continuous communication with her husband.

John started to turn things around considerably on July 21st, when the Beatles began recording "Come Together"—the song that would set the *Abbey Road* album into motion, as well as the penultimate composition that John would ever write expressly for production by the group.[2] "It's a funky record," Lennon remembered. "It's one of my favorite Beatles tracks" (qtd. in Dowlding 277). On May 30th, Timothy Leary had met with John during the bed-in for peace that he and Yoko held in Room 1742 of Montreal's Hôtel Reine-Elizabeth. The counterculture guru asked John to compose a song based on the slogan for Leary's 1970 California gubernatorial campaign, "Come Together—Join the Party!" The next day, John and Yoko famously recorded "Give Peace a Chance" in their bedclothes. Strumming his Jumbo, John was joined on vocals by Leary, Allen Ginsberg, Murray the K, and Derek Taylor, among others. The embryo for the song had been born the day before, when

Lennon told a reporter that "all we are saying is give peace a chance." John imagined that the song would emerge as a peace anthem in the same vein as the gospel standard "We Shall Overcome." In spite of its titular call for coalition, "Come Together" shares little in common with "Give Peace a Chance"— or, for that matter, with Leary's unifying political slogan, which went for naught after the candidate was jailed for a 1968 drug arrest.

In composing "Come Together," Lennon was influenced by Chuck Berry's 1956 hit "You Can't Catch Me," in which the pioneering rock-and-roller sings, "Here come up flattop he was movin' up with me." The Beatles had improvised a version of "You Can't Catch Me" on January 14th during the *Get Back* sessions. Lennon's slight revisioning of the lyric into "Here come 'ol flattop he was movin' up slowly" would find him on the losing end, at least initially, of a protracted lawsuit with Berry's publisher Morris Levy.[3] "Come Together" witnesses the Beatles at their groovy zenith, with John's soulful lead vocal, George on his Gibson Les Paul Standard, and Ringo fashioning a slick tom-tom roll for the song's motto. In addition to the distinctive looping bass sound that he achieved on his Rickenbacker, Paul had fond memories of playing the Fender Rhodes electric piano: "Whenever [John] did praise any of us, it was great praise, indeed, because he didn't dish it out much," McCartney recalled. "If ever you got a speck of it, a crumb of it, you were quite grateful. With 'Come Together,' for instance, he wanted a piano lick to be very swampy and smoky, and I played it that way and he liked it a lot. I was quite pleased with that" (qtd. in Dowlding 277). As with the sessions that concluded the *Get Back* project, the group's work on "Come Together" was loose and effortless, with John good-naturedly ad-libbing "got to get some bobo" and "Eartha Kitt, man!" (qtd. in Winn, *That Magic Feeling* 332). Lyrically, the song's nonsensicality most closely resembles the idiosyncratic verbal textures of "I Am the Walrus," as opposed to the superficial automobile homage afforded by Berry's "You Can't Catch Me." Prefaced by Lennon's come-hither call to heroin—he sings "shoot me" during the composition's introductory phrases—"Come Together" offers a positively grotesque illustration of yet another one of the band's patent outsiders. In contrast with Eleanor Rigby, the character's unkempt, smarmy persona is the product of his self-isolating nature, his desire to choose his own exile and intentionally seek out the marginalizing power of loneliness. With his "joo-joo eyeball," his "toe-jam football," and the "disease" festering in his armchair, he is decidedly unashamed of what his alienation has wrought. In its vile depiction of humanity's inner repugnance, "Come Together" offers a masterful reading of the corrosive effects of loneliness.[4]

Harrison's songwriting career with the Beatles would reach its stunning apex with "Something," a composition that he had written, as with Paul's "The

Long and Winding Road," with Ray Charles in mind. Having begun working on "Something" during *The White Album* sessions, George had borrowed the song's opening lyric from Apple artist James Taylor's "Something in the Way She Moves." The Beatles created an eight-minute version of "Something" during the song's lengthy production, including a substantial countermelody and piano part played by Lennon (mostly deleted), as well as Billy Preston on Hammond organ. During this period, George had begun developing his signature slide-guitar sound, an aspect of his musicianship that was enhanced by the Leslie speaker that Clapton had given him several months earlier. With "Something," Harrison had finally come into his own. It "was the first time he ever got an A-side, because Paul and I always wrote both sides anyway," John later observed. "Not because we were keeping him out, 'cause, simply, his material wasn't up to scratch" (*All We Are Saying* 165). "Something" would be Harrison's crowning achievement and the classic tune that Frank Sinatra would famously dub "the greatest love song of the past 50 years," although the crooner would often mistakenly ascribe it as a Lennon-McCartney composition. The sessions for "Something" were relatively convivial, although Geoff Emerick recalls Harrison asking Paul to simplify his bass part. McCartney pointedly refused to oblige, ironically setting up one of the duo's finest moments on record. For much of the song, Harrison's soaring guitar dances in delectable counterpoint with McCartney's jazzy, melodic bass. Instrumentally, the fusion of their guitar-work produces an exquisite musical tapestry as "Something" meanders toward Harrison's most unforgettable and magisterial of guitar solos, the tune's greatest lyrical feature—even more lyrical, interestingly enough, than the lyrics themselves. A masterpiece of aesthetic simplicity, Harrison's solo on his Gibson Les Paul Standard reaches toward the sublime, wrestles with it in a bouquet of downward syncopation, and hoists it yet again in a moment of supreme grace.

The grandeur established by "Something" is quickly extinguished by Paul's "Maxwell's Silver Hammer," yet another composition that finds its roots in the *Get Back* sessions. It was also affected by George's purchase of a Moog synthesizer in early 1969. Originally designed by Robert Moog, the electronic keyboard instrument employs oscillators to produce a series of basic tones. The keyboard activates a bank of sound modules that allows the user to create a host of sounds, which can then be manipulated in terms of pitch and timbre. The Moog played a central role in the song's fruition, as did the anvil upon which Mal Evans would bang in order to signal Maxwell Edison's homicidal tendencies. In "Maxwell's Silver Hammer," McCartney's psychopathic protagonist subscribes to the "pataphysical" branch of metaphysics as delineated in the work of Parisian playwright Alfred Jarry. Pataphysics is a form of antiphilosophy in which every occurrence throughout the universe, no matter how mundane or routine, is treated as an extraordinary and, hence, meaning-ful event. In "Maxwell's Silver Hammer," this phenomenon is made manifest in Paul's song through Maxwell's unprovoked, largely motive-free killing spree. As McCartney later observed: "'Maxwell's Silver Hammer' is my analogy for when something goes wrong out of the blue, as it so often does, as I was beginning to find out at that time in my life. I wanted something symbolic of that, so to me it was some fictitious character called Maxwell with a silver hammer. I don't know why it was silver," he added. "It just sounded better than Maxwell's ham-mer. It was needed for scanning. We still use that expression now when some-thing unexpected happens" (qtd. in Miles 554). In spite of the song's well-wrought origins, Lennon remained decidedly unimpressed. "I hate it. 'Cuz all I remember is the track—he made us do it a hundred million times," John later recalled. Paul "did *everything* he could to make it a hit single and it never was and it never could've been" (*All We Are Saying* 202).

In terms of *Abbey Road*'s larger textual progress, "Maxwell's Silver Ham-mer" is a proverbial fish out of water, an odd conduit from the opulence of George's "Something" to the vintage rock and roll panache of Paul's "Oh! Dar-ling." As "another audience-distancing performance of a performance," in the words of Walter Everett, "Maxwell's Silver Hammer" finds its composer increasing the notion of authorial distance between artist and listener by depicting ordinary happenings—a young couple going to the movies, a way-ward pupil staying after class—with mind-numbingly improbable conse-quences (*Revolver through the Anthology* 251). Lyrically, McCartney treats this strange nexus of events with an intensely jarring sense of detachment and nar-ratorial nonchalance: "Bang, bang, Maxwell's silver hammer / Came down upon her head," Paul sings about the untimely demise of quizzical Joan at the hands of her unbalanced suitor. "Bang, bang, Maxwell's silver hammer / Made sure that she was dead."

Worse yet, the song's inherent insincerity affords listeners with a damn-ingly ineffectual transition into "Oh! Darling," an impassioned musical throw-back that deserved a much better framing device. Inspired by the rock and roll ballads of the late 1950s—particularly such bombastic vocal showcases as Jackie Wilson's "Lonely Teardrops"—"Oh! Darling" features George propelling the fiery track on his Rosewood Telecaster, while Paul turns in a searing vocal performance arrayed against a 12/8 time signature. Produced under the work-ing title of "I'll Never Do You No Harm," "Oh! Darling" offers one of McCart-ney's most deftly crafted vocal performances: "When we were recording this track," he remembered, "I came into the studios early every day for a week to sing it by myself because at first my voice was too clear. I wanted it to sound as though I'd been performing it on stage all week" (qtd. in Dowlding 282). As with its charming precursor, Ringo's "Octopus's Garden" offers a playful message about the innate powers of peace and harmony. Written by Ringo on a family vacation in Sardinia during his August 1968 hiatus from the Beatles, "Octopus's Garden" had been inspired by a fisherman's tale about undersea life: "He told me all about octopuses, how they go 'round the sea bed and pick up stones and shiny objects and build gardens," Ringo recalled. "I thought, 'How fabulous!' 'cause at the time I just wanted to be under the sea, too. I wanted to get out of it for a while" (qtd. in Dowlding 283). The song's distinctive underwater ambience was created by George on the Moog, although Ringo was especially keen on effecting the sound of blowing bubbles in order to enhance his lead vocal: "After some experimentation," Emerick writes, "I discovered that feeding the vocals into a compressor and triggering it from a pulsing tone (which I derived from George Harrison's Moog synthesizer) imparted a distinctive wobbly sound, almost like gargling. It was weird, almost like something out of a cheesy science-fiction movie, but Ringo loved the result" (283). With Harrison establishing a jaunty, country and western sound on his Fender Strat and McCartney providing a jangly piano backdrop, "Octopus's Garden" brings Ringo's serene aquamarine vision delightfully to life.

As both the first and last song recorded for *Abbey Road*, Lennon's "I Want You (She's So Heavy)" was ironically begun at Trident Studios (as opposed to EMI Studios) back on February 22nd. The original recording session featured John on his Casino, Paul on his Rickenbacker, and Ringo behind the drums. In mid-April, Lennon and Harrison began constructing the composition's massive guitar sound by doubling the existing arpeggiated Casino track and adding two more layers via George's heavily distorted Les Paul. A few days later, Billy Preston contributed a groovy Hammond organ part, while Ringo punctuated the lengthy musical bridge—as Paul's funky Rickenbacker solo took center stage—with a supple conga. On April 20th, the song's distinctive white noise was generated by Ringo on a wind machine from the Studio Two percussion cupboard, with Lennon augmenting the din on Harrison's Moog. As with "Strawberry Fields Forever," "I Want You" was made possible by editing various discrete sections together. During an August 20th session, the song was assembled with the introductory passages transitioning into John and George's guitar strata prior to the extended musical bridge. Lennon's vocal proper reemerges in the vicinity of the composition's midway point, before achieving its scorching climax with the needle literally driving into the red at 4:28. For the remaining three minutes, "I Want You" increases perceptibly in intensity. "Louder! Louder!" Lennon implored Emerick during the mixing process. "I want the track to build and build and build, and then I want the

white noise to completely take over and blot out the music altogether." With
only twenty-one seconds remaining of the original recording, "all of a sudden
he barked out an order" to the Beatles' engineer, "Cut the tape here!" (qtd. in
Emerick 301). As a brute study on the urgency and ferocity of desire, "I Want
You" bookends the ephemeral puppy love of "Love Me Do" with a sultry,
libidinous moan.

"I Want You" was originally supposed to conclude the record, with the
medley running its thematic course on side one instead. While the decision to
bring the album and the Beatles' recording career to a close with a symphonic
suite makes perfect sense—and who would really want it any other way?—the
sudden, unexpected resolution of "I Want You" would have made for an
alarming end to *Abbey Road*, as well as to the Fab Four's musical fusion, in and
of itself. The album's second side begins with George's "Here Comes the Sun,"
his exuberant final composition as a member of the Beatles. Harrison had
written the song's lush melody while strolling around Eric Clapton's garden on
a break from the group's relentless business meetings: "The relief of not having
to go and see all those dopey accountants was wonderful," George later
recalled, "and I was walking around the garden with one of Eric's acoustic guitars and wrote 'Here Comes the Sun'" (qtd. in Dowlding 285). Strumming his
capoed Gibson J-200 and playing the Moog to great effect, Harrison's work on
"Here Comes the Sun" is arguably one of the most magnificent instances in his
storied career. In contrast with "Yesterday," which exists as the Beatles' most
genuinely sad composition, "Here Comes the Sun" is easily the most buoyant
and optimistic entry in their entire catalogue. Signaling the ethereal, pastoral
beauty of a sunrise, "Here Comes the Sun" begins with George's gentle
acoustic guitar part, complemented in melodic parallel by his luminous Moog,
which softly pans from left to right as if to unveil the dawn of a new day. The
song's brightly arrayed middle-eight—"Sun, sun, sun, here it comes"—is con-
figured by a quintet of increasingly vibrant musical passages before erupting
in the swirl of color and light that brings the track to its transcendent conclusion. "Here Comes the Sun" is neatly countered by the somber quietude of
"Because." John was inspired to write the song after hearing Yoko play the first
movement of Beethoven's *Moonlight Sonata* on the piano. Intrigued by its delicate structure and counterpoint, he asked her to play the sonata backward,
and, with the recomposition of yet another found object, "Because" was born.
As with the mere dozen words that comprise the lyrics of "I Want You,"
"Because" employs a paucity of language in order to capture the simple truth
and nature of love, preferring instead to denote romantic expression via Martin's delicate Baldwin Electric Harpsichord and Harrison's Moog synthesizer
adornments. The song's most salient feature is John, Paul, and George's exqui-

site three part-harmony, which they recorded three times in order to achieve a blissful layered effect.

While there is some critical debate about precisely which song inaugurates the *Abbey Road* medley, Thomas MacFarlane argues rather convincingly that "Because"—with its gentle musings about the all-encompassing power of love as a universalizing force—functions as the overture for the so-called "huge medley" that concludes the album. The idea for the suite was probably hatched at Olympic Studios on May 6th, as the Beatles worked on Paul's multipart "You Never Give Me Your Money."[5] As MacFarlane points out, much of the medley's composition occurred in the studio, as McCartney and Martin began to craft a miniature pop opera—or "popera," in contemporary parlance: "The final version of the medley seems to have as much to do with the recording process as it does with traditional methods of composition," MacFarlane observes. "In that sense, the creation of the medley could properly be termed, *composing to tape*" (137–38). In the weeks directly preceding his car accident on July 1st, John evinced particular excitement about the Beatles' symphonic suite: "Paul and I are now working on a kind of song montage that we might do as one piece on one side," he remarked in an interview with the *New Musical Express*. "We've got about two weeks to finish the whole thing, so we're really working on it" (qtd. in Doggett 49). Yet in later years, Lennon would damn the medley's inclusion on *Abbey Road*, even going so far as to suggest that it lacked his authorial imprimatur, that it was the pet project of McCartney and Martin. This sudden change of heart may have been due to the fact that much of the suite was recorded in his absence. As he lay in a hospital bed recuperating in Scotland, the others had recorded the basic track for "Golden Slumbers" and "Carry That Weight," while George had debuted and recorded "Here Comes the Sun" almost in its entirety. Perhaps John felt understandably left out during such crucial instances in the album's production?

As the Beatles went about the business of recording their musical finale, McCartney and Martin began assembling the medley during July and August. "I wanted to do something bigger, a kind of operatic moment," McCartney remembered (qtd. in Lewisohn 14). In contrast with the pop-operas of that era by the Who ("A Quick One While He's Away"), Frank Zappa and the Mothers of Invention (*Absolutely Free*), and Keith West ("Excerpt from a Teenage Opera"), the Beatles' medley essentially consists of an assortment of unfinished songs. Yet McCartney and Martin's inspired post-production efforts ensured that the medley enjoys a cohesiveness from which we can draw larger musical and lyrical motifs. While the medley highlights the Beatles' penchant for balladry via such literary characters as Mean Mr. Mustard, Polythene Pam, and the eccentric female protagonist who meanders in and out of the narrative of "She Came in through the Bathroom Window," the sequence reaches its most profound instances during such poignant numbers as "You Never Give Me Your Money," "Golden Slumbers," and "Carry That Weight." As quite literally their farewell performance, the suite pointedly grapples with nostalgia and its equally complex relationship with regret. With the medley, the group also elevates the universal significance of love as humanity's last desperate hope for achieving wholeness in an increasingly fragmented world. As W. H. Auden famously observed in "September 1, 1939," a poem written on the eve of the Second World War, "We must love one another or die" (246). Although they invariably recognized contemporary life's inherent complexities and conundrums, for the Beatles the equation for transcendence and joy had always been ineluctably simple: "Love is all and love is everyone"; "with our love we could save the world"; "all you need is love"; "love you forever and forever"; and, even more recently in "Because," "love is all, love is you." It's the word, "love."

Written in response to the Beatles' crippling managerial crisis, "You Never Give Me Your Money" is yet another example, as with "Happiness Is a Warm Gun," of a "through-composed" song comprised of discrete individual components.[6] In "You Never Give Me Your Money," McCartney's plaintive piano strains give way to Lennon and Harrison's dueling rhythm guitars, as well as to one of the Beatles' most organic musical fusions. As Harrison later observed, the song "does two verses of one tune, and then the bridge is almost like a different song altogether, so it's quite melodic" (qtd. in Dowlding 287). In the composition's beginning, the speaker muses upon his lack of personal freedom in comparison with the responsibilities associated with his present-day wealth and fame:

> You never give me your money.
> You only give me your funny paper.
> And in the middle of negotiations,
> You break down.

Tethered to the establishment—and fettered by his money—the speaker begins to reflect upon his more liberated youth when he was genuinely free from the self-mollifying dictates of the crowd. He remembers enjoying a "magic feeling" with "nowhere to go" during those carefree early years, a time when "going nowhere" was a virtue, rather than a putdown. As the music transports the speaker from one period of his past to another, his lyrics bespeak the tragedies of misspent youth and runaway fame: "Out of college, money spent / See no future, pay no rent / All the money's gone, nowhere to go." As "You Never Give Me Your Money" comes to a close, the song's bluesy guitar riffs transform into the chorus of a nursery rhyme, with a layer of wind chimes and cicadas underscoring the speaker's childhood bliss: "One, two, three, four, five, six, seven / All good children go to heaven." As Wilfrid Mellers shrewdly points out, the subsequent "electronic gibbering and beeping belies the nursery-rhyme paradise of the words," ultimately producing an emotional response that is "more scary than ecstatic" (119).

As Paul's tape loops consisting of birds, crickets, and cicadas effect an early evening ambience, John's "Sun King" lumbers into view. Influenced by Fleetwood Mac's wistful instrumental hit "Albatross," "Sun King" had been rehearsed earlier during the *Get Back* sessions. With Paul on harmonium and Martin on Lowrey organ, "Sun King" fashions a tranquil mood in which the regal appearance of King Louis XIV—*Le Roi Soleil* himself—is met with happiness, joviality, and communal warmth. With John's bizarre admixture of *faux* Romance languages, "Sun King" seems purposeless, in terms of the medley's larger thematics, except only to effect the atmospherics that Ringo abruptly destroys with the entrance of "Mean Mr. Mustard" to the sound of five staccato drumbeats. John's inspiration for the song came from yet another found object, a newspaper article about a man who is so parsimonious that he secrets £5 notes within his nether regions. In "Mean Mr. Mustard," Lennon tells the story of a dirty old man who has become invisibilized by his society, the larger insensate crowd that has no use for him beyond his potential for sideshow grotesquerie. His inherent malevolence is the logical conclusion of alienation, of loneliness run amok. As Suzanne Sherman observes regarding the Beatles' fables about the dehumanizing effects of loneliness: "One discovers that isolation in a self-made world allows the intangible things in life to be destroyed. The feeling of despair that grasps man can be lifted if he breaks with tradition (time and materialism) and seeks freedom from the artificial world" (623). In Mean Mr. Mustard's case, living in an artificially fashioned personal reality offers his only genuine means for interacting with the real world of interhuman life. As a kind of anti-Father Mackenzie, Mean Mr. Mustard blithely shouts out obscenities in order to force people to notice him while he sounds his own "barbaric yawp" to the world.

"Mean Mr. Mustard" concludes in a headlong 12/8 time signature before giving way to "Polythene Pam," whose protagonist Lennon drew from an eccentric Beatles fan named Pat Hodgett who was well-known for eating polythene, the tough, light, translucent thermoplastic made by polymerizing ethylene (*OED*). Originally named Shirley in an earlier version of the composition, Polythene Pam's deviant nature finds its roots in August 1963, when John was introduced to Stephanie, the polythene-wearing girlfriend of British Beat poet Royston Ellis (Spizer 170). "Perverted sex in a polythene bag," John later recalled. "Just looking for something to write about" (*All We Are Saying* 203). Strumming away on his Hootenanny, John intentionally uses a thick Liverpudlian accent in order to connote the character's North Country origins and coarse demeanor. "Well, you should see Polythene Pam," Lennon sings. "She's so good looking, but she looks like a man." Wearing the intriguing ensemble of a polythene bag, a pair of jackboots, and a kilt, Pam wanders the nighttime streets, looking "killer diller" and making her way into the sleazy tabloid pages of the *News of the World* because of her freakish get-up. As with her brother Mean Mr. Mustard, Pam craves attention. As a kind of anti-Eleanor Rigby, she earns her notoriety by wearing an attention-getting ensemble, a masculinized wardrobe consisting of combat boots and a Scottish kilt. Could Polythene Pam be a drag queen in the tradition of Sweet Loretta Martin of "Get Back" fame? Polythene Pam's appearance in the *News of the World* underscores society's prurient interest in her sexuality in spite of its own condemnatory beliefs about her perversions. As with Lady Madonna and the hardhearted characters in "Happiness Is a Warm Gun," Mean Mr. Mustard and Polythene Pam are byproducts of a bitter urban locale beset by the psychological effects of loneliness and despair. As "Polythene Pam" comes to a close, John appropriately sings a sneering "yeah, yeah, yeah," invoking the seamy underbelly of "She Loves You" in the process.

Recorded as a single track along with "Polythene Pam," Paul's "She Came in through the Bathroom Window" may have been inspired by a March 1969 burglary at McCartney's Cavendish home, although the Beatles had actually rehearsed a version of the composition in January during the *Get Back* sessions. Recorded under the working title of "Bathroom Window," the song depicts a protagonist who may be every bit as deviant as Polythene Pam—in fact, given the song's lack of any obvious antecedent, she may even *be* Pam herself—but she pointedly represents an ethical turn away from the perverted mores of her aberrant precursors. Although it evokes childhood memories of *Mother Goose* nursery rhymes, the song's conspicuous reference to a silver spoon suggests that the protagonist is a cocaine addict, as opposed to the beneficiary of a world of wealth and privilege, while the fifteen clubs that she frequents on a daily basis imply that she works as a stripper in exceedingly popular demand. Yet for all of her vice and immodesty, the protagonist exercises intriguing limits in a seemingly limitless consumer culture: "She could steal," the speaker tells us, "but she could not rob." While she can carry out the impersonal crime of petty theft without troubling her conscience in the slightest, the personal violation inherent in robbery is simply beyond the protagonist's moral ken. After the pomp and circumstance of "Sun King," Mean Mr. Mustard and Polythene Pam exist as sad reminders of contemporary social disarray in contrast with an ostensibly happier era. With such cautionary tales emerging from an unremittingly corruptive urban landscape, Louis XIV's seventeenth-century reign seems like halcyon days indeed. Perhaps the dancer in "She Came in through the Bathroom Window"—with her quaint stripper's ethics preventing her from doing any lasting harm—offers the faintest glimmer of hope in the psychosocial nether world depicted so vividly in "Revolution 9" and beyond?

As Lennon and McCartney's ultimate vehicle for their nostalgic journey to a comparatively genial, untarnished past, the medley finds the Beatles staging elaborate backward glances in order to seek out and posit the essence of humanity in an inhospitable present. As the medley's final act, the triumvirate of "Golden Slumbers," "Carry That Weight," and "The End" affords listeners with the pure concatenation of the Beatles' art—from the tender anguish of "Golden Slumbers" and the nostalgic fanfare of "Carry That Weight" through the rock and roll bluster of "The End," the band's fond farewell to their international stage, their audience, and, ultimately, to themselves. A traditional English lullaby originally penned by Elizabethan playwright Thomas Dekker, "Golden Slumbers" came into Paul's orbit during a visit to his father's Cheshire home in 1968. The elder McCartney had married thirty-four-year-old Angela Williams back in November 1964, and her nine-year-old daughter Ruth was trying her hand at the piano when her twenty-six-year-old Beatle stepbrother encountered "Golden Slumbers" in one of her piano books. Inspired by the four hundred-year-old poem, Paul began writing his own musical accompaniment to Dekker's original lyrics:

> Golden slumbers kiss your eyes,
> Smiles awake you when you rise.
> Sleep pretty wantons, do not cry,
> And I will sing a lullaby;
> Rock them, rock them, lullaby.

Paul debuted his refashioned "Golden Slumbers" along with "Carry That Weight" as a single unit on January 7th during the *Get Back* sessions, with the Beatles recording them for posterity on July 2nd (Sulpy and Schweighardt 80). With McCartney's bittersweet nostalgia on full display—"Once there was a way to get back homeward. / Once there was a way to get back home"— "Golden Slumbers" acknowledges that the reclamation of a metaphorical sense of home, of a communal, comforting past, is no longer possible in the comparatively vexing world of adulthood. As recently as "Two of Us," the songwriter had allowed his nostalgia to run free, to enable both himself and his audience to imagine a sense of reconnection with the past. By contrast,

"Golden Slumbers" finds Paul renouncing his youthful dreams for a return to spiritual oneness, suggesting instead that our only hope for enjoying genuine succor and relief is to lose ourselves in the lullabies of our pasts for as long as their manna might sustain our weary souls. MacFarlane sagely asserts that the lullaby at the heart of "Golden Slumbers" exists as an explicit response to the nursery rhyme that concludes "You Never Give Me Your Money." In this manner, the medley takes on a much wider thematic arc in which the relative innocence of a cradle song is answered by a pensive lullaby for a melancholy middle age.

As the medley progresses toward its symphonic conclusion, the heartrending nostalgia inherent in "Golden Slumbers" yields itself to a larger realization, in the intensely autobiographical "Carry That Weight," that we inevitably shoulder the past's frequently irredeemable burden for the balance of our lives. In "Carry That Weight," McCartney addresses his own culpability in the Beatles' rapidly encroaching dissolution. Paul's rather humbling, self-conscious lyrics extend an olive branch to his increasingly distant chums by admitting his own failure to provide consolation—to share his "pillow" in an act of reassurance and contrition. Only the hubris of the human ego has prevented him, it seems, from fomenting the peace and goodwill that were entirely within his grasp. Paul's lyrics find him spiraling into self-oblivion amidst the heartbreaking—albeit no less triumphant—fanfare of Martin's puissant string and brass accompaniment as it cannily reprises the melody of "You Never Give Me Your Money." Played on his beloved Rosewood Telecaster, Harrison's impassioned guitar solo paves the way for McCartney to deliver his most soul-scathing and self-lacerating confession on record:

> I never give you my pillow.
> I only send you my invitations.
> And in the middle of the celebrations,
> I break down.

Having accepted the harrowing truth of his own culpability in the Beatles' malaise, Paul can only contemplate the awesome burden of the past, of his memories: "Boy, you're gonna carry that weight," the bandmates sing in unison. "Carry that weight a long time."

In its highly polished, final form, the *Abbey Road* medley encounters the Beatles at the height of their literary faculties. In many ways, the medley functions as McCartney's clever reconfiguration of Shakespeare's "seven ages of man" in *As You Like It*. From "You Never Give Me Your Money" through "The End," his lyrics impinge upon the inherent difficulties that come with growing up and growing older. Only the power of memory, it seems, can placate our inevitable feelings of nostalgia and regret—not only for our youthful days, but for how we lived them. As "Carry That Weight" comes to its sudden close, the medley's remorseful tones are displaced by the hard-driving guitar rock of "The End." As an old-style rock and roll revue in which the musicians show off their chops before the curtain sends the audience into the night, "The End" begins amidst the swagger and strut of rock concert rhetoric: "Oh, yeah, alright," Paul sings. "Are you gonna be in my dreams tonight?" And then, one by one, the bandmates take the spotlight, signaling their farewell to the stage with a final burst of electric gusto for the road. Mathematician Marc Kac has famously asked, "Can one hear the shape of a drum?" By placing a dozen microphones around Ringo's kit, Emerick makes it possible for listeners to experience every thump and throb of the drummer's rousing, pounding rumble as it ushers "The End" into being against a wall of sound of the Beatles' own making. "Love you, love you," they sing, before releasing a fusillade of guitar solos into the mix.[7] With Paul on his Fender Esquire, George on his Gibson Les Paul Standard, and John on his Casino, each guitarist succeeded in improvising a two-bar solo for the ages. Played by three different musicians on three different makes of guitars along with three separate amplifiers, each solo takes on a highly distinctive sound as Paul, George, and John parade their stuff—with McCartney at his inventive best, Harrison jousting with the sublime, and Lennon heartily engorging in his unquenchable thirst for grunge.[8] As Emerick later recalled: "John, Paul, and George looked like they had gone back in time, like they were kids again, playing together for the sheer enjoyment of it. More than anything, they reminded me of gunslingers, with their guitars strapped on, looks of steely-eyed resolve, determined to outdo one another. Yet there was no animosity, no tension at all—you could tell that they were simply having fun" (295).

As John drives his Casino into the quagmire, "The End" evaporates into stop-time, with a single piano note emerging from the murk. Paul appropriately concludes the medley with a quasi-Shakespearean couplet—"a cosmic, philosophical line," in Lennon's words (qtd. in Dowlding 292): "And in the end the love you take / Is equal to the love you make." As "The End" comes to a close, a series of guitar flourishes coalesce with Martin's orchestration, establishing a sense of an ending amidst the warmth of the musicians' harmonics. It is worth pointing out that while "A Day in the Life" climaxes in a darker hue—with the inherent tension and uncertainty of an E-major chord—"The End" reaches the finish line with the comparative serenity of C major before giving way to what feels like an inexorable silence.[9] But after the passage of some twenty seconds of quietude, the Beatles erupt back into being, if only briefly, with "Her Majesty," the album's belated coda. Originally recorded as the postscript for "Mean Mr.

Mustard," "Her Majesty" was spliced out of the mix after Paul astutely recognized that the twenty-three-second song made for a problematic segue into "Polythene Pam." Tape editor John Kurlander retained the snippet, realizing that EMI policy required all Beatles output to be strictly preserved. Not wishing to question the studio's rigid chain-of-command, Kurlander judiciously spliced "Her Majesty" onto the conclusion of "The End," along with twenty seconds of red leader tape. After hearing the final mix, McCartney was intrigued by the jarring manner in which "Her Majesty" explodes the silence in the wake of the seeming finality of "The End." As with "Hello Goodbye," "Helter Skelter," and "Get Back," the false ending undercuts, in true Beatles style, the utter plausibility of ascribing concrete endings to the twists and turns of human experience. In itself, the massive chord that punctuates "Mean Mr. Mustard" represents all four Beatles giving way to Paul for one last ditty on his Martin D-28. As an ironic footnote to the medley, "Her Majesty" cleverly subverts our accepted notions of Queen Elizabeth II's regal decorum—"Her Majesty's a pretty nice girl," Paul sings, "but she doesn't have a lot to say."[10] By normalizing her persona, the speaker's playfully nostalgic memories of the Queen's youth transport us back to a more innocent time, as with the group's more carefree, pre-Beatlemania days, before the onset of adulthood's inevitable compromises and burdens. And with the sudden terminus of "Her Majesty," the Beatles' silence returns with a vengeance.

∼

In addition to *Four in the Bar, All Good Children Go to Heaven*, and the patently absurd *Billy's Left Foot*, the Beatles had considered naming the album *Everest* in honor of the brand of cigarettes that Emerick smoked. "We were stuck for an album title," Paul remarked during an interview with Mark Lewisohn, "and the album didn't appear to have any obvious concept, except that it had all been done in the studio and it had been done by us. And Geoff Emerick used to have these packets of Everest cigarettes always sitting by him, and we thought, 'That's good. It's big and it's expansive.'" The band ultimately balked at the idea when they realized that they didn't want to go to the enormous trouble of journeying to Tibet to shoot the album's cover art. Besides, Paul added, "You can't name an album after a ciggie packet!" (13). Suddenly out of options, they turned to the studio from whence they had made their name. "Fuck it," Ringo reportedly said. "Let's just step outside and name it *Abbey Road*" (qtd. in Emerick 297). And with that, the Beatles gathered outside the stately gates of 3 Abbey Road for the photo shoot, which took place shortly before noon on Friday, August 8th, 1969. While the London Metropolitan

Police helpfully cleared the area of traffic, Iain MacMillan stood atop a ladder and took the famous cover photograph of the bandmates walking across the zebra crossing only a few yards from the main entrance to EMI Studios. With a long-maned Lennon leading the way in a crisp white suit, Ringo following behind in a black frock coat with a barefoot, out-of-step Paul on his heels, and denim-clad George shoring up the rear, the album cover pointedly depicts the Beatles striding *away* from the studio and into the waiting arms of history.

Released to widespread critical and commercial acclaim in September 1969, *Abbey Road* is the veritable synthesis of the Beatles' lyricism and musicianship. From the smooth R&B of "Come Together" and the pop-music majesty of "Something" through the raw metal of "I Want You" and the sheer beauty of "Here Comes the Sun," the album posits a moveable feast of imagery and sound. And then there's the passion play of the symphonic suite and its role in consolidating their aesthetic. With the medley, the Beatles—particularly McCartney—make a crucial shift in terms of their philosophy regarding the place of nostalgia in their art. It is the moment in which their hitherto reflective nostalgia transforms into a restorative mode that offers possibilities for authentic transcendence beyond the dreamworld of the self. In Svetlana Boym's conception, reflective nostalgia involves the act of lingering on the personal ruins of the past and meditating on the passage of time—as Lennon and McCartney had done so memorably with "Strawberry Fields Forever" and "Penny Lane"—while restorative nostalgia requires an act of critical judgment in which individuals recognize their own places in the interhuman continuum (49–50). With the *Abbey Road* medley, the group affords a sense of resolution to their textual musings about nostalgia's salvelike, albeit highly illusory, possibilities. By entreating the band's listeners to move beyond superficial reflections about the past and to recognize the fleeting temporality of our existence, the medley offers sobering wisdom about the frailty of our condition. Again, as "Golden Slumbers" so presciently reminds us, "*Once* there was a way to get back homeward. / *Once* there was a way to get back home." In so doing, the Beatles suggest that comprehending our earthly transience is the first step toward a more evolved understanding of our humanity and the heavy burden of the past. Only then can we begin to discern our place in the universe and recognize that we are fated to shoulder the weight of the past, the present, and an unknowable future from the cradle to the grave.

As with Shakespeare's *The Tempest*, the Beatles recognize that what's past is invariably prologue. Ultimately, the restorative nostalgia inherent in the *Abbey Road* medley finds its flight in the Beatles' enduring humanism, which exists as yet another aspect of their modernism—and particularly among the work of such "high modernists" as James Joyce, William Butler Yeats, and

D. H. Lawrence. As Sanford Pinsker observes, "High modernism was fashioned from richer, more humane stuff, as anyone who takes the time to compare Joyce's Leopold Bloom with Pynchon's Benny Profane will readily attest.
And that is really the essential point about the humanism that high modernism reflected," he continues. "High modernism taught us to see the work
of art as sacrosanct, and its difficulties as worthy of our best efforts." Are
Lennon and McCartney—fascinated, as they were, with the literary nuances
of irony, memory, and the inevitable pull of the past—really so different from
Joyce, Yeats, Lawrence, and their ilk? James O. Brecher interprets cultural phe-
nomena like the Beatles and the Beat poets as "the link between the 'high' art
of the modernists and the popular 'art' of the masses" (122). By acting as a
bridge to the past—as a virtual conduit for their vast audience of listeners
searching for a reprieve from the ills of an encroaching postmodern world—
the Beatles espouse a sense of hope and the promise of humanity and sameness in the face of an increasingly inexplicable present. Yet they also assert
that we are complicit in our own destinies, that we must never abdicate the
necessity of respecting otherness. "And in the end," they sing, "the love you
take is equal to the love you make." And so it goes. It is a message that never
fades with age, that never drifts into the shadows of obscurity.

Notes

1. The Northern Songs calamity continues into the present day. After wresting control of the Lennon-McCartney songbook in September 1969, ATV maintained a
majority interest in Northern Songs until 1985, when the company was put up for sale.
McCartney was famously outbid for Northern Songs by Michael Jackson, with whom
he had recently collaborated on a pair of hit singles ("The Girl Is Mine" on Jackson's
Thriller [1982] and "Say Say Say" on McCartney's *Pipes of Peace* [1983]). The self-
styled "King of Pop" paid $47.5 million for the publishing company. In 1995, Jackson
agreed to merge ATV with Sony Music for some $95 million in order to ease his finan-
cial problems. In recent years, Jackson's fiscal woes have grown considerably, leaving
his future ownership role with Sony/ATV Music Publishing in considerable doubt.
While Sony/ATV Music Publishing owns the copyrights for most of the Lennon-
McCartney songwriting catalogue, the Beatles' sound recordings remain in the possession and control of the EMI Group.

2. Sometime in late August, John debuted "Cold Turkey"—a composition that narrates his harrowing effort to kick his heroin addiction—for consideration as the next
Beatles' single. His bandmates' dismissal of the highly personal and confessional song
undoubtedly contributed, in its own small way, to their ensuing breakup (see Winn,
That Magic Feeling 344–45). "Cold Turkey" also featured prominently in Lennon's
November 25th, 1969, letter to Queen Elizabeth II in which he returned his MBE as an
antiwar gesture: "Your Majesty, I am returning my MBE as a protest against Britain's

involvement in the Nigeria-Biafra thing, against our support of America in Vietnam, and against 'Cold Turkey' slipping down the charts. With Love, John Lennon."

3. In his out-of-court settlement with Berry's publisher, Lennon promised to record other songs in Levy's stable, several of which appeared on the Beatle's 1975 solo album *Rock 'n' Roll*. The saga involving "Come Together" involved various other permutations, including Phil Spector's absconding of the album's master tapes, which led to Capitol Records paying some $90,000 in ransom to the eccentric producer for their return. Impatient with Lennon over the disposition of the out-of-court settlement, Levy marketed a television mail-order version of the album's rough mix, entitled *Roots*. Capitol Records' subsequent lawsuit against Levy plunged the music publisher's label Adam VIII, Ltd. into bankruptcy. The lawsuit also directed Levy to pay Lennon $42,000 in damages for harming his professional reputation.

4. Walter Everett interprets the song as John's attempt to provide listeners with a composite rendering of the individual Beatles' personae: "The gobbledygook may be heard as a disguise for Lennon's portrayal of the band members, one per verse: George as the long-haired holy roller, Paul as the good-looking player of Muddy Waters licks, and Lennon himself through images of the Walrus, Ono, and Bag Productions and a 'spinal cracker' reference to his car accident, but Ringo is harder to make out so clearly" (*Revolver through the Anthology* 246).

5. Paul would reprise the song's distinctive melody in "Every Night," a selection from his eponymous solo album *McCartney*.

6. As Paul later recalled, "This was me directly lambasting Allen Klein's attitude to us: no money, just funny paper, all promises and it never works out. It's basically a song about no faith in the person, that found its way into the medley on *Abbey Road*. John saw the humor in it" (qtd. in Miles 556).

7. For his drum solo on "The End," Ringo admittedly (and liberally) borrows from Ron Bushy's drumwork for Iron Butterfly's seventeen-minute magnum opus "In-a-Gadda-Da-Vida."

8. Walter Everett intriguingly reads the brevity of the guitar solos on "The End" as symptomatic of the Beatles having reached their musical peak: "The guitarists displayed fascinating pretensions on 'The End,' but they likely realized that the two-bar breaks were as far as they could go in that direction. Or, apparently, any direction" (*Revolver through the Anthology* 269).

9. An alternate version of "The End" was mixed in which the song concluded with a reprise of the E-major chord (replayed in reverse) that was recorded back in February 1967 for "A Day in the Life." This version of "The End" is included on *Anthology 3*.

10. For "Her Majesty," McCartney was undoubtedly influenced by the work of George Formby, an early twentieth-century British singer and comedian, as well as one of Liverpool's favorite sons in his own right. As with McCartney's breezy treatment of Queen Elizabeth II in "Her Majesty," Formby was famous for taking a lighthearted approach to serious subjects (see MacFarlane 185). At the end of the Beatles' "Free as a Bird," Lennon can be heard quoting Formby's signature catchphrase, "Turned out nice again," which was recorded backward in the song's final mix.

Chapter 14

Long Live the Dream

The moral sense in mortals is the duty
We have to pay on mortal sense of beauty.
—VLADIMIR NABOKOV, *LOLITA*

Fare thee well, and if for ever,
Still for ever, fare thee well.
—LORD BYRON

Twenty-three seconds.

At the end of the Beatles' career as recording artists, there were twenty-three seconds. But for the Beatles, the end was merely the beginning of something much larger and more lasting. Their days at EMI Studios may have been once and truly over, but their legend was only in its infancy.

As the history of twentieth-century culture well knows, the echo of the group's achievement continues to resound beyond the grave. Yet for all of the band's artistic accomplishments, we continue to hypothesize *ad nauseum* about the circumstances of their dissolution, rather than about the nature and quality of their creative fusion. All told, we have spent nearly forty years speculating about the reasons behind their breakup as an artistic unit. Was it Yoko? Linda? Allen Klein? Paul's megalomania? John's frustration with the group's musical direction? George's desire to strike out on his own? In many ways, their disbandment is the most uninteresting aspect of their narrative, yet we cannot help but wonder how *anyone* could walk away from such a momentous and indelibly influential partnership. A more perceptive question might consider how the bandmates managed to stay together in the first place—especially during the mind-numbing emotional cliffs and valleys of the post-Epstein era, a

301

period that saw them continuing to challenge the boundaries of their craft even as their personal and financial lives began to spiral out of their control. How, indeed, did they succeed in righting their ship, if only temporarily, after the *Magical Mystery Tour* debacle? Was it their timely sojourn in India? The collective shedding of their psychedelic personae in favor of a grittier rock and roll sound? Was it the dream of getting back to their pre-Beatlemania roots?

In Allan Kozinn's estimation, the vexing issue of authorship acted as the deciding factor in the Beatles' disintegration. He attributes their growing "insularity" to the simple fact that by the advent of the recording sessions for the *White Album*, "Lennon, McCartney, and Harrison were by this point only fully engaged in the recording of their own songs" (176). Although the Beatles still relied on the processes of multiple authorship that they had honed after years of working together in the studio, they had begun to feel, quite understandably, "that their musical destinies lay in different directions" (209). This is undeniably true for John, who found the Beatles' internal political chemistry to be increasingly constricting, with Paul exerting greater control over the band's creative efforts. In a taped conversation with McCartney in September 1969—only scant days before Lennon would announce his "divorce" from the band—John expressed his irritation with the Beatles' lopsided state of affairs:[1] "You'd come up with a *Magical Mystery Tour*," he told Paul, but "I didn't write any of that except 'Walrus.' I'd accept it and you'd already have five or six songs, so I'd think, 'Fuck it, I can't keep up with that.' So I didn't bother, you know?" (qtd. in Miles 562). In many ways, it was no different from Harrison's dismay with Lennon and McCartney back in January 1969. Their fecundity had become, of all things, their curse.

But whatever the reason behind the dissolution of their partnership—and, make no mistake about it, the causes were many and varied, as with any long-term emotional relationship—their breakup was, in large part, the logical conclusion of four men experiencing the throes of adulthood and its attendant responsibilities and changes. When asked about her own ostensible role in the band's demise, Yoko suggests that they were responding to internal forces—perhaps even involving individual needs and desires related to growing up—rather than to external pressures: "I don't think you could have broken up four very strong people like them, even if you tried. So there must have been something that happened within them—not an outside force at all" (*All We Are Saying* 144). McCartney couldn't have agreed more, as he remarked during an interview with CNN's Larry King, "I think it was time. I always remember the old song 'Wedding Bells (Are Breaking Up That Old Gang of Mine),' you know. The army buddies, the band, and you're going to grow up. You're going to get married. You're going to get girlfriends and have babies and things, and you don't do that in a band." Ringo seconded Paul's conclusions about the group's dissolution in an interview with *Rolling Stone* magazine's John Harris: "I think the reason the Beatles split up was because we were 30, and it was, 'Hey, I've got married, I've got kids, I've got a few more friends.' We didn't have the energy to put into it" (44).

The disbanding of the Beatles, although disconcerting for legions of music lovers, makes perfect sense when understood in the context that Paul and Ringo describe. Indeed, how many people complete the developmental tasks commonly associated with maturity—including marriage, child-rearing, and the assumption of more expansive leadership positions in work and family life—in the company of their childhood mates? In this sense, isn't the breakup more usefully construed as the result of the individual Beatles going in decidedly different directions as they approach midlife and all that growing older entails? Disintegration may have been a necessary phase alright, but it would take years for the band members' emotional wounds to begin to heal. For John, the group's demise continued to be a bone of contention at the relatively late date of September 1980. "It's very complicated and there are a lot of mixed emotions," Lennon observed. "But don't get me wrong—I still love those guys. The Beatles are over, but John, Paul, George, and Ringo go on" (*All We Are Saying* 151). Years later, George confessed to becoming disengaged, slowly but surely, from the Beatles' myth. The finer points of their breakup had been dulled by life's vicissitudes, with time having done its inevitable work on the recesses of the human memory. "When people see me," said Harrison, "they see a Beatle. But for me it was all such a long time ago. Sometimes I ask myself if I was really there or whether it was all a dream" (qtd. in Huntley 302).

~

For the Beatles, dispersal was an essential phase in their life cycle, but the work of art—the musical artifacts of their creation—will survive for the ages. While it is impossible to deny the significance of Harrison and Starr to the band's fusion, the Lennon-McCartney partnership—even after that partnership had visibly splintered during the latter years of the band's existence—was the central aspect of the group's extraordinary critical and commercial success. Whether explicitly working together or having become separated by the rites of songwriterly competition, their relationship was the combustion engine that propelled the group ever forward. It has become a critical and cultural commonplace to describe Lennon and McCartney as a creative union of opposites—John's inner pessimism in relentless struggle with Paul's unvarnished optimism. It's a description that they not only came to believe themselves, but that they ultimately helped to perpetuate. In truth, it is a fool's enterprise, a zero-sum game, to believe that two Liverpool lads—the novice rock-and-rollers who came together in July 1957 in that much-vaunted churchyard—were so very different from one another when they shared virtually the same heritage, having been born and bred among a homogeneous North Country mindscape. Rather than ascribing their success to a creative marriage of contradictory natures, we can understand the strength of their association by considering their inability as solo artists to equal their accomplishments with the Beatles. As Allan F. Moore points out: "It is no exaggeration to claim that, on the dissolution of the songwriting partnership, neither writer alone was able to reproduce the strength of interaction (as McCartney may presciently have observed in *Abbey Road*'s 'Carry That Weight')" (24). Even more significantly, we can comprehend the nature of their greatness by recognizing the comparatively subtle difference in their roles in the fabric of the Beatles—if not in the larger realm of popular music and culture. On the one hand, Lennon was a pop-music visionary, a songwriter with the innate musical talent to breathe reality into his artistic revelations. He had the breadth of mind to render far-reaching observations about the human condition, to realize the inherent complexities of our existence even as he dared us to live deeply and embrace one another in community. On the other hand, McCartney was a pop-music virtuoso, a timeless composer who concocted musical and lyrical images with exquisite ease. With the natural ability to play nearly any instrument—and often better than his contemporaries could ever dream—he was at home in virtually any musical style and gifted with the capacity for crafting rich, evocative melodies. John and Paul's partnership wasn't a marriage of opposites—it was a marriage made in heaven. And for the Beatles, it made all the difference.[2]

The kitschy world of popular culture is often too quick to memorialize the Beatles—and so many other icons of musical fame, for that matter—as mere nostalgia acts, as historical markers for highly particularized moments in time. But the abiding power and influence of the band's achievement was made possible by much more than a fortuitous appearance on the *Ed Sullivan Show*, metal lunchboxes, or a spate of relatively innocuous feature films. From their earliest days in the front parlor of Paul's family home on Forthlin Road to the bitter end at EMI Studios, Lennon and McCartney nurtured a work ethic driven by commitment and faith in the Beatles as the creative vehicle for their music. As a collective whole, the bandmates channeled all of the energy that they could reasonably muster and then some into bringing the Lennon-McCartney songbook to life. It's a remarkable accomplishment in itself—especially given the incredible amount of extra-textual baggage that accompanied their lives among the rock and roll elite. Indeed, the Beatles' most impressive narrative concerns their simple ability to toil as hard and as long as it took to refine their work. As Norman Maclean writes in *A River Runs through It* (1976), "All good things come by grace and grace comes by art and art does not come easy" (8). It is nearly impossible, of course, to overstate George Martin's role in immortalizing their art, in fashioning the sound that first caught the attention of British and American ears. The A&R men at Decca may have genuinely believed that guitar-oriented music was on its last legs, but Martin clearly heard something different in the unpolished, stage-honed thrashings of John, Paul, George, and Ringo. With his guidance, the Beatles dared to experiment with their sound, to revivify it with irony and nostalgia, to adorn it with a string quartet, a full-blown orchestra, and even a sitar. Martin afforded them with the courage and the know-how to tinker with their sound as far as their artistry would take them. And, as history has shown, their prolific imaginations traversed well beyond the boundaries of their musicality, transmogrifying Western culture's conceptions of hope, love, and the idea—whimsical as it may seem—of an everlasting peace.

For the Beatles, the textual artifact is everything. It is the only genuine record of their attainment, the only meaningful representation of the realization of their artistic vision—from the simple ebullience of "She Loves You" and the gentle nostalgia of "In My Life" to the bone-crushing terror of "Helter Skelter" and the cultural apocalypse of "I Am the Walrus." The text—the music, the lyrics, the élan—is the thing. As Sean Cubitt observes, "The recorded performance is a *revenant*, a representation of something which is already past (if indeed, with modern technology, it ever took place as a single event)" (213). The Beatles' carefully delineated art works from precisely such a well-honed illusion of undiluted textuality. But what makes all the difference, what really matters in the grand sweep of time, is the insight that they derive from their backward glances into the hearts and minds of humankind. The group's luminosity—the central, driving intelligence of their music—finds its origins in an innate sense of purpose and magnitude. The perceptive, discerning quality of the Beatles—of Lennon and McCartney in particular—concerns a writerly attempt to get to the heart of the matter. In the provocative, self-critical master-texts of "Eleanor Rigby," "A Day in the Life," "Happiness Is a Warm Gun," the "Revolution" series, and the *Abbey Road* medley, the Beatles mine the inherent truth in Socrates's famous dictum that "the unexamined life is not worth living" (*Apology* 38a; qtd. in Plato 92). By questioning the external world in relation to our internal human frailties, the songwriters pit the reality of social disarray against the needs and desires manifested by our own worst (and best) individual instincts. In so doing, they invite us to look inward even as we attempt to diagnose the problems and malaise of the outer world.

"We must struggle even though we are all rats and valueless," George remarked in *I Me Mine*, and "try to become better human beings" (312). It is only then, when we have summoned up the courage to confront our own worst demons, that we can begin to glimpse the angels of real and abiding change. By sharing our journeys of the self, the Beatles urge us to embrace the restorative powers of love, friendship, and a universalizing belief in a redeemable past—a past to which, if our aim is really true, we can get back to where we once belonged.

With an embarrassment of artistic riches that includes *Rubber Soul*, *Revolver*, *Sgt. Pepper*, *The White Album*, and *Abbey Road*, the Beatles fashioned an enduring legacy based upon our intrinsically human needs for hopefulness and reconciliation. "I'm really glad that most of the songs dealt with love, peace, and understanding," McCartney later recalled. "There's hardly any one of them that says: 'Go on, kids, tell them all to sod off. Leave your parents.' It's all very 'All You Need Is Love' or John's 'Give Peace a Chance.' There was a good spirit behind it all, which I'm very proud of" (*Anthology* 357). The Beatles' cultural apotheosis is so well-known and so pervasive that it has become a veritable cliché. We take the pure talent and musicianship of their art for granted. We intuitively understand their cultural significance and the enormity of their accomplishment. They loom so large in our collective global consciousness that we have become impotent in our efforts to comprehend, much less explain in words, the measure of their majesty. Leave it to Kurt Vonnegut—a twentieth-century master in his own right—to capture the essence of their virtuosity. "The function of the artist is to make people like life better than they have before," Vonnegut observes. "When I've been asked if I've ever seen that done. I say, 'Yes, the Beatles did it'" (qtd. in Brinkley 110).

In the end—as in the beginning—it is the authentic performance of the Beatles' peculiar, elaborate, unfettered art that matters. It is the performance that makes the text possible in the first place, that imbues it with the heartbreaking reality of our transitory existence. It is the impermanence of the moment—rendered seemingly permanent by magnetic tape and celluloid—that is so vexing in its realness that it somehow seems immutable. Take the rooftop concert, with London's blustery, wintry winds swirling up from the streetscape as John, Paul, George, and Ringo make one last play for greatness after a month of soul-destroying misery. They climbed the stairs above 3 Savile Row and willed a final, breathtaking performance for the ages. It is the primal image of the Beatles having become lost in the pure joy of their sound, just as they had done so many years before in the Cavern and not so very long ago in Studio Two. Everything else—the gossip, the intrigue, the emotional collapse—suddenly becomes moot, irrelevant even, as Ringo keeps the backbeat strong and true on his Ludwigs, while George furrows his brow as he drives his Rosewood Telecaster home. And John and Paul, smiling at each other across the staves of memory, play their hearts out one more time. The rest is silence.

Notes

1. On September 20th, 1969, John declared his intent to "divorce" his bandmates during an Apple board meeting. Although George was away in Cheshire visiting his ailing mother, the other three Beatles agreed to keep their impending breakup a secret in order to avoid upsetting Allen Klein's contract renegotiations with EMI and Capitol. As Lennon later recalled, "Paul and Allen both said that they were glad that I wasn't going to announce it, and that I wasn't going to make an event out of it. I don't know whether Paul said 'don't tell anybody,' but he was darned pleased that I wasn't going to. He said, 'Oh, that means that nothing's really happened if you're not going to say anything'" (qtd. in Badman 466). On April 10th, 1970, McCartney publicly announced the Beatles' dissolution on the eve of releasing his first solo album, *McCartney*, which appropriately features a metaphorical spilt bowl of cherries as its cover art.

2. Todd Compton offers a penetrating examination of the Lennon-McCartney partnership in "McCartney or Lennon?: Beatle Myths and the Composing of the Lennon-McCartney Songs."

Acknowledgments

A book of this magnitude would not have been possible without the encouragement and advice of a wide circle of friends and colleagues. Special thanks are due to William Baker, Lori Bower, Dick Caram, Lee Ann De Reus, Bill Engelbret, Bruce Hersey, David Kasdorf, John Knapp, Carl Larsen, Kate Latterell, Heather McCoy, Maggie McNulty, Dana Miller, Patti Mills, Nick Miskovsky, Kevin Moist, Mary Lou Nemanic, Laura "The Bulldog" Rotunno, Stuart Selber, Valerie Stratton, Bob Trumpbour, Andy Vavreck, L. A. Wilson, Michael Wolfe, and Julian Wolfreys.

I am grateful to the many scholars who so generously lent me their time and expertise, including Walter Everett, Philip Gossett, Maura Ives, Howard Kramer, Anna Lindberg, Robin Reese, Russell Reising, Dave Villani, Gary Weisel, Tim Wherry, Sheila Whiteley, and Jerry Zolten. I am especially indebted to Carole Bookhamer, Barb Brunhuber, Aaron Heresco, Michele Kennedy, Jacki Mowery, Judy Paul, Deb "The Q" Shandor, Amy Wilkes, and Deb "The Boss" Wilshire for their generous and unfailing assistance.

From start to finish, my work on this volume benefited from the unwavering kindness and support provided by Lori Bechtel, Brian Black, Tom Liszka, Ian Marshall, Dinty W. Moore, and Rebecca Strzelec. I particularly appreciate the efforts of Todd Davis, James Decker, and Amy Mallory-Kani, who offered painstaking and valuable editorial guidance along the way. I am thankful for the vision and zeal of David Barker, my editor at Continuum, as well as for the work of Assistant Managing Editor Jeffrey McCord and Gabriella Page-Fort, a truly skilled and imaginative designer. I owe a special debt of thanks to the students in my Beatles seminars at Penn State University's Altoona College. Your affection and enthusiasm for the Beatles' art afforded me with deep reservoirs of inspiration throughout the duration of this project.

Finally, I would like to express my enduring gratitude to the family members whose warmth and wisdom gave me the strength to make it through life's wild and windy nights: Ryan, Becca, and Tori Harshbarger, Bill and Colleen Lumadue, Justin and Mellissa Lumadue, Gerty MacDowell, Andy and Melissa Womack, Fred and Jennifer Womack, Ken Zimmerman, and especially Jeanine Womack, whose vast reserves of love, energy, and insight made it all possible. Thank you for sharing my journey along these long and winding roads.

Bibliography

Attali, Jacques. *Noise: The Political Economy of Music.* Trans. Brian Massumi. Minneapolis: U of Minnesota P, 1985.

Atwood, Margaret. *The Handmaid's Tale.* Toronto: McClelland and Stewart, 1985.

Auden, W. H. *The English Auden: Poems, Essays, and Dramatic Writings, 1927–1939.* Ed. Edward Mendelson. London: Faber and Faber, 1977.

Axelrod, Mitchell. *Beatletoons: The Real Story Behind the Cartoon Beatles.* Pickens: Wynn, 1999.

Babiuk, Andy. *Beatles Gear: All the Fab Four's Instruments, from Stage to Studio.* San Francisco: Backbeat, 2001.

Bacon, Tony, and Gareth Morgan. *Paul McCartney: Bassmaster.* San Francisco: Backbeat, 2006.

Badman, Keith. *The Beatles Off the Record: Outrageous Opinions and Unrehearsed Interviews.* London: Omnibus, 2001.

Barlow, Hugh. "George Not So Quiet." *Wairarapa Times* [New Zealand]. 3 December 2001. <timesage.co.nz/news2001/011203b.html>.

Barnard, Charles P., and Ramon Garrido Corrales. *The Theory and Technique of Family Therapy.* Springfield: Thomas, 1979.

Barrow, Tony. *John, Paul, George, Ringo, and Me: The Real Beatles Story.* New York: Thunder's Mouth, 2006.

———. *The Making of the Beatles' Magical Mystery Tour.* London: Omnibus, 1999.

———. "The Story behind *A Hard Day's Night.*" *Beatles Monthly Book* 204 (September 1993): 5–11.

———. "The Story behind *Yellow Submarine.*" *Beatles Monthly Book* 204 (April 1993): 8–13.

Bartlett, Bruce. *Glossary of Recording Terms.* 2004. <www.tape.com/Bartlett_Articles/recording_terms.html>.

The Beach Boys. *Pet Sounds.* Capitol, 1966.

———. *Smiley Smile.* Capitol, 1967.

311

The Beatles. *Abbey Road*. 1969. Parlophone, 1987.

———. *Anthology 1*. Capitol, 1995.

———. *Anthology 2*. Capitol, 1996.

———. *Anthology 3*. Capitol, 1996.

———. *The Beatles* [*The White Album*]. 1968. Parlophone, 1987.

———. *Beatles '65*. Capitol, 1964.

———. *The Beatles Anthology*. San Francisco: Chronicle, 2000.

———. *The Beatles Anthology*. Television Documentary. ABC, 1995; DVD Release. EMI, 2003.

———. *Beatles for Sale*. 1964. Parlophone, 1987.

———. *The Beatles Lyrics: The Songs of Lennon, McCartney, Harrison, and Starr*. Milwaukee: Leonard, 1993.

———. *The Beatles' Second Album*. Capitol, 1964.

———. *Beatles VI*. Capitol, 1965.

———. *The Capitol Albums, Volume 1*. Capitol, 2004.

———. *The Capitol Albums, Volume 2*. Capitol, 2006.

———. *A Collection of Beatles Oldies*. Parlophone, 1966.

———. *Complete Scores*. Milwaukee: Leonard, 1989.

———. *The Early Beatles*. Capitol, 1964.

———. *From Kinfauns to Chaos*. Vigo, 1999.

———. *Get Back: The Glyn Johns Final Compilation*. Vigotone, 1999.

———. *A Hard Day's Night*. 1964. Parlophone, 1987.

———. *A Hard Day's Night*. United Artists, 1964.

———. *Help!* 1965. Parlophone, 1987.

———. *Help!* Capitol/United Artists, 1965.

———. *Hey Jude*. Capitol/Apple, 1970.

———. *Let It Be*. 1970. Parlophone, 1987.

———. *Let It Be . . . Naked*. Capitol, 2003.

———. *Live at the BBC*. Capitol, 1994.

———. *Live! at the Star-Club in Hamburg, Germany, 1962*. Lingasong, 1977.

———. *Long Tall Sally*. Parlophone, 1964.

———. *Love*. Capitol, 2006.

———. *Magical Mystery Tour*. 1967. Parlophone, 1987.

———, dirs. *Magical Mystery Tour*. Apple Films, 1967.

———. *Meet the Beatles!* Capitol, 1964.

———. *Past Masters, Volume 1*. Parlophone, 1988.

———. *Past Masters, Volume 2*. Parlophone, 1988.

———. *Please Please Me*. 1963. Parlophone, 1987.

———. *Revolver*. 1966. Parlophone, 1987.

———. *Revolver*. Capitol, 1966.

———. *Rubber Soul*. 1965. Parlophone, 1987.

———. *Rubber Soul*. Capitol, 1965.

———. *Sgt. Pepper's Lonely Hearts Club Band*. 1967. Parlophone, 1987.

————. *Something New.* Capitol, 1964.

————. *With the Beatles.* 1963. Parlophone, 1987.

————. *Yellow Submarine.* 1969. Parlophone, 1987.

————. *Yellow Submarine Songtrack.* Capitol, 1999.

————. *Yesterday . . . and Today.* Capitol, 1966.

"Beatles' 'Yesterday' a Cover of Old Neapolitan Song, Producer Claims." *Monsters and Critics* 19 July 2006. <music.monstersandcritics.com/news/article_ 1182243. php/Beatles_Yesterday_a_cover_of_old_Neapolitan_song_ producer_claims>.

Beckett, Samuel. *Waiting for Godot: A Tragicomedy in Two Acts* [*En attendant Godot*]. 1952. New York: Grove, 1954.

Benedek, László, dir. *The Wild One.* Columbia Pictures, 1953.

Bernstein, Leonard, and Stephen Sondheim. *West Side Story: Original Broadway Cast Recording.* Columbia, 1957.

Berry, Chuck. *The Definitive Collection.* Chess, 2006.

Bhagavad Gita. Trans. Eknath Easwaran. 1961. Petaluma: Nilgiri, 1985.

Bjørnson, Bjørnstjerne. "Konge-Kvadet." *The Lied and Art Song Texts Page.* 2003. <www.recmusic.org/lieder/get_text.html?TextId=2652>.

Bloom, Harold. *The Anxiety of Influence: A Theory of Poetry.* Oxford: Oxford UP, 1973.

"Bob Dylan." *Last FM: The Social Music Revolution.* <www.last.fm/music/Bob+ Dylan/+wiki>.

Bogart, Anne. "Violence." *A Director Prepares: Seven Essays on Art and Theatre.* London: Routledge, 2001. 43–60.

Bogart, Anne, and Tina Landau. *The Viewpoints Book: A Practical Guide to Viewpoints and Composition.* New York: Theatre Communications Group, 2005.

Booth, Wayne C. *The Rhetoric of Fiction.* 1961. 2nd ed. Chicago: U of Chicago P, 1983.

Boulting, Roy, dir. *The Family Way.* Warner, 1966.

Bowles, Paul. *The Sheltering Sky.* 1949. New York: Vintage, 1990.

Boym, Svetlana. *The Future of Nostalgia.* New York: Basic, 2001.

The Bran Flakes. *I Don't Have a Friend.* Lomo, 2001.

Brecher, James O. "Connections: Modernism to the Beats and Beatles and on to a Future American Literature." Diss. U of South Florida, 2002.

Brinkley, Douglas. "Vonnegut's Blues: Why America's Darkest Humorist Isn't Laughing Anymore." *Rolling Stone* 24 August 2006: 77–78, 110.

Bromell, Nick. *Tomorrow Never Knows: Rock and Psychedelics in the 1960s.* Chicago: U of Chicago P, 2000.

Brown, Peter, and Steven Gaines. *The Love You Make: An Insider's Story of the Beatles.* New York: McGraw-Hill, 1983.

Browning, Robert. *Selected Poems.* Ed. Daniel Karlin. London: Penguin, 1989.

Burke, John. *The Beatles in A Hard Day's Night.* New York: Dell, 1964.

Burns, Gary. "Refab Four: Beatles for Sale in the Age of Music Video." Inglis, *The Beatles, Popular Music, and Society* 176–88.

Byron, George Gordon. *Lord Byron: The Major Works*. Ed. Jerome J. McGann. Oxford: Oxford UP, 1986.

Cage, John. "The Future of Music: Credo." 1937. *Silence: Lectures and Writings*. Middletown: Wesleyan UP, 1961. 3–6.

———, ed. *Notations*. New York: Something Else, 1969.

Campbell, Colin, and Allan Murphy. *Things We Said Today: The Complete Lyrics and a Concordance to the Beatles' Songs, 1962–1970*. Ann Arbor: Pierian, 1980.

Carroll, Lewis. *The Complete Works of Lewis Carroll*. New York: Modern Library, 1936.

Cashmere, Paul. "Paul McCartney, Madison Square Garden, September 30, 2005." *Undercover* 2 October 2005. <www.undercover.com.au/news/2005/oct05/20051001_paulmccartney.html>.

Center for Black Music Research. "Project Stop-Time." Columbia College Chicago. 2006. <www.cbmr.org/perform/stoptime.htm>.

Chopin, Kate. *The Awakening and Selected Stories*. London: Penguin, 1984.

Chopra, Deepak. "Deepak Chopra on His Friend George Harrison." Interview by Steve Waldman. *Beliefnet* December 2001. <www.beliefnet.com/story/94/story_9434_1.html>.

Clayson, Alan. *Ringo Starr*. London: Sanctuary, 2003.

Compton, Todd. "McCartney or Lennon?: Beatle Myths and the Composing of the Lennon-McCartney Songs." *Journal of Popular Culture* 22.2 (1998): 99–131.

Cooke, Deryck. "The Lennon-McCartney Songs." *Vindications: Essays on Romantic Music*, by Cooke. Cambridge: Cambridge UP, 1982. 196–200.

Costello, Elvis. Foreword. Emerick and Massey, *Here, There, and Everywhere* ix–xi.

———. *Mighty Like a Rose*. Warner, 1991.

Covach, John. "From 'Craft' to 'Art': Formal Structure in the Music of the Beatles." Womack and Davis, *Reading the Beatles* 37–53.

Cross, Craig. *The Beatles: Day-by-Day, Song-by-Song, Record-by-Record*. New York: iUniverse, 2005.

Cubitt, Sean. "'Maybellene': Meaning and the Listening Subject." *Popular Music* 4 (1984): 207–24.

cummings, e. e. *Complete Poems, 1913–1962*. New York: Harcourt Brace Jovanovich, 1972.

Davis, Fred. *Yearning for Yesterday: A Sociology of Nostalgia*. New York: Free, 1979.

Dickinson, Emily. *The Complete Poems of Emily Dickinson*. Ed. Thomas H. Johnson. Boston: Little, Brown, 1960.

Didion, Joan. *The White Album*. New York: Simon and Schuster, 1979.

Disney, Walt, prod. *Snow White and the Seven Dwarfs*. Walt Disney Pictures, 1937.

DJ BC. "Mother Nature's Rump." <www.djbc.net/beastles>.

DJ Danger Mouse. *The Grey Album*. 2004.

Doggett, Peter. *Abbey Road/Let It Be: The Beatles.* New York: Schirmer, 1998.

Dowlding, William J. *Beatlesongs.* New York: Simon and Schuster, 1989.

Dunning, George, dir. *Yellow Submarine.* United Artists, 1968.

Du Noyer, Paul. "Across the Universe." Trynka, *The Beatles* 80–83.

Dylan, Bob. *Blonde on Blonde.* 1966.

———. *The Freewheelin' Bob Dylan.* Columbia, 1963.

———. *Highway 61 Revisited.* Columbia, 1965.

———. *John Wesley Harding.* Columbia, 1967.

———. *The Times They Are a-Changin'.* Columbia, 1964.

Eliot, George. *Felix Holt, the Radical.* 1866. Ed. William Baker and Kenneth Womack. Peterborough: Broadview, 2000.

Eliot, T. S. *Collected Poems, 1909–1962.* San Diego: Harcourt Brace Jovanovich, 1963.

Emerick, Geoff, and Howard Massey. *Here, There, and Everywhere: My Life Recording the Music of the Beatles.* New York: Gotham, 2006.

Epstein, Brian. *A Cellarful of Noise: The Autobiography of the Man Who Made the Beatles.* 1964. New York: Pocket, 1998.

Everett, Walter. *The Beatles as Musicians: The Quarry Men through Rubber Soul.* Oxford: Oxford UP, 2001.

———. *The Beatles as Musicians: Revolver through the Anthology.* Oxford: Oxford UP, 1999.

———. "Painting Their Room in a Colorful Way: The Beatles' Exploration of Timbre." Womack and Davis, *Reading the Beatles* 71–94.

Faulkner, William. *Requiem for a Nun.* 1951. New York: Vintage, 1975.

———. *The Sound and the Fury.* 1929. New York: Vintage, 1991.

Ford, Ford Madox. *The Good Soldier: A Tale of Passion.* 1915. Ed. Kenneth Womack and William Baker. Peterborough: Broadview, 2003.

Forster, E. M. *Howards End.* 1910. New York: Vintage, 1989.

Frost, Robert. *The Road Not Taken and Other Poems.* New York: Holt, 1916.

Gambaccini, Paul. *Paul McCartney: In His Own Words.* New York: Flash, 1976.

Gardiner, Sandy. "Heavy Disc Dose Spreads Disease in England." *Ottawa Journal* 9 November 1963. <beatles.ncf.ca/sandyg.html>.

Gibran, Kahlil. *Sand and Foam: A Book of Aphorisms.* 1926. New York: Knopf, 1995.

Glynn, Stephen. *A Hard Day's Night.* London: I. B. Taurus, 2005.

Goldman, Albert. *The Lives of John Lennon.* New York: Morrow, 1988.

Goranson, Ted. *Beatles Archive.* <homepage.mac.com/tedgoranson/Beatles Archives/>.

Gray, Michael. *Song and Dance Man III: The Art of Bob Dylan.* New York: Continuum, 2000.

Haines, John. "The Skipper's Lament." <www.lulu.com/Josh-Rogan>.

Handy, Hank. "Beatles Mash-Up Medley." 2005.

Harris, John. "Syntax Man." Trynka, *The Beatles* 118–19.

Harrison, George. *All Things Must Pass*. Apple, 1970.

———. *Brainwashed*. Dark Horse, 2002.

———. *Extra Texture (Read All about It)*. Apple, 1975.

———. *George Harrison*. Dark Horse, 1979.

———. *Gone Troppo*. Dark Horse, 1982.

———. *I Me Mine*. 1980. San Francisco: Chronicle, 2002.

———. "The Pirate Song." *Rutland Weekend Television*. BBC, 1976.

———. *Thirty Three & 1/3*. Dark Horse, 1976.

———. *Wonderwall Music*. Apple, 1968.

Harry, Bill. *The Ultimate Beatles Encyclopedia*. New York: Hyperion, 1992.

———. "When We Were Very Young." Trynka, *The Beatles* 12–17.

Hartley, L. P. *The Go-Between*. London: Penguin, 1953.

Herrera, Nancy Cooke de. *All You Need Is Love: An Eyewitness Account of When Spirituality Spread from the East to the West*. San Diego: Jodere, 2003.

Herrmann, Bernard. *Fahrenheit 451*. Uni, 1995.

———. *Psycho: The Complete Motion Picture Score*. Varese Sarabande, 1997.

Hertsgaard, Mark. *A Day in the Life: The Music and Artistry of the Beatles*. New York: Delta, 1995.

Hieronimus, Robert R. *Inside the Yellow Submarine: The Making of the Beatles' Animated Classic*. Iola: Krause, 2002.

Hopkin, Nick, and Michael Maier, dirs. *Live 8*. Capitol, 2005.

Houston, Frank. "Sir George Martin." *Salon Magazine* 25 July 2000. <archive. salon.com/people/bc/2000/07/25/martin/index.html>.

Hoyde, Ellen, Albert Maysles, David Maysles, and Muffie Meyer, dirs. *Grey Gardens*. Portrait Films, 1975.

Hunt, Chris. "Fantasy Island." Trynka, *The Beatles* 262–63.

Huntley, Elliot J. *Mystical One: George Harrison after the Breakup of the Beatles*. Toronto: Guernica, 2004.

Inglis, Ian. "'The Beatles Are Coming!': Conjecture and Conviction in the Myth of Kennedy, America, and the Beatles." *Popular Music and Society* 24.2 (2000): 93–108.

———, ed. *The Beatles, Popular Music, and Society*. New York: St. Martin's, 2000.

Iron Butterfly. *In-a-Gadda-Da-Vida*. ATCO, 1968.

Jackson, Michael. *Thriller*. Epic, 1982.

Jameson, Fredric. *Postmodernism or, The Cultural Logic of Late Capitalism*. Durham: Duke UP, 1991.

Jay-Z. *The Black Album*. Def Jam, 2003.

Jimi Hendrix and the Experience. *The Jimi Hendrix Experience*. Universal, 2000.

Joyce, James. *Finnegans Wake*. 1939. London: Penguin, 1999.

———. *Ulysses*. 1922. New York: Modern Library, 1961.

Kac, Mark. "Can One Hear the Shape of a Drum?" *American Mathematical Monthly* 73.4 (1966): 1–23.

Kermode, Frank. *The Sense of an Ending: Studies in the Theory of Fiction.* Oxford: Oxford UP, 1966.

Koskimäki, Jouni. "Happiness Is . . . a Good Transcription: Reconsidering the Beatles' Sheet Music Publications." Diss. U of Jyväskylä, 2006.

Kozinn, Allan. *The Beatles.* London: Phaidon, 1995.

Kramer, Lawrence. *Musical Meaning: Toward a Critical History.* Berkeley: U of California P, 2002.

Lahr, John. "Czechs and Balances." *The New Yorker* 24 July 2006: 78–80.

Lamb, Charles. *Poems, Plays, and Miscellaneous Essays.* New York: Armstrong, 1893.

Lapidakis, Michalis. "Variations on Gustav Mahler." *Musicology* 12–13 (2000). <www.musicology.gr/issue012013/lapidakis1en.html>.

Larkin, Philip. *High Windows.* London: Faber and Faber, 1974.

Leary, Timothy, Ralph Metzner, and Richard Alpert. *The Psychedelic Experience: A Manual Based on the Tibetan Book of the Dead.* New Hyde Park: University Books, 1964.

Leigh, Spencer. "The Axe Files." Trynka, *The Beatles* 36–37.

———. "Nowhere Man?" Trynka, *The Beatles* 20–21.

Lennon, Cynthia. *John.* London: Hodder and Stoughton, 2005.

———. *A Twist of Lennon.* London: Star Books, 1978.

Lennon, John. *Anthology.* Capitol, 1998.

———. "Being a Short Diversion on the Dubious Origins of Beatles." *Mersey Beat* 6 July 1961. <www.triumphpc.com/mersey-beat/archives/dubious.shtml>.

———. *Imagine.* Apple, 1971.

———. *In His Own Write.* London: Jonathan Cape, 1964.

———. *John Lennon/Plastic Ono Band.* Apple, 1970.

———. *Lennon Remembers.* Interview by Jann Wenner. 1970. New York: Verso, 2000.

———. *Rock 'n' Roll.* Apple, 1975.

———. *Skywriting by Word of Mouth and Other Writings.* New York: Harper & Row, 1986.

———. *A Spaniard in the Works.* London: Jonathan Cape, 1965.

Lennon, John, and Yoko Ono. *All We Are Saying: The Last Major Interview with John Lennon and Yoko Ono.* Interview by David Sheff. Ed. G. Barry Golson. New York: Griffin, 2000.

———. *Double Fantasy.* Geffen, 1980.

———. *Unfinished Music No. 1: Two Virgins.* Track, 1968.

Lennon, John, Paul McCartney, Stevie Wonder, Harry Nilsson, Jesse Ed Davis, and Bobby Keys. *A Toot and a Snort in '74.* Mistral Music, 1992.

Lester, Richard, dir. *A Hard Day's Night.* United Artists, 1964.

———, dir. *Help!* United Artists, 1965.

———, dir. *How I Won the War.* United Artists, 1967.

Lewisohn, Mark. *The Beatles Live!* London: Pavilion, 1986.

———. *The Complete Beatles Chronicle.* London: Pyramid, 1995.

————. *The Complete Beatles Recording Sessions: The Official Abbey Road Studio Session Notes, 1962–1970.* New York: Harmony, 1988.

————. "The Day of Reckoning." Trynka, *The Beatles* 40–46.

————. "High Times." Trynka, *The Beatles* 182–83.

Lindsay-Hogg, Michael, dir. *Let It Be.* United Artists, 1970.

————, dir. *Rock and Roll Circus.* ABKCO Films, 1996.

Long, Harry Alfred. *Personal and Family Names: A Popular Monograph on the Origin and History of the Nomenclature of the Present and Former Times.* 1883. Detroit: Gale, 1968.

MacDonald, Ian. *Revolution in the Head: The Beatles' Records and the Sixties.* New York: Holt, 1994.

MacFarlane, Thomas. "The *Abbey Road* Medley: Extended Forms in Popular Music." Diss. New York U, 2004.

Maclean, Norman. *A River Runs Through It.* 1976. Chicago: U of Chicago P, 1989.

Mann, William. "What Songs the Beatles Sang." *Times* 27 December 1963. <jolomo.net/music/william_mann.html>.

Marcus, Greil. "The Beatles." *The Rolling Stone Illustrated History of Rock and Roll.* Ed. Jim Miller. New York: Rolling Stone, 1976. 177–89.

Marks, J., and Linda Eastman. *Rock and Other Four-Letter Words.* New York: Bantam, 1968.

Marquand, Christian, dir. *Candy.* Cinerama, 1968.

Marquand, Richard, dir. *The Birth of the Beatles.* ABC, 1979.

Marshall, Ian. "'I am he as you are he as you are me and we are all together': Bakhtin and the Beatles." Womack and Davis, *Reading the Beatles* 9–35.

Martin, Bill. *Avant Rock: Experimental Music from the Beatles to Björk.* Chicago: Open Court, 2002.

Martin, George, and His Orchestra. *Off the Beatle Track.* Parlophone, 1964.

Martin, George, with Jeremy Hornsby. *All You Need Is Ears.* 1979. New York: St. Martin's, 1994.

Martin, George, with William Pearson. *With a Little Help from My Friends: The Making of Sgt. Pepper.* Boston: Little, Brown, 1994.

Massot, Joe, dir. *Wonderwall.* Cinecenta, 1968.

Matteo, Steve. *Let It Be.* New York: Continuum, 2004.

McCartney, Paul. *Back in the US.* Capitol, 2002.

————. *Chaos and Creation in the Backyard.* Parlophone, 2005.

————. *Flaming Pie.* Capitol, 1997.

————. *Give My Regards to Broad Street.* Parlophone, 1984.

————. Interview by Larry King. *Larry King Live.* CNN. 12 June 2001.

————. Interview by Mark Lewisohn. Lewisohn, *The Complete Beatles Recording Sessions* 6–15.

————. *McCartney.* Apple, 1970.

————. *McCartney II.* Columbia, 1980.

————. *Pipes of Peace.* Columbia, 1983.

————. *Tripping the Live Fantastic.* Capitol, 1990.

————. *Wingspan: Hits and History.* Capitol, 2001.

McCartney, Paul, and Linda McCartney. *Ram.* Apple, 1971.

McCartney, Paul, and Wings. *Band on the Run.* Apple, 1973.

McGrath, Joseph, dir. *The Magic Christian.* Commonwealth United Entertainment, 1969.

McKenzie, Scott. *Stained Glass Reflections: Anthology, 1960–1970.* Raven, 2001.

McKinney, Devin. *Magic Circles: The Beatles in Dream and History.* Cambridge: Harvard UP, 2003.

Mellers, Wilfred. *Twilight of the Gods: The Music of the Beatles.* New York: Schirmer, 1973.

Mendelsohn, John. Rev. of *Let It Be. Rolling Stone* 11 June 1970. <www.rolling stone.com/artists/thebeatles/albums/album/230618/review/5940857/let_it_be>.

Miles, Barry. *Paul McCartney: Many Years from Now.* New York: Holt, 1997.

Moore, Allan F. *The Beatles: Sgt. Pepper's Lonely Hearts Club Band.* Cambridge: Cambridge UP, 1997.

More, Thomas. *Utopia.* 1516. Ed. Edward Surtz. New Haven: Yale UP, 1964.

Münch, Christopher. *The Hours and Times.* Antarctic Pictures, 1992.

Nabokov, Vladimir. *The Annotated Lolita.* 1955. Ed. Alfred Appel, Jr. New York: Vintage, 1991.

Neaverson, Bob. *The Beatles Movies.* London: Cassell, 1997.

Norman, Philip. *Shout!: The Beatles in Their Generation.* New York: Simon and Schuster, 1981.

Nussbaum, Martha C. *Upheavals of Thought: The Intelligence of Emotions.* Cambridge: Cambridge UP, 2001.

O'Donnell, Shaugn. "Sailing to the Sun: *Revolver*'s Influence on Pink Floyd." Reising, "*Every Sound There Is*" 169–86.

O'Gorman, Martin. "Take 137!" Trynka, *The Beatles* 242–43.

Ono, Yoko. *Grapefruit: A Book of Instructions and Drawings by Yoko Ono.* 1964. New York: Simon and Schuster, 2000.

Oxford English Dictionary. <dictionary.oed.com>.

Pearce, Lynne. *Romance Writing.* Cambridge: Polity, 2006.

Peel, Ian. *The Unknown Paul McCartney: McCartney and the Avant-Garde.* London: Reynolds & Hearn, 2002.

Phillips, Bruce. "The Beatles in Washington." *The Ottawa Citizen* 13 February 1964. <beatles.ncf.ca/phillips.html>.

Pinsker, Sanford. "Was High Modernism a Humanism?" *The Midwest Quarterly* 36 (1995). <www.english.swt.edu/cohen_p/Postmodern/Pinsker.html>.

Plato. *Four Texts on Socrates: Plato's Euthyphro, Apology, and Crito, and Aristophanes's Clouds.* Ed. and trans. Thomas G. West and Grace Starry West. Ithaca: Cornell UP, 1998.

Pollack, Alan W. "Alan W. Pollack's 'Notes On' Series." 2000. <www.recmusic beatles.com/public/files/awp/awp.html>.

Presley, Elvis. *The King of Rock and Roll: The Complete 50s Masters*. BMG, 2000.

Proust, Marcel. *Du côté de chez Swann* [*Swann's Way*]. 1913. Trans. C. K. Scott Moncrieff and Terence Kilmartin. New York: Modern Library, 1992.

Quantick, David. *Revolution: The Making of the Beatles' White Album*. Chicago: Chicago Review, 2002.

The Quarry Men and the Beatles. *Puttin' on the Style*. Black Dog, 1998.

Reeve, Andru J. *Turn Me On, Dead Man: The Beatles and the "Paul Is Dead" Hoax*. Bloomington: Authorhouse, 2004.

Reising, Russell. "'It is not dying': *Revolver* and the Birth of Psychedelic Sound." Reising, *"Every Sound There Is"* 234–53.

———. "*Vacio Luminoso*: 'Tomorrow Never Knows' and the Coherence of the Impossible." Womack and Davis, *Reading the Beatles* 111–28.

———, ed. *"Every Sound There Is": The Beatles' Revolver and the Transformation of Rock and Roll*. Aldershot: Ashgate, 2002.

Richmond, Len, with Gary Noguera, eds. *The New Gay Liberation Book: Writings and Photographs about Gay (Men's) Liberation*. 1973. Palo Alto: Ramparts, 1979.

Richmond, W. Edson. "The Value of the Study of Place Names." *The Study of Place Names*. Ed. Ronald L. Baker. Terre Haute: Indiana Council of Teachers of English, 1991. 23–31.

Riley, Tim. *Tell Me Why: A Beatles Commentary*. New York: Knopf, 1988.

Ritivoi, Andreea Deciu. *Yesterday's Self: Nostalgia and the Immigrant Identity*. Lanham: Rowman and Littlefield, 2002.

Roessner, Jeffrey. "We All Want to Change the World: Postmodern Politics and the Beatles' *White Album*." Womack and Davis, *Reading the Beatles* 147–58.

The Rolling Stones. *Singles Collection: The London Years*. Decca, 2002.

Rooksby, Rikky. "Harrison, George (1943–2001)." *Oxford Dictionary of National Biography*. Ed. Colin Matthew and Brian Harrison. Oxford: Oxford UP, 2004. <www.oxforddnb.com>.

Roos, Michael E. "The Walrus and the Deacon: John Lennon's Debt to Lewis Carroll." *Journal of Popular Culture* 18 (1984): 19–29.

Russell, Jeff. *The Beatles Complete Discography*. New York: Universe, 2006.

Ryan, Kevin, and Brian Kehew. *Recording the Beatles: The Studio Equipment and Techniques Used to Create Their Classic Albums*. Houston: Curvebender, 2006.

Rydell, Bobby. *The Best of Bobby Rydell: Cameo Parkway, 1959–1964*. ABKCO, 2005.

Sauceda, James. *The Literary Lennon: A Comedy of Errors*. Ann Arbor: Pierian, 1983.

Schaffner, Nicholas. *The Beatles Forever*. Harrisburg: Cameron House, 1977.

Schreuders, Piet, Mark Lewisohn, and Adam Smith. *The Beatles London*. New York: St. Martin's, 1994.

Schultz, Michael, dir. *Sgt. Pepper's Lonely Hearts Club Band*. Universal Pictures, 1978.

Schwartz, Francie. *Body Count*. New York: Straight Arrow, 1972.

Scott, Ken. "Shooting to Thrill." Interview by Joe Chiccarelli. *EQ* December 2005: 38–53.

Service, Robert. *Collected Poems of Robert Service*. New York: Putnam, 1907.

Shakespeare, William. *The Riverside Shakespeare*. Ed. G. Blakemore Evans. Boston: Houghton Mifflin, 1974.

Sherman, Suzanne. "*The Yellow Submarine*: A Fable for Our Time." *Journal of Popular Culture* 8 (1974): 619–23.

Shotton, Pete, and Nicholas Schaffner. *John Lennon: In My Life*. New York: Stein and Day, 1983.

"Sir James Paul McCartney, MBE." *BBC: h2g2*. 30 September 2005. <www.bbc.co. uk/dna/ww2/A5972718>.

Smith, Alan. "My Broken Tooth—by Paul McCartney." *New Musical Express* 24 June 1966: 3.

Smith, Kimberly K. "Mere Nostalgia: Notes on a Progressive Paratheory." *Rhetoric & Public Affairs* 3.4 (2000): 505–27.

Spitz, Bob. *The Beatles: The Biography*. Boston: Little, Brown, 2005.

Spizer, Bruce. *The Beatles on Apple Records*. New Orleans: 498 Productions, 2003.

Starr, Ringo. "Ringo Solo." Interview by John Harris. *Rolling Stone* 17 April 2003: 43–44.

Stevens, Wallace. *The Collected Poems of Wallace Stevens*. New York: Knopf, 1954.

Stratton, Valerie N., and Annette H. Zalanowski. "The Effects of Music and Cognition on Mood." *Psychology of Music* 19 (1991): 121–27.

Sullivan, Henry W. *The Beatles with Lacan: Rock 'n' Roll as Requiem for the Modern Age*. New York: Lang, 1995.

Sulpy, Doug, and Ray Schweighardt. *Get Back: The Unauthorized Chronicle of the Beatles' Let It Be Disaster*. New York: Griffin, 1997.

Taylor, Alistair. *With the Beatles*. London: John Blake, 2003.

Taylor, James. *James Taylor*. Apple, 1968.

Tears for Fears. *The Seeds of Love*. Mercury, 1989.

Thomas, Dylan. *Collected Poems of Dylan Thomas, 1934–1952*. New York: New Directions, 1971.

Thompson, Thomas. "The New Far-Out Beatles." *Life* 16 June 1967: 100–06.

Thoreau, Henry David. *Walden, or Life in the Woods*. 1854. Ed. Bill McKibben. Boston: Beacon, 1997.

Tompkins, Jane. "I Want to Hold Your Hand." Womack and Davis, *Reading the Beatles* 215–19.

Trynka, Paul, ed. *The Beatles: Ten Days That Shook the World*. London: Dorling Kindersley, 2004.

Turner, Steve. *A Hard Day's Write: The Story Behind Every Beatles Song*. New York: HarperCollins, 1994.

Twentieth-Century Blues: The Songs of Noël Coward. Ichiban Old Indie, 1999.

Wainwright, Rufus. *Poses*. DreamWorks, 2001.

Warwick, Jacqueline. "*I'm* Eleanor Rigby: Female Identity and *Revolver.*" Reising, *"Every Sound There Is"* 58–68.

West, Nancy Martha. *Kodak and the Lens of Nostalgia.* Charlottesville: UP of Virginia, 2000.

Whiteley, Sheila. "'Love, love, love': Representations of Gender and Sexuality in Selected Songs by the Beatles." Womack and Davis, *Reading the Beatles* 55–69.

Whitley, Ed. "The Postmodern *White Album.*" Inglis, *The Beatles, Popular Music, and Society* 105–25.

Wikipedia. <en.wikipedia.org>.

Wilson, Brian. *Smile.* Nonesuch, 2004.

Wings. *At the Speed of Sound.* Capitol, 1976.

———. *Back to the Egg.* Columbia, 1979.

———. *Venus and Mars.* Capitol, 1975.

———. *Wild Life.* Apple, 1971.

———. *Wings over America.* Capitol, 1975.

Winn, John C. *That Magic Feeling: The Beatles' Recorded Legacy, Volume Two: 1966–1970.* Sharon, VT: Multiplus, 2003.

———. *Way Beyond Compare: The Beatles' Recorded Legacy, Volume One: 1957–1965.* Sharon, VT: Multiplus, 2003.

Womack, Kenneth. "The Beatles as Modernists." *Music and Literary Modernism: Critical Essays and Comparative Studies.* Ed. Robert McParland. London: Cambridge Scholars, 2007. 222–47.

———. "Editing the Beatles: Addressing the Roles of Authority and Editorial Theory in the Creation of Popular Music's Most Valuable Canon." *TEXT: An Interdisciplinary Annual of Textual Studies* 11 (1998): 189–205.

Womack, Kenneth, and Todd F. Davis, eds. *Reading the Beatles: Cultural Studies, Literary Criticism, and the Fab Four.* Albany: State U of New York P, 2006.

Woolf, Virginia. *To the Lighthouse.* 1927. San Diego: Harcourt Brace Jovanovich, 1989.

World Wildlife Fund. *No One's Gonna Change Our World.* Regal Starline, 1969.

Yeats, William Butler. *Selected Poems and Three Plays of William Butler Yeats.* 3rd ed. Ed. M. L. Rosenthal. New York: Collier, 1996.

You Can't Do That: The Making of A Hard Day's Night. VCI, 1994.

Zolten, Jerry. *Great God A'mighty! The Dixie Hummingbirds: Celebrating the Rise of Soul Gospel Music.* Oxford: Oxford UP, 2002.

Index